The Eastern Paths to Philosophic Self-Enlightenment

An Introduction to Eastern Philosophies

Chánh Công Phan, Ph.D.
San Jose State University

KENDALL/HUNT PUBLISHING COMPANY
4050 Westmark Drive   Dubuque, Iowa 52002

CONTENTS

v

It is wonderful that there are so many valuable anthologies and sourcebooks and interpretative works on Eastern philosophies *already* in circulation. It seems desirable, then, to explain why I have added *The Eastern Paths to Philosophic Self-Enlightenment* to their growing number.

The Comparative and Historical Framework

The Eastern Paths to Philosophic Self-Enlightenment is an anthology of selected scriptural writings of Eastern sages and philosophers to be used for an introductory course to Eastern philosophies at San Jose State University. In the course of my teaching during the past ten years, I have used a number of anthologies, sourcebooks, and interpretive works on Eastern philosophies, but, none has satisfied adequately the special curriculum requirements of the course in particular and the intellectual curiosities of my students in general.

The various philosophical inquiries and special topics about life and reality, that my students want to know, have revealed the wide range of their concerns and interests. Among the curriculum requirements of the course is the use of a "textual analysis" method (*hermeneutics*) that should be philosophically critical, imaginative, and comparative. This philosophical method, which I use in my teaching, can be viewed as the functional expression of *the academic task of doing philosophy*, both in the *praxis* of those who teach and those who learn Eastern philosophies.

In pursuit of the above stated academic objectives, *The Eastern Paths to Philosophic Self-Enlightenment* is structured to *give* an intellectually comparative framework of topically oriented philosophical issues that may yield a comparative philosophical perspective for its readers. The anthology is, therefore, organized into nine parts encompassing five main fields of philosophy:

1. Space, Time, and Spirit of Eastern Philosophies (Part A)
2. The Inner Powers of Philosophic Consciousness (Part B)
3. Eastern Philosophies of Life (Part C)
4. Eastern Ethics and Political Thoughts (Part D)
5. Eastern Cosmological Traditions and Universal Equality (Part E)
6. Eastern Views of the Human Self and Self-Knowledge (Part F)
7. Eastern Views of Reality and Philosophic Self-Enlightenment (Part G)
8. Appendices (Part H)

Concerning the internal comparative framework of any given Part of the text, which happens to belong to a specific field of philosophy, then, the Hindu, Buddhist, Confucianist, and Taoist views are organized into sequentially separate chapters, whenever *textually* possible. It is hoped that this internal comparative framework can provide the reading materials for students or any interested reader to gain the desired *comparative philosophical understanding* of Eastern philosophies through the methods of critical textual analysis and comparative philosophical thinking.

I am now convinced that I can never come closer to an understanding of the philosophies of the ancient East without *also* learning many aspects of the philosophies and sciences of the West. One may not understand the true nature of one's own *Platonic cave*, unless, one has completely left it behind to enter a new world, and then back to it one will return with a totally new perspective. So, this small anthology is *a philosophical invitation* to those who wish to understand their own Western philosophical and scientific traditions (Platonic caves) by learning some aspects of the philosophies of the East.

If "philosophy" is the highest expression of the intellect of a thinker or the minds of many generations of a nation's leading thinkers, then, learning Eastern philosophies is one of the best possible ways to understand the hearts and minds of Asian peoples and their cultures and histories. Given the ongoing processes of globalization and regional integration, a general knowledge of Eastern philosophies is no longer a mere intellectual curiosity for a few rare scholars. A general knowledge of Eastern philosophies may have *now* become "a new intellectual need" to be cultivated and mastered by any Westerner who interacts or does business with Asians here in the West or there in the East. If the West should be historically fated to confront the Chinese in a military showdown when China has attained the true status of a world superpower, the time to get intellectually prepared may be now.

One may not really know what an Asian or even an Asian-American thinks, why he/she acts, what he/she rethinks, and why he/she makes a new move, unless one is familiar with his/her mind and heart. Inside the mind and heart of an Asian or even an Asian-American is an intellectual paradigm by which his/her thinking and acting are programmed and re-programmed. That which governs the self-programming paradigms of Asian minds and hearts is their thought-system, which can be traced back to the guiding principles of Buddhism, Confucianism, Hinduism, Taoism, and Yi Li (v. Dịch Lý [Philosophy of Change]). An Asian may think and act or may pretend to think and act *as* a Buddhist, or *as* a Confucianist, or *as* a Hindu, or *as* all the above mentioned at the same time, shifting his/her intellectual paradigm in response to the rationalistic paradigm of any Western minds. But most important, it is hoped that a self-reflective reading of this anthology may lead one to one's own *philosophic self-enlightenment*, the ultimate end, pursued by all Eastern philosophies.

The Multicultural Perspective

Another feature of *The Eastern Paths to Philosophic Self-Enlightenment* is its *multicultural perspective* concerning the cultural histories of Eastern philosophies in contrast to the ideologically entrenched Sinocentrism and Indocentrism of past and present Asian studies. By the "multicultural perspective," I mean the pluralistic view of human cultures, which demands, in the words of Charles Taylor, that "we all *recognize* the equal value of different cultures; that we not only let them survive, but acknowledge their *worth*." Precisely, because, each culture is true to itself and authentic with the same right and the same status as any other, none can claim a priority over the other.

Therefore, the philosophy of any culture should be viewed as the highest intellectual expression of that culture. Respect and give credit back to *each culture* of the classical East (1500–221 BCE); honor the right people who had created and practiced it as their established way of life. That is the first *mantra* of applied Asian studies multiculturalism. Respect and give back *each philosophy* of the classical East to its right culture because it had been its highest intellectual expression. That is the second *mantra* of applied Asian studies multiculturalism.

Sinocentrism and Indocentrism have seriously impaired past and present Asian studies scholarship, since they have dogmatically asserted that "China" and "India" were the only two givers of culture and civilization in the traditional and ancient East. Thus, Sinocentrism has *expropriated* all the philosophical schools of ancient East Asian cultures by making them *the* philosophies of "ancient China" (that is "ancient Ch'in" [221–206 BCE] which gave "China" its name). The *multicultural* perspective views all the philosophical schools that had once flowered in the mainland of ancient East Asia before the birth of "China" (221 BCE) as *the schools of ancient East Asian philosophies* or the philosophical schools of the different ancient East Asian cultures.

Therefore, the "school of ancient East Asian Confucianism," by which I mean the thoughts of K'ung Fu Tzu (v. Khổng Phu Tử), Meng Tzu (c. Mạnh Tử), and Hsun Tzu (v. Tuân Tử), is considered to have belonged to the Lu (v. Lỗ), Tsou (v. Trâu), and Chao (v. Triệu) cultures, because, Confucius, Mencius, and Hsun Tzu (v. Tuân Tử) came from these northern cultures.

The "school of ancient East Asian Taoism," by which I mean the thoughts of Lao Tzu (v. Lão Tử) and Chuang Tzu (v. Trang Tử), is viewed to have belonged to the non-Sinic Ch'u (v. Sở) culture, because the Taoist founder came from this Southern wet-rice cultural tradition.

The "school of ancient East Asian Legalism" belongs to the political thoughts of Shang Yang (v. Thương Uởng) from the Kingdom of Wei (v. Vệ), Han Fei Tzu (v. Hàn Phi Tử) from the Kingdom of Han (v. Hàn), Lui Pu Wei (v. Lã Bất Vi) from the Kingdom of Chao (v. Triệu) or Wei (v. Vệ), and Li Ssu (v. Lý Tư) from the Kingdom of Ch'u (v. Sở). The Legalist political ideology of the Ch'in Dynasty should be considered to have belonged *both* to the Ch'in culture *before* its power conquest and the later Chinese Civilization *after* Ch'in Shih Huang Ti (v. Tần Thủy Hoàng Đế) created "China" in 221 BCE. All the remaining schools of ancient East Asian philosophies should be attributed to the cultural landscapes or the cultural kingdoms which their respective philosophers recognized as home.

The philosophies of all the ancient East Asian schools should, therefore, be viewed as *"the intellectual properties"* of the ancient East Asian sages and thinkers rather than "the Chinese sages" as uncritically asserted by Sinocentrists. And all the schools of ancient East Asian philosophies should also be *re*-considered as *the multiculturally common intellectual heritage* of the later *national philosophies* of traditional East Asia (Chinese Philosophy, Japanese Philosophy, Korean Philosophy, and Vietnamese Philosophy). Consequently, any philosophical system that was introduced *after* the formal creation of China (in 221 BCE) and within that territory should be scholarly established to be *authentically* belonging to the "Chinese Philosophy."

A distinction is herein made between the "ancient East Asian philosophies," which had been historically pre-Chinese (prior to 221 BCE), and the later "national philosophies," which are historically post-Chinese (posterior to 221 BCE). Thus, the ancient East Asian philosophies should be *multiculturalistically* re-established as the *common regional philosophical heritage* and cannot be *subsumed* under the *national philosophical tradition* of "Chinese Philosophy" as Sinocentrism has *culturoimperialistically* done.

Indocentrism has claimed that all the philosophical traditions that had flourished in the so-called "ancient India" belong to the "Indian Philosophy" (Radhakrishnan 1923). Instead, the *multicultural* perspective *views* the philosophical traditions that had once prospered in the peninsula of ancient South Asia before the *"parinirvana"* of the Buddha (483 BCE or 360 BCE) as *the ancient South Asian philosophies* or the philosophies of different ancient South Asian cultures. They should be considered as *"the intellectual properties"* of the ancient South Asian sages and philosophers who had once lived in the vast subcontinent of ancient South Asia. The ancient

South Asian philosophies that had been popular before the *"parinirvana"* of the Buddha are here *re*-established to have belonged to the two culturally different branches of ancient South Asian philosophies, the *"heterodox"* (non-Aryan [Hindu]) and the *"orthodox"* (Aryan [Hindu]). The non-Aryan philosophical traditions include the Jain philosophy, Carvaka philosophy, and Buddhaian philosophy (the Buddha's philosophy). The "orthodox" Hindu philosophical branch includes the Upanishadic Brahmanism and six *darshanas* (Nyaya, Vaisheshika, Samkhya, Yoga, Mimamsa, and Vedanta). Out of these two branches of the ancient South Asian philosophies the later "Indian Philosophy" finally emerged around 400 BCE.

The ancient East Asian language, used by the *Ju* (v. *Nho* [Literati]) of ancient East Asia and also used and developed by the Chinese, Japanese, Korean, and Viêtnamese intellectuals, is historically known as *"Ju tzu"* (v. *Nho tự* [the script of flexible utility]). The *Ju* (v. *Nho*) terms in the anthology will be spelled primarily according to the old Wade-Giles Romanination System rather than the current Pin-yin Romanization System, because they were mostly romanized as such in the borrowed translations of the ancient Ju (v. Nho) texts. Due to the "extremely phonetic poverty" of the modern Pekinese as Bernhard Karlgren points out, the Wade-Giles Romanization System is supplemented by the Việt Nho (c. Yüeh Ju) system, which has been used in the Viêtnamese tradition. The Việt Nho system, "with the old sounds of the Ts'in period attached to the written characters. . . . [and-ccp] with a necessary allowance for decay and self-divergence," as Terrien de Lacouperie says, "rightly deserves the qualification of the most archaic of the Chinese [ancient *Nho*-ccp] dialects."

Acknowledgements

To all the people, who have supported my efforts in bringing this anthology to its completion and final birth, I would like to express my lasting appreciation and gratitude. For their ideas and spiritual support, I would like to thank Professors Selma Burkom, Don Ciraulo, Scot Guenter, Chris Jochim, Richard Keady, Thomas Leddy, Trị Đình Trần, and the graduate student of philosophy Tony Nguyễn. For other forms of support, I would like to thank Kim-Anh Nguyên and Vương Vũ.

Part A

Space, Time, and Spirit of
Eastern Philosophies

CHAPTER 1

Historical Contexts, Periods, and Schools of Eastern Philosophies

History of Indian Thought

Sarvepalli Radhakrishnan

The Introduction

Sarvepalli Radhakrishnan (1888–1975) was recognized internationally for his remarkable ability as teacher, lecturer, scholar, philosopher, and statesman. Not only being the most respected of modern Indian philosophers, Dr. Radhakrishnan also served as President of India from 1962–1967. For his important works on ancient South Asian and Indian philosophies, see his *Indian Philosophy* (1923), and his translations of *The Principal Upanishads* (1953), and *The Bhagavadgita* (1971). Concerning his philosophical method and cultural history orientation, he remained a faithful Indocentrist because he subsumed all ancient non-Vedic thoughts (pre-Ashoka) under the later "Indian philosophy."

This selection is taken from the "General Introduction" to *A Sourcebook in Indian Philosophy* (1957) that was edited by Sarvepalli Radhakrishnan and Charles A. Moore.

At the very outset, it should be emphasized that Indian philosophy has had an extremely long and complex development, much more complex than is usually realized, and probably a longer history of continuous development than any other philosophical tradition. While the historical perspective is undoubtedly of immense importance in the study of such a tradition, it is impossible to present an exact historical survey of this development. Because of the Indians' lack of concern for chronology, many of the details of the chronological sequence of the writings either are lost or no record of them was kept. In a sense, the history of Indian philosophy can be written, if only in broadest outline, but no history of philosophy can be complete without some acquaintance with the philosophers who were responsible for the doctrines and for the development of thought. However, so unhistorical, or perhaps so deeply-philosophical, was the nature of the ancient Indians that much more is known about the philosophies than about the philosophers. Relatively few of the great philosophers of ancient Indian thought are known to us and some of the most famous names to which history attributes certain philosophical doctrines or systems are now admitted to be legendary. On the one hand, we are occasionally aware of the author of some doctrines but, as in the case of Indian materialism and some other movements, original texts are not available and the details of the systems are completely unknown.

In broad outline, Indian philosophy may be said to have had four major periods of development up to the time of its serious decline about A.D. 1700. The Vedic Period is dimmed by obscurity, but it may be placed approximately between 2500 and 600 B.C. This is the period during which the Āryans, having come down into India from central Asia, settled their new homeland and gradually expanded and developed their Āryan culture and civilization. In the technical sense of the term, this can hardly be called a philosophical age. It is to be thought of as an age of groping, in which religion, philosophy, superstition, and thought were inextricably interrelated and yet in perpetual conflict. It is an age of philosophical development, however, and its culminating doctrines, those expounded in the major Upaniṣads, have determined the tone if not the precise pattern of the Indian philosophical development ever since.

The literature of this period consists of the four Vedas (*Ṛg Veda*, *Yajur Veda*, *Sāma Veda*, and *Atharva Veda*), each of which has four parts, known as Mantras, Brāhmaṇas, Āraṇyakas, and Upaniṣads. The Mantras (hymns), especially the later ones in the *Ṛg Veda*, constitute the actual beginning of Indian philosophy. By progressing from the not unusual polytheism of the early Vedas, through monotheism, to suggestions of monism, these poems and songs paved the way for the monistic tendencies of the Upaniṣads. The Brāhmaṇas are chiefly religious documents, including ritualistic precepts and sacrificial duties. The Āraṇyakas and the Upaniṣads constitute the concluding parts of the Brāhmaṇas, and in these philosophical problems are discussed. The

Brāhmaṇas provide the ritual to be observed by the householder, but when the householder has reached old age, he resorts to the forest and needs a substitute for the ritual he has known as a householder. The Āraṇyakas, which come between the Brāhmaṇas and the Upaniṣads, supply this need by encouraging meditation for those who live in the forest. The Āraṇyakas form the transition link between the ritual of the Brāhmaṇas and the philosophy of the Upaniṣads. While the hymns are the creation of poets, the Brāhmaṇas are the work of priests, and the Upaniṣads are the meditations of philosophers. The Upaniṣads, though in one sense a continuation of the Vedic religion, are in another sense a strong philosophical protest against the religion of the Brāhmaṇas. It is in the Upaniṣads that the tendency to spiritual monism, which in one form or another characterizes much of Indian philosophy, was first established and where intuition rather than reason was first recognized as the true guide to ultimate truth.

The second period of philosophical development is the Epic Period, dated approximately from 500 or 600 B.C. to A.D. 200. This period is characterized by the indirect presentation of philosophical doctrines through the medium of nonsystematic and nontechnical literature, especially the great epics, the *Rāmāyaṇa* and the *Mahābhārata*. In addition, however, the period includes the rise and early development of Buddhism, Jainism, Śaivism, and Vaiṣṇavism. The *Bhagavad-gītā*, which is a part of the *Mahābhārata*, ranks as one of the three most authoritative texts in Indian philosophical literature. Furthermore, the beginnings of the orthodox schools of Indian philosophy also belong to this period. Most of the systems had their beginnings about the time of the rise of Buddhism, and developed side by side for centuries. The systematic works of the major schools were written later, but the origin of the doctrines of the several schools most probably occurred during the Epic Period. This was one of the most fertile periods of philosophy in India as well as in several other parts of the world—Greece, China, Persia, and elsewhere. A great amount of philosophical or semiphilosophical material was produced during the period, and it is very probable that our knowledge of the doctrines developed at that time merely scratches the surface of the wealth, depth, and variety of philosophical speculation that took place. It was during this period that such philosophies as skepticism, naturalism, materialism, etc., arose along with the other heterodox systems of Buddhism and Jainism and what were later to be known as the orthodox systems of Hinduism. It is out of this wealth of material that the later systems—the orthodox systems of Hinduism and the unorthodox systems of the Cārvāka, Buddhism, and Jainism—were perforce brought into clearer perspective by the construction of systematic treatises.

It was also during this period that many of the Dharmaśāstras, treatises on ethical and social philosophy, were compiled. These, like the rest of the philosophical texts of the period, are classed as smṛtis, that is, traditional texts, as contrasted with the literature of the Vedic Period, which is known as śruti, revealed scriptures or authoritative texts. The Dharmaśāstras are systematic treatises concerning the conduct of life among the Āryans, describing their social organization and their ethical and religious functions and obligations.

The third period is the Sūtra Period, which is dated approximately from the early centuries of the Christian era. In this period the systematic treatises of the various schools were written and the systems took the basic form they were to preserve henceforth. The doctrines of each of the systems were presented in orderly, systematic, and logically developed sets of aphorisms, extremely brief, sometimes enigmatic, statements which, according to some interpretations, are merely reminders for the initiated to enable them to recall the details of philosophical systems to which they belonged and whose fuller doctrines were known only to those within the fold of the system. During this period the critical attitude in philosophy was

distinctly developed along with the systematic, and the Sūtras themselves contain not only the positive developments of the systems but also keen and comprehensive polemics against opposing systems. Whereas during the preceding period philosophical thought and discussion had their origin, they were at that time carried on at the precritical level. In the Sūtras, however, we have self-conscious thought and reflection and no longer merely constructive imagination and spontaneous insights.

The six Hindu systems presented in sūtra form during this period are the Nyāya or logical realism; the Vaiśesika or realistic pluralism; the Sāmkhya or evolutionary dualism; the Yoga or disciplined meditation; the Pūrva Mīmāmsā or earlier interpretative investigations of the Vedas, relating to conduct; and the Uttara Mīmāmsā or later investigations of the Vedas, relating to knowledge, also called Vedānta, the "end of the Vedas".

The fourth period, the Scholastic Period, is that in which commentaries were written upon the Sūtras in order to explain them. Without elaboration and explanation the Sūtras are almost unintelligible. Not only were commentaries written upon the Sūtras, but also commentaries upon commentaries, and commentaries upon these, almost without limit. It is impossible to provide dates for this period with any great degree of certainty. It is dated generally from the Sūtra Period to the seventeenth century. The literature of this period is primarily explanatory, but is also strongly and sometimes grossly polemical. There is a brood of "Schoolmen," noisy controversialists, indulging in oversubtle theories and finespun arguments, who fought fiercely over details of philosophical doctrines and who were in constant philosophical conflict with representatives of other schools. Sometimes the commentaries are more confusing than enlightening. Instead of clear explanation and thought, one often finds mere words; instead of philosophy, logic-chopping. Obscurity of thought, subtlety of logic, and intolerance of opposition are marks of the worst types of commentators. The better types, however, are invaluable and are respected almost as much as the creators of the systems themselves. Śaṁkara, for example, the writer of a famous commentary on the *Sūtra* of the Vedānta system, is thought of more highly as a philosopher than is Bādarāyaṇa, the seer who wrote the original *Vedānta Sūtra* (also called the *Brahma Sūtra*). The Scholastic Period is one of explanation of the original *Sūtras,* but, like any scholastic period, it has also produced quibbling and unphilosophical debates which are relatively worthless. On the other hand, it has brought forth some of the greatest of all Indian philosophers. Among these, in addition to Śaṁkara, are Kumārila, Śrīdhara, Rāmānuja, Madhva, Vācaspati, Udayana, Bhāskara, Jayanta, Vijñānabhikṣu, and Raghunātha. These great thinkers have been much more than commentators on ancient systems, although, in their modesty, they have claimed to be no more. In fact, however, they have been, to all intents and purposes, creators of their own systems. In the guise of commentators, they have elaborated points of view which, though capable of being related to the original system of which they are supposed to be commentaries, are new expositions rather than mere explanations. For example, the three major forms of Vedānta, those developed by Śaṁkara, Rāmānuja, and Madhva, are distinct and elaborate systems, although they all stem from the same *Vedānta Sūtra* of Bādarāyaṇa. This type of development is indicative of the unique way in which Indian philosophers have maintained their traditional respect for the past and their recognition of the value of authority in philosophy, but, without seeming to break this tradition, have also carried along the free development of thought as their insight and reason directed.

While, in a sense, the Scholastic Period is still in progress, since interpretations of ancient ideas and systems are still being written, Indian philosophy lost its dynamic spirit about the sixteenth century when India became the victim of outside powers. First the Muslims and then the British assumed control of the country, not only physically but also in the realm of thought. The Muslims undermined Āryan culture and thought as far as possible, and the British, in their time, did as much as they could to belittle the thought of traditional India. For a long time, the English-educated Indians were apparently ashamed of their own philosophical tradition, and it became the mark of intelligence as well as expediency to be as European and as English in thought and in life as possible. While the coming of the British brought about a revival in education, the resulting revival of Indian thought was unintentional, to say the least. During this period indigenous reform movements like that of the Brāhmo Samāj and the Ārya Samāj took a leading part in India's philosophical and religious renaissance. More recently, especially since the nationalist movement began, and more especially since the re-establishment of India as a free and independent nation, the revival of Indian philosophy as such and the consciousness of the greatness of India's philosophical past have been the most prominent developments in the field. During the twentieth century, the Indian mind has been affected by the Western, but the Western mind has also been influenced by the Indian more than ever before, through the writings of contemporary poets, sages, and philosophers. To be sure, the revival of the Indian consciousness of the greatness of its own philosophical past has tended in recent years to develop a nationalistic tone in philosophy as well as in politics. The resulting tendency of extremists to minimize or reject the revival and development of philosophy which was effected by the contact of Indians and Westerners has not been a healthy sign. We of today are able to see further than our predecessors, since we have climbed on their shoulders. Instead, therefore, of resting content with the foundations so nobly laid in the past, we must build in harmony with ancient endeavor as well as with contemporary thought. The future development of Indian philosophy, if one may hazard a guess, will be in terms of a more synthetic approach to Indian and Western points of view.

Study Questions

A.1.1 Sarvepalli Radhakrishnan, History of Indian Thought

1. Identity the "four major periods" of ancient South Asian and Indian philosophies and their respective dates.
2. Identify the main scriptures that were introduced during each period and their main ideas.
3. Identify the philosophical traditions and schools of ancient South Asia and India, including the philosophies that emerged during each period and their respective founders and most representative philosophers.

The Spirit of Indian Philosophy

Sarvepalli Radhakrishnan

The Introduction

Unlike Fung Yu-lan, who takes the *pragmatism* of "Chinese philosophy" (theory-practice unity) to be its "spirit" (A.I.5), Radhakrishnan does not restrict the "spirit of Indian philosophy" to its *practicality* alone but takes into account its other aspects as well.

This selection is taken from the "General Introduction" to *A Sourcebook in Indian Philosophy* (1957) that was edited by Sarvepalli Radhakrishnan and Charles A. Moore.

Indian philosophy, it has been noted, is extremely complex. Through the ages the Indian philosophical mind has probed deeply into many aspects of human experience and the external world. Although some methods, such as the experimental method of modern science, have been relatively less prominent than others, not only the problems of Indian philosophy but also the methods used and the conclusions reached in the pursuit of truth have certainly been as far-reaching in their extent, variety, and depth as those of other philosophical traditions. The six basic systems and the many subsystems of Hinduism, the four chief schools of Buddhism, the two schools of Jainism, and the materialism of the Cārvāka are evidence enough of the diversity of views in Indian philosophy. The variety of the Indian perspective is unquestionable. Accordingly, it is very difficult to cite any specific doctrines or methods as characteristic of Indian philosophy as a whole and applicable to all the multitudinous systems and subsystems developed through nearly four millenniums of Indian philosophical speculation.

Nevertheless, in certain respects there is what might be called a distinct spirit of Indian philosophy. This is exemplified by certain attitudes which are fairly characteristic of the Indian philosophical mind or which stand as points of view that have been emphasized characteristically by Indians in their philosophies.

(1) The chief mark of Indian philosophy in general is its concentration upon the spiritual. Both in life and in philosophy the spiritual motive is predominant in India. Except for the relatively

minor materialistic school of the Cārvāka and related doctrines, philosophy in India conceives man to be spiritual in nature, is interested primarily in his spiritual destiny, and relates him in one way or another to a universe which is also spiritual in essential character. Neither man nor the universe is looked upon as physical in essence, and material welfare is never recognized as the goal of human life, except by the Cārvāka. Philosophy and religion are intimately related because philosophy itself is regarded as a spiritual adventure, and also because the motivation both in philosophy and in religion concerns the spiritual way of life in the here-and-now and the eventual spiritual salvation of man in relation to the universe. Practically all of Indian philosophy, from its beginning in the Vedas to the present day, has striven to bring about a socio-spiritual reform in the country, and philosophical literature has taken many forms, mythological, popular, or technical, as the circumstances required, in order to promote such spiritual life. The problems of religion have always given depth and power and purpose to the Indian philosophical mind and spirit.

(2) Another characteristic view of Indian philosophy is the belief in the intimate relationship of philosophy and life. This attitude of the practical application of philosophy to life is found in every school of Indian philosophy. While natural abundance and material prosperity paved the way for the rise of philosophical speculation, philosophy has never been considered a mere intellectual exercise. The close relationship between theory and practice, doctrine and life, has always been outstanding in Indian thought. Every Indian system seeks the truth, not as academic "knowledge for its own sake," but to learn the truth which shall make men free. This is not, as it has been called, the modern pragmatic attitude. It is much larger and much deeper than that. It is not the view that truth is measured in terms of the practical, but rather that the truth is the only sound guide for practice, that truth alone has efficacy as a guide for man in his search for salvation. Every major system of Indian philosophy takes its

beginning from the practical and tragic problems of life and searches for the truth in order to solve the problem of man's distress in the world in which he finds himself. There has been no teaching which remained a mere word of mouth or dogma of schools. Every doctrine has been turned into a passionate conviction, stirring the heart of man and quickening his breath, and completely transforming his personal nature. In India, philosophy is for life; it is to be lived. It is not enough to *know* the truth; the truth must be *lived*. The goal of the Indian is not to know the ultimate truth but to *realize* it, to become one with it.

Another aspect of the intimate inseparability of theory and practice, philosophy and life, in Indian philosophy is to be found in the universally prevalent demand for moral purification as an imperative preliminary for the would-be student of philosophy or searcher after truth. Śaṁkara's classic statement of this demand calls for a knowledge of the distinction between the eternal and the noneternal, that is, a questioning tendency in the inquirer; the subjugation of all desire for the fruits of action, either in this life or in a hereafter, a renunciation of all petty desire, personal motive, and practical interest; tranquillity, self-control, renunciation, patience, peace of mind, and faith; and a desire for release (*mokṣa*) as the supreme goal of life.

(3) Indian philosophy is characterized by the introspective attitude and the introspective approach to reality. Philosophy is thought of as *ātmavidyā*, knowledge of the self. Philosophy can start either with the external world or with the internal world of man's inner nature, the self of man. In its pursuit of the truth, Indian philosophy has always been strongly dominated by concern with the inner life and self of man rather than the external world of physical nature. Physical science, though developed extensively in the Golden Age of Indian culture, was never considered the road to ultimate truth; truth is to be sought and found within. The subjective, then, rather than the objective, becomes the focus of interest in Indian philosophy, and, therefore,

psychology and ethics are considered more important as aspects or branches of philosophy than the sciences which study physical nature. This is not to say that the Indian mind has not studied the physical world; in fact, on the contrary, India's achievements in the realm of positive science were at one time truly outstanding, especially in the mathematical sciences such as algebra, astronomy, and geometry, and in the applications of these basic sciences to numerous phases of human activity. Zoology, botany, medicine, and related sciences have also been extremely prominent in Indian thought. Be this as it may, the Indian, from time immemorial, has felt that the inner spirit of man is the most significant clue to his reality and to that of the universe, more significant by far than the physical or the external.

(4) This introspective interest is highly conducive to idealism, of course, and consequently most Indian philosophy is idealistic in one form or another. The tendency of Indian philosophy, especially Hinduism, has been in the direction of monistic idealism. Almost all Indian philosophy believes that reality is *ultimately* one and *ultimately* spiritual. Some systems have seemed to espouse dualism or pluralism, but even these have been deeply permeated by a strong monistic character. If we concentrate our attention upon the underlying spirit of Indian philosophy rather than its variety of opinions, we shall find that this spirit is embodied in the tendency to interpret life and reality in the way of monistic idealism. This rather unusual attitude is attributable to the nonrigidity of the Indian mind and to the fact that the attitude of monistic idealism is so plastic and dynamic that it takes many forms and expresses itself even in seemingly conflicting doctrines. These are not conflicting doctrines in fact, however, but merely different expressions of an underlying conviction which provides basic unity to Indian philosophy as a whole.

Materialism undoubtedly had its day in India, and, according to sporadic records and constant and determined efforts on the part of other systems to denounce it, the doctrine apparently enjoyed widespread acceptance at one time. Nevertheless, materialism could not hold its own; its adherents have been few in number, and its positive influence has been negligible. Indian philosophy has not been oblivious to materialism; rather, it has known it, has overcome it, and has accepted idealism as the only tenable view, whatever specific form that idealism might take.

(5) Indian philosophy makes unquestioned and extensive use of reason, but intuition is accepted as the only method through which the ultimate can be known. Reason, intellectual knowledge, is not enough. Reason is not useless or fallacious, but it is insufficient. To know reality one must have an actual experience of it. One does not merely *know* the truth in Indian philosophy; one *realizes* it. The word which most aptly describes philosophy in India is *darśana*, which comes from the verbal root *dṛś*, meaning "to see." "To see" is to have a direct intuitive experience of the object, or, rather, to realize it in the sense of becoming one with it. No complete knowledge is possible as long as there is the relationship of the subject on one hand and the object on the other. Later developments in Indian philosophy, from the time of the beginning of the systems, have all depended in large part upon reason for the systematic formulation of doctrines and systems, for rational demonstration or justification, and in polemical conflicts of system against system. Nevertheless, all the systems, except the Cārvāka, agree that there is a higher way of knowing reality, beyond the reach of reason, namely, the direct perception or experience of the ultimate reality, which cannot be known by reason in any of its forms. Reason can demonstrate the truth, but reason cannot discover or reach the truth. While reason may be the method of philosophy in its more intellectualistic sense, intuition is the only method of comprehending the ultimate. Indian philosophy is thus characterized by an ultimate dependence upon intuition, along with the recognition of the efficacy of reason and intellect when applied in their limited capacity and with their proper function.

(6) Another characteristic of Indian philosophy, one which is closely related to the preceding one, is its so-called acceptance of authority. Although the systems of Indian philosophy vary in the degree to which they are specifically related to the ancient *śruti*, not one of the systems—orthodox or unorthodox, except the Cārvāka—openly stands in violation of the accepted intuitive insights of its ancient seers, whether it be the Hindu seers of the Upaniṣads, the intuitive experience of the Buddha, or the similarly intuitive wisdom of Mahāvīra, the founder of Jainism, as we have it today. Indian philosophers have always been conscious of tradition and, as has been indicated before, the great system-builders of later periods claimed to be merely commentators, explaining the traditional wisdom of the past. While the specific doctrines of the past may be changed by interpretation, the general spirit and frequently the basic concepts are retained from age to age. Reverence for authority does not militate against progress, but it does lend a unity of spirit by providing a continuity of thought which has rendered philosophy especially significant in Indian life and solidly unified against any philosophical attitude contradicting its basic characteristics of spirituality, inwardness, intuition, and the strong belief that the truth is to be lived, not merely known.

The charge of indulging in an exaggerated respect for authority may be legitimately leveled against some of Indian philosophy, but this respect for the past is rooted in the deep conviction that those who really know reality are those who have *realized* the truth and that it is to them that we must turn ultimately, beyond all our power of reasoning, if we are to attain any comprehension of the truth which they saw and realized. As has been said, India has produced a great variety of philosophical doctrines and systems. This has been true despite universal reverence for and acceptance of the authority of the ancient seers as the true discoverers of wisdom. The variety of the systems, even in their basic conceptions, looked at in the light of the prevalent acceptance of authority, reveals the fact that this reverence has not made Indian philosophy a dogmatic religious creed, as is often alleged, but rather a single tone or trend of thought on basic issues. How completely free from traditional bias the systems are is seen, for example, by the fact that the original Sāṁkhya says nothing about the possible existence of God, although it is emphatic in its doctrine of the theoretical undemonstrability of his existence; the Vaiśeṣika and the Yoga, especially the latter, admit the existence of God, but do not consider him to be the creator of the universe; the Mīmāṃsā speaks of God but denies his importance and efficacy in the moral ordering of the world. To emphasize the point further, reference should be made also to the early Buddhist systems, which reject God, and to the Cārvākas, who deny God without qualification.

(7) Finally, there is the over-all synthetic tradition which is essential to the spirit and method of Indian philosophy. This is as old as the *Ṛg Veda*, where the seers realized that true religion comprehends all religions, so that "God is one but men call him by many names." Indian philosophy is clearly characterized by the synthetic approach to the various aspects of experience and reality. Religion and philosophy, knowledge and conduct, intuition and reason, man and nature, God and man, noumenon and phenomena, are all brought into harmony by the synthesizing tendency of the Indian mind. The Hindu is prone to believe even that all the six systems, as well as their varieties of subsystems, are in harmony with one another, in fact, that they complement one another in the total vision, which is one. As contrasted with Western philosophy, with its analytic approach to reality and experience, Indian philosophy is fundamentally synthetic. The basic texts of Indian philosophy treat not only one phase of experience and reality, but of the full content of the philosophic sphere. Metaphysics, epistemology, ethics, religion, psychology, facts, and value are not cut off one from the other but are treated in their natural unity as aspects of one life and experience or of a single comprehensive reality.

It is this synthetic vision of Indian philosophy which has made possible the intellectual and religious tolerance which has become so pronounced in Indian thought and in the Indian mind throughout the ages. Recent squabbles between religious communities, bred of new political factionalism, are not outgrowths of the Indian mind but, instead, are antagonistic to its unique genius for adaptability and tolerance, which takes all groups and all communities into its one truth and one life.

In addition to these general characteristics of Indian philosophy from the intellectual or theoretical point of view, there is also a fundamental unity of perspective in the practical realm. This has several aspects. In the first place, there is the fact, mentioned earlier, that all philosophies in India—Hindu, Buddhist, Jaina, and Cārvāka—have a practical motivation, stemming from man's practical problems of life, his limitations and suffering, and culminating in every case except the Cārvāka in a consideration of his ultimate liberation. In every case, including the Cārvāka, the motivation is practical rather than theoretical, for the Cārvāka is interested not in theory for its own sake, but in living a life of pleasure since it believes the world is conducive to that type of life and justifies no other. The goal of life in Hinduism, Buddhism, and Jainism is essentially the same. *Mokṣa* (liberation) is the ultimate objective for Hinduism and Jainism, and *nirvāṇa* is the goal in Buddhism. The precise meanings of liberation vary among the different schools, even among those within the framework of Buddhism and Hinduism, but the essential meaning of both *mokṣa* and *nirvāṇa* is emancipation or liberation from turmoil and suffering and freedom from rebirth. In some instances, the goal seems to be negative, consisting essentially of freedom from pain and freedom from rebirth, but in reality it is the positive achievement of a richer and fuller life and the attainment of infinite bliss. The spirit re-achieves its original purity, sometimes by becoming identical with the Absolute, sometimes by a life of communion with God, sometimes simply by the eternal existence of the pure spirit in its individuality, but in all cases free from the limitations and entanglements of life.

The several schools and systems of Indian philosophy are of one mind not only with reference to the goal of life, but also with reference to the good life on earth. The essential spirit of the philosophy of life of Hinduism, Buddhism, and Jainism is that of non-attachment. This is an attitude of mind with which the individual fulfills his part in life and lives a "normal" everyday existence in company with his fellow men, without being entangled in or emotionally disturbed by the results of his actions. He attains a mental and spiritual superiority to worldly values and is never enslaved by them. This is not negativism or escapism, for one takes part in everyday activities in accordance with his place in society. However, it is living and acting without any sense of attachment to the things of this world and without any selfishness whatsoever.

Hinduism, Buddhism, and Jainism, in all their branches, also accept the underlying doctrines of *karma* and rebirth. All of these schools believe that man must be morally and spiritually perfected before he can attain salvation. They also believe that justice is the law of the moral life exactly as cause-and-effect is the law of the natural world. What one sows one must reap. Since justice and moral and spiritual perfection are not achievable in one life, all these systems believe in rebirth, so as to provide the opportunity for moral progress and eventual perfection. Throughout Indian philosophy, from the earliest Vedas to the latest developments, the moral order of the universe has been an accepted doctrine of all Indian thinkers except the Cārvākas. *Karma* and rebirth are the instrumentalities by which the moral order of the universe is worked out in the life of man.

There is a further common element which unifies all schools of Hindu philosophy in the practical realm, although the heterodox schools, the Cārvāka, Buddhism, and Jainism, do not conform to this pattern. The way of life accepted by all schools of Hinduism, regardless of metaphysical and epistemological variations, includes the fourfold division of society, the four stages of life, and the four basic values which man seeks. In Hinduism, society is divided into four groups (*varṇa*, frequently translated as castes) determined generally according to occupational ability, namely, the priest-teacher (*brāhmin*), the king or political and military leader (*kṣatriya*), the merchant (*vaiśya*), and the laborer (*śūdra*). The first three of these are called the twice-born, that is, they are religiously initiated Hindus, whereas *śūdras* are not so accepted. The lives of the twice-born are to consist of the four stages of the student (*brahmacārin*), the householder (*gṛhastha*), the forest-dweller (*vānaprastha*), and the wandering monk (*sannyāsin* or *saṃnyāsin*). In this social scheme, one does not enter the life of asceticism until after he has fulfilled his obligations to his fellow man as a student and as a householder, but in the later stages of life one is to concentrate more and more upon the spiritual and upon his search for liberation. The goals of life which are accepted by all Hindus are righteousness or obedience to the moral law (*dharma*), wealth or material welfare (*artha*), pleasure (*kāma*), and emancipation (*mokṣa*). *Dharma* prevails throughout life, that is, neither pleasure nor wealth is to be obtained through violation of the rules of morality. *Mokṣa* is the ultimate goal to which all men should aspire. This social philosophy is accepted without question by all Hindus. It is presented in the literature of the Dharmaśāstras, but is not found in any elaboration or with any philosophical justification in the basic technical philosophical texts. This common ideal life of all Hindus provides a spirit of unity to the social and moral life of the country, although Buddhists and Jainas, who are greatly in the minority, do not follow the same specific pattern of life.

Study Questions

A.1.2 Sarvepalli Radhakrishnan, The Spirit of Indian Philosophy

1. List the seven "general characteristics" that constitute the "spirit" of ancient South Asian and Indian philosophies.
2. Identify the elements of each general characteristic and what philosophical tradition(s) and school(s) they are said to characterize.
3. Discuss the *problematics* of the concept of spirit.
   a. Is Radhakrishnan correct in taking the "general characteristics" to be the theoretical *contents* of the spirit of Indian philosophy?
   b. How should we understand the concept of "spirit" itself before we can redetermine the "spirit" of ancient South Asian and Indian philosophies?

Causes for the Development of Philosophy During the Period of the Philosophers

Fung Yu-Lan

The Introduction

Fung Yu-Lan (1895–1990) has a fascinating ideologically self-balancing life, since, in the words of Professor Michael C. Brannigan, he "went from being an ardent defender of traditional Confucianism to finally becoming a defender of Marxist-Maoist thought." (Brannigan 2000:37). Educated at Peking and Columbia universities, he taught at the universities of Pennsylvania and Hawaii, and finally went back to China where he lived out his life. He is best known for the scholarly work of his *History of Chinese Philosophy* (Fung 1952).

Concerning his method and cultural history orientation, Dr. Fung Yu-Lan is a Sinocentrist, since, he subsumes all pre-China philosophies under the banner of "Chinese philosophy." However, he does recognize the national origins and philosophical contributions of ancient East Asian philosophers, including: Hsun Tzu (v. Tuân Tử) and Kung-Sun Lung (v. Công Tôn Long) from the kingdom of Chao (v. Triệu), Tsou Yen (v. Trâu Diên) and others from the kingdom of Ch'i (v. Tề), Lao Tzu (v. Lão Tử) and others from the kingdom of Ch'u (v. Sở), K'ung Fu Tzu (v. Khổng Phu Tử) and others from the kingdom of Lu (v. Lỗ), and Meng Tzu (v. Mạnh Tử) from the kingdom of Tsou (v. Trâu).

In Chinese history, the age extending from the Ch'un Ch'iu period (722–481 B.C.) down to the beginning of the Han dynasty (206 B.C.–A.D. 220) is one of general emancipation, in which political institutions, social organization, and economic structure all undergo fundamental changes. The early Chou dynasty had been a time of rule by a feudal aristocracy, under which each of the feudal states was either a fief created by the Royal House of Chou, or a state that had already existed before the Chou. The ministers and great officers within these states were also all members of the ruling houses, and held their offices in hereditary perpetuity, whereas the common people were

[Source: Taken from Fung Yu-Lan, *A History of Chinese Philosophy*, volume I (Princeton: Princeton University Press, 1952), pp. 9–10, 12–14].

denied all share in the political power. The *Tso Chuan*,[1] under the year 535 B.C., states: "As the days have their divisions in periods of ten each, so men have their ten ranks. It is by these that inferiors serve their superiors, and that superiors perform their duties to the spirits. Therefore the king has the ruler (of each feudal state) as his subject; the rulers have the great prefects as their subjects; the prefects have their officers; the officers have their subalterns; the subalterns have their multitude of petty officers; the petty officers have their assistants; the assistants have their employees; the employees have their menials. For the menials there are helpers, for the horses there are grooms, and for the cattle there are cowherds. And thus there is provision for all things" (p. 616). With a government thus maintained by a feudal aristocracy holding hereditary offices and fiefs, it was inevitable that the social organization should also be based on an elaborately graded hierarchy.

The outstanding characteristic of the Warring States period (403–221 B.C.), however, was the gradual collapse of the feudal system, resulting in marked changes in the earlier rigid social system. This phenomenon was marked, on the one hand, by the rise during the Warring States period of many men, of comparatively lowly origin, to positions of great political importance; while on the other it was marked by the fall from power of many of the former ruling families. This movement reached a climax in 221 B.C., when Ch'in Shih-huang succeeded in unifying all China under the rule of the House of Ch'in, and dealt feudalism a decisive blow by relegating the royal families of all states except that of Ch'in to the level of the common people.

During the several years of civil warfare following the death of Ch'in Shih-huang in 210, it is true, several of the members of the former ruling families succeeded in raising armies and returning to power. And when unification was once more effected through the founding of the Han dynasty in 206, the first Han ruler, despite the fact that he was of plebeian origin, allowed feudalism

to be revived by granting fiefs to his meritorious ministers and to members of his own family, as well as by allowing several of the former nobles to retain their rank. The feudalism thus revived was only a shadow of its former self, however, and especially after a revolt of several nobles occurring in 154 B.C., it was greatly circumscribed by restrictive measures, among them one that all governing officials should be directly appointed by the Emperor. The final blow was dealt by the gradual establishment of the examination system under Emperor Wu-ti (140–87 B.C.), so that after that time feudalism almost ceased to exist.

We can find evidence of the breakdown of feudalism beginning already during the Ch'un Ch'iu period. Thus it is recorded that Ning Ch'i, a mere carter, while feeding his oxen, attracted the attention of Duke Huan of Ch'i (685–643) and so obtained office, and that Po-li Hsi, while a prisoner of war, was ransomed by Duke Mu of Ch'in (659–621) for the price of five ram skins, and so became the latter's counsellor. At the same time there was a corresponding decline of the aristocracy. The *Tso Chuan*, for example, under the year 539 B.C., makes the statement: "The Luan, the Ch'i, the Hsü, the Yüan, the Hu, the Hsü, the Ch'ing and the Po (all descendants of great families of the Chin state) are reduced to the position of menials" (p. 589). Confucius himself originally belonged to the nobility of the state of Sung, but because of poverty entered office and was 'once a keeper of stores,' and 'once in charge of the public fields,' both lowly offices. All this indicates how the nobles were gradually losing their positions and becoming a part of the common people. Institutions that had been based upon a graded hierarchy likewise gradually fell into oblivion, so that by the time of the founding of the Han dynasty, it was possible for a man of the common people to become Emperor.

Intimately connected with feudalism was the economic system known as the 'well-field' or *ching t'ien* system. According to this, all land was divided into large squares, each subdivided into nine smaller squares. Each of the eight outer of these nine squares was cultivated by one family

---

[1] *Cf. Mencius, Vb, 5.*

for its own use, while the produce of the ninth central square, cultivated in common by the eight families and called the 'public field,' went to the support of the overlord.[2] Under this system all land was ultimately the possession of the ruler. Thus the *Shih Ching* (Book of Odes) says: "Under the whole heaven, every spot is the sovereign's ground; to the borders of the land, every individual is the sovereign's subject" (II, vi, Ode 1, 2). The *Tso Chuan* also states, under the year 535: "The dominion of the Son of Heaven extends everywhere. The feudal lords have their own defined boundaries. Such is the ancient rule. Within the state and the kingdom, what ground is there which is not the ruler's? What individual of all whom the ground supports is there who is not the ruler's subject?" (p. 616).

Such terms as 'king's land' and 'king's subject' were in later times regarded merely as political concepts, but during the ancient feudal period they had economic meaning as well. The graded ranks of society which have been described above, were likewise not merely political and social, but also economic. In short, under the feudal system of ancient China, the Emperor (Son of Heaven), feudal lords, and ministers and great officers, were all overlords of the people, not only politically but also economically, and so when the Royal House of Chou invested the male branches of its family with land grants, those so invested acted both as political rulers and as economic landholders. These feudal lords, in their turn, divided this land among their relatives, and these relatives again among the common people for cultivation. The common people could not themselves own land, and so were mere agricultural serfs of their political and economic overlords. Consequently we find that the records of government of that time, as found in the *Tso Chuan* and *Kuo Yü*,[3] describe no more than the activities of a few noble families. As for the common people, they were required to labor for their lords in time of peace, while in time of war they had to be ready to sacrifice their lives. The relationship of serf to overlord is described by the historian Hsia Tseng-yu (died 1924), in his discussion of the question of the *ching t'ien* system:

"The truth of the matter probably is that the land was exclusively the possession of the nobles, and that the peasants were all attached to this land as serfs, this forming the basis of the distinction between the ordinary people and those who belonged to the Hundred Names (i.e., who bore a recognized family name, in contradistinction to the nameless serfs). Such a condition lasted until Lord Shang, of the state of Ch'in, abolished it. This act marked one phase of social progress."

The histories tell us that Shang Yang "destroyed the *ching t'ien* system, and opened up the paths and furrows between the fields . . . . . . The (ancient) imperial regulations thereupon disappeared, there was no limit upon encroachments, and among the common people there were wealthy men who accumulated millions (of coins)." This suffices to indicate how the agricultural serfs, following their emancipation, seized power and came into control of large land areas. The decay of the so-called *ching t'ien* system was undoubtedly one of the main tendencies of that age, and Shang Yang, by making especial use of political power, did no more than give it a conscious and exemplary impetus.

Another of the tendencies of the time was the changing status of the merchant class, which gradually rose till it acquired great power. Thus the *Ch'ien Han Shu* (History of the Former Han Dynasty) says:

"With the decline of the House of Chou, the rites (*li*) and laws fell into decay. . . . . . This falling

---

[2] The word *ching* or 'well,' as used here, represents the square fields, into which the land was divided under this system.—TR.

[3] 'Sayings of the States,' a collection of historical conversations which cover about the same period as the *Tao Chuan*, but are grouped geographically according to states, rather than chronologically.—TR.

away (from the old standards) reached the point where, among the officials and common people, there were none who did not set the (old) regulations aside and spurn what is fundamental (i.e., agriculture). The peasants became few and the merchants numerous. Of grain there was an insufficiency, and of (commercial) goods a superfluity. . . . . . Thereupon the merchants circulated goods difficult to obtain (i.e., rare and expensive luxuries); the artisans produced objects of no real utility; and the scholars instituted conduct subversive to morality, in their pursuit for immediate benefits and search for worldly wealth . . . . . . The grounds and groves of the rich underwent elaborate adornment, and their dogs and horses had a superabundance of meat and grain . . . . While among the common people, though all were (theoretically) of equal rank, some by the power of their wealth could become the masters of others" (ch. 91, p. 3).

Looked at from the economic point of view, it is evident that the collapse of feudalism was brought about through this continual increase of economic power of the former agricultural serfs and of the merchants, with the result that 'the imperial regulations disappeared,' and 'the rites and laws fell into decay.' The rise of the merchant class may be illustrated by such men as Hsien Kao, who, while a mere merchant, successfully protected the state of Cheng from the surprise attack of the state of Ch'in; and Lü Pu-wei, who, from the position of a great trader, became minister of the Ch'in state. These are examples of 'capitalists' who became directly involved in the political affairs of their day. Summing up, we may say that the breakdown of the system of hereditary revenues, and of the *ching t'ien* organization; the emancipation of the common people; and the amassing of private fortunes, were the outstanding changes in the economic structure during the ancient period.

These great changes began during the Ch'un Ch'iu period, and came to an end about the middle of the Han dynasty.

During this gradual collapse of the old institutions of an entire society, it is natural that there should have been a tendency among conservatives, seeing that "the spirit of the age is not that of antiquity, and men's hearts daily decline," to arise as upholders of these ancient institutions. Confucius was a man of this sort. Before these institutions had been shaken, the mere fact of their antiquity was sufficient to awaken in men's hearts a feeling of reverence. But once that they were actually in danger, their preservers, if they wished to gain a genuine following among the rulers and men of their time, were obliged to supply reasons for upholding the past and its institutions. Confucius had already begun this sort of work; the later Confucians continued it; and in this rests one of their great contributions.

The general tendency of the time was such, however, that these ancient institutions continued to disintegrate despite the attempts of the Confucians to uphold them. From the age of Confucius onward, there arose men who criticized or opposed these institutions; who wished to revise them; who wished to establish new institutions in their place; or who were opposed to all institutions whatsoever. The age was one of transition, during which the institutions of the past had lost their authority, and those of the new age had not yet been definitely formulated. It was inevitable, then, that it should also be one of uncertainty and divergence. Thus when the Confucians had advanced their arguments for the preservation of the past, other philosophers, holding divergent views, were forced, if they wished to gain a following, to explain in their turn the reasons why they considered their own doctrines superior. The Confucian philosopher, Hsün Tzŭ, refers to this situation when he says about the doctrines of twelve opposing philosophers: "What they support (all) seems reasonable; their teachings are (all) plausible" (*Hsün Tzŭ*, pp. 78, 79).

In this way men became accustomed to emphasis being laid upon logical presentation, a fact which resulted in the rise of the School of

Dialecticians, with its discussions on such subjects as 'the hard and the white, similarity and difference,' and its purely logical interest. Thus we see that the beginnings of rationalism coincide with the beginnings of philosophizing.

A number of quotations from contemporary literature allude to the prevailing intellectual anarchy of the time. The *Mencius* states:

"Sage-kings cease to arise, the feudal lords give rein to their lusts, and unemployed scholars indulge in unreasonable discussions" (III*b*, 9.)

The *Chuang-tzŭ* (ch. 33) says similarly:

"The world is in great confusion, the virtuous and the sage are obscured, morality and virtue have lost their unity, and there are many in the world who have seized a single aspect of the whole for their self enjoyment. . . . . Everyone in the world

does what he wishes and is a rule unto himself" (p. 439).

And the *I-wen Chih* (catalogue of the Imperial Han library, forming Chapter XXX of the *Ch'ien Han Shu*) states:

"The various philosophers belonged to ten schools, but there are only nine worthy of notice. They all began when royal control was lessening and the feudal nobles were becoming more powerful and differed widely in what they preferred and disliked. Just so the differing practices of the nine schools swarmed forth and had a common development. Each school picked a single point which was exalted as the good and was discussed so as to win the favor of the feudal lords" (*Aids*, p. 64).

Study Questions

A.1.3 Fung Yu-Lan, Causes for the Development of Philosophy During the Period of the Philosophers

1. Describe the changes of dynastic powers in the Central Plains (c. Chung Yuan [v. Trung Nguyên]) from the Spring–Autumn (Ch'un Ch'iu [v. Xuân Thu]) Period to the reign of Emperor Wu-Ti (v. Vũ Đế' 140–87 BCE).
2. Describe Fung's reconstruction of the "great changes" that "began during the Spring–Autum Period, and came to an end about the middle of the Han dynasty."
3. Explain Fung's reconstruction of the causes for the emergence of the various schools of ancient East Asian philosophies and make your critical response.

The Discussion of the Essentials of the Six Schools

Ssu-Ma T'an (v. Tử Mã Đàm)

The Introduction

Ssu-Ma T'an (v. Tử Mã Đàm [died 110 BCE]) was the father of Ssu-Ma Ch'ien (v. Tử Mã Thiên), the famous Han-Chinese Grand Historian (145-c. 86 BCE), who wrote the monumental *Shih Chi* (v. *Sử Ký*). The *Shih Chi* is the first general history of the ancient East Asian mainland and Han China, extending from their *legendary* beginnings down to the reign of Wu-ti (v. Vũ Đế 140–87 BCE) of the Han Dynasty. For the English translation, read *Records of the Grand Historian of China*, translated from the *Shih Chi* of Ssu-Ma Ch'ien by Burton Watson, 2 vols (New York: Columbia University Press, 1961).

There is no certainty as to the exact number of philosophical "schools" that had existed in the mainland of ancient East Asia *before* and during the "Period of the Hundred Schools of Philosophers" (551-c. 233 BCE). By the time of Meng Tzu (v. Mạnh Tử [ca. 371–289 BCE]), numerous schools were contending for public recognition. They are mentioned in the *Nan Hua Ching* (v. *Nam Hoa Kinh*) of Chuang Tzu (v. Trang Tử) as "the doctrines of the Hundred Schools." (chapter 33). By the middle of the Han Dynasty, the number of schools of thought might have been reduced to a total of six schools as classified by Ssu-Ma T'an. But the *I-wen Chih* (catalogue of the Imperial Han library), forming chapter XXX of the *Ch'ien Han Shu* (v. *Tiền Hán Thư*), fixes the number at 10: "The various philosophers belonged to ten schools, but there are only nine worthy of notice." [Fung 1952:14]

The "Great Commentary" on the *Book of Changes* says: "There is one moving force, but from it a hundred thoughts and schemes arise. All have the same objective, though their ways are different." [Hsi Tz'u 2:3b]. The schools of the yin-yang, the Confucianists, the Moists, the Logicians, the Legalists, and the Taoists all strive for good Government. It is simply that they follow and teach different ways, and some are more penetrating than others.

It has been my observation that the yin-yang school in its theories puts strong emphasis upon omens and teaches a great many things to be shunned and tabooed. Hence it causes men to feel restrained and bound by fear. But in its work of arranging correctly the all-important succession of the four seasons it fills an essential need.

The Confucianists are very broad in their interests but do not deal with much that is essential. They labor much and achieve but slight success. Therefore their discipline is difficult to carry out to the fullest. But in the way they order the rules of decorum between lord and subject and father and son, and the proper distinctions between husband and wife and elder and younger, they have something that cannot be altered.

The Moists are too stern in their parsimony to be followed and therefore their teachings cannot be fully applied. But in their emphasis upon what is basic [agriculture] and upon frugal usage they have a point that cannot be overlooked.

The Legalists are very strict and of small mercy. But they have correctly defined the distinctions between lord and subject, and between superior and inferior, and these distinctions cannot be changed.

The Logicians cause men to be overnice in reasoning and often to miss the truth. But the way in which they distinguish clearly between names and realities is something that people cannot afford not to look into.

The Taoists teach men to live a life of spiritual concentration and to act in harmony with the unseen. Their teaching is all-sufficient and embraces all things. Its method consists in following the seasonal order of the yin-yang school, of selecting what is good from the Confucian and Moist teachings, and adopting the important points of the Logical and Legalist schools. It modifies its position with the times and responds to the changes which come about in the world. In establishing customs and practices and administering affairs it does nothing that is not appropriate to the time and place. Its principles are simple and easy to practice; it undertakes few things but achieves much success.

Study Questions

A.1.4 Ssu-Ma T'an, The Discussion of the Essentials of the Six Schools

1. List the names of the six schools of ancient East Asian philosophies that Ssu-ma T'an (v. Tư Mã Đàm) identifies.
2. Explain the significance of each school and compare it with the others.
3. Explain the one common aspect that all the six schools share according to Ssu-ma T'an.

The Spirit of Chinese Philosophy

Fung Yu-Lan

There are many people who say that Chinese philosophy is a this-worldly philosophy. This opinion cannot be said to be either wholly right or wholly wrong.

On a superficial view these words are not wholly wrong, because on that view Chinese philosophy, irrespective of its different schools of thought, directly or indirectly concerns itself with government and ethics. It appears to emphasize society not the universe, the daily functioning of human relations and not hell and heaven, man's present life and not his life in a world to come. Mencius said, "The sage is the acme in human relations," and the sentence taken literally means that the sage is the morally perfect man in society. This ideal man being of this world, it seems that what Chinese philosophy calls a sage is a very different order of person from the Buddha in Buddhism and the saint in the Christian religion.

This, however, is only the superficial view of the question. Chinese philosophy cannot be understood in this over-simple way. So far as the main tenets of its tradition are concerned, if we understand them, they cannot be said to be wholly this-worldly, just as, of course, they cannot be said to be wholly other-worldly. We may use a newly

coined expression and say that this philosophy is world-transcending. The meaning of this is that it is both of this world and of the other world.

Chinese philosophy has one main tradition, one main stream of thought. This tradition is that it aims at a particular kind of highest life. But this kind of highest life, high though it is, is not divorced from the daily functioning of human relations. Thus it is both of this world and of the other world, and we maintain that it "both attains to the sublime and yet performs the common tasks". What Chinese philosophy aims at is the highest of realms, one which transcends the daily functioning of human relations, although it also comes within the scope of this daily functioning. That is: "It is not divorced from daily regular activity, yet it goes straight to what was before the heavens." The first of these two expressions represents the this-worldly side, the second the other-worldly side. That is to say that, both sides being present, Chinese philosophy is what we describe it to be, namely world-transcending. Because it is of this world it is concerned with common activity: because it is other-worldly it reaches up to the sublime: its attention is directed to both worlds, its concern is with both worlds.

Having this kind of spirit, it is at one and the same time both extremely idealistic and extremely realistic, extremely practical, though not in a shallow way. So also it is positive, but not in the sense of a man taking the wrong road and the faster he walks the more he deviates from the right road.

This-worldliness and other-worldliness stand in contrast to each other as do idealism and realism; and this is the antithesis between what we describe as the sublime and common activity. In ancient Chinese philosophy the antithesis was made between what was called "the inner" and "the outer", "the root," and "the branches" and "the fine" and "the coarse"; and after the Han era there was the contrast between what was called "the abstruse" and "the daily task", the contrast between abandoning the world and being in the world, between the active and the contemplative, between the essence and its functioning. All these contrasts are perhaps the same as the contrast between the sublime and the common, or (at any rate) these contrasts are of the same kind. In a world-transcending philosophy and its accompanying manner of life all these contrasts do not continue to be antithetical. This does not mean that, to put it shortly, they are abolished, but that according to the world-transcending view-point they are made to become a whole. The sublime and the common still exist with all their differences, but they are synthesized into one whole. How can this be done? This is one problem which Chinese philosophy attempts to solve, and herein lies the spirit of that philosophy, whilst in the solution it gives lies the contribution which it makes to the study of philosophy.

The philosophers of China hold that the highest life of all, that at which philosophy aims, is both this-worldly and other-worldly; and that the men who are in possession of this highest life are the sages. The life of the sage is a transcendent one, and the spiritual achievement of the Chinese sages corresponds to the saint's achievement in Buddhism and the West. They all come under the same head. But to transcend the world does not mean to be divorced from the world, and therefore the Chinese sage is not the kind of sage who is so sublime that he is not concerned about the business of the world. His character is described as one of sageness in its essence and kingliness in its manifestation. That is to say that in his inner sageness he accomplishes spiritual cultivation, in his outward kingliness he functions in society. It is not necessary that a sage should be the actual head of the government in his society. With regard to practical politics, for the most part the sage certainly has no opportunity to be such; and when the statement is made "sage within and king without" it only means that he who has the noblest spirit should theoretically be king. As to whether he actually had or had not the opportunity to be king, that is immaterial.

Since the character of the sage is one of sageness within and kingliness without, philosophy, according to the Chinese tradition, is a branch of learning which exists to enable men to possess this kind of character. Therefore what philosophy discusses is what the philosophers of China describe as the Tao (Way) of "sageness within and kingliness without".

In China, whatever the school of thought, all Chinese philosophy maintains this Tao in one way or another. But not every school satisfies the criterion of both attaining to the sublime and performing the common task. There are some schools which over-emphasize the sublime, some which over-emphasize the common. This means that some of the philosophies in China are near to being other-worldly, others near to being this-worldly. In the history of Chinese philosophy, from first to last, the more influential philosophers have been those who have attempted to synthesize the two sides, the sublime and the common.

Study Questions

A.1.5 Fung Yu-Lan, The Spirit of Chinese Philosophy

1. What is the "spirit of Chinese philosophy" according to Fung Yu-Lan?
2. Historically, would the "spirit of Chinese philosophy" as Fung Yu-Lan calls it be more appropriately designated the "spirit of ancient East Asian philosophies?" (Please note that Fung Yu-Lan says that he takes "the *T'ien Hsia* Chapter, in the *Chuang Tzu Book*" [Fung 1962:5] to be the textual basis for his characterization of the so-called "spirit of Chinese philosophy"? In the "T'ien Hsia" (v. Thiên Hạ) chapter of his *Nan Hua Ching* (v. *Nam Hoa Kinh*), Chuang Tzu (v. Trang Tử) talks about the moral and political orientations of ancient East Asian sages [pre-China]).
3. Should the "sageness within and kingliness without" be called the "spirit of Chinese philosophy" or the "spirit of ancient East Asian philosophies," if, "*spirit*" is understood as their highest essence?
4. Would it be more appropriate to consider the "sageness within and kingliness without" to be the "spirit of ancient East Asian political ideologies," which later became the "spirit of Chinese political ideology," if, "*spirit*" is understood as their highest political ideal?
5. If the "sageness within and kingliness without" is the highest ideal of ancient East Asian political *praxis* or one of the spirits of ancient East Asian and later Chinese philosophies, then, what were the true spirits of ancient East Asian and later Chinese philosophies? Can the approach that Radhakrishnan uses to characterize "the spirit of Indian philosophy" be applied to the task of redetermining the spirits of ancient East Asian and later Chinese philosophies?

A.1.6

The Southern Origin of Taoism

N. J. Girardot

The Introduction

"Taoism" (v. Đạoism) is normally divided into "Philosophical Taoism" (Tao Chia [v. Đạo Gia]) and "Religious Taoism" (Tao Chiao [v. Đạo Giáo]). Since Religious Taoism did not become operational as an organized religion until the time of the Later Han Dynasty (25–220 CE), the determination of the geocultural origins of Taoism must begin with the search for the "founder" of Philosophical Taoism.

Who was the "founder" of Philosophical Taoism? "Lao Tzu" (v. Lão Tử) is generally recognized to have enjoyed the status of "the founder of Taoism." In his monumental *Shih Chi* (v. *Sử Ký* [*Historical Records*]), Ssu Ma Ch'ien, the Grand Historian of China, offers the first biography of Lao Tzu in these words: "Lao Tzu was a native of Ch'u-jen hamlet, in Li-hsiang, in the district of K'u, in the state of Ch'u. His proper name was Erh, his pseudonym was Tan, and his family name was Li. . . . Lao Tzu practiced the Way (*Tao*) and the Power (*Te*)." [Cited in Fung Yu Lan 1952:171]. Concerning the ancient Southern kingdom of Ch'u (v. Sở), Dr. Fung Yu Lan explains: "Li Erh was a native of Ch'u, a large state on the southern periphery of the civilized China of ancient times, occupying much of present Honan, Hunan, Hupeh and Anhuei. It was in this state, according to the *Shih Chi*, that Confucius met most of the recluses who were mentioned in the *Lun Yu*. . . . Ch'u was inhabited by a people largely non-Chinese in origin, who had risen to prominence later than those of the other feudal states of China, and who were comparatively lacking in culture." [Fung Yu Lan 1952:175]

Lao Tzu (v. Lão Tử) was according to this account *not* a "civilized" Northerner but a "Southern barbarian" (*Nan man*). But whether this was true or not is yet to be decided. It is interesting to note that the "non-Chinese" people of the wet-rice growing Ch'u (v. Sở), who "were comparatively lacking in culture," had an "Old Master" (Old Baby), whose naturalistic philosophy is rather profound beyond anything the "civilized North" could match. It is also interesting to note that "most of the recluses" whom Confucius is said to have met preferred to live among *a* people who were "comparatively lacking in culture" rather than among the "civilized" peoples of the North.

Concerning the geocultural origins of Taoism, there are other alternative approaches that can be introduced for a scholarly search. One of the *multiculturally* creative approaches, that looks towards the Southern geocultural origins of Philosophical Taoism, was developed and executed with admirable scholarship by Professor N. J. Girardot. The approach that Professor Girardot uses in his *Myth and*

Meaning in Early Taoism is to analyze the intricate theoretical connections between "*the theme of chaos (hun-tun)*" in the *Tao Te Ching* (v. Đạo Đúc Kinh) and *Chuang Tzu* (v. Trang Tử) and the creation myths of the ancient barbarian South (now South China, Indochina, and insular Southeast Asia). Furthermore, the naturalistic philosophy in the Tao Te Ching tends to point to the wet rice growing South of the "Pa Yüeh" (v. Bách Việt) to be its geocultural roots.

On the archaeological culture of the Pa Yüeh (v. Bách Việt), see William Meacham, "Origins and Development of the Yueh Coastal Neolithic: A Microcosm of Culture Change on the Mainland of East Asia," in *The Origins of Chinese Civilization*, ed. David N. Keightley (Berkeley: University of California Press, 1983), pp. 147–75.

An examination of the cultural and mythological origins of Taoist tradition is crucial for a fuller understanding of the chaos theme; but I want to emphasize that no final solution is possible. The issue of tracing the cultural and historical origins of a civilizational tradition as complex as Taoism is always fraught with intractable problems relating to the paucity of historical evidence and the presuppositions of methodology. There is, however, sufficient evidence to say that most of the mythic units associated with the exposition of the *hun-tun* theme generally suggests a "southern" focus of cultural origin.

For some scholars such as Izutsu and Fung a belief in the southern origin of Taoism is prompted by what is seen to be a special connection with the ancient tradition of Ch'u, especially Ch'u shamanism, which was an important cultural component in the development of Chinese civilization during the Chou period.[1] There is, no doubt, a good deal of truth in this observation but it is, at the same time, too much of an oversimplification. A more expansive and balanced perspective on the "southern" origins of the mythology associated with the chaos theme is indicated by the work of several scholars who point to the general linguistic and cultural significance of the so-called Austroasiatic and Austronesian (=Mayalo-Polynesian) traditions or, more particularly, to the role of various local tribal traditions in the ancient cultural areas of south China, Indo-China, and insular southeast Asia.[2]

Moreover, while the ultimate origins of Ch'u probably go back to "northern" cultural sources (northeastern, northwestern, or "Hunnish"), even to the extent of having possible connections with the ancient Shang tradition and showing some traces of Altaic and Indo-European influence, the traditional (i.e., post-Chou) significance of the Ch'u culture is at least to some degree related to this same complex of "southern" local cultures.[3]

Maspero and Erkes were the first to emphasize the importance of primitive tribal culture and mythology for the study of Chinese myth and, as Inez de Beauclair notes for the tribal folklore of the Miao, "the motives of their myths, which they share with a number of peoples of southeast Asia and certain islands of the Pacific, may preserve the clue to the ancient Chinese cosmogony."[4] The implications of this for a reconstruction of ancient Chinese mythology have been especially developed by Eberhard, who traces "chains" of mythology and ritual back to specific archaic local cultures that were formative factors in the shaping of Chinese civilization. In this way he finds that the chain linked with the *hun-tun* theme is primarily reflective of an extremely ancient southern Liao[b] (=Lao) culture, along with traits coming from the Yao[b] and Thai cultures. For Eberhard this cultural matrix most probably can be traced back to an Austroasiatic cultural sphere. Eberhard concludes that "it is a chain that was important for the high culture during the earliest times."[5]

Eberhard's theory of "local cultures" and identifiable "chains" is controversial in theory and not wholly demonstrable in terms of evidence; but the work of Porée-Maspero, Kaltenmark, and Ho Ting-jui helps to substantiate and develop many of his findings, especially with regard to the cultural underpinnings of the *hun-tun* theme. Thus, Porée-Maspero's study of the Cambodian cycle of calendric rites is primarily addressed to an analysis of the myth-ritual pattern that she calls the ancient Man cultural complex. For Porée-Maspero, the Man Complex represents a religio-cultural pattern that is to some degree connected with Central Asiatic (especially the Shaka, Yue-Tche, Hun, and Parthians), Austroasiatic, and Austronesian language families and underlies many aspects of "barbarian" Chinese (i.e., such traditional Chinese ethnic groups as the Jung, Ti, I, Miao, Man, Yao[b], Liao[b], etc.),[6] Indo-Chinese, and southeast Asian traditions. Ho's work is similarly directed toward a comparative analysis of the folklore and mythology associated with insular, south Chinese, and Indo-Chinese cultures that can be traced back to Asiatic and Austronesian origins.[7]

Finally, Kaltenmark's monograph on the legends and symbolism associated with the honorary Chinese military title of *Fu-po chiang chün* ("general tamer of the flood") builds on the earlier work of Maspero and is directly pertinent to these considerations.[8] The legends of the Fu-po go back to the later Han period, or earlier, and are attributed to the historical figure of Ma Yüan who suppressed the revolt of the ancient Annamite tribes of Indo-China in A.D. 42. As Kaltenmark points out, the title of Fu-po, while applied to a historical figure and incident, harbors complex mythological motifs and refers to the heroic taming of the southern barbarians who had not been fully incorporated into the Chinese empire. From the Chinese point of view, the barbarians were usually understood in mythical terms so that the "flood" referred to in this official title suggests the mythic equation of "barbarian" with the *ssu-hai* or "four seas" outside the boundaries of the central kingdom.[9]

A parallel instance of a foundational "history" of a hero rooted in mythic themes is provided by Porée-Maspero, who analyzes the Chinese accounts of Hun-hui (or Hun-t'ien[b]), a barbarian hero from the south, and the origins of the kingdom of Fu-nan in Indo-China. It is significant, as Porée-Maspero remarks, that the name of the hero, Hun-hui, most probably represents a mythic theme transformed into a historical account since "*hun*, or *kun*, designates 'troubled waters,' a chaos, and *hui* has the sense of a 'river which has overflowed its banks' or 'disorder, confusion.'"[10] Moreover, it might also be noted that the alternate term for *hui* is *t'ien* (or *tien, chen*), which connotes the "settlement" of a kingdom or, more mythically, the rumbling and crashing sounds of drums and thunder. Porée-Maspero concludes, therefore, that the "name of the hero was 'deluge.' Can it be simply by chance that the accounts of the origins of Fu-nan reveal a story of the hero-saviour of the deluge?"[11]

Kaltenmark demonstrates that, in the process of civilizing the barbarians, the mythology and legends of the southern tribes were adopted or sinicized into an official Chinese ideology of cosmological and historical order. The symbolism related to the figure of the Fu-po was originally derived from various southern barbarian myths dealing with a demiurge hero (especially in the form of a dog, horse, or serpent) who orders the chaotic waters of the creation time. In this way, for example, the dog god P'an-hu of the Man culture is similar to the demiurge P'an-ku—"both are related with the deluge and chaos."[12] More generally, the figure of the Fu-po assimilates the mythological symbolism of the barbarian myths "where a demiurge puts an end to the deluge" and subsequently gives rise to a new creation.[13] The ambivalent hero of the creation time is at least partially identified with the vanquished chaos condition since in the creative act of establishing the ordered or human world, the demiurge always "risks reconstituting a new chaos by reuniting the assailed Heaven and submerged Earth into a single unformed mass."[14] As in the Emperor Hun-tun story from the *Chuang Tzu* where "lightning [Hu and Shu] put an end to Chaos by giving his sack-like form a human figure, Fu-po, as a great military figure, puts an end to anarchy by subduing the barbarians with the thunder of his drums and the virtue of his arrows [these are also details in the Hun-hui accounts]. . . . The Chinese tried to 'sinicize' the barbarian divinities: their military becomes the thunder which represents celestial justice; the vanquished divinities, chained to a column, become the guardians of the Chinese order."[15]

As indicated by this quotation, many of the mythic motifs uncovered by Kaltenmark are identical with the theme of chaos found in the Taoist texts. Kaltenmark's findings, therefore, support the contention that there is a special southern or "barbarian" focus for the mythological symbolism associated with hun-tun. Kaltenmark's analysis also helps to clarify the process of "sinicization" or the "Chinese" reinterpretation of elements from various local cultures—that is, the process whereby mythic themes from local religious cults are reworked into an official sacred history that validates the imperial order. The imperial or Confucianized "sinicization" of the barbarian myths associated with the figure of Fu-po represents an obverse parallel to the Taoist assimilation of many of the same materials. Whereas in the official version the emphasis is on the heroic triumph over a destructive chaos condition (deluge, barbarian revolt, etc.) and the reestablishment and preservation of the civilized order, the Taoist reinterpretation of similar mythic themes stresses the artificiality of the human order and the need to reidentify with the condition or creature of chaos. Furthermore, it is important to realize that in the Confucian and Taoist sinicized versions of tribal mythology the original demiurgic figure (animal ancestor) is fundamentally ambiguous with respect to the chaos condition and can be either the heroic "tamer of the flood" or the agent responsible for, and identified with, the return of chaos.

Both Ho and Porée-Maspero's findings, along with Kaltenmark's corroborating work, will prove to be valuable in the next chapter when I set out

the salvation pattern of egg-gourd-deluge; but at this point I would like only to stress the relevance of Porée-Maspero's thesis for suggesting a general linguistic, historical, and cultural foundation for the "foreign" or "barbarian" connotations associated with the hun-tun theme in Taoism. Porée-Maspero, in fact, describes the overall religio-cultural pattern of the southern Man tradition as the "k'un-lun complex" or what could also be called the hun-tun complex.[16] Functionally, as I will develop below, the K'un-lun mythology (themes of deluge, animal ancestor, and the salvation of a primal couple in a gourd-drum boat) is closely related to many of the primary symbolic motifs found in the Taoist use of the chaos theme. K'un-lun is a term (as well as the term hun-tun) initially related to the ancient Jung tribes in Chinese texts and "the name of K'un-lun was equally used to designate the populations of Indo-China: Chams, Khmers, inhabitants of the Prome region."[17] Porée-Maspero goes on to say:

> K'un-lun was primitively the name of one of the Jung tribes, and it is in relation to the Jung that we find the first historical mention of bronze drums. Certain Jung were also said to be born from a dog and they are also associated with the downfall of the Yin [Shang] . . . M. Rolf Stein has shown that the theme of the calabash-gourd as a perfect closed world, grotto or ancestral cavern, and the cornucopia motifs, are all equivalent to the idea of k'un-lun which is also related to the theme of chaos as the vast watery condition of the flood.[18]

In this sense the myth-ritual pattern reconstructed by Porée-Maspero depicts K'un-lun as a veritable Mt. Ararat, which appeared in the midst of the chaotic waters of the deluge and served as the landing place for the gourd-drum-boat of the primordial couple. This was also the place for the subsequent creation of man and the regeneration of the world.[19]

Porée-Maspero notes that the use of coupled words where only the initial sound is differentiated, such as *hun-tun* and *k'un-lun* (as well as many archaic Sanskrit words like *Pulinda-Kulinda, Anga-Vanga, Kosala-Tosala,* etc.), may betray the influence of the ancient Man cultural complex and, linguistically speaking, reveal a linkage with that "vast family of Austroasiatic languages which in India is related to the Munda, or Kolarian, languages."[20] There is, however, no monolithic solution to the problem of linguistic origins since the word *hun*[d] shows a complex affinity with various central and western Asiatic nomadic cultures (i.e., the Huns and the Hsuing-nu), which have perhaps some ultimate connection with Indo-European languages and traditions.[21]

From the standpoint of the imperial Chinese tradition, inculcated with the chauvinistic values of Confucianism, words like *hun-tun* and *k'un-lun*, which were originally associated with mythologies of the deluge and chaos, became general derogatory expressions for uncouth, uncivil, or "barbarian" peoples. Maenchen-Helfen points out, for example, that the term *hun*[d] was used by the Chinese as a "transcription of **aryun* 'half-breed,' the offspring of a mixed marriage"; and Link has noted that the famous Buddho-Taoist Tao-an was called "Little K'un-lun"—an epithet that was "used as a vulgar term of opprobrium in a somewhat similar way that 'little Darky' has been used in our own language."[22]

Despite the general "barbarian," "asiatic," or "southern" (used broadly to refer to a mixture of cultural factors some of which originally had a central or northwestern cultural origin) locus of this terminology, it is important to reiterate that this does not make the *hun-tun* theme in Taoism essentially non-Chinese. Different local cultures go back to the very beginnings of the Chinese civilization in the neolithic and Shang periods and were integral factors in the shaping of the high tradition throughout the Chou and Han periods.[23] The real issue of the foreignness of the *hun-tun* terminology is more a matter of the evaluation and interpretation of Chinese civilization from the standpoint of what became the official or orthodox ideology of Confucianism. It must be remembered

that Confucianism itself also harbors important traits that may be labeled as "barbarian" in origin.[24] It is therefore not so much the case that *kun-lun* or *hun-tun* were really foreign words or concepts but that they were terms applied to those elements outside the norms of the self-defined Great Tradition of Confucianism.

Pertinent to this whole discussion is the need to avoid theories that tend to resolve the contrast between Confucianism and Taoism into a simple north-south cultural polarity—the view that the more ancient and more properly "Chinese" northern cultural matrix engendered Confucianism as its basic ideological and symbolic mode of expression and that later extrinsic additions from southern "barbarian" cultures nurtured Taoism as a basic mode of expression.[25] The problem is that such theories grow out of the attempt to validate the traditional self-image of Confucianism as the purest manifestation of Chinese culture. From a more neutral historical perspective that respects the complexity of Chinese cultural origins, it is almost possible to stand this type of xenophobic theory on its head. Thus the so-called "southern" cultures, or what more properly involves a complex blend of Austroasiatic, Austronesian, and central, or originally "northern" and "western" Asiatic (Altaic as well as Indo-European) elements are crucial in the development of Chinese civilization. Furthermore, such "foreign" cultural elements may also have played a role in the evolution of the earliest Chinese neolithic and Shang traditions.[26] It is sufficient to emphasize that if the *hun-tun* theme possesses "le caractère méridional," this does not necessarily mean that it is foreign or peripheral to the mainstream of Chinese tradition.[27]

As a final point on the issue of cultural origins, it would be disingenuous if I did not stress that, while there is much merit in the theory of a special connection between the *hun-tun* theme in Taoism and a "southern" cultural sphere, such an identification has only a very general applicability and relevance. It is helpful comparatively since it provides some clues as to a specific context of culture and myth, but it cannot be taken as a controlling factor in my analysis. Even more so than with the unresolved problems associated with the Indo-European hypothesis, there is still a great deal of controversy concerning the origin, nature, coherence, and interrelationship of those languages and cultures called "Austroasiatic" and "Austronesian."[28] Despite the wealth of detailed evidence and suggestive argument provided by Porée-Maspero, these problems are only compounded when one postulates the existence of an ancient Indo-Chinese cultural tradition known as the Man or K'un-lun complex.[29]

Notes

1. See above, chapter 3 [of Giradot's book-ccp], for Izutsu's views; and Fung Yu-Lan, *A History of Chinese Philosophy*, trans. Derk Bodde (Princeton: Princeton University Press, 1952) 1:175–176.

2. Besides the works of Eberhard, Kaltenmark, Porée-Maspero, and Ho cited below, see Obayashi Taro, "The Origins of Japanese Mythology," *Acta Asiatica* 31 (1977): 1–23; Franz Numazawa, "Background of Myths on the Separation of Sky and Earth from the Point of View of Cultural History," *Scientia* (Milan) 88 (1953): 28–35; Leopold Walk, "Das Flut-Geschwisterpaar als Ur- und Stammelternpaar der Menschheit. Ein Beitrag zur Mythengeschichte Süd-un Südostasiens," *Mitteilungen der Anthropologischen Gesellschaft in Wien* 78–79 (1949): 60–115; Toichi Mabuchi, *The Ethnology of the Southwestern Pacific* (Taipei: Orient Cultural Service, 1974), pp. 65–160, 221–242; and Chang Kwang-chih, "Prehistoric and Early Historic Culture Horizons and Transitions in South China," *Current Anthropology* 5 (1964): 359–406.

3. See Major, "Research Priorities," pp. 227–230; and Eberhard, *LC* [*The Local Cultures of South and East China*-ccp], pp. 70–71 (especially in relation to the Yao).

4. Inez de Beauclair, *Tribal Cultures of Southwest China* (Taipei: Orient Cultural Service, 1974). p. 99. Maspero's "Legendes mythologiques" points to the comparative significance of the White and Black Thai myths in Indochina; and Erkes in his "Chinesisch-Amerikanischen Mythenparallelen," *T'oung Pao* 24 (1941), provides an even broader base of comparison (i.e. myths of the Battak of Sumatra, the Semang of Malacca, and the Goldi of Amur). On "southern" local cultures see H. J. Wiens, *Han Chinese Expansion in South China* (n.p.: Shoe String Press, 1967); and F. M. Lebar, G. C. Hickey, and J. K. Musgrave, *Ethnic Groups of Mainland Southeast Asia* (New Haven: Human Relations Area Files, 1964).

5. Eberhard, *LC*, p. 446.

6. E. Porée-Maspero, *Étude sur les rites agraires des Cambodgiens* (Paris: Muton and Co., 1962, 1964, 1969), 3 vls., pp. 567–569, 703 ff., 771 ff.

7. Ho, *Myths and Legends*, pp. 165 ff.

8. M. Kaltenmark, "Le Dompteur des flots," *Han-hiue* (Peking) 3 (1948), pp. 1–112.

9. Ibid., p. 1.

10. Porée-Maspero, *Rites agraires*, p. 795.

11. Ibid., p. 796. See also pp. 532–533.

12. Kaltenmark, "Le Dompteur des flots," p. 76.

13. Ibid., p. 78.

14. Ibid.

15. Ibid., pp. 79–80.

16. Porée-Maspero, *Rites agraires*, pp. 703 ff., 783 ff. See also Kachorn Sukhabanji, "Two Thai MSS on the K'un Lun Kingdom," in *Symposium on Historical Archaeological, and Linguistic Studies on Southern China, South-East Asia, and the Hong Kong Region*, ed. F. S. Drake (Hong Kong University Press, 1967), pp. 70–74.

17. Porée-Maspero, *Rites agraires*, p. 786.

18. Ibid., p. 787. See also L. de Saussure, "L'etymologie du nom des monts K'ouen-louen," *T'oung Pao* 20 (1921): 370–371.

19. Porée-Maspero, *Rites agraires*, pp. 832–833; and Kaltenmark, "Dompteur des flots," p. 56.

20. Porée-Maspero, *Rites agraires*, p. 780.

21. O. Maenchen-Helfen, "The Ethnic Name Hun," in *Studia Serica Bernhard Kalgren Dedicata*, ed. Sören Egerod (Copenhagen: E. Munksgaard, 1959), pp. 223–238. See also B. Laufer, *Sino-Iranica* (1919; reprint ed., Taipei: Ch'eng-Wen, 1967), pp. 248–249. On the linguistic relation between Malayo-Polynesian and Sino-Tibetan, see especially Chang Kwang-Chih, "A Working Hypothesis for the Early Cultural History of South China," *Bulletin of the Institute of Ethnology, Academia Sinica* 7 (1959): 95–97.

22. Maenchen-Helfen, "Ethnic Name," p. 224; and A. Link, "The Biography of Shih Tao-an," *T'oung Pao* 46 (1958): 10.

23. See especially Eberhard, *LC*, on this, pp. 1–31; and also Judith Triestman, *The Prehistory of China* (New York: Doubleday and Co., 1970), pp. 103–143.

24. As, for example, found in the official cosmological-historical theories of Tsou-yen and Tung Chung-shu see John S. Major, "Myth, Cosmology, and the Origins of Chinese Science," *Journal of Chinese Philosophy* 5 (1978), pp. 1–20.

25. See P. Pelliot, *T'oung Pao* 28 (1931): 468; and Granet, *Pensee*, p. 412.

26. See, for example, Major, "Research Priorities," pp. 231–233; and his review of K. C. Chang and Ping-ti Ho's works on Chinese cultural origins in *Isis* 68 (1977): 639–640. See also David Keightley's review, "Ping-ti Ho and the Origins of Chinese Civilization," *Harvard Journal of Asiatic Studies* 37 (1977): 381–411. For possible Indo-European influence see E. G. Pulleyblank, "Chinese and Indo-Europeans," *Journal of the Royal Asiatic Society* (1966): 304; Tor Ulving, "Indo-European Elements in Chinese," *Anthropos* 63/64 (1968/1969): 944–951: Major, "Myth and Origins," passim; and Prusek, *Chinese Statelets*, pp. 9–20. For a discussion that essentially supports the view adopted here see Chang Kwang-chih, "A Working Hypothesis for the Early Cultural History of South China," pp. 75–103. Chang considers the ancient cultural complex of south China to be a "Lungshanoid" extension of the north China neolithic, a perspective that recognizes that "various local phases came into being in the South as the result of adaptation to various kinds of environment and of different historical experience" (p. 94).

27. See Pelliot, *T'oung Pao* 28 (1931): 428.

28. See, for example, Nancy Kleiber, "The Controversy About the Austronesian Homeland," *Anthropologica* 11 (1969): 151–163; Isidore Dyen, "The Austronesian Languages and Proto-Austronesian," in *Current Trends in Linguistics*, ed. Thomas A. Sebeok (The Hague: Mouton, 1963) 8:5–12; Paul K. Benedict, *Austro-Thai Language and Culture* (New Haven: Human Relations Area Files, 1975), pp. 464–490 ("Austro-Thai and Austroasiatic"); B. J. Terwiel, "The Origin of the T'ai Peoples Reconsidered," *Oriens Extremus* 25 (1978): 239–258; and most recently, Donn Bayard, "The Roots of Indochinese Civilization: Recent Developments in the Prehistory of Southeast Asia," *Pacific Affairs* 53 (1980): 89–114.

29. See Frank Reynolds, "Buddhism and the Anthropologists: Some Comments Concerning Recent Works on Southeast Asia," *History of Religions* 11 (1972): 303–313; and A de Hauteclocque, "Agriculture et religion: rites et légendes des cambodgiens," *Annales Economies-Sociétés-Civilizations* 18 (1963): 102–1006. Some note should be taken of the panbabylonian theories of Ling Shun-shen who argues for a linguistic and cultural origin of K'un-lun symbolism in the tradition of Mesopotamian ziggurats see his "K'un-lun chiu yu Hsi Wang Mu," *Bulletin of the Institute of Ethnology, Academia Sinica* 22 (1966): 235–255 (English summary). Occam's razor suggests that this kind of hypothesis is least probable as a satisfactory explanation of the material.

Study Questions

A.1.6 N. J. Girardot, The Southern Origin of Taoism

1. Describe how Girardot questions the validity of a belief in "the special connection" between "the southern origin of Taoism" with "the ancient tradition of Ch'u [v. Sở-ccp], especially Ch'u shamanism, which was an important cultural component in the development of Chinese civilization during the Chou period."
2. Describe why Girardot maintains that there is "the need to avoid theories that tend to resolve the contrast between Confucianism and Taoism into a simple north-south cultural polarity—the view that the more ancient and more properly 'Chinese' northern cultural matrix engendered Confucianism as its basic ideological and symbolic mode of expression and that later extrinsic additions from southern 'barbarian' cultures nurtured Taoism as a basic mode of expression."
3. Show how Girardot demonstrates the "merit" of the theory that sees "a special connection between the *hun-tun* [v. *hỗn độn*-ccp] theme in Taoism and a 'southern' cultural sphere" as the cultural basis for any authentic reconstruction of "the southern origin of Taoism."

The Parable of the Raft

The Buddha

The Introduction

The "Buddha" (563–483 BCE) is one of the many titles of Siddhartha Gautama that he was honored by his followers. Many fascinating aspects of his life and teachings were later fictionalized to assure the continued success of Buddhism as an all-Asian religious movement. But a few items can be viewed as historical facts. The first fact is that Siddhartha Gautama was born a prince to the family of King Suddhodana and Empress Maya of the *non-Aryan* Shakya kingdom (now Nepal). Together with Yasodhara, he fathered a son, whom he named Rahula (Chain). By the age of twenty-nine, facing the first intellectual crisis of his life after supposedly witnessing the four sights of life (an old man, a sick man, a dead man, and an ascetic), Siddhartha Gautama renounced the world in order to search for their true causes.

The second fact is that Siddhartha Gautama claimed or was claimed by his disciples that he achieved his "Buddhahood" (Enlightenment) at the foot of a *bodhi* tree (tree of knowledge) in the town of Bodh Gaya after six years of learning and ascetic practice since his "Great Departure." Siddhartha Gautama became the "Buddha" (Awakened One or Enlightened One). What did he awake from? He awoke from the state of his own ignorance when he came to know *self-consciously* the true cause of *samsara* (cycle of rebirth) and the best solution for its complete removal and a truly happy life (*nirvana*).

The third fact revealed that the Buddha was not only a great philosopher but also the greatest man of action that the ancient South Asian peninsula had ever known. After carefully deliberating whether he should or should not teach others about his Buddhahood experience, the Buddha went to the Deer Park in Benaras, the holiest city of Hinduism, where, he delivered the "First Sermon" to his former five ascetic companions. This first missionary activity of the Buddha won him his original disciples for his future Sangha (monastic order) that he launched for the historically unprecedented mass conversion of all people to his Dharma (Doctrine or Teachings).

The initial act of abandoning his family, his kingdom, and his princeship for the purpose of discovering the true causes of birth, sickness, aging, and death, Siddhartha Gautama made himself a student of philosophy. The conscious decision to meditate at the foot of a *bodhi* tree for his self-discovery of the true nature of life and reality until he died if he failed and the self-realization of his Buddhahood earned Siddhartha Gautama the status of a true philosopher. For this philosophical achievement, we salute the Shakyamuni and the Shakya culture! His philosophy of life we shall call the Buddhaian philosophy and its cultural root we credit the Shakya culture. But the very moment when the Buddha accepted his first disciples to his future sangha, he finally *left* the realm of philosophy and entered the realm of religion. From the unceremonial death of a philosopher emerged the greatest missionary of ancient South Asia.

Was the Buddha truly self-enlightened as he claimed?

That is the philosophical question for those who search for self-enlightenment to ponder!

"Monks, I will teach you Dhamma—the Parable of the Raft—for crossing over, not for retaining. Listen to it, attend carefully, and I will speak.

"A man going along a high-road might see a great stretch of water, the hither bank dangerous and frightening, the farther bank secure, not frightening. But if there were no boat for crossing by or a bridge across for going from the not-beyond to the beyond, he might think: 'If I were to collect sticks, grass, branches, foliage and to tie a raft, then, depending on the raft and striving with my hands and feet, I might cross over safely to the beyond.' If he carried out his purpose, then, crossed over, gone beyond, it might occur to him: 'Now, this raft has been very useful to me. Depending on it and striving with my hands and feet, I have crossed over safely to the beyond.

Suppose now, having put this raft on my head or lifted it on to my shoulder, I should proceed as I desire?' Now, monks, in doing this is that man doing what should be done with that raft?"

"No, Lord."

"But, monks, it might occur to him after he has crossed over and gone beyond: 'Now, this raft has been very useful to me. Depending on it and striving with my hands and feet, I have crossed over safely to the beyond. Suppose now, having beached this raft on the dry ground or having submerged it in the water, I should proceed as I desire?' In doing this, monks, that man would be doing what should be done with that raft. Even so is the Parable of the Raft Dhamma taught by me for crossing over, not for retaining."

Study Questions

A.1.7 The Buddha, The Parable of the Raft

1. Explain the functional status of Buddhism as taught by the Buddha through "The Parable of the Raft."
2. Taking the *spirit* of "The Parable of the Raft" as intended by the Buddha, explain how you would view a particular Eastern philosophy or the whole body of Eastern philosophies *while* you are studying them and *after* you have studied them.
3. Should the *spirit* of the Buddhaian teaching be applied to all doctrines that one happens to learn, whether a religious doctrine, a political ideology, a scientific theory, or a personal belief?

Methodology in Writing a Philosophical Article and Yoga and Buddhist Meditation for Classroom Management

An Upanishadic Yoga for Whole Being Self-Control

The Shvetashvatara Upanishad

The Introduction

What is yoga? It is difficult to define yoga. According to Professor Mircea Eliade, etymologically, the word "yoga" is derived from "the root *yuj*, 'to link together,' 'to bind closely,' 'to harness,' 'to bring under the yoke,' and this root also is the source of the Latin *jungere* and *jugum*, the English *yoke*, etc." [Eliade 1969:9] He further states that yoga is used to distinguish "every *technique of asceticism* and every *method of meditation*." But with this etymology of the word, yoga, according to Professor Haridas Chaudhuri, "literally means union and control." [Chaudhuri 1974:21] By "control," he means "appropriate self-discipline." And by "union," he explains: "It signifies the union of man with God, of the individual with the universal reality, of each with the All of existence. It means union of the mortal with the eternal. It implies union of the mind with the inmost centre of one's own being, the self or *atman*—union of the conscious mind with the deeper levels of the unconscious—resulting in the integration of personality." [*Ibid*]

In his famous *Yoga Sutra*, Patanjali (2nd century BCE) gives this definition of yoga: "Yoga is contemplation (samadhi), and it is a characteristic of the mind pervading all its planes." [Cited in Radhakrishnan and Moore 1957:454] Concerning this meaning, the *Tattva-vaisharadi* of Vacaspati Mishra (ca. 850 CE) offers this explanation: "The commentator now removes the doubt as to the meaning of the word '*yoga*,' which arises from its ordinary connotation. Thus says he, '*Yoga* is contemplation.' The word '*yoga*' is derived from the root *yuj*, to contemplate, and not from the root *yujir*, to join, in which latter case it would mean conjunction." [*Ibid*] Since the human mind is viewed to have the "three qualities" (the nature of illumination, activity, and inertia), the *Yoga Sutra* says "Yoga is the restraint of mental modifications."

Yoga has enjoyed a superior status in all the religious and philosophical traditions of India as it had in the peninsula of ancient South Asia. There are different kinds of yoga: Jnana Yoga (Yoga of Knowledge), Bhakti Yoga (Yoga of Religious Devotion), Karma Yoga (Yoga of Selfless Service), Raja Yoga (Yoga of Kingliness), and Hatha Yoga (Yoga of Physical Exercise). Of the Yoga of Knowledge, there are six darshanas (six schools of Hindu philosophy). One of these six yoga darshanas is called the Yoga school, which shares a dualistic metaphysics with the Samkhya school.

35

Yoga is normally claimed to have been invented by the Hindu sages of ancient Vedic times (ca. 1500–400 BCE). But yoga might have originated with the Dravidian (Indus Valley) Civilization because about half a dozen Indus seals show figures in yogic posture. One seal shows "a personage, apparently with three faces, seated in yoga on a low dais, before which stand two opposed gazelles. Four beasts surround him in the four directions: a tiger, elephant, rhinoceros, and water buffalo. His immense headdress of horns with its towering crown between suggests (like the headdress of the goddess in the tree) the form of a trident (*trishula*). And the phallus, exposed, is erect." [Campbell 1976:168–69 with figure]

The *Shvetashvatara Upanishad* is one of the collection of philosophical scriptures, known collectively as the *Upanishads*. For background information on the *Upanishads*, see C.4.1 (Part C, chapter 4, topic 1).

Rules and Results of Yoga

8. Holding his body steady with the three [upper parts[1]] erect,
    And causing the senses with the mind to enter into the heart,
    A wise man with the Brahma-boat should cross over
    All the fear-bringing streams.
9. Having repressed his breathings here in the body, and having his movements checked,
    One should breathe through his nostrils with diminished breath.
    Like that chariot yoked with vicious horses,[2]
    His mind the wise man should restrain undistractedly.
10. In a clean level spot, free from pebbles, fire, and gravel,
    By the sound of water and other propinquities
    Favorable to thought, not offensive to the eye,
    In a hidden retreat protected from the wind, one should practise Yoga.
11. Fog, smoke, sun, fire, wind,
    Fire-flies, lightning, a crystal, a moon—
    These are the preliminary appearances,
    Which produce the manifestation of Brahma in Yoga.

12. When the fivefold quality of Yoga has been produced,
    Arising from earth, water, fire, air, and space,[3]
    No sickness, no old age, no death has he
    Who has obtained a body made out of the fire of Yoga.
13. Lightness, healthiness, steadiness,[4]
    Clearness of countenance and pleasantness of voice,
    Sweetness of odor, and scanty excretions—
    These, they say, are the first stage in the progress of Yoga.

The Vision of God

14. Even as a mirror stained by dust
    Shines brilliantly when it has been cleansed,
    So the embodied one, on seeing the nature of the Soul (Ātman),
    Becomes unitary, his end attained, from sorrow freed.
15. When with the nature of the self, as with a lamp,
    A practiser of Yoga beholds here the nature of Brahma,
    Unborn, steadfast, from every nature free—

[3] That is, the five cosmic elements.
[4] Or, with another reading, *alolubhatvam*, 'freedom from desires.'

[1] Head, chest, and neck—so prescribed at BhG. 6. 13.
[2] Described at Katha 3. 4.

[Source: Taken from the *Shvetashvatara Upanishad* 3.2, printed in R. E. Hume, trans., *The Thirteen Principal Upanishads* (London: Oxford University Press, Humphrey Milford, 1921), pp. 398–99].

By knowing God (*deva*) one is released from all fetters!

The Immanent God

16. That God faces all the quarters of heaven. Aforetime was he born, and he it is within the womb.

He has been born forth. He will be born. He stands opposite creatures, having his face in all directions.[5]

17. The God who is in fire, who is in water, who has entered into the whole world, who is in plants, who is in trees—to that God be adoration!—yea, be adoration!

[5] This stanza = VS. 32. 4.

Study Questions

A.2.1 An Upanishadic Yoga for Whole Being Self-Control

1. Explain how and where to practice yoga.
2. List the three types of benefits that yogic practice can bring.
3. Meditate on the *universal* immanence of God during the second part of your yogic practice.
4. First, close your eyes and practice yoga as instructed in the text. Then, after your yogic practice, write down whatever problems you had with your mind and body while you were practicing yoga.
5. Then, close your eyes and practice yoga as before, but, now, focus your mind on your breath *single-mindedly* by following it *closely* when you inhale and exhale as a specific device for self-control (mind and body). After you are through, write down *the results* of your yogic practice.
6. Should each student control one's mind and body in class? Explain your response.

A.2.2

Buddhist Meditation for Classroom Mindfulness

The Introduction

Buddhist meditation (*dhyana*), which is originally derived from Hindu yoga, began with the meditative practice of the Buddha. The master of yoga, while sitting at the foot of the *bodhi* tree in the town of Bodh Gaya, Siddhartha Gautama, decided to employ yoga for his philosophical meditation on the true nature of life and reality. After seven days of concentrated meditation in the highest and purest degree, Siddhartha Gautama attained Buddhahood (Awakening or Enlightenment). Using the spiritual power of yogic meditation as his philosophical method, Siddhartha Gautama came to understand that *dukkha* (suffering) is the true nature of life, which is caused by human "*tanha*" (desire or craving), and the Noble Eightfold Path is the remedy. Because of its whole-being harmonizing and heuristic powers, yogic meditation became the Buddha's established method of teaching and all-purpose self-cultivation. The tradition of Buddhist meditation had thus originated and has continued until today.

One main theoretico-methodological distinction between the original Buddhian method of meditation and the later Buddhist mindfulness should be pointed out here. The Buddha made use of deep meditation (dhyana) as the main philosophical method to contemplate about the nature of human life and the new alternative lifestyle for self-liberation, which are revealed in his "First Sermon" rather than about the nature of reality (totality of the natural world). The later Buddhist method of mindfulness focuses on the whole-being self-awareness and self-mastery of both the subjective and objective realities. The philosophical end is to *personally* comprehend "*shunyata*" (*emptiness*) as the true nature of all that is. Being armed with this "*prajnaparamita*" (*perfection of wisdom*), one can achieve total self-liberation by freeing oneself from one's own dualistic thinking, which is the ultimate cause of "*avidya*" (*ignorance*), and the immediate cause of *dukkha*.

Was the Buddha still trapped in dualistic thinking when he declared in his "First Sermon" that "*tanha*" (desire or craving) is the true cause of dukkha and his Dharma is the ultimate vehicle for one to cross over the other shore of "*nirvana*" from this worldly "*samsara*" (cycle of rebirth)?

Monks, there is one road, one path for beings to purify themselves, to transcend sorrow and grief, to overcome suffering and melancholy, to attain the right way, to realize nirvana: that is the fourfold establishment of mindfulness. What are the four mindfulnesses? They are . . . the mindful contemplation of the body . . . the mindful contemplation of the feelings . . . the mindful contemplation of thoughts . . . and the mindful contemplation of the elements of reality.

How does a monk practice the mindful contemplation of the body? In this way: He goes to the forest, or to the foot of a tree, or to an empty room, and he sits down, cross-legged, keeps his back straight, and directs his mindfulness in front of him. Mindfully, he breathes in, mindfully, he breathes out; breathing in a long breath, he knows "I am breathing in a long breath"; breathing out a long breath, he knows "I am breathing out a long breath"; breathing in a short breath, he knows "I am breathing in a short breath"; breathing out a short breath, he knows "I am breathing out a short breath.". . .He should be like a lathe operator who knows that "I am making a long turn" when he is making a long turn and that "I am making a short turn" when he is making a short turn. . . . Thus a monk practices mindfully contemplating his body.

Furthermore, when a monk is walking, he knows "I am walking," and when he is standing, knows "I am standing," and when he is sitting, knows "I am sitting," and when he is lying down, knows "I am lying down." Whatever posture his body may take, he knows that he is taking it. . . . Thus a monk practices mindfully contemplating his body.

And also, a monk is fully mindful of what he is doing, both going and coming, looking straight ahead and looking away, holding out his bowl or retracting it, putting on his robes, carrying his bowl, eating, drinking, chewing, tasting, defecating, urinating, moving, standing, sitting, sleeping, waking, talking, being quiet. . . . Thus a monk practices mindfully contemplating his body.

And also, a monk considers his body itself, from the soles of his feet upward and from the top of his head downward, wrapped as it is in skin and filled with all sorts of impurities. He reflects, "In this body, there is hair, body-hair, nails, teeth, skin, flesh, sinews, bones, marrow, kidneys, heart, liver, pleura, spleen, lungs, colon, intestines, stomach, feces, bile, phlegm, pus, blood, sweat, fat, tears, lymph, saliva, snot, synovia, and urine." . . . Thus a monk practices mindfully contemplating his body.

And also, a monk considers his body . . . with regard to the elements that compose it. He reflects, "In this body, there is earth, water, fire, and air. . . ." He should think of these elements that make up the body as though they were pieces of the carcass of a cow that a butcher had slaughtered and displayed in a market. . . . Thus a monk practices mindfully contemplating his body.

And also, if a monk should see a corpse abandoned in a cemetery, dead one day or two or three, swollen, turning blue, and beginning to fester, he should concentrate on his own body and think, "This body of mine is just like that one; it has the same nature, and it will not escape this fate." . . . And should he see a corpse abandoned in a cemetery, being eaten by crows, hawks, vultures, dogs, jackals, or various kinds of vermin, he should concentrate on his own body and think, "This body of mine is just like that one; it has the same nature, and it will not escape this fate." . . . And should he see a corpse abandoned in a cemetery, a skeleton still covered with some flesh and blood and held together by tendons, or without flesh but smeared with blood and still held together, or without flesh or blood but still held together, or just bones no longer held together but scattered in different directions—here the bones of a hand, there the bones of a foot, here a tibia, there a femur, here a hipbone, there a backbone, over there a skull—he should concentrate on his own body and think, "This body of mine is just like that; it has the same nature, and it will not

[Source: Taken from the *Satipatthanasutta* 10.1–9, printed in V. Trenckner, *The Majjhima-Nikaya*, volume I (London: Pali Text Society, 1888), pp. 55–63].

escape this fate . . . ." And should he see a corpse abandoned in a cemetery, bones bleached white as shells, old bones in a heap, bones that have completely decayed and become dust—he should concentrate on his own body and think, "This body of mine is just like that; it has the same nature, and it will not escape this fate." . . . Thus a monk keeps mindfully contemplating his body.

And how, monks, does a monk practice the mindful contemplation of feelings? In this way: Experiencing a pleasant feeling, he knows "I am experiencing a pleasant feeling"; experiencing an unpleasant feeling, he knows "I am experiencing an unpleasant feeling." Experiencing a feeling that is neither pleasant nor unpleasant, he knows "I am experiencing a feeling that is neither pleasant nor unpleasant." Experiencing a pleasant physical feeling, he knows "I am experiencing a pleasant physical feeling"; experiencing a pleasant spiritual feeling, he knows "I am experiencing a pleasant spiritual feeling"; experiencing an unpleasant physical feeling . . . an unpleasant spiritual feeling . . . a physical feeling that is neither pleasant nor unpleasant . . . a spiritual feeling that is neither pleasant nor unpleasant, he knows he is experiencing those feelings. . . . Thus a monk practices mindfully contemplating feelings.

And how, monks, does a monk practice the mindful contemplation of thoughts? In this way: He knows a passionate thought to be a passionate thought; he knows a passionless thought to be a passionless thought; he knows a hate-filled thought to be a hate-filled thought; he knows a hate-free thought to be a hate-free thought; he knows a deluded thought . . . an undeluded thought . . . an attentive thought . . . a distracted thought . . . a lofty thought . . . a lowly thought . . . a mediocre thought . . . a supreme thought . . . a concentrated thought . . . a diffused thought, . . . a thought that is free . . . a thought that is still bound . . . to be such thoughts as they are. Thus a monk practices mindfully contemplating his thoughts.

And how, monks, does a monk practice the mindful contemplation of the elements of reality? In this way: He practices the mindful

contemplation of the elements of reality with regard to the five hindrances. And how does he do that? In this way: When there is within him sensual excitement, he knows that "sensual excitement is occurring within me"; when there is within him no sensual excitement, he knows that "sensual excitement is not occurring within me." . . . When there is within him some ill will, he knows that "ill will is occurring within me"; when there is within him no ill will, he knows "ill will is not occurring within me." . . . And similarly he knows the presence and the absence within himself of laziness and lethargy, agitation and worry, and doubt. . . . Thus he practices mindfully contemplating elements of reality within himself, he practices mindfully contemplating elements of reality outside of himself, . . . and he practices mindfully contemplating elements of reality as they arise . . . and as they pass away. . . . And thinking that "this is an element of reality," he is concerned with it only insofar as he needs to be for the sake of knowledge and recognition; so he abides free from attachment and does not cling to anything in this world.

A monk also practices the mindful contemplation of the elements of reality with regard to the five aggregates of attachment. And how does he do that? In this way: He reflects "Such is physical form, such is the origin of physical form, such is the passing away of physical form." "Such is feeling, such is the origin of feeling, such is the passing away of feeling." "Such is perception, such is the origin of perception, such is the passing away of perception." "Such are karmic constituents, such is the origin of karmic constituents, such is the passing away of karmic constituents." "Such is consciousness, such is the origin of consciousness, such is the passing away of consciousness . . . ."

A monk also practices the mindful contemplation of the elements of reality with regard to the six senses and sense-objects. How does he do this? In this way: He knows his eyes, he knows visible forms, and he knows the attachments that develop in connection with the two of them. . . . Similarly he knows his ears, and he knows sounds. . . . He knows his nose and he knows smells. . . . He knows his tongue and he knows tastes. . . . He knows his body and he knows tactile things. . . . He knows his mind and he knows thoughts. And he knows the attachments that develop in connection with any of them. . . .

A monk also practices the mindful contemplation of the elements of reality with regard to the seven factors of enlightenment. How does he do that? In this way: When the first factor of enlightenment, which is mindfulness, is within him, he knows it to be present; when it is not within him, he knows it to be absent. . . . And similarly, he knows the presence and absence within himself of the other factors of enlightenment: the investigation of Dharma . . . energetic effort . . . enthusiasm . . . serenity . . . meditative concentration . . . and equanimity. . . .

A monk also practices the mindful contemplation of the elements of reality with regard to the Four Noble Truths. How does he do that? In this way: He knows "suffering" the way it really is, and he knows "the origination of suffering" the way it really is, and he knows "the cessation of suffering" the way it really is, and he knows "the way leading to the cessation of suffering" the way it really is.

Study Questions

A.2.2 Buddhist Meditation for Classroom Mindfulness

1. List the five benefits that the practice of mindfulness can produce.
2. List the "four mindfulnesses" or "the fourfold establishment of mindfulness."
3. Explain *step by step* what the Buddha means by "mindfulness," then, put your knowledge of his doctrine of mindfulness into practice.
4. Can the practice of Buddhist meditation help one to achieve self-knowledge and knowledge of reality as claimed by the Buddha and Buddhist philosophers?

Philosophical Essays: Critical Examination of a View

Jay F. Rosenberg

The Introduction

Philosophical discourse (verbal karma) and philosophical writing (physical and intellectual karma) are the two concrete expressions of the intellectual activity of *philosophical thinking* (intellectual karma). What and how one thinks determines what and how one speaks and writes. But, what and how one speaks and writes also determines what and how one thinks. The thinking-talking-writing relationships are always *dialectical*, i.e., they mutually complement, mutually contradict, and mutually negate each other, either sequentially and/or simultaneously.

But *what* and *how* one thinks, one speaks, and one writes *may not be philosophical in form and content*, because philosophical thinking, philosophical discourse, and philosophical writing are different from other ways of thinking, speaking, and writing. In order to think philosophically, one has to learn the method of philosophical thinking because without proper knowledge, one may not know *how* to practice philosophical thinking the correct way. The same rule applies to philosophical discourse and philosophical writing. One must conscientiously practice philosophical writing before one can write a good philosophical paper, therefore, one has to learn the writing-a-philosophical-essay method as taught by Professor Rosenberg.

So, please read the selection carefully, and many times until you know for sure the writing-a-philosophical-essay method.

The primary medium for working through a philosophical dialectic is the philosophical essay. This is a distinctive form which ranges from brief discussion notes in professional journals to works of book length. As a student of philosophy, you will (or should) be called upon to try your hand at writing philosophical essays. In any case, you will surely be reading some, and so a thorough discussion of the form is appropriate here.

A philosophical essay is neither a research paper, a scholarly collection and arrangement of diverse sources (although the standards and forms of scholarly documentation should, of course, be observed whenever relevant and necessary), nor is it a literary exercise in self-expression. It does not deal with feelings or impressions. It is not a report or a summary. Fundamentally, it is the *reasoned defense of a thesis.* That is, there must be some point or points to be *established* in the essay, and considerations must be offered in *support* of them in such a way that the considerations can be seen *to* support them.

Clarity of exposition, precision of statement, organization of ideas, and logical rigor and consistency in the treatment of those ideas are thus among the primary demands of philosophical writing. It follows that literacy and sound literary style are essential preconditions of a successful philosophical essay (indeed, I would add, of any writing). At a minimum, a philosophical essay should be written in coherent and articulate prose which adheres to the accepted rules and conventions of English grammar and composition. Enthusiasm cannot compensate for un-intelligibility, nor can a superficial facility with technical terms effectively substitute for a sound understanding of the ideas and principles that such terminology has evolved to express. You should particularly avoid ponderous "academic" forms. Philosophy has had a bad press in this regard. It is notorious for being a "deep" subject, and those who write about it all too often aspire to a corresponding impenetrability. Well, deep philosophy may be—but the deep lucidity of a glacier-fed mountain lake, not the deep murkiness of a mist-laden swamp, should be your model and inspiration.

Philosophical essays come in a variety of *species*, each of which has its own characteristic structure. Perhaps the most basic of these, mastery of which serves as a point of entry to all the others, is the critical examination of a view.

The critical examination of a view, of course, presupposes a view to be critically examined. That is, you are confronted at the beginning with something that *itself* has fundamentally the form of a philosophical essay—a piece of writing within which some claim or thesis is advanced and considerations are offered in favor of accepting or adopting that claim. Correspondingly, a critical examination of a view may be broadly divided into two parts: the exposition and the critique. Exposition consists in setting out for study and discussion the view, position, claim, or thesis at issue together with the structure of argumentation offered in support of it. Critique is the assessment or evaluation of that view through an examination of the structure and content of the supporting reasoning. One useful way to approach the writing of such a philosophical essay, then, is with something like the following checklist of questions in mind:

Introduction:
Does my essay have an introductory paragraph? In my introductory paragraph, do I

____ give a brief description of what the essay is about?
____ state what I plan to accomplish in the essay?
____ summarize how I plan to go about accomplishing it?

The Exposition:
When reconstructing an argument, have I clearly explained

____ what conclusion the philosopher is working toward?
____ what reasons, both implicit and explicit, the philosopher offers to support that conclusion?
____ why and how the philosopher thinks those reasons support the conclusion?

The Critique:
When raising an objection, have I

____ made it clear what aspect of the argument I object to?
____ explained the reasons why I object to that aspect of the argument?
____ assessed the severity of my objection?
____ thought about and discussed how the philosopher might respond to my objection?

___ discussed one objection thoroughly rather than many objections superficially?

General Concerns:
Throughout my paper, do I periodically tell the reader

___ what I've just done?
___ what remains to be done?
___ what the reader should expect to happen next?
___ whether what I am saying is an interpretation or a criticism?

Does my essay have a clear and articulate structure?

___ Does each paragraph work to support my thesis?
___ Do I have transitions between paragraphs that make it clear why one paragraph follows the one which precedes it?
___ Does each sentence within a paragraph work to support or explain the topic of that paragraph?

Have I satisfactorily explained

___ any important special terminology that the author employs?
___ the interpretation of any passages that I quote?
___ the nature and point of any examples that I offer?

As helpful as such a brief checklist can often be, however, both the idea of a philosophical exposition and, especially, the topic of a philosophical critique deserve a more extensive discussion.

Views are usually somebody's views. The expository task is thus primarily exegetical. The business of setting out a position together with its supporting argumentation will usually be a matter of reading, understanding, reconstructing, and lucidly reporting the content of some philosophical work. This undertaking has its own strategies and hazards, some of which I will have occasion to discuss later.

As I have repeatedly stressed, the most important fact about a philosophical critique is that it does not end with disagreement. That is where it begins. Philosophical criticism is *reasoned* disagreement. Since the view up for assessment will be supported by its own structure of reasoned considerations, a negative philosophical evaluation of a thesis requires that the arguments supporting the position, and not merely the position itself, be critically engaged. That's Rule One. It is, you will recall, thus never sufficient simply to point out that a philosophical conclusion looks, or even is, false or paradoxical. If you wish effectively to call the conclusion into question, what you need to discover and demonstrate are the inadequacies of the reasoning offered in support of it.

As we have seen, there are two directions which a critical thrust can take. You may address the form of the argument—its validity or invalidity—or you may address its content. I have already said most of what can usefully be said about the first type of criticism outside the confines of a course in formal logic. The exposition of the argument to be evaluated is clearly crucial to this mode of criticism. The argument must be set out with sufficient clarity and precision and in sufficient orderly detail to allow for the extraction of a "logical skeleton" that in fact fairly and accurately represents the pattern of reasoning actually being employed. Unfortunately, nothing short of the kind of familiarity and practice that only repeated experience brings suffices to indicate what the argument is likely to be and how much detail is needed to uncover its operative logical structure. Even if you've successfully accomplished this rather tough job, however, your ability to demonstrate the argument's invalidity (if it *is* invalid) is still limited by your insight in recognizing it for what it is, and by your creativity in coming up with an appropriate model to *demonstrate* invalidity by exhibiting a further instance of that pattern of reasoning with indisputably true premises and an indisputably false conclusion. Alas, as I remarked earlier, both insight and creativity sadly fall outside the limits of what is teachable.

Usually, however, you will be dealing with patterns of reasoning that are formally correct. In that case, your critique will need to address the specific content of the argument. The way you do this, you surely remember, is to construct an *internal* criticism. That is, you attempt to establish that the various premises and presuppositions used in the argument cannot all consistently be held together. You try to show that anyone who accepts all of those premises and presuppositions at the same time—and in particular, then, the philosopher who offered the argument in the first place—lands in trouble.

What kind of trouble? I have repeatedly spoken of uncovering an inconsistency or an incoherence in some philosopher's views. It is now time to talk about this matter in more detail. What kinds of incoherence or inconsistency are there?

And what do they look like when you uncover them?

In a sense, there is only one *basic* form of inconsistency or incoherence—a self-contradiction. In the most straightforward case, a person contradicts himself by saying two things which cannot both be true at the same time. At one point in the dialectic he says X; at another, he says *not-X*. In a somewhat less straightforward case, however, he may, so to speak, say both X and *not-X* at the same time. This sounds a bit mysterious, but in fact you've already seen at least one example of it. A person who claimed that all paintings were forgeries would be contradicting himself in this way, for he would in effect be saying both that some paintings are originals (for the forgeries to be copies of) and that no paintings are originals, both X and *not-X*.

Study Questions

A.2.3 Jay F. Rosenberg, Philosophical Essays: Critical Examination of a View

1. Explain what Professor Rosenberg means by "a philosophical essay."
2. Explain what Professor Rosenberg means by "a thesis."
3. List "the primary demands of philosophical writing" as stated by Professor Rosenberg.
4. Explain what Professor Rosenberg means by "the critical examination of a view."
5. List the items that you must include in the "Introduction" of a philosophical essay.
6. List the items that you must include in the "Exposition" of a philosophical essay.
7. List the items that you must include in the "Critique" of a philosophical essay.
8. In your own words, explain what Professor Rosenberg means by "the most important fact about a philosophical critique" that you need to know.
9. List all the items to be covered under the "General Concerns" in a philosophical essay.

A.2.4

The Conception of *Ming* in Early Confucian Thought

Edward (Ted) Slingerland

The Introduction

Ted Slingerland was a doctoral candidate in Religious Studies at the Stanford University when he published the selected article (1996). Currently, Edward G. (Ted) Slingerland is a member of the Department of Religious Studies and the Department of East Asian Languages and Cultures at the University of Southern California.

We hang in perpetual suspense between life and death, health and sickness, plenty and want; which are distributed amongst the human species by secret and unknowable causes, whose operation is oft unexpected, and always unaccountable.

David Hume, *The Natural History of Religion*

The Duke of She asked Zi-lu about Confucius. Zi-lu did not answer. [Hearing of this] Confucius said, "Why did you not say something like this: He is the kind of man who so passionately pursues self-cultivation that he forgets to eat, who has attained a joy that allows him to forget worries concerning external things, and who grows old without even noticing it."

Analects 7.19

The role of *ming* (variously translated as "fate," "destiny," "mandate") in early Confucian thought has been subject to a range of interpretations.[1] From its literal meaning of "command" or "order," and its predominant pre-Confucian use as the revocable "mandate" bestowed by Heaven (*tian*) upon the rulers of a particular dynasty, it had evolved by the time of the Confucian *Analects* into a force that plays a role at the level of the individual. Its significance for the process of self-cultivation is reflected in Confucius' observation in *Analects* 2.4 that "by the age of fifty I had understood the heavenly *ming*," as well as such passages as *Analects* 20.3, in which Confucius notes that "One who does not understand *ming* has not the means by which to become a gentleman."[2]

The importance of *ming* in the Confucian project is clear. The point of controversy concerns its precise nature, as well as the character of its influence on the individual. As Kwong-loi Shun has noted, the various interpretations of *ming* can generally be characterized as either "descriptive" or "normative."[3] At one extreme, the descriptive interpretation (exemplified by Robert Eno)[4] takes *ming* to refer to an impersonal force outside human control, similar to Hume's "secret and unknown causes, whose operation is oft unexpected and always unaccountable."[5] This view can be seen as fostering a fatalistic attitude toward life, and its apparent usefulness in explaining the political failure of the early Confucian school is emphasized by Eno. At the other end of the spectrum is the more normative interpretation (exemplified by Tang Junyi), according to which *ming* is to be taken as functionally equivalent to *yi* (duty or righteousness): everything being ordained by Heaven, accepting and following the dictates of *ming* is seen not as fatalistic surrender but rather as an extension of the other "duties" prescribed to the individual by the principle of *yi*. In addition to these two views, a middle course between an exclusively descriptive or normative interpretation is charted by such scholars as D. C. Lau, who takes *ming* when it occurs in isolation in a descriptive sense but also sees it as possessing normative significance when coupled with heaven in the compound *tian ming* (a combination which occurs only twice in the *Analects*).[6]

The position advanced in this essay can best be characterized as descriptive, although it differs somewhat from Eno's view (as will be explained below). In my opinion, one finds in both the *Analects* and the *Mencius* a bifurcation of reality into two distinct realms: *nei* (inner) and *wai* (outer).[7] *Ming* refers to forces that lie in the outer realm—that is, the realm beyond the bounds of proper human endeavor, or the area of life in which "seeking does not contribute to one's getting it."[8] This external world is not the concern of the gentleman, whose efforts are to be concentrated on the self—the inner realm in which "seeking contributes to one's getting it."[9] This is the arena in which the struggle for self-cultivation must be carried out. Once one has achieved success there, the vicissitudes of the outside world—life and death, fame and disgrace, wealth and poverty—can be faced "without worry and without fear,"[10] for one will have attained the internal joy described by Confucius, who was able "to grow old without even noticing it." The Confucian response to an apparently capricious and often inexplicable fate is thus neither an attempt to control it through supplication or prayer (an endeavor that Hume saw as the origin of all human religion) nor a type of pessimistic resignation to a meaningless life. It is, on the contrary, a realistic and mature redirection of human energy toward the sole area of life in which one does have control—the cultivation and moral improvement of one's own self—coupled with a faith in the ability of self-cultivation to produce in one an attitude of joyful acceptance of all that life may bring. Such an attitude springs naturally from a conception of human existence that emphasizes an inner-outer bifurcation of reality.

At this point, it might be useful to consider briefly two possible objections to the inner-outer dichotomy upon which this discussion of *ming* will be based. First, the category of "inner"—with its attendant implications of a capacity for mental reflection and a concern for emotive states—might be viewed with suspicion by scholars such as Herbert Fingarette, who has criticized the consideration of inner psychological states in an early Chinese, particularly Confucian, context as merely a reflection of Western "psychological bias." While Fingarette's caution against a reading of our own cultural biases into a text from a significantly different culture is well taken, there would seem to be considerable textual evidence for a "psychological" reading of Confucius and Mencius, as will be demonstrated below. For instance, it is difficult to see precisely how such phrases as "examining oneself inwardly" (*nei xing*) could be explained without reference to some sort of personal, psychic state.[11]

A second, more troubling difficulty concerns an issue that casts doubt on the validity of the inner-outer distinction itself: the question of how one defines the individual or self and its relation to the cosmos as a whole. It is undeniable that certain passages in the *Analects* and the *Mencius*, particularly those concerning the power of the gentleman's virtue (*de*) to influence the world[12] and the discussion of the "flood-like *qi*,"[13] suggest a degree of response and correspondence between the individual and the cosmos as a whole—a theme that is later developed at length in Neo-Confucianism. The paradigmatic example of such a correspondence is the orderly progression from investigating things (*ge wu*) and cultivating the self to ultimately pacifying the world that is described in the beginning of the "Great Learning" (*Da xue*). It is clear that once the distinction between the individual and the cosmos begins to be blurred in this fashion, the dichotomy between inner and outer realms becomes increasingly difficult to maintain. While not wishing to overlook the importance of this issue, it is nevertheless my opinion that the correspondence between the self and the cosmos is a theme only latently present in pre-Qin orthodox Confucianism, and that the emphasis on and explicit development of this theme is a later Neo-Confucian development. The inner/outer dichotomy proposed in this essay is more characteristic of early Confucianism. In this regard one should note the relative infrequency of passages implying a unity of individual and cosmos in the *Analects* and *Mencius,* as well as the fact that although the "Great Learning," for instance, is certainly an early text, it is not even necessarily pre-Han, and in any case was only a minor chapter in the *Book of Rites* (*Li ji*) until

raised to prominence by Song Neo-Confucians.

Despite its possibly problematic nature, then, the inner-outer dichotomy can still be seen as a useful conceptual tool for exploring the early Confucian conception of *ming*. Since this dichotomy is formulated most clearly in the *Mencius* (particularly 7A:1–3), I will begin my discussion there, noting the identification of *ming* with the external realm as well as the definition of the proper scope of a gentleman's *yu* (worry) and *huan* (concern)—in short, a gentleman worries about self-cultivation, but is free from concern about external matters. Terms such as *yu* and *huan* are important, for while *ming* is not explicitly discussed with reference to external or internal realms in the *Analects*, *yu* and *huan* clearly are, and the link between *ming* and *yu/huan* serves as a conceptual bridge allowing us to see the *ming* of Confucius in terms of the *nei/wai* dichotomy formulated by Mencius. Finally, the views of Tang Junyi and Robert Eno on *ming* will be discussed in light of my own interpretation.

Mencius

The clearest expression of the inner-outer dichotomy in the *Mencius* is found in passage 7A:3:

> Mencius said: "Simply seek them out and you will get them, simply let them go and you will lose them."[14] This refers to a case in which seeking helps one to get it, because the search lies within oneself. "Seeking for it involves a method, getting it involves *ming*." This refers to a case in which seeking does not help one to get it, because the search lies outside oneself.

The "them" referred to in this allusion to 6A:6 are the four Confucian virtues of humanity, duty, ritual propriety, and wisdom, which are explained in that passage also in terms of outer and inner:

> Humanity, duty, ritual propriety, and wisdom are not things simply welded onto me from the outside—they are things that I possess inherently.

Thus, the phrase "seeking helps one to get it" points toward the process of self-cultivation, for the "sprouts" (*duan*) of the four virtues are rooted in the self, in the inner realm. Effort expended in this sort of "seeking" will inevitably bear fruit. On the other hand, seeking "outside oneself" is futile—such activity will never "help one to get it" because the forces at work in this external realm are beyond human control.[15] Mencius identifies these forces as *tian* (Heaven) and *ming*. Discussing the vagaries of dynastic succession in 5A:6, Mencius explains:

> This was all due to Heaven—this type of thing is not something that people are able to bring about. When something comes to be although no one has caused it to be, it is due to Heaven. When something comes about although no one has brought it about, it is due to *ming*.

The proper attitude of a gentleman toward this external realm is exemplified in 5A:8, where Confucius displays indifference toward the external realm (political office) while directing his attention toward the inner realm (ritual propriety and duty):

> Mi-zi said to Zi-lu, "If Master Kung will lodge with me, the office of minister of Wei could be his." Zi-lu reported this to Confucius, who replied, "This is a matter of *ming*." Confucius entered in accordance with ritual propriety, and retired as required by duty. With regard to getting it (the office) or not getting it, he said, "This is a matter of *ming*."

This attitude is explained in a more abstract sense in 7A:1, where the heavenly (*tian*) is identified with human nature and the mind (the internal realm), and where *ming* is identified with the length of one's life span (the external realm):

> Mencius said, "One who exhaustively investigates the mind will know the nature (*xing*); one who knows nature will know the heavenly.

> "Preserving one's mind and nourishing one's nature are the means by which to serve Heaven. Considering as one an untimely death or long life, and cultivating oneself in order to await it, these are the means by which to establish *ming*."[16]

What does it mean to "establish *ming*"? This is somewhat further clarified in the next passage, 7A:3:

> Mencius said: "There is nothing that is not subject to *ming*, yet one should acquiesce to and accept only one's proper *ming*. For this reason, one who comprehends *ming* does not stand beneath a crumbling wall. Dying after having exhausted one's *dao* (way)—this is proper *ming*. Dying in shackles—this is not proper *ming*."

Thus, to "establish *ming*" means to realize one's proper *ming*, which is accomplished by "exhausting one's *dao*"—that is, fully comprehending the mind and cultivating the self.[17] Once one is on the path toward self-cultivation, the proper frame of mind required to accept one's lot in life will naturally follow and one will not be inclined to "tempt fate" by standing under crumbling walls. On the contrary, one who ignores self-cultivation (the inner realm) and blindly pursues things that lie outside the proper realm of human agency is just looking for trouble—such a one will most likely end up meeting a disgraceful and untimely end.

The scope of the proper realm of human activity has thus been clearly delineated: the gentleman is concerned solely with cultivating the inner realm (the four virtues, the mind, nature), and once this is done, concerns of the outer realm (length of life span, honor and disgrace, etc.) will take care of themselves. In 4B:28, Mencius formulates this in terms of "worries" (*yu*) and "concerns" (*huan*):

> Mencius said, "A gentleman is different from other people in that he preserves

his mind. The gentleman preserves his mind by means of humanity and ritual propriety. The humane person cares for others, and the ritually correct person shows respect for others. One who cares for others will be cared for in turn, and one who respects others will also be treated with respect.

"Now, if treated by someone in a contrary and perverse manner, the gentleman invariably looks into himself: 'It must be that I am not being humane; it must be that I am not ritually correct. How else could this come to pass?' If, however, he looks into himself and finds that he has been both benevolent and humane, and yet this contrary and perverse treatment nonetheless persists, the gentleman will invariably look into himself and say, 'It must be that I am not faithful.' If, however, he looks into himself and finds that he has been faithful, and yet this contrary and perverse treatment nonetheless persists, the gentleman says, 'This is simply an ignorant person. Someone like this is no better than an animal! How can one be troubled by an animal?'

"It is for this reason that a gentleman has worries (*yu*) his entire life, but never one moment of concern (*huan*). Now, the sort of worries he has are of this sort: Shun was a man. I am also a man. Shun served as a model for the world worth passing down to later generations, while I am still a common villager. This is something worth worrying about. What is to be done about this worry? One should merely try to become like Shun, that is all.[18]

"Being like this, the gentleman is therefore free of concerns. If something is not humane, he does not do it; if an activity is not ritually correct, he does not engage in it. Thus, even if some sort of problem (*huan*) arises, the gentleman is not concerned."

Confucius

The presence in the *Analects* of an inner-outer dichotomy with regard to "seeking" (*qiu*) is hinted at in 15.21:

The gentleman seeks for it in himself; the petty person seeks for it in others.

However, the words *yu* (worry) and *huan* (concern) are not distinguished as referring, respectively, to the inner and outer realms, as they are in the *Mencius* 4B:28 passage cited above. Rather, they are both used in the same general sense of being concerned or worried about something, the appropriateness of the feeling being determined by whether the object of concern is something internal or external:

Si-Ma Niu asked about the gentleman.

The Master said, "The gentleman is without worry and without fear."

"Is that all there is to being a gentleman?"

"If one examines oneself (*nei xing*) and finds that one is without fault, then what is there to fear? What is there to worry about?"

Si-Ma Niu was worried (*yu*) and said, "Everyone else has brothers. I alone have none."

Zi-xia said, "I have heard it said that with regard to life and death there is *ming*, and that [the distribution of] riches and honor lies with Heaven. If the gentleman is reverent and without error, respectful of other people and observant of ritual propriety, then everyone within the Four Seas will be his brother. So why should the gentleman be concerned (*huan*) about not having brothers?"[19]

As in the *Mencius*, we find such matters as life and death, riches and honors, and the specifics of one's family situation (e.g., the possession of biological brothers) attributed to *ming* and to Heaven. This is the external realm, with regard to which it is possible to be free from concern as long as one can examine oneself and find no fault within. Thus we have the observation in 9.29 that "one who is humane is without worry" (*ren zhe bu yu*).

However, *yu* is warranted when the object of concern is the internal realm—for example, one's state of self-cultivation or learning:

> The Master said, "To fail to cultivate virtue, to neglect to further elaborate what I have learned, to be unmoved when informed of my duty, and to be unable to change what is not good in myself— these are my worries."[20]

> The Master said, "Do not be concerned that you have no position—rather concern yourself with that by which you would establish yourself. Do not be concerned that no one knows of you— rather seek to become someone worth being known."[21]

> "The gentleman worries about the *Dao* and not about poverty."[22]

We are now in a position to understand better *Analects* 20.3, "One who does not understand *ming* has not the means by which to become a gentleman." If one does not understand *ming*— that is, what is internal and what is external to the project of self-cultivation—one will lack a sense of what is important and so misuse one's energies. Such a person is the disciple Si, of whom Confucius notes, "Si does not accept his *ming* and instead engages in money making."[23] An emphasis on external things not only diverts energy away from the process of self-cultivation, but is also pointless in a purely practical sense, since these things lie outside human control:

> Gong Bo-liao made accusations about Zi-lu to Ji Sun. Zi-fu Jing-bo reported this, saying, "Gong Bo-liao is definitely succeeding in confusing my master,[24] but I still have enough influence to have his corpse exposed in the market place."

> The Master said, "Whether or not the *Dao* is to be put into practice is a matter of *ming*; whether or not the *Dao* is to fall into decline is a matter of *ming*. How could Gong Bo-liao possibly have an effect on *ming*?"[25]

Although the realm of *ming* lies beyond one's control, this does not imply that one should flippantly disregard it altogether. The proper attitude of an individual toward *ming* is one of respect—it is not becoming of a gentleman to tempt fate by standing beneath crumbling walls. Thus we have *Analects* 16.8, in which the heavenly *ming* is mentioned as one of the three things of which a gentleman stands in awe. This awe is, however, rather passive in the sense that it pertains to something beyond the realm of human agency. Just as one should "show reverence to ghosts and spirits but keep them at a distance,"[26] one should maintain a healthy respect for the power of *ming* while nonetheless concentrating on the task at hand—self-cultivation. This is what Confucius has in mind in snubbing Jilu, in 11.12:

> Ji-Lu asked about serving the ghosts and spirits.

> The Master said, "You are not yet even capable of serving people—how would you be able to serve ghosts?"

> He requested to hear about death.

> Confucius replied, "You do not yet even understand life—how could you possibly understand death?"

We can thus see in the *Analects* that although *ming* is not explicitly characterized as being external, a definite inner-outer dichotomy is developed, primarily in terms of the proper and improper objects of the gentleman's "worry" or "concern." Furthermore, things having to do with *ming* are clearly of the latter category. Although there is often a danger of reading too much Mencius into Confucius, it would appear that in this case the Mencian conception of inner and outer realms of action is merely a more explicit development of a view already present in the *Analects*.[27]

Interpretation

Tang Junyi, in his identification of *ming* with *yi*, makes much of such passages as *Analects* 16.8, in which it is said that the gentleman stands in awe of the heavenly *ming*, Confucius' emphasis on the importance of knowing *ming*,[28] and especially the phrase *wu yi wu ming* ([this is] without *yi* and without *ming*) in *Mencius* 5A:8, where he takes the repetition of *ming* to be an indication of their functional synonymy.[29] It becomes clear, however, that this functional identification de-emphasizes the inner-outer dichotomy. In his section on "The Humane *Dao* of Confucius," Tang Junyi explains how the heavenly *ming* is ultimately the source of *yi*:

> When Heaven causes me to encounter elders, it also commands (*ming*) me to seek to care for them; when Heaven causes me to have friends, it commands me to seek to be trusted by them; when Heaven causes me to encounter juniors, it commands me to seek to cherish them. Extending this argument, we can say that when people in their lives encounter different things, the appropriate way to carry out *yi* also differs . . . and so at the source of all this we can see the Heavenly *ming*.[30]

He proceeds to claim that even the existence of the self is due to Heaven; therefore, it does not make sense to speak of an autonomous moral agent making decisions concerning *yi*:

> When Heaven bestows a new *ming* upon me, it is at the same time the case that this is something that I demand (*ming*) of myself: things such as being a filial son or compassionate parent are all such things. However, we can not actually say that we demand it of ourselves, for if there is no "I" (*wo*), then it is impossible that there could be this self-demanding (*zi ming*), and without the things that "I" am brought into contact with, there could also be no self-demanding. Looking at it in this way, we can thus generally say that all cases of "me demanding something from myself" can, if we leave out the "me," be explained as cases in which the things which I encounter command (*ming*) me—that is, this is all something which Heaven has commanded.[31]

This vision of *yi* as a sort of moral imperative mandated by the heavenly *ming* is certainly powerful, but in de-emphasizing the inner-outer dichotomy some of the complexity of the early Confucian vision is lost.[32] First of all, *ming* and *yi* seem to appear in Tang Junyi's interpretation as a monolithic moral reality, which one can choose to accept or not. This blending of the two concepts leaves little room for doubt—for instance, the sort of doubt that one would find in an individual striving to adhere to internal moral values in the face of an often inexplicable and sometimes actively perverse external world. It is precisely this sort of doubt that we find, for instance, expressed after Yen Yuan's death in *Analects* 11.9 ("Oh, Heaven has bereft me! Heaven has bereft me!") or in *Analects* 6.10:

> Bo-niu was sick, and the Master went to visit him. Holding his hand through the window, he lamented, "We are going to lose him. It must be due to *ming*! Such a person with such an illness. . . . Oh, such a person with such an illness!"

Furthermore, if one eliminates the "I" as an active moral agent (as Tang Junyi, at least in the passage cited above, seems to do), determinism seems unavoidable: it is difficult to see how one would even be able to decide whether to accept the *ming-yi* order of the universe or not, or be able through self-cultivation to "establish one's proper *ming*."[33]

Moving away from the normative extreme represented by Tang Junyi,[34] I find myself more inclined toward the sort of descriptive interpretation offered by Robert Eno. In general, my interpretation of *ming* as a force external to the individual shares many similarities with the theory of *ming* advanced in *The Confucian Creation of Heaven*. I have, however, some reservations concerning Eno's position, particularly with regard to the motivations he attributes to a descriptive conception of *ming*. Commenting on the use of *ming* in *Analects* 14.36, he notes:

> Here Confucius is pictured using *ming* in much the way he used T'ien in A: 3.13, as a defensive political fatalism that protects him from compromising his ideals and engaging in political intrigue. . . .
>
> There is a sense here that the decree that determines the failure of the Ruist political mission almost frees the Ruist, extricating him from the toils of political responsibilities and allowing him to retire, at least partially, into the pure ritual practice of the Ruist community.[35]

Perhaps it is my rejection of Eno's general conception of the "Ruists" ("a group of eccentrically costumed disciples assembled at their Master's house, carefully stepping through an intricately scripted and choreographed ritual under the eyes of their teacher")[36] that causes me to disagree with him on this particular point. It would seem that, were one compelled to analyze the possible motives behind the descriptive conception of *ming*, it might be well to consider what the Confucians themselves saw as informing their project. "In ancient times people studied for themselves," laments Confucius in 14.24; "Now

people study for the sake of others." In 6A:11 and 13, Mencius pointedly notes:

> If a person's chickens or dogs have wandered off, he knows to go after them, but doesn't know to do the same when it is his mind that has strayed. The path of learning is none other than this: simply going after a mind that has strayed.
>
> If people want to grow a *tong* or *zi* tree one or two spans thick, everyone knows how to go about nourishing it. When it comes to the self, though, no one knows how to nourish it. Is it because people love a *tong* or *zi* tree more than themselves? No, it is because they don't give the slightest thought to it.

The *Analects* and the *Mencius* are full of such reproaches. The motivation informing these texts is the desire to change people's views of what is and what is not important, to redirect people's energy and efforts from the external realm (position, wealth, physical concerns) to the internal realm of self-cultivation. The conception of *ming* is employed in order to mark off, in effect, the outer boundaries of one's proper realm of action. Understood this way, an otherwise puzzling passage, *Mencius* 7B:24, becomes more comprehensible:

> Mencius said, "With regard to the mouth in its pursuit of flavors, the eye in its pursuit of beauty, the ear in its pursuit of pleasing sounds, the nose in its pursuit of scents, and the four limbs in their pursuit of ease and comfort—this is all [part of] human nature (*xing*), but since there is *ming* involved in [getting it], the gentleman does not refer to it as human nature.
>
> "With regard to humanity as put to use by fathers and sons, duty as put to use by rulers and vassals, ritual as put to use by guests and hosts, wisdom as put to use by worthies, and the sagely person

as put in the service of the heavenly *Dao*—this is all [subject to] *ming*, but since human nature is involved in [its application], the gentleman does not refer to it as subject to *ming*."

The point is that *all* "appetites"—whether physical or moral—are not only grounded in human nature, but also subject to *ming* with regard to their satisfaction. That food and sex and physical ease are not always to be obtained is clear; what is equally true is that the practice of morality does not necessarily bring one success, as the perfectly filial Shun's treatment at the hands of his family and the perfect sage Confucius' fate at the hands of Heaven demonstrate quite dramatically. However, that the gentleman refers to the first class of appetites as *ming* (i.e., something to be ignored as beyond one's control) and the second as human nature (i.e., something actively to be pursued and cultivated) is due to the fact that the cultivation of the physical desires in themselves adds nothing to one as a person. The gentleman thus dismisses such concerns as *ming*. The engendering and practice of the "moral appetites," on the other hand, is an end in itself—the central task in the project of self-cultivation. This, then, is the object upon which the gentleman concentrates his attention.

It would appear, then, that the conception of *ming* as being something outside human control is not a fatalistic excuse for retiring to a life of ritual, but rather an observation designed to redirect the student's attention from the pursuit of external goals (official position, etc.) toward the project of self-cultivation. The belief that the success or failure of the *Dao* in the political arena is a matter of *ming* should not be viewed as a thinly veiled political cop-out, but rather as the expression of a mature and realistic assessment of the limits of human power coupled with a firm resolution to attend to one's proper task.

Notes

1. By "early Confucian thought," I am referring specifically to the Confucian tradition as expressed in two texts: the *Lunyu* of Confucius and the *Mengzi* of Mencius. The distinction I would like to maintain between this pre-Qin orthodox tradition and later strains of Confucianism (particularly the *Lixue* or Neo-Confucianism school) is discussed in greater detail below.
2. All translations from the classical Chinese are my own, unless otherwise noted.
3. Kwong-loi Shun, unpublished manuscript.
4. Cf. Eno 1990.
5. Hume 1956, p. 29.
6. Cf. Lau 1979, pp. 27–30.
7. What it might mean precisely to say that something is "inner" as opposed to "outer" is subject to different interpretations. In the case of both Mencius and Confucius, that something belongs to the "inner" realm would seem to mean both that it pertains to the personal realm (heart/mind, moral character) and that its attainment lies entirely within my control, as will be discussed below. "Inner" has the further implication in Mencius of being something with which one has been endowed and that one must merely bring to fruition, as opposed to being something that one does not yet possess. I am inclined to see this as the position of Confucius as well, but a discussion of relative theories of human nature would stray too far from the purpose of this essay.
8. *Mencius* 7A:3.
9. Ibid., 7A:3.
10. *Analects* 12.4.
11. For a discussion of this problem, cf. Schwarz 1985, pp. 71–75.
12. For example, cf. *Analects* 2.1, 12.19, 15.5.
13. Cf. *Mencius* 2A:2 ff.
14. A reference to 6A:6.
15. The phrase "not helping [one to get it]," *wu yi*, is found also in Mencius' comment on the story, in 2A:2, of the farmer from Song who tried to help his rice sprouts grow by pulling on them: "Those who think that nothing will help [one to get it] and so give up [the task of cultivation of the mind] are like those who neglect to weed their rice paddies; those who try to help them grow are like those who pull on the rice sprouts—not only does

this not help, but it actually causes harm." Weeding one's rice paddy and pulling on the sprouts to make them grow are two paradigmatic examples of, respectively, how "seeking helps one to get it" and how "seeking does not help one to get it."

16. Although the direct object of the verb "to await" (*si*) in this passage is the indefinite pronoun "it" (*zhi*), the identity of "it" is most likely *ming*, as is indicated by a parallel passage in 7B:33: "The gentleman merely follows what is naturally given in order to await *ming*." The indefinite pronoun was likely employed in order to avoid a stylistically unpleasant repetition of *ming*, an aesthetic decision I have followed in my translation.

17. An interesting observation that argues against Tang Junyi is that if *ming* were to be read as functionally equivalent to *yi*, it would make no sense to speak of something being "proper *ming*" or not "proper *ming*."

18. I.e., one should not worry about one's position or lack of recognition per se, but rather that in cultivating oneself one has not yet become the equal of Shun.

19. *Analects* 12.4, 12.5.

20. Ibid., 7.3.

21. Ibid., 4.14.

22. Ibid., 15.32.

23. Ibid., 11.18. It is important to note that Si will not necessarily be unsuccessful in his speculatory endeavors—it is merely that the determination of success or failure in this arena of action is not within his control, whereas virtue is there for the taking if he would only choose to concentrate his efforts on himself. In examples such as this the line between the normative and descriptive sense of *ming* begins to blur, a phenomenon that is discussed at greater length below.

24. Referring to Ji Sun.

25. *Analects* 14.36.

26. Ibid., 6.22.

27. Although this essay is focused on the conception of *ming* in the *Analects* and the *Mencius*, it is interesting to note the distinction between Heavenly and human—i.e., outer and inner—realms that we find described quite explicitly in the other major pre-Qin Confucian work, the *Xunzi*:

> The king of Chu has a retinue of a thousand chariots, but not because he is wise. The gentleman must eat boiled greens and drink water, but not

because he is stupid. These are accidents of circumstance [*jie ran*—glossed by Yang Liang as referring to *ming*]. To be refined in purpose, rich in virtuous action, and clear in understanding; to live in the present and yet have your heart set on the past—these are things which are within your own power. Therefore the gentleman cherishes what is within his power and does not long for what is within the power of Heaven alone. The petty man, however, puts aside what is in his power and longs for what is in the power of Heaven. Because the gentleman cherishes what is within his power and does not long for what is within Heaven's power, he goes forward day by day. Because the petty man sets aside what is within his power and longs for what is within Heaven's power, he goes backward day by day. The same cause impels the gentleman forward day by day, and the petty man backward. What separates the two originates in this one point alone. (Adapted from Watson 1963, p. 83)

28. *Analects* 2.4, 16.8, 20.3.

29. It is just as easy and, in my opinion at least, more satisfying to read this as a "neither/nor" statement ("this is not only without *yi*, but moreover without *ming*")—that is, as indicating that had Confucius decided to lodge with Yung Ju and Ji Juan he would have been going against the external flow of events as well as internal morality.

30. Tang 1973, p. 118.

31. Ibid., p. 118. Compare this apparent de-emphasis of human agency with Benjamin Schwartz' observation: "Heaven has in the past also made manifest to man the normative order that should govern human society, but the task of 'completing' or actualizing this order devolves upon the human being who must actualize it. The order is not immanent in the society in the sense that human beings are not preprogrammed to realize it" (Schwartz 1985, p. 124).

32. A similar point is made by Heiner Roetz, who characterizes the type of "cosmologism" one finds in thinkers such as Tang Junyi as a "typical Neo-Confucian stereotype" (Roetz 1993, p. 228).

33. *Mencius* 7A:1; cf. the discussion of this passage above.

34. In the discussion above of Tang Junyi's position, I have chosen to emphasize its normative slant. However, as Kwong-loi Shun notes, it is not necessary to see Tang's position as precluding an

inner-outer dichotomy—it could very well be the case that such a dichotomy is present, but is merely not emphasized in the conception of *ming*. A normative interpretation is not necessarily devoid of a descriptive component: Tang's conception of *ming* could be seen as merely highlighting the ethical content of what are normally viewed as purely external constraints. As Shun describes it, "*ming* is used primarily to highlight two dimensions of human ethical experience—that in moments of frustrated efforts one can also discern certain ethical constraints on how one responds to the situation, and that ethical constraints are themselves experienced as something that comes beyond oneself" (Kwong-loi Shun, personal correspondence). The distinction between a "normative" and a "descriptive" conception of *ming* can perhaps best be viewed as a convenient heuristic device, for the boundaries between the two often begin to blur upon close examination.

35. Eno 1990, pp. 92–93.
36. Ibid., p. 33.

Bibliography

Eno, Robert. *The Confucian Creation of Heaven.* Albany: State University of New York Press, 1990.

Fingarette, Herbert. *Confucius: The Secular As Sacred.* New York: Harper and Row, 1972.

Hume, David. *The Natural History of Religion.* Stanford: Stanford University Press, 1956.

Lau, D. C., trans. *Confucius: The Analects.* Middlesex, England: Penguin Books, 1979.

Roetz, Heiner. *Confucian Ethics in the Axial Age.* Albany: State University of New York Press, 1993.

Schwartz, Benjamin. *The World of Thought in Ancient China.* Cambridge: Harvard University Press, 1985.

Tang Junyi. *Zhongguo zhexue yuanlun.* Vol. 1, *Yuandao pian.* Hong Kong: Xinshuyuan Yanjiusuo, 1973.

Watson, Burton, trans. *Hsün-tzu: Basic Writings.* New York: Columbia University Press, 1963.

Xunzi. Shanghai: Shanghai Guji Chubanshe, 1989.

Zhu Xi. *Sishu zhangzhu jishu.* Shanghai: Shanghai Shudian, 1987.

Study Questions

A.2.4 Edward (Ted) Slingerland, The Conception of *Ming* in Early Confucian Thought

1. Explain the main points that Ted Slingerland makes in the "introduction" of his essay.
2. Identify the "position" (thesis) that Ted Slingerland advances in his essay and write the whole *thesis* down in your notes.
3. Explain the "two possible objections to the inner-outer dichotomy" that Ted Slingerland makes and how he defends himself.
4. Identify and list the textual sources that Ted Slingerland uses to make his argument(s).
5. Critically explain the argument(s) that Ted Slingerland makes in support of his thesis.
6. Explain the way Ted Slingerland prepared his "NOTES" and consider it for your adoption.
7. Explain the way Ted Slingerland prepared his "BIBLIOGRAPHY" and consider it for your adoption.
8. Using Rosenberg's method of writing a philosophical essay as your model, evaluate and critique the method that Ted Slingerland used in his article.

Part B

The Inner Powers of Philosophic Consciousness

CHAPTER 3

Eastern Forms of Non–Dualistic Contemplation, Meditation, and Thinking

The Buddhist Forms of "Middle Way" Meditation

The Introduction

Buddhism is also known as the Middle Way Dharma (Doctrine or Teaching). The concept of the "Middle Way" was introduced by the Buddha in his "First Sermon" to his former five ascetic companions in the Deer Park after he attained Buddhahood. His "First Sermon" was later given a scriptural form and is known as *The Sutra on Setting in Motion the Wheel of the Dharma*. He identifies the two ways of life, one, the life of self-indulgence that he himself and most people of his time pursued, and the other, a life of self-mortification that ascetics of his time pursued (asceticism). He characterizes them as the "two extremes"of life and rejects them wholesale. Finally, he advocates for the "Middle Way" which he also calls the "Noble Eightfold Path."

What does the Buddha really mean by the "Middle Way"? Later Buddhist answers to this question led to conflicting interpretations and further philosophical developments of the concept of the "Middle Way" within both the Theravadin and Mahayanist traditions. Of the Buddhist Middle Way traditions, there are at least three main forms of "middle way" perceiving and thinking and doing: the Buddhaian form started by the Buddha, the Theravadin form, and the Mahayanist form.

The Buddhist doctrines of the Middle Way have their own unique characteristics and can be viewed as the third alternative to the Aristotelian doctrine of the Mean and the ancient East Asian Confucianist doctrine of the Mean. A scholarly study of these doctrines and their practical applications can be rewarding, both intellectually and existentially. A comparative study of the Buddhist doctrine of the Middle Way and the ancient East Asian Confucianist doctrine of Chung Yung (v. Trung Dung) is encouraged for students of this anthology.

B.3.1.a

The Buddha Taught the Middle Way of Thinking and Living

The Buddhaian Form of the Middle Way Thinking and Living

17. The Blessed One thus addressed the five Bhikkhus: 'There are two extremes, O Bhikkhus, which he who has given up the world ought to avoid. What are these two extremes? A life given to *pleasures*, devoted to pleasures and lusts: this is degrading, sensual, vulgar, ignoble, and profitless; and a life given to *mortifications*: this is painful, ignoble, and profitless. By avoiding these two extremes, O Bhikkhus, the Tathâgata has gained the knowledge of the Middle Path which leads to insight, which leads to wisdom, which conduces to calm, to knowledge, to the Sambodhi, to Nirvâna.

18. 'Which, O Bhikkhus, is this Middle Path the knowledge of which the Tathâgata has gained, which leads to insight, which leads to wisdom, which conduces to calm, to knowledge, to the Sambodhi, to Nirvâna? It is the *holy eightfold Path*, namely, Right Belief, Right Aspiration, Right Speech, Right Conduct, Right Means of Livelihood, Right Endeavour, Right Memory, Right Meditation. This, O Bhikkhus, is the Middle Path the knowledge of which the Tathâgata has

gained, which leads to insight, which leads to wisdom, which conduces to calm, to knowledge, to the Sambodhi, to Nirvâna.

19. 'This, O Bhikkhus, is the Noble Truth of *Suffering*: Birth is suffering; decay is suffering; illness is suffering; death is suffering. Presence of objects we hate, is suffering; Separation from objects we love, is suffering; not to obtain what we desire, is suffering. Briefly, the fivefold clinging to existence[1] is suffering.

20. 'This, O Bhikkhus, is the Noble Truth of the *Cause of suffering*: Thirst, that leads to re-birth, accompanied by pleasure and lust, finding its delight here and there. [This thirst is threefold] namely, thirst for pleasure, thirst for existence, thirst for prosperity.

21. 'This, O Bhikkhus, is the Noble Truth of the *Cessation of suffering*: [it ceases with] the complete cessation of this thirst—a cessation

[1]The 'five clingings' are: corporality, feeling, perception, mental formation, consciousness. Buddhism sums up in this way all the elements of our (illusory) bodily and spiritual personality.

[Source: Taken from the *Mahavagga* 1.16.17–22, printed in M. Muller, ed., *Sacred Books of the East*, volume XIII (London: Oxford University Press, 1881), pp. 94–6].

which consists in the absence of every passion—with the abandoning of this thirst, with the doing away with it, with the deliverance from it, with the destruction of desire.

22. 'This, O Bhikkhus, is the Noble Truth of the *Path* which leads to the cessation of suffering; That holy eightfold Path, that is to say: Right Belief, Right Aspiration, Right Speech, Right Conduct, Right Means of Livelihood, Right Endeavour, Right Memory, Right Meditation.'

Study Questions

B.3.1.a The Buddha Taught the Middle Way Thinking and Living

1. Explain what the Buddha means by the "two extremes" of life.
2. Explain what the Buddha means by the "Middle Path" in relation to the two extremes.
3. Analyze the Buddhaian mode of the *"middle way"* thinking and living that the Buddha presents in the opening of his "First Sermon."
4. Explain what the Buddha really means by the "Middle Way" as a mode of thinking and living. For your thinking options, the following theses are possible:

    a. Middle Way as "centrality."
    b. Middle Way as "moderation."
    c. Middle Way as "a new alternative way of life."
    d. Middle Way as "dependent origination."
    e. Middle Way as "emptiness."

5. Critically explain whether the Buddha might have violated the principles of his "middle way" thinking and living when he introduces his "Four Noble Truths" and the "Noble Eightfold Path."
6. Explain how you would resolve such a *problem* as the result of your critique.
7. In what way can you apply the Buddhaian middle way doctrine to your thinking and living?

B.3.1.b

Ananda Taught Channa the Middle Way

The Introduction

What did the Buddha really mean by the "Middle Way"? This question has remained theoretically problematic not only for students of Buddhism but also for Buddhist thinkers and philosophers. By the "Middle Way," did the Buddha mean: the "Noble Eightfold Path" or *moderation* or *centrality* or *a third alternative way of life* or *dependent origination* or their combination?

Each of the stated interpretations is theoretically possible and has its own theoretical and practical problems. But, which interpretation is true to the original meaning that the Buddha might have intended? If, by the "Middle Way," the Buddha means "moderation" between two extremes, then, how should this interpretation deal with the problem of "moderation" between "killing" and "not-killing" as two extremes?

This textual selection shows how Ananda, who is known to be the Buddha's closest disciple, understands the "Middle Way" himself. Does Ananda understand the "Middle Way" as "centrality" or something else? Regardless of what interpretation of Ananda's Middle Way view is correct, it is considered here as a Theravadin version of the Middle Way doctrine. The selection portrays the story of the monk Channa (how he learns and comprehends the Middle Way view as it is applied to the doctrine of anatman), which "reflects the real struggle Buddhists underwent to grapple with this question of anatman, not just as an intellectual issue but also existentially as a matter of actual realization." [Strong 1995:96]

Once several elders were staying in Benares at Isipatana in the Deer Park. One evening, the Venerable Channa came out of his meditational retreat, took his door key, and going from one lodging to the next, he said this to the elders: "Please, venerable sirs, exhort me, teach me, preach to me, so that I may come to see the Dharma!"

Thus addressed, the elders said this to the Venerable Channa: "Brother Channa, physical form is impermanent, feelings are impermanent, perceptions are impermanent, karmic constituents are impermanent, consciousness is impermanent. Physical form is not the Self, feelings are not the Self, perceptions are not the Self, karmic constituents are not the Self, consciousness is not the Self. . . . "

[Source: Taken from *The Samyutta-Nikaya*, ed. Léon Feer (London: Pali Text Society, 1890), 3:132–35]

"I know all of that! . . . " exclaimed the Venerable Channa, "but my mind fails to experience the calming of all conditioned states, the complete rejection of the bases of rebirth, the destruction of craving, the achievement of passionlessness, cessation, nirvāṇa! Agitated, I find no satisfaction, no stability, no release! Attachment arises, and I keep coming back to the thought 'Well, then, what *is* the Self?' I just cannot understand the Dharma in this way. Isn't there anyone who can teach it to me in such a way that I will see it?"

Then it occurred to Channa that the Venerable Ānanda was staying in Kosambī in the Ghosita Park and that the Master had praised and honored him as foremost among his learned co-practitioners. "The Venerable Ānanda," he reflected, "will be able to teach me the Dharma, in such a way that I will come to see it." . . .

So Channa left his lodging, took his robe and bowl, and went to Ghosita Park in Kosambī, where the Venerable Ānanda was staying. There, [after telling him all about his quest and his inability to experience the Truth of the Buddha's teachings, he explained his motivation in coming], saying: "Please, Venerable Ānanda, exhort me, teach me, preach to me, so that I may come to see the Dharma."

"All this is pleasing to me, Channa," Ānanda replied. "You have indeed made things clear. You are like a field ready for planting. Listen to me, for you are capable of truly knowing the Dharma!"

And at these words—that he would really be able to know the Dharma—there arose in the Venerable Channa an exhilarating joy and gladness.

Then the Venerable Ānanda said: "With my own lips, Channa, I will impart to you what I heard from the very lips of the Blessed One, as he was instructing the monk Kaccānagotta. 'Kaccāna,' he said, 'the world, as a rule, depends on dualism: things are said to exist or not to exist. But, Kaccāna, one who sees the arising of the world as it truly happens, with right wisdom, cannot maintain the nonexistence of the world; and one who sees the cessation of the world as it truly happens, with right wisdom, cannot maintain the existence of the world. Kaccāna, for the most part, people in this world seek support in schemes and are tied to tendencies. But those who do not resort to or depend on schemes or mental obstinacies, tendencies and biases, do not decide, "This is my Self."

"'What arises is suffering; what ceases is suffering—one who knows this has no doubts, is not distracted, has knowledge that does not depend on others. This, Kaccāna, is the extent of right view.

"'Everything exists—that, Kaccāna, is one extreme. Everything does not exist—that is the other extreme. The Tathāgata, Kaccāna, teaches a doctrine that goes down the middle, avoiding both extremes. Dependent on ignorance are karmic constituents; dependent on karmic constituents is consciousness, and so forth. In this way, this whole mass of suffering arises. But with the doing away of passion and the complete cessation of ignorance comes the cessation of karmic constituents, and so forth. In this way, this whole mass of suffering ceases.'"

"Venerable Ānanda," Channa responded, "this is what we brethren get who have co-practitioners such as you, who are compassionate, who long for our welfare, who are exhorters, teachers. Indeed, by hearing you preach the doctrine, Venerable Ānanda, I have come to realize the Dharma."

[1]Alternative English translation, F. L. Woodward, *The Book of the Kindred Sayings* (London: Pali Text Society, 1925), 3:111–14.

Study Questions

B.3.1.b Ananda Taught Channa the Middle Way

1. Explain the theoretical and methodological problems that the Venerable Channa faces.
2. Explain how and why the Venerable Ananda teaches Channa the middle way thinking.
3. Explain what and how Channa might have understood the "middle way" as he claims that he "has come to realize the Dharma."
4. As he teaches Channa, explain what Ananda might have understood the "middle way" to be.
5. If, by the "middle way," the Tathāgata (the Buddha) teaches "the doctrine that goes down the middle, avoiding both extremes" as Ananda interprets, then, explain any problems that you may discover in Ananda's teaching.
6. In what way can you apply the Theravadin middle way doctrine to your thinking and living?

An Ancient East Asian Confucianist Form of Thinking and Doing by the Mean

The Chung Yung (v. Trung Dung)

The Introduction

Like Hinduism and Buddhism, Chinese Confucianism, which was the ruling political ideology and moral philosophy of Chinese monarchy (206 BCE–1911 CE), had its own system of scriptures (*ching* [v. *kinh*]). The standard system of Confucianist scriptures, which was organized according to the numerology of the number 9, consisted of the "Five Classics" (Wu Ching [v. Ngũ Kinh]) and the "Four Books" (Ssu Shu [v. Tứ Thư]).

The Five Classics are the *Chou Yi Ching* (v. *Chu Dịch Kinh* [*Classic of Universal Change*]), the *Shih Ching* (v. *Thi Kinh* [*Classic of Poetry*]), the *Shu Ching* (v. *Thư Kinh* [*Classic of History*]), the *Ch'un Ch'iu Ching* (v. *Xuân Thu Kinh* [*Classic of Spring and Autumn*]), and the *Li Ching* or *Li Chi* (v. *Lễ Kinh* or *Lễ Ký* [*Classic of Rites*]).

The Four Books are the *Lun Yu* (v. *Luận Ngữ* [*Analects* of Confucius], the *Meng Tzu* (v. *Mạnh Tử* [*Book of Mencius*]), the *Ta Hsueh* (v. *Đại Học* [*Great Learning*]), and the *Chung Yung* (v. *Trung Dung* [*Doctrine of the Mean*]).

The *Doctrine of the Mean* and the *Great Learning* are often mentioned together, since they used to form a chapter in the *Classic of Rites* until Chu Hsi (1130–1200 ACE) selected them to make the "Four Books." The two became the influential texts for Chinese civil service examinations from 1313 until 1905. Concerning their theoretical contents, Professor Wing-Tsit Chan observes: "The *Great Learning* deals with social and political matters, while the *Doctrine of the Mean* is a discourse on psychology and metaphysics. The *Great Learning* discusses the mind but not human nature, whereas with the *Doctrine of the Mean* the opposite is true. The *Great Learning* emphasizes method and procedure, whereas the *Doctrine of the Mean* concentrates on reality. The *Great Learning* is generally rational in tone, but the *Doctrine of the Mean* is religious and mystical." [Chan 1963:95]

The date and authorship of the *Doctrine of the Mean* have remained historically problematic and unresolved. This is also the case of the *Great Learning* and the case for most of the Five Classics and the Four Books. The *Doctrine of the Mean* is traditionally attributed to the authorship of Tzu Ssu (v. *Tử Tư* [492–431 BCE]), Confucius' grandson. But there is no evidence for this arbitrary attribution, an ideologically characteristic practice of Chinese Confucianists. This attribution can be interpreted as ideologically intended by Han and later Chinese scholars to *legitimize* the *Doctrine of the Mean* as an authentic Confucianist text, because it was authored by Confucius' grandson! "Many modern scholars," notes Dr. Wing-Tsit Chan, "refuse to accept the theory; some have dated it around 200 B.C. The work is not consistent [with Confucianism-ccp] either in style or in thought. It may be a work of more than one person over a considerable period in the fifth or fourth century B.C." [Chan 1963:97, note 6]

The *Chung Yung* (v. *Trung Dung*), which James Legge translates as *The Doctrine of the Mean*, is one of the Chinese-Confucianist system of Four Books and Five Classics.

Chapter I.

1. What Heaven has conferred is called the Nature; an accordance with this nature is called the Path of duty; the regulation of this path is called Instructions.
2. The path may not be left for an instant. If it could be left, it would not be the path. On this account, the superior man does not wait till he sees things, to be cautious, nor till he hears things, to be apprehensive.
3. There is nothing more visible than what is secret, and nothing more manifest than what is minute. Therefore the superior man is watchful over himself, when he is alone.
4. While there are no stirrings of pleasure, anger, sorrow, or joy, the mind may be said to be in the state of Equilibrium. When those feelings have been stirred, and they act in their due degree, there ensues what may be called the state of Harmony. This Equilibrium is the great root *from which grow all the human actings* in the world, and this Harmony is the universal path *which they all should pursue.*
5. Let the states of equilibrium and harmony exist in perfection, and a happy order will prevail throughout heaven and earth, and all things will be nourished and flourish.

Chapter II.

1. Chung-ni said, "The superior man *embodies* the course of the Mean; the mean man acts contrary to the course of the Mean.

2. "The superior man's embodying the course of the Mean is because he is a superior man, and so always maintains the Mean. The mean man's acting contrary to the course of the Mean is because he is a mean man, and has no caution."

Chapter III.

1. The Master said, "Perfect is the virtue which is according to the Mean! Rare have they long been among the people, who could practice it!"

Chapter IV.

1. The Master said, "I know how it is that the path *of the Mean* is not walked in: —The knowing go beyond it, and the stupid do not come up to it. I know how it is that the path of the Mean is not understood: —The men of talents and virtue go beyond it, and the worthless do not come up to it.
2. There is no body but eats and drinks. Both there are few who can distinguish flavours.

Chapter V.

The Master said, "Alas! How is the path of the Mean untrodden!"

Chapter VI.

The Master said, "There was Shun: —He indeed was greatly wise! Shun loved to question

[Source: Taken from *The Doctrine of the Mean* in James Legge, trans., *The Chinese Classics*, volumes I-II (London: Oxford University Press, 1893), chapters cited].

others, and to study their words, though they might be shallow. He concealed what was bad in them, and displayed what was good. He took hold of their two extremes, *determined* the Mean, and employed it in *his government of* the people. It was by this that he was Shun!"

Chapter VII.

The Master said, "Men all say, `We are wise;' but being driven forward and taken in a net, a trap, or a pitfall, they know not how to escape. Man all say, `We are wise;' but happening to choose the course of the Mean, they are not able to keep it for a round month."

Chapter VIII.

"The Master said, "This was the manner of Hui: —he made choice of the Mean, and whenever he got hold of what was good, he clasped it firmly, as if wearing it on his breast, and did not lose it."

Chapter VIX.

The Master said, "The kingdom, its States, and its families, may be perfectly ruled; dignities and emoluments may be declined; naked weapons may be trampled under the feet; —but the course of the Mean cannot be attained to."

Chapter X.

1. Tze-lu asked about energy.
2. The Master said, "Do you mean the energy of the South, the energy of the North, or the energy which you should cultivate yourself?
3. "To show forbearance and gentleness in teaching others; and not to revenge unreasonable conduct: —this is the energy of the Southern regions, and the good man makes it his study.
4. "To lie under arms; and meet death without regret: —this is the energy of the Northern regions, and the forceful make it their study.
5. "Therefore, the superior man cultivates *a friendly* harmony, without being weak. — How firm is he in his energy! He stands erect in the middle, without inclining to either side. —How firm is he in his energy! When bad principles prevail in the country, he maintains his course to death without changing. —How firm is he in his energy!

Chapter XI.

3. [The Master said,] "The superior man accords with the course of the Mean. Though he may be all unknown, unregarded by the world, he feels no regret. —It is only the sage who is able for this."

Chapter XII.

1. The way which the superior man pursues, reaches wide and far, and yet is secret.
2. Common men and women, however ignorant, may intermeddle with the knowledge of it; yet in its utmost reaches, there is that which even the sage does not know. Common men and women, however much below the ordinary standard of character, can carry it into practice; yet in its utmost reaches, there is that which even the sage is not able to carry into practice. . . .

Chapter XIV.

1. The superior man does what is proper to the station in which he is; he does not desire to go beyond this.
2. In a position of wealth and honour, he does what is proper to a position of wealth and honour. In a poor and low position, he does what is proper to a poor and low position. Situated among barbarous tribes, he does what is proper to a situation among barbarous tribes. In a position of sorrow and difficulty, he does what is proper to a position of sorrow and difficulty. The superior man can find himself in no situation in which he is not himself.
3. In a high situation, he does not treat with contempt his inferiors. In a low situation, he does not court the favour of his superiors. He rec-

tifies himself, and seeks for nothing from others, so that he has no dissatisfactions. He does not murmur against Heaven, nor grumble against men.

4. Thus it is that the superior man is quiet and calm, waiting for the appointments of *Heaven*, while the mean man walks in dangerous paths, looking for lucky occurrences.

5. The Master said, "In archery we have something like the way of the superior man. When the archer misses the centre of the target, he turns round and seeks for the cause of his failure in himself."

Chapter XV.

1. The way of the superior man may be compared to what takes place in travelling, when to go to a distance we must first traverse the space that is near, and in ascending a height, when we must begin from the lower ground.

Study Questions

B.3.2 The Chung Yung (v. Trung Dung): An Ancient East Asian Confucianist Form of Thinking and Doing by the Mean

1. Explain the relationships between "Nature," "Path of duty," and "Instructions."
2. Explain what is meant by "the state of Equilibrium" and "the state of Harmony." How do they relate?
3. Identify and analyze different aspects of acting according to the Mean (Chung Yung [v. Trung Dung]).
4. Explain the method by which Emperor Shun (v. Thuẩn) practices the thinking and doing by the Mean in contrast to "the energy of the South" and "the energy of the North."
5. Explain how the "superior man" should practice the method of thinking and doing by the Mean in contrast to the "mean man."
6. Critique this ancient East Asian Confucianist doctrine of thinking and doing by the Mean.

An Ancient East Asian Form of Categorical Thinking

The White Horse Is Not a Horse

Kung Sun Lung (v. Công Tôn Long)

The Introduction

One of the schools of ancient East Asian philosophies is known as the "Ming Chia" (v. Danh Gia [School of Names]) or "Ming Pien" (v. Danh Biện [Scholars of Names and Debaters]) or "Pien Che" (v. Biện Giả [Logicians]). This school has been given different names in English. Derk Bodde renders "pien che" (v. biện giả) into English as "Dialecticians" (Fung 1952:192). Wing-Tsit Chan prefers the name "Logicians" for this school. And A. C. Graham calls the "pien che" as "Sophists" [Graham 1989:75]. Dr. Graham explains that "the label 'Sophist' does call attention to a configuration of tendencies at the birth of rational discourse which is common to Greece and China. In both traditions we meet thinkers who delight in propositions which defy common sense, and consequently are derided as frivolous and irresponsible. In both, these thinkers belong to the early period when reason is a newly discovered tool not yet under control, seeming to give one the power to prove or disprove anything. In both, the exuberance with which they play with this astonishing new toy leads not only to 'sophistries' but to paradoxes of lasting philosophical significance. In both, the pride and pleasure in logical acrobatics call attention to the relation between words and things." [*Ibid*].

Among the most prominent thinkers of the school of Logicians (Pien Che [Biện Giả]), we can name Hui Shih (v. Huệ Thi) and Kung Sun Lung (v. Công Tôn Long). Thus, in his *Nan Hua Ching* (v. *Nam Hoa Kinh* [chapter 33]), Chuang Tzu (v. Trang Tử) has this to say: "Through such sayings [paradoxes–ccp], Hui Shih made a great show in the world, and taught them to the Dialecticians. The Dialecticians in the world were delighted with them. . . . Huan T'uan and Kung-sun Lung were followers of the Dialecticians" [translated and cited in Fung 1952:192].

Unlike Kung Sun Lung (v. Công Tôn Long), who tends to be extreme in his philosophical view of things, Hui Shih (v. Huệ Thi) tends to be relativistic in his philosophical stand. This may be due in part to the influence of ancient East Asian Taoism because Hui Shih (v. Huệ Thi) was a friend of Chuang Tzu (v. Trang Tử), who was in turn influenced by the former.

The works of the school of Logicians or Ming Chia (v. Danh Gia [School of Names]) are all lost, except the partially preserved *Kung-sun Lung Tzu* (v. *Công Tôn Long Tử*). It is a short treatise in six chapters, but it is mostly unintelligible due to its textual corruption. It is from "On the White Horse" (chapter 2) of the *Kung-sun Lung Tzu* (v. *Công Tôn Long Tử*) that this selection is chosen. It begins with this question: "Is it correct to say that a white horse is not a horse?" What follows is the arguments for the positive answer to the question.

B. "Because 'horse' denotes the form and 'white' denotes the color. What denotes the color does not denote the form. Therefore we say that a white horse is not a horse."

A. "There being a horse, one cannot say that there is no horse. If one cannot say that there is no horse, then isn't [it] a horse? Since there being a white horse means that there is a horse, why does being white make it not a horse?"

B. "Ask for a horse, and either a yellow or a black one may answer. Ask for a white horse, and neither the yellow horse nor the black one may answer. If a white horse were a horse, then what is asked in both cases would be the same. If what is asked is the same, then a white horse would be no different from a horse. If what is asked is no different, then why is it that yellow and black horses may yet answer in the one case but not in the other? Clearly the two cases are incompatible. Now the yellow horse and the black horse remain the same. And yet they answer to a horse but not to a white horse. Obviously a white horse is not a horse."

A. "You consider a horse with color as not a horse. Since there is no horse in the world without color, is it all right [to say] that there is no horse in the world?"

B. "Horses of course have color. Therefore there are white horses. If horses had no color, there would be simply horses. Where do white horses come in? Therefore whiteness is different from horse. A white horse means a horse combined with whiteness. [Thus in one case it is] horse and [in the other it is] a white horse. Therefore we say that a white horse is not a horse."

A. [Since you say that] before the horse is combined with whiteness, it is simply a horse, before whiteness is combined with a horse it is simply whiteness, and when the horse and whiteness are combined they are collectively called a white horse, you are calling a combination by what is not a combination. This is incorrect. Therefore it is incorrect to say that a white horse is not a horse."

B. "If you regard a white horse as a horse, is it correct to say that a white horse is a yellow horse?"

A. "No."

B. "If you regard a white horse as different from a yellow horse, you are differentiating a yellow horse from a horse. To differentiate a yellow horse from a horse is to regard the yellow horse as not a horse. Now to regard a yellow horse as not a horse and yet to regard a white horse as a horse is like a bird flying into a pool or like the inner and outer coffins being in different places. This would be the most contradictory argument and the wildest talk."

A. "[When we say that] a white horse cannot be said to be not a horse, we are separating the whiteness from the horse. If [the whiteness] is not separated from [the horse], then there would be a white horse and we should not say that there is [just] a horse. Therefore when we say that there is a horse, we do so simply because it is a horse and not because it is a white horse. When we say that there is a horse, we do not mean that there are a horse [as such] and another horse [as the white horse]."

B. "It is all right to ignore the whiteness that is not fixed on any object. But in speaking of the white horse, we are talking about the whiteness that is fixed on the object. The object on which whiteness is fixed is not whiteness [itself]. The term `horse' does not involve any choice of color and therefore either a yellow horse or a black one may answer. But the term `white horse' does involve a choice of color. Both the yellow horse and the black one are excluded because of their color. Only a white horse may answer. What does not exclude [color] is not the same as what excludes [color]. Therefore we say that a white horse is not a horse." (SPPY, 3b-5b)

Study Questions

B.3.3 An Ancient East Asian Form of Categorical Thinking. Kung Sun Lung (v. Công Tôn Long), The White Horse Is Not a Horse

1. Identify and analyze all the arguments that Công Tôn Long (c. Kung Sun Lung) makes in support of his thesis.
2. Critically explain how Kung Sun Lung (v. Công Tôn Long) views the whiteness-horseness relationship and make your response: Do they remain as the two independent constitutive categories that form a new third entity or transform themselves to give rise to a new third entity?
3. In what way can you apply the Kungian (v. Côngian) method of categorical thinking to your own thinking and doing?

Ancient East Asian Taoist Forms of Contemplation

The Semi-Dialectic of Thinking and Doing

Lao Tzu (v. Lão Tử)

The Introduction

Lao Tzu (v. Lão Tử) is generally regarded as the "founder" of Taoism and "author" of the *Tao Te Ching* (v. *Đạo Đức Kinh* [*Classic of the Way and Its Virtue*]). The word "lao" (v. lão) means "old" or "well seasoned" or "widely experienced." The word "tzu" (v. tử) means "master" or "baby" or "infant." "Lao Tzu" (v. Lão Tử) means therefore the "Old Master" or "Old Baby." The title may express an existentially unique Taoist (v. Đạoist) view of life, which takes the "sage" (a person of perfect wisdom and goodness) to be the ideal for a baby to achieve, and the "baby" (a symbol of natural purity and innocence) to be the ideal for the sage to return to his true being. A cycle of life is thus completed.

The *Tao Te Ching* (v. *Đạo Đức Kinh*) is also known as the *Lao Tzu* (v. *Lão Tử*). Currently, there are two main versions of the *Tao Te Ching*, the traditionally circulated text, and the archaeologically unearthed text at Ma Wang Tui (v. Mã Vương Đội). The traditionally circulated text consists of eighty-one chapters of short stanzas, over half of which are rhymed. The 81 chapters (9 times 9) were then divided into two books in harmony with the Yin-Yang dichotomy. Book I, the *Tao* (v. Đạo [Way]), consists of thirty-seven chapters (1–37). Book II, the *Te* (v. Đức [Virtue]), consists of forty-four chapters (38–81). The internal organization and theoretical importance of the concepts of *tao* and *te* of the text caused it to be called the *Tao Te Ching* (v. *Đạo Đức Kinh*). The date of the traditional text has remained unresolved and is still a subject of much debate. William H. Baxter divides all dating schemes of the traditional text into "three main theories." The first traditional theory dates "the Lao-tzu at somewhere around 500 B.C.E." The second traditional theory dates it "about 375 B.C.E." And the modern theory takes "225 B.C.E." to be its proximate date. [Baxter 1998:232–33]

The archaeologically unearthed text of the *Tao Te Ching* is called the "*Ma-wang-tui* text" after its place of discovery. In 1973, students of Taoism welcomed the archaeological discovery of the two ancient silk manuscripts of the *Tao Te Ching* in the Han Tom No. 3 at Ma-wang-tui (v. Mã Vương Đội), the grave of the son of the marquis of Tai (v. Thái) in early Han times. These two ancient silk manuscripts can be dated around the 2nd century BCE, because according to Professor Robert G. Henricks, "an inventory slip in the tomb informs us that this man was buried on the equivalent in the Western calendar of April 4, 168 BCE" [Henricks 1989:xiii]. One of the differences between the *Ma-wang-tui* text and the traditional text is its internal organization, namely, the order of its two books is reversed, the *Te Tao Ching*.

Read 1 of section

[1] The Tao (Way [v. Đạo]) that can be told of is
   not the eternal Tao;
The name that can be named is not the eternal
   name.
The Nameless is the origin of Heaven and Earth;
The Named is the mother of all things [lit. 10,000
   wu [v. vạn vật]-ccp],
Therefore let there always be non-being [wu (v.
   vô)] so we may see their subtlety [v. *diệu*],
And let there always be being [yu (v. hữu)] so we
   may see their outcome,
The two are the same,
But after they are produced, they have different
   names.
They both may be called deep and profound
   (*hsüan* [v. *huyền*]).
Deeper and more profound,
The door of all subtleties! (*TTC*:1).

[2] When the people of the world all know beauty
   as beauty, there arises the recognition of
   ugliness.
When they all know the good as good, there arises
   the recognition of evil.
Therefore:

   Being and non-being produce each other;
   Difficult and easy complete each other;
   Long and short contrast each other;
   High and low distinguish each other;
   Sound and voice harmonize with each
      other;
   Front and back follow each other.
   Therefore the sage manages affairs
      without action (*wu-wei* [v. *vô vi*]).
   And spreads doctrines without words.

All thing arise, and he does not turn away
   from them.
He produces them, but does not take
   possession of them.
He acts, but does not rely on his own
   ability.
He accomplishes his task, but does not
   claim credit for it.
It is precisely because he does not claim
   credit that his accomplishment
   remains with him. (*TTC*:2 ["*TTC*"
   stands for *Tao Te Ching* and "7" stands
   for the chapter number.])

[3] Heaven is eternal and Earth everlasting.
They can be eternal and everlasting because they
   do not exist for themselves,
And for this reason can exist forever.
Therefore the sage places himself in the back-
   ground, but finds himself in the foreground.
He puts himself away, and yet he always remains.
Is it not because he has no personal interests are
   fulfilled. (*TTC*:7).

[4] Attain complete vacuity,
Maintain steadfast quietude.
All things come into being,
And I see thereby their returns.
All things flourish,
But each one returns to its root.
This return to its root means tranquillity.
It is called returning to its destiny.
To return to destiny is called the eternal (Tao).
To know the eternal is called enlightenment.
Not to know the eternal is to act blindly to result
   in disaster.

He who knows the eternal is all-embracing.
Being all-embracing, he is impartial.
Being impartial, he is kingly (universal).
Being kingly, he is one with Nature [lit. Heaven—ccp].
Being one with Nature, he is in accord with Tao.
Being in accord with [the-cc] Tao, he is everlasting,
And is free from danger throughout his lifetime. (*TTC*:16).

[5] To yield is to be reserved whole.
To be bent is to become straight.
To be empty is to be full.
To be worn out is to be renewed.
To have little is to possess.
To have plenty is to be perplexed.
Therefore the sage embraces the one
And becomes the model of the world.
He does not show himself; therefore he is luminous.
He does not justify himself; therefore he becomes prominent.
He does not boast of himself; therefore he is given credit.
He does not brag; therefore he can endure for long.
It is precisely because he does not compete that the world cannot compete with him.
Is the ancient saying, "to yield is to be preserved whole," empty words?
Truly he will be preserved and (prominence, etc.) will come to him. (*TTC*:22).

[6] In order to contract,
It is necessary first to expand.
In order to weaken,
It is necessary first to strengthen.
In order to destroy,
It is necessary first to promote.
In order to grasp,
It is necessary first to give.
This is called subtle light.
The weak and the tender overcome the hard and the strong.
Fish should not be taken away from water.
And sharp weapons of the state should not be displayed to the people. (*TTC*:36).

[7] The softest things in the world overcome the hardest things in the world. (*TTC*:43).

[8] When the government is non-discriminative and dull,
The people are contented and generous.
When the government is searching and discriminative,
The people are disappointed and contentious.
Calamity is that upon which happiness depends;
Happiness is that in which calamity is latent.
Who knows when the limit will be reached?
Is there no correctness (used to govern the world?)
Then the correct again becomes the perverse
And the good will again become evil.
The people have been deluded for a long time.
Therefore the sage is as pointed as a square but does not pierce.
He is as acute as a knife but does not cut.
He is as straight as an unbent line but does not extend.
He is as bright as light but does not dazzle. (*TTC*:58).

[9] When man is born, he is tender and weak.
At death, he is stiff and hard.
All things, the grass as well as trees, are tender and supple while alive.
When dead, they are withered and dried.
Therefore the stiff and the hard are companions of death.
The tender and the weak are companions of life.
Therefore if the army is strong, it will not win.
If a tree is stiff, it will break.
The strong and the great are inferior, while the tender and the weak are superior. (*TTC*:76).

[10] True words are not beautiful;
Beautiful words are not true.
A good man does not argue;
He who argues is not a good man.
A wise man has no extensive knowledge;
He who has extensive knowledge is not a wise man.
The sage does not accumulate for himself.

The more he uses for others, the more he has himself.

The more he gives to others, the more he possesses of his own.

The way of Heaven is to benefit others and not to injure.

The way of the sage is to act but not to compete. (*TTC*:81).

Study Questions

B.3.4.a Lao Tzu (v. Lão Tử), The Semi-Dialectic of Thinking and Doing

1. Identify and list all the pairs of opposites mentioned by Lao Tzu (v. Lão Tử) and explain their relationship and meanings.
2. Recognizing the existence of pairs of opposites as Lao Tzu (v. Lão Tử) does but he does not fall victim to *dualistic thinking* as Socrates and Plato do. Explain his philosophical reasons. To answer this question, please see *also* G.18.1.a (Laoian ontology of the Tao [v. Đạo]).
3. Explain the method of semi-dialectial thinking that Lao Tzu (v. Lão Tử) uses when he thinks about any practical problem and when he contemplates the nature of reality.
4. Explore the possible principles that lie behind the semi-dialectical method of action that Lao Tzu (v. Lão Tử) recommends. For instance: "In order to grasp, It is necessary first to give."

B.3.4.b

Forms and Levels of Thinking

Chuang Tzu (v. Trang Tử)

The Introduction

In this short introduction, I will discuss Chuang Tzu (v. Trang Tử), the man, and his work (the *Nam Hua Ching* [v. *Nam Hoa Kinh*]).

Chuang Tzu (v. Trang Tử), who styles himself as "Chuang Chou" (v. Trang Chu), is traditionally honored as the early master of "Philosophical Taoism" (v. Đạoism) after Lao Tzu (v. Lão Tử), the founder of Taoist philosophy.

The biography of Chuang Tzu in Ssu Ma Ch'ien's *Shih Chi* (v. *Sử Ký*) tells us that Chuang Tzu (v. Trang Tử) came from the district of Meng (v. Mông) and lived during the reigns of King Hui of Liang (v. Lương [370–319 BCE]) and King Hsuan of Ch'i (v. Tề [319–301 BCE]). Chuang Tzu was therefore a contemporary of Meng Tzu (v. Mạnh Tử), Hui Tzu (v. Huệ Tử), Aristotle, Zénon, and Epicure. Scholars are not sure whether Chuang Tzu was a native of the ancient kingdom of Sung (v. Tống) or the ancient kingdom of Liang (v. Lương) because Meng (v. Mông) cannot be determined to be a district of either kingdom.

Chuang Tzu (v. Trang Tử) treasured freedom and life; submersing himself in the midst of Nature and people. He says of himself: "He did not condemn right or wrong, so he was able to get along with ordinary people. His writings, though they have a grand style, are not opposed to things and so are harmless. His phrases, though full of irregularities, are yet attractive and full of humor. The richness of his ideas cannot be exhausted. Above he roams with the Creator (*Tsao-wu-che* [v. Tạo vật giả-ccp]). Below he makes friends of those who, without beginning or end, are beyond life and death." [Translated cited in Fung 1952:174]

Valuing his private life more than political power and wealth, Chuang Tzu (v. Trang Tử) also practiced political "wu wei" (v. vô vi [non-action]). Thus, he prefers to "drag my tail in the mud" like a tortoise does rather than taking the high political office offer of the King of Ch'u (v. Sở).

The book of Chuang Tzu is known as the *Nan Hua Ching* (v. *Nam Hoa Kinh* [*Classic of Southern Flowers*]), but most American scholars prefer to call it the *Chuang Tzu*. The *Nan Hua Ching* (v. *Nam Hoa Kinh*), as it was abridged by the commentator Kuo Hsiang (died 312 CE), is divided into three main parts: The "Inner Chapters" (chs. 1–7), the "Outer Chapters" (chs. 8–22), and the "Mixed Chapters" (chs. 23–33). This division is still too loose for A. C. Graham, who dissects the text into "five main elements" with different dates as follows:

1. Writings of Chuang-tzu (c. 320 B.C.)
2. Writings classable only as 'School of Chuang-tzu'.
3. The essay of a writer we here label the 'Primitivist', datable with unusual precision to the period of civil war between the fall of Ch'in and victory of Han, between 209 and 202 B.C.
4. The Yangist chapters, from approximately the same period.
5. The final Syncretist stratum, 2nd century B.C.

The forms and levels of thinking that Chuang Tzu discusses in the textual selection from his *Nan Hua Ching* (v. *Nam Hoa Kinh*) can be viewed as his creative reconstruction of the ancient East Asian forms and levels of thinking that might have been current during his time *multiculturally*.

For speech is not merely the blowing of breath. The speaker has something to say, but what he says is not final. Has something been said? Or has something not been said? It may be different from the chirping of chickens. But is there really any difference? Or is there no difference?

How can Tao be so obscured that there should be a distinction of true and false? How can speech be so obscured that there should be a distinction of right and wrong? Where can you go and find Tao not to exist? Where can you go and find speech impossible? Tao is obscured by petty biases and speech is obscured by flowery expressions. Therefore there have arisen the controversies between the Confucianists and the Moists, each school regarding as right what the other considers as wrong, and regarding as wrong what the other considers as right. But to show that what each regards as right is wrong or to show that what each regards as wrong is right, there is no better way than to use the light (of Nature).

There is nothing that is not the "that" and there is nothing that is not the "this." Things do not know that they are the "that" of other things; they only know what they themselves know. Therefore I say that the "that" is produced by the "this" and the "this" is also caused by the "that." This is the theory of mutual production. Nevertheless, when there is life there is death, and when there is death there is life. When there is possibility, there is impossibility, and when there is impossibility, there is possibility. Because of the right, there is the wrong, and because of the wrong, there is the right. Therefore the sage does not proceed along these lines (of right and wrong, and so forth) but illuminates the matter with Nature. This is the reason.

The "this" is also the "that." The "that" is also the "this." The "this" has one standard of right and wrong, and the "that" also has a standard of right and wrong. Is there really a distinction between "that" and "this"? Or is there really no distinction between "that" and "this"? When "this" and "that" have no opposites, there is the very axis of Tao. Only when the axis occupies the center of a circle can things in their infinite complexities be responded to. The right is an infinity. The wrong is an infinity. Therefore I say that there is nothing better than to use the light (of Nature).

To take a mark (*chih*) to show that a mark is not a mark is not as good as to take a non-mark to show that a mark is not a mark. To take a horse to show that a [white] horse is not a horse (as such) is not as good as to take a non-horse to show that a horse is not a horse. The universe is but one mark, and all things are but a horse. When [people say], "All right," then [things are] all right. When people say, "Not all right," then [things are] not all right.

Chan, Wing-tsit. *A Source Book in Chinese Philosophy*. Copyright © 1963 by Princeton University Press. Reprinted by permission of Princeton University Press.

A road becomes so when people walk on it, and things become so-and-so [to people] because people call them so-and-so. How have they become so? They have become so because [people say they are] so. How have they become not so? They have become not so because [people say they are] not so. In their own way things are so-and-so. In their own way things are all right. There is nothing that is not so-and-so. There is nothing that is not all right. Let us take, for instance, a large beam and a small beam, or an ugly woman and Hsi-shih (famous beauty of ancient China), or generosity, strangeness, deceit, and abnormality. The Tao identifies them all as one. What is division [to some] is production [to others], and what is production [to others] is destruction [to some]. Whether things are produced or destroyed, [Tao] again identifies them all as one.

Only the intelligent knows how to identify all things as one. Therefore he does not use [his own judgment] but abides in the common [principle]. The common means the useful and the useful means identification. Identification means being at ease with oneself. When one is at ease with himself, one is near Tao. This is to let it (Nature) take its own course. He has arrived at this situation, and does not know it. This is Tao.

Those who wear out their intelligence to try to make things one without knowing that they are really the same may be called "three in the morning." What is meant by "three in the morning"? A monkey keeper once was giving out nuts and said, "Three in the morning and four in the evening." All the monkeys became angry. He said, "If that is the case, there will be four in the morning and three in the evening." All the monkeys were glad. Neither the name nor the actuality has been reduced but the monkeys reacted in joy and anger [differently]. The keeper also let things take their own course. Therefore the sage harmonizes the right and wrong and rests in natural equalization. This is called following two courses at the same time.

"Suppose you and I argue. If you beat me instead of my beating you, are you really right and am I really wrong? If I beat you instead of your beating me, am I really right and are you really wrong? Or are we both partly right and partly wrong? Or are we both wholly right and wholly wrong? Since between us neither you nor I know which is right, others are naturally in the dark. Whom shall we ask to arbitrate? If we ask someone who agrees with you, since he has already agreed with you, how can he arbitrate? If we ask someone who agrees with me, since he has already agreed with me, how can he arbitrate? If we ask someone who disagrees with both you and me to arbitrate, since he has already disagreed with you and me, how can he arbitrate? If we ask someone who agrees with both you and me to arbitrate, since he has already agreed with you and me, how can he arbitrate? Thus among you, me, and others, none knows which is right. Shall we wait for still others? The great variety of sounds are relative to each other just as much as they are not relative to each other. To harmonize them in the functioning of Nature and leave them in the process of infinite evolution is the way to complete our lifetime."

"What is meant by harmonizing them with the functioning of Nature?"

"We say this is right or wrong, and is so or is not so. If the right is really right, then the fact that it is different from the wrong leaves no room for argument. If what is so is really so, then the fact that it is different from what is not so leaves no room for argument. Forget the passage of time (life and death) and forget the distinction of right and wrong. Relax in the realm of the infinite and thus abide in the realm of the infinite."

The Shade asks the Shadow, "A little while ago you moved, and now you stop. A little while ago you sat down and now you stand up. Why this instability of purpose?"

"Do I depend on something else to be this way?" answered the Shadow. "Does that something on which I depend also depend on something else? Do I depend on anything any more than a snake depends on its discarded scale or a cicada on its new wings? How can I tell why I am so or why I am not so?"

Once I, Chuang Chou, dreamed that I was a butterfly and was happy as a butterfly. I was conscious that I was quite pleased with myself, but I did not know that I was Chou. Suddenly I awoke, and there I was, visibly Chou. I do not know whether it was Chou dreaming that he was a butterfly or the butterfly dreaming that it was Chou. Between Chou and the butterfly there must be some distinction. [But one may be the other.] This is called the transformation of things. (NHCC, 1:18a–48b)

Study Questions

B.3.4.b Chuang Tzu (v. Trang Tử), The Forms and Levels of Thinking

1. Identify and analyze the different levels and forms of thinking that Chuang Tzu (v. Trang Tử) discusses in the selected writing.
2. "The 'this' is also the 'that.' The 'that' is also the 'this'."
    a. Explain the theoretico-methodological status and function of the "this" and the "that" as they are intended by Chuang Tzu (v. Trang Tử).
    b. Take two concrete things as examples of the this and the that, then, explain how they are identical.
    c. Characterize the theoretical nature of this form of thinking and critique it.
3. Compare the different levels and forms of thinking and explain which one can help you to better understand the nature of the world in relation to your own being.
4. "Only the intelligent knows how to identify all things as one."
    a. Explain how and why the "intelligent" thinks that way according to Chuang Tzu (v. Trang Tử).
    b. Explain the meaning of the "one" according to Chuang Tzu (v. Trang Tử).
    c. Characterize the theoretical nature of this form of thinking and critique it.

The Zen of Self-Enlightenment

The Introduction

"Zen" is the Japanese form of "Meditative Buddhism" (*Dhyana*), just like "*Ch'an*" the Chinese form, "*Son*" the Korean form, and "*Thiền*" the Viêtnamese. All these East Asian forms of Meditative Buddhism have their respective national characteristics as they have diversified from their Ch'an ancestry. The word "Zen," meaning "meditation," is derived from the Chinese term "*ch'an*," which is a mispronunciation of the Sanskrit word "*dhyana*" (meditation). But thanks to the popularization of Japanese Zen by the works of D. T. Suzuki and others, Zen has become identical with Meditative Buddhism.

The two schools of Japanese Zen, the Rinzai and the Soto, were derived from the Lin-chi and Ts'ao-tung sects of Chinese Ch'an. Like the Lin-chi, the Rinzai school, whose founder was Eisai (1141–1214), emphasizes *sudden* enlightenment through the use of *koans* (riddles). The Soto school, whose founder was Dogen (1200–1253), stresses the path of *gradual* enlightenment through the practice of *zazen* (sitting meditation). The Rinzai and Soto differ in their approaches but "*satori*" is the ultimate goal they share. What is satori? To attain satori is to gain "an illuminating insight into the very nature of things." Suzuki further explains the nature of this form of enlightenment: "Satori is a sort of inner perception—not the perception, indeed, of a single individual object but the perception of Reality itself, so to speak." [Suzuki 1948:93]

Meditative Buddhism began with the arrival of Bodhidharma, the 28th Patriarch of Indian Buddhism, in Southern China (Canton) around 475 (or 520 or 527). The *legendary* founder of Meditative Buddhism was received by Emperor Wu of the Liang Dynasty in Nanjing (v. Nam Kinh). A devout Buddhist himself, he failed to make sense of Bodhidharma's Buddhistically "strange" utterances. For example, concerning Emperor Wu's question on the "meritoriousness" of all the works he did for Chinese Buddhism, Bodhidharma said: "No merit whatsoever!" Concerning the essence of Buddhism, Bodhidharma said: "Vast emptiness!" To Emperor Wu's trap question regarding who he was, Bodhidharma answered: "I don't know!"

The emperor did not understand and Bodhidharma left. But no such meeting was mentioned in the earliest records of Ch'an Buddhism. Eventually, Bodhidharma is said to have resided at the Shaolin Temple on Mount Sung, in Honan Province, southwest of Loyang. It was on Mount Sung's western Shaoshih Peak that Bodhidharma is said to have spent nine years in meditation, facing the rock wall of a cave about a mile from the temple. Shaolin later became the famous center for training monks in kung fu, and Bodhidharma is honored as the founder of this marshall art as well. In his *Transmission of the Lamp*, Tao Yuan says that Bodhidharma died in 528 on the fifth day of the tenth month, poisoned by a jealous monk, after he had transmitted the patriarchship of his lineage to Hui K'o [Pine 1987:xiv].

The spirit of the principal teaching of Meditative Buddhism is contained in the following message (normally attributed to Bodhidharma):

> A direct transmission outside the scriptures;
> No dependence upon words and letters;
> Direct pointing at the mind of man;
> Seeing into one's nature and the attainment of Buddhahood.
> [Thich Thien-An 1975:17]

With this free spirit of its methodology, from the very beginning of the Buddha's experience of self-enlightenment (Buddhahood), Meditative Buddhism teaches that human *dualistic thinking* is the cause of human *avidya* (ignorance) which perpetuates human *dukkha* (suffering). By centering on *shunyata* (emptiness), which can be interpreted as the ultimate "Middle Way," where all dualities meet to be intellectually transcended, one is free. The poem that Shen Hsiu (606–706 CE) submitted for the succession contest reveals that he was still a victim of his own dualistic thinking. The following is the English translation of his poem:

> The body is the Bodhi-tree,
> The mind is like a mirror bright.
> Take heed to keep it always clean,
> And let not dust collect on it. [*Ibid*:30]

The poem that Hui Neng (v. Huệ Năng) submitted for the patriarchship contest reveals that he was free from dualistic thinking. The following is the English translation of his poem:

> The Bodhi is not like the tree,
> The mirror bright is nowhere shining.
> As there is nothing from the first,
> Where can the dust itself collect? [*Ibid*:31]

With this poem, Hui Neng (638–713 CE) was chosen to be the Sixth Patriarch, and his teaching became known later as the "Southern School of Ch'an" in contrast to the "Northern School" headed by Shen Hsiu (v. Thần Tú). Shen Hsiu stresses *gradual* enlightenment of the mind, whereas, Hui Neng prefers *sudden* enlightenment. But from the ninth century CE onward, the Southern School overshadowed the Northern School and became almost identical with Ch'an Buddhism in particular and Meditative Buddhism in general.

In conclusion, Meditative Buddhism can be viewed as the philosophical expression of East Asian Mahayana Buddhism with Pure Land Buddhism as its religious expression.

1. A Cup of Tea

Nan-in, a Japanese master during the Meiji era (1868–1912), received a university professor who came to inquire about Zen.

Nan-in served tea. He poured his visitor's cup full, and then kept on pouring.

The professor watched the overflow until he no longer could restrain himself. "It is overfull. No more will go in!"

"Like this cup," Nan-in said, "you are full of your own opinions and speculations. How can I show you Zen unless you first empty your cup?" [Paul Reps: 5]

2. Muddy Road

Tanzan and Ekido were once traveling together down a muddy road. A heavy rain was still falling.

Coming around a bend, they met a lovely girl in silk kimono and sash, unable to cross the intersection.

"Come on, girl," said Tanzan at once. Lifting her in his arms, he carried her over the mud.

Ekido did not speak again until that night when they reached a lodging temple. Then he no longer could restrain himself. "We monks don't go near females," he told Tanzan, "especially not young and lovely ones. It is dangerous. Why did you do that?"

"I left the girl there," said Tanzan. "Are you still carrying her?" [Paul Reps: 18]

3. The Sound of One Hand

The master of Kennin temple was Mokurai, Silent Thunder. He had a little protégé named Toyo who was only twelve years old. Toyo saw the older disciples visit the master's room each morning and e'vening in which they were given koans to stop mind-wandering.

Toyo wished to do sanzen also.

"Wait a while," said Mokurai. "You are too young."

But the child insisted, so the teacher finally consented.

In the evening little Toyo went at the proper time to the threshold of Mokurai's sanzen room. He struck the gong to announce his presence, bowed respectfully three times outside the door, and went to sit before the master in respectful silence.

"You can hear the sound of two hands when they clap together," said Mokurai. "Now show me the sound of one hand."

Toyo bowed and went to his room to consider this problem. From his window he could hear the music of the geishas. "Ah, I have it!" he proclaimed.

The next evening, when his teacher asked him to illustrate the sound of one hand, Toyo began to play the music of the geishas.

"No, no," said Mokurai. "That will never do. That is not the sound of one hand. You've not got it at all."

Thinking that such music might interrupt, Toyo moved his abode to a quiet place. He meditated again. "What can the sound of one hand be?" He happened to hear some water dripping. "I have it," imagined Toyo.

When he next appeared before his teacher, Toyo imitated dripping water.

"What is that?" asked Mokurai. "That is the sound of dripping water, but not the sound of one hand. Try again."

For more than ten times Toyo visited Mokurai with different sounds. All were wrong. For almost a year he pondered what the sound of one hand might be.

At last little Toyo entered true meditation and transcended all sounds. "I could collect no more," he explained later, "so I reached the soundless sound."

[Source: *Zen Flesh, Zen Bones: A Collection of Zen and Pre-Zen Writings Compiled by Paul Reps* (New York: An Anchor Press Book Doubleday, n.d.), pages already indicated].

Toyo had realized the sound of one hand. [Paul Reps:25–26]

4. Kyogen Mounts the Tree

Kyogen said: "Zen is like a man hanging in a tree by his teeth over a precipice. His hands grasp no branch, his feet rest on no limb, and under the tree another person asks him: 'Why did Bodhidharma come to China from India?'

"If the man in the tree does not answer, he fails, and if he does answer, he falls and loses his life. Now what shall he do?" [Paul Reps: 94]

5. Bodhidharma Pacifies the Mind

Bodhidharma sits facing the wall. His future successor stands in the snow and presents his severed arm to Bodhidharma. He cries: "My mind is not pacified. Master, pacify my mind."

Bodhidharma says: "If you bring me that mind, I will pacify it for you."

The successor says: "When I search my mind I cannot hold it."

Bodhidharma says: "Then your mind is pacified already." [Paul Reps 121–122]

6. This Mind Is Buddha

Daibai asked Baso: "What is Buddha?"

Baso said: "This mind is Buddha." [Paul Reps: 114]

Mumon's Comment: If anyone wholly understands this, he is wearing Buddha's clothing, he is eating Buddha's food, he is speaking Buddha's words, he is behaving as Buddha, he is Buddha.

This anecdote, however, has given many a pupil the sickness of formality. If one truly understands, he will wash out his mouth for three days after saying the word Buddha, and he will close his ears and flee after hearing "This mind is Buddha."

Under blue sky, in bright sunlight,
One needs not search around.
Asking what Buddha is
Is like hiding loot in one's pocket and
declaring oneself innocent.
[Paul Reps: 114–115]

Study Questions

B. 3.4.5 The Zen of Self-Enlightenment

1. Construct the *Zen* way of thinking and meditation (principles and characteristics).
2. Explain the reason(s) why the Zen way of thinking and meditation can lead to self-enlightenment (understanding the true nature of reality and one's being).

Part C

Eastern Philosophies of Life

CHAPTER 4

The Hindu Philosophy of Life

C.4.1

An Upanishadic View of Life

The Katha Upanishad

The Introduction

The *Upanishads* contain the earliest Hindu philosophy of life along with other fields of philosophy. The Upanishadic philosophy of life is common to all the *Upanishads* but many *Upanishads* have their own unique ideas. An example of the Upanishadic philosophy of life is found in the selection from the *Katha Upanishad* 2.1–22. In essence, the Upanishadic philosophy of life is spiritually oriented because it prefers spiritual values above material interests.

The Sanskrit word *"Upanishad"* is, according to Sarvepalli Radhakrishnan and Charles Moore, derived from *"upa*, near, *ni*, down, and *sad*, to sit. Groups of pupils sat near the teacher to learn the truth by which ignorance is destroyed." [Radhakrishnan and Moore 1957:37] There are over 200 *Upanishads* of which only 108 are traditionally considered authentic. Of these, ten are the principal *Upanishads*: *Isha, Kena, Katha, Prashna, Mundaka, Mandukya, Taittiriya, Aitareya, Chāndogya,* and *Brhadāranyaka.* The *Upanishads* are found at the end of each of the four *Vedas* (*Books of Wisdom*) and thus also called the "Vedanta" (End of the Veda). There are two main divisions of Hindu scriptures, the *Shruti* (That Which Is Heard) and the *Smrti* (That Which Is Remembered), with the *Upanishads* belonging to the former.

The authorship and dates of the *Upanishads* (namely, who wrote them and when they were written) have remained unknown and are almost impossible to determine. Radhakrishnan and Moore assign "the eighth and seventh centuries B.C." as the dates of most of the ten principal *Upanishads* [*Ibid*]. The one most important feature of the *Upanishads* is their philosophical and theological orientation. What makes the *Upanishads* "much more philosophical" than the rest of the *Vedas* is their attempt "Not only do they try to explain the fundamental principles of existence, but they also show a recognition of the need to supply reasons for their claims." [Koller and Koller 1998:19] What is still missing is the philosophical method of formal analysis, by which, the truth can be determined in light of the relationship between the theoretical speculation of human reason and the empirical evidence of reality.

Death. There is the path of joy, and there is the path of pleasure. Both attract the soul. Who follows the first comes to good; who follows pleasure reaches not the End.

The two paths lie in front of man. Pondering on them, the wise man chooses the path of joy; the fool takes the path of pleasure.

You have pondered, Nachiketas, on pleasures and you have rejected them. You have not accepted that chain of possessions wherewith men bind themselves and beneath which they sink.

There is the path of wisdom and the path of ignorance. They are far apart and lead to different ends. You are, Nachiketas, a follower of the path of wisdom: many pleasures tempt you not.

Abiding in the midst of ignorance, thinking themselves wise and learned, fools go aimlessly hither and thither, like blind led by the blind.

What lies beyond life shines not to those who are childish, or careless, or deluded by wealth. 'This is the only world: there is no other', they say; and thus they go from death to death.

Not many hear of him; and of those not many reach him. Wonderful is he who can teach about him; and wise is he who can be taught. Wonderful is he who knows him when taught.

He cannot be taught by one who has not reached him; and he cannot be reached by much thinking. The way to him is through a Teacher who has seen him: He is higher than the highest thoughts, in truth above all thought.

This sacred knowledge is not attained by reasoning; but it can be given by a true Teacher. As your purpose is steady you have found him. May I find another pupil like you!

I know that treasures pass away and that the Eternal is not reached by the transient. I have thus laid the fire of sacrifice of Nachiketas, and by burning in it the transient I have reached the Eternal.

Before your eyes have been spread, Nachiketas, the fulfillment of all desire, the dominion of the world, the eternal reward of ritual, the shore where there is no fear, the greatness of fame and boundless spaces. With strength and wisdom you have renounced them all.

When the wise rests his mind in contemplation on our God beyond time, who invisibly dwells in the mystery of things and in the heart of man, then he rises above pleasures and sorrow.

When a man has heard and has understood and, finding the essence, reaches the Inmost, then he finds joy in the Source of joy. Nachiketas is a house open for thy Atman, thy God.

Nachiketas. Tell me what you see beyond right and wrong, beyond what is done or not done, beyond past and future.

Death. I will tell you the Word that all the *Vedas* glorify, all self-sacrifice expresses, all sacred studies and holy life seek. That Word is OM.

That Word is the everlasting Brahman: that Word is the highest End. When that sacred Word is known, all longings are fulfilled.

It is the supreme means of salvation: it is the help supreme. When that great Word is known, one is great in the heaven of Brahman.

Atman, the Spirit of vision, is never born and never dies. Before him there was nothing, and he is ONE for evermore. Never-born and eternal, beyond times gone or to come, he does not die when the body dies.

If the slayer thinks that he kills, and if the slain thinks that he dies, neither knows the ways of truth. The Eternal in man cannot kill: the Eternal in man cannot die.

Concealed in the heart of all beings is the Atman, the Spirit, the Self; smaller than the smallest atom, greater than the vast spaces. The man who surrenders his human will leaves sorrows behind, and beholds the glory of the Atman by the grace of the Creator.

Resting, he wanders afar; sleeping, he goes everywhere. Who else but my Self can know that God of joy and of sorrows?

When the wise realize the omnipresent Spirit, who rests invisible in the visible and permanent in the impermanent, then they go beyond sorrow.

Study Questions

C.4.1 *The Katha Upanishad*, An Upanishadic View of Life

1. Is there a causal relationship between ignorance and pleasure-seeking or wisdom and pleasure-avoidance, as assumed by the author(s) of the selection from the *Katha Upanishad*?
2. "When the wise rests his mind in contemplation on our God beyond time, who invisibly dwells in the mystery of things and in the heart of man, then he rises above pleasures and sorrow."
    a. Explain whether or not such a result is possible and the possible reasons why that is so.
    b. Explain whether or not you agree or disagree with the Upanishadic thesis concerning the universal immanence of God and the possible consequences if this profound thesis is universally accepted by all humans.

The Four Stages and Duties of Hindu Life

The Laws of Manu

The Introduction

All Hindu scriptures are divided into two main divisions, the Shruti ("That Which Is Heard or Revealed"), and the Smrti ("That Which Is Remembered"). The *Laws of Manu* or *Code of Manu* (*Manu Shastra*) belong to the Smrti. Being a metrical work of 2,685 verses, the *Laws of Manu* deals with a wide range of religious, social, political, ethical, and legal matters. Concerning its practical orientation, S. Radhakrishan writes: "The book discusses certain philosophical topics and offers solutions based on the Samkhya and the Vedanta, but its aim is not the exposition of a philosophical system." [Radhakrishnan and Moore 1957:172] Of existential interest, the *Laws of Manu* offer what can be called "a philosophy of life." Two key aspects of its philosophy of life are the doctrine of the four stages of life and the four aims of life. These aspects are discussed in this textual selection. These two existential aspects of human life are linked to the "divine" model of society that Manu offers.

The *Laws of Manu* is generally considered to be the product of the Epic Period of Hinduism (ca. 500 BCE–200 CE). The *Laws of Manu* belongs to the category of *Dharma shastras*, and the *Mahabharata* and *Ramayana* belong to the category of epics. The primary objective of the *shastras* is the firm maintenance of the Hindu social order enabling the realization of material and spiritual interests through proper ethical conduct of all social members.

87. The student, the householder, the hermit, and the ascetic, these (constitute) four separate orders, . . . (VI.87 [Repeated])

(a) The Student

165. An Āryan must study the whole Veda together with the Rahasyas [Upaniṣads], performing at the same time various kinds of

[Source: Taken from Manu, *Manu Smrti* (II.36, 68–9, 108, 145–6, 148, 165, 173, 175–80, 182, 188, 199, 201, 225–6, 233–4, 237; III.1, 2, 4, 12–13, 75, 77–8; IV.1–3, 11–12, 15–19, 21; V.169; VI.1–5, 8, 26–34, 36–8, 41–3, 45, 49, 65, 73–5, 80–1, 83, 85, 89–90), printed in G. Buhler, trans., *The Laws of Manu*, *The Sacred Books of the East*, vol. XXV (Oxford: The Clarendon Press, 1886)].

austerities and the vows prescribed by the rules (of the Veda) (II.165)

36. In the eighth year after conception, one should perform the initiation (*upanāyana*) of a *brāhmin*, in the eleventh [year] after conception (that) of a *kṣatriya*, but in the twelfth that of a *vaiśya*. (II.36)

68. Thus has been described the rule for the initiation of the twice-born, which indicates a (new) birth, and sanctified; learn (now) to what duties they must afterwards apply themselves.

69. Having performed the (rite of) initiation, the teacher must first instruct the (pupil) in (the rules of) personal purification, of conduct, of the fire-worship [fire sacrifice], and of the twilight [morning and evening] devotions. (II.68–9)

108. Let an Āryan who has been initiated, (daily) offer fuel in the sacred fire, beg food, sleep on the ground and do what is beneficial to his teacher, until (he performs the ceremony of) *Samāvartana* [the rite of returning home] (on returning home). (II.108)

173. The (student) who has been initiated must be instructed in the performance of the vows [acts of discipline, *vrata*], and gradually learn the Veda, observing the prescribed rules. (II.173)

175. . . . a student who resides with his teacher must observe the following restrictive rules, duly controlling all his organs, in order to increase his spiritual merit.

176. Every day, having bathed, and being purified, he must offer libations of water to the gods, sages and manes, worship (the images of) the gods, and place fuel on (the sacred fire).

177. Let him abstain from honey, meat, perfumes, garlands, substances (used for) flavouring (food), women, all substances turned acid, and from doing injury to living creatures.

178. From anointing (his body), applying collyrium to his eyes, from the use of shoes and of an umbrella (or parasol), from (sensual) desire, anger, covetousness, dancing, singing, and playing (musical instruments),

179. From gambling, idle disputes, backbiting, and lying, from looking at and touching women, and from hurting others.

180. Let him always sleep alone, . . .

182. Let him fetch a pot full of water, flowers, cowdung, earth, and *Kuśa* grass, as much as may be required (by his teacher), and daily go to beg food. (II.175–80, 182)

188. He who performs the vow (of studentship) shall constantly subsist on alms, (but) not eat the food of one (person only); the subsistence of a student on begged food is declared to be equal (in merit) to fasting. (II.188)

199. Let him not pronounce the mere name of his teacher (without adding an honorific title) behind his back even, and let him not mimic his gait, speech, and deportment.

201. By censuring (his teacher), though justly, he will become (in his next birth) an ass, by falsely defaming him, a dog; he who lives on his teacher's substance, will become a worm, and he who is envious (of his merit), a (larger) insect. (II.199, 201)

225. The teacher, the father, the mother, and an elder brother must not be treated with disrespect, especially by a *brāhmin*, though one be grievously offended (by them).

226. The teacher is the image of *Brahman*, the father the image of Prajāpati (the lord of created beings), the mother the image of the earth, and an (elder) full brother the image of oneself. (II.225–6)

233. By honouring his mother he gains this (nether) world, by honouring his father the middle sphere, but by obedience to his teacher the world of *Brahman*.

234. All duties have been fulfilled by him who honours those three; but to him who honours them not, all rites remain fruitless.

237. By (honouring) these three all that ought to be done by man, is accomplished; that is clearly the highest duty, every other (act) is a subordinate duty. (II.233–4, 237)

145. The teacher is ten times more venerable than a sub-teacher, the father a hundred times more than the teacher, but the mother a thousand times more than the father.

146. Of him who gives natural birth and him who gives (the knowledge of) the Veda, the giver

of the Veda is the more venerable father; for the birth for the sake of the Veda (ensures) eternal (rewards) both in this (life) and after death.

148. But that birth which a teacher acquainted with the whole Veda, in accordance with the law, procures for him through the Sāvitrī, is real, exempt from age and death. (II.145–6, 148)

1. The vow (of studying) the three Vedas under a teacher must be kept for thirty-six years, or for half that time, or for a quarter, or until the (student) has perfectly learnt them. (III.1)

(b) Householder

77. As all living creatures subsist by receiving support from air, even so (the members of) all orders subsist by receiving support from the householder.

78. Because men of the three (other) orders are daily supported by the householder with (gifts of) sacred knowledge and food, therefore (the order of) householders is the most excellent order. (III.77–8)

89. And in accordance with the precepts of the Veda and of the traditional texts, the housekeeper, [householder] is declared to be superior to all of them [the other three orders]; for he supports the other three.

90. As all rivers, both great and small, find a resting-place in the ocean, even so men of all orders find protection with householders. (VI.89–90)

2. (A student) who has studied in due order the three Vedas, or two, or even one only, without breaking the (rules of) studentship, shall enter the order of householders.

4. Having bathed, with the permission of his teacher, and performed according to the rule the rite on returning home, a twice-born man shall marry a wife of equal caste who is endowed with auspicious (bodily) marks. (III.2, 4)

12. For the first marriage of twice-born men (wives) of equal caste are recommended; but for those who through desire proceed (to marry again) the following females, (chosen) according to the (direct) order (of the castes), are most approved.

13. It is declared that a *śūdra* woman alone (can be) the wife of a *śūdra*, she and one of his own caste (the wives) of a *vaiśya*, those two and one of his own caste (the wives) of a *kṣatriya*, those three and one of his own caste (the wives) of a *brāhmin*.(III.12–13)

75. Let (every man) in this (second order, at least) daily apply himself to the private recitation of the Veda, and also to the performance of the offering to the gods; for he who is diligent in the performance of sacrifices, supports both the movable and the immovable creation. (III.75)

1. Having dwelt with a teacher during the fourth part of (a man's) life, a *brāhmin* shall live during the second quarter (of his existence) in his house, after he has wedded a wife.

2. A *brāhmin* must seek a means of subsistence which either causes no, or at least little pain (to others), and live (by that) except in times of distress.

3. For the purpose of gaining bare subsistence, let him accumulate property by (following those) irreproachable occupations (which are prescribed for) his (caste), without (unduly) fatiguing his body.

11. Let him never, for the sake of subsistence, follow the ways of the world; let him live the pure, straightforward, honest life of a *brāhmin*.

12. He who desires happiness must strive after a perfectly contented disposition and control himself; for happiness has contentment for its root, the root of unhappiness is the contrary (disposition).

15. Whether he be rich or even in distress, let him not seek wealth through pursuits to which men cleave, nor by forbidden occupations, nor (let him accept presents) from any (giver whosoever he may be).

16. Let him not, out of desire (for enjoyments), attach himself to any sensual pleasures, and let him carefully obviate an excessive attachment to them, by (reflecting on their worthlessness in) his heart.

17. Let him avoid all (means of acquiring) wealth which impede the study of the Veda; (let him maintain himself) anyhow, but study, because

that (devotion to the Veda-study secures) the realisation of his aims.

18. Let him walk here (on earth), bringing his dress, speech, and thoughts to a conformity with his age, his occupation, his wealth, his sacred learning, and his race.

19. Let him daily pore over those Institutes of science which soon give increase of wisdom, those which teach the acquisition of wealth, those which are beneficial (for other worldly concerns), and likewise over the *Nigamas* which explain the Veda. (IV.1–3, 11–12, 15–19)

21. Let him never, if he is able (to perform them), neglect the sacrifices to the sages, to the gods, to the *bhūtas* [elementary forces], to men, and to the manes. (IV.21)

169. (Living) according to the (preceding) rules, he must never neglect the five (great) sacrifices, and, having taken a wife, he must dwell in (his own) house during the second period of his life. (V.169)

(c) The Forest-Dweller

1. A twice-born *snātaka*, who has thus lived according to the law in the order of householders, may, taking a firm resolution and keeping his organs in subjection, dwell in the forest, duly (observing the rules given below).

2. When a householder sees his (skin) wrinkled, and (his hair) white, and the sons of his sons, then he may resort to the forest.

3. Abandoning all food raised by cultivation, and all his belongings, he may depart into the forest, either committing his wife to his sons, or accompanied by her.

4. Taking with him the sacred fire and the implements required for domestic (sacrifices), he may go forth from the village into the forest and reside there, duly controlling his senses.

5. Let him offer those five great sacrifices according to the rule, with various kinds of pure food fit for ascetics, or with herbs, roots, and fruit.

8. Let him be always industrious in privately reciting the Veda; let him be patient in hardships, friendly (towards all), of collected mind, ever

liberal, and never a receiver of gifts, and compassionate towards all living creatures.

26. Making no effort (to procure) things that give pleasure, chaste, sleeping on the bare ground, not caring for any shelter, dwelling at the roots of trees.

27. From *brāhmins* (who live as) ascetics, let him receive alms, (barely sufficient) to support life, or from other householders of the twice-born (castes) who reside in the forest.

28. Or (the hermit) who dwells in the forest may bring (food) from a village, receiving it either in a hollow dish (of leaves), in (his naked) hand, or in a broken earthen dish, and may eat eight mouthfuls.

29. These and other observances must a *brāhmin* who dwells in the forest diligently practise, and in order to attain complete (union with) the (supreme) Self, (he must study) the various sacred texts contained in the Upaniṣads,

30. (As well as those rites and texts) which have been practised and studied by the sages (*ṛṣis*), and by *brāhmin* householders, in order to increase their knowledge (of *Brahman*), and their austerity, and in order to sanctify their bodies;

31. Or let him walk, fully determined and going straight on, in a north-easterly direction, subsisting on water and air, until his body sinks to rest.

32. A *brāhmin*, having got rid of his body by one of those modes practised by the great sages, is exalted in the world of *Brahman*, free from sorrow and fear. (VI.1–5, 8, 26–32)

(d) The Wandering Ascetic

33. . . . . having thus passed the third part of (a man's natural term of) life in the forest, he may live as an ascetic during the fourth part of his existence, after abandoning all attachment to worldly objects.

34. He who after passing from order to order, after offering sacrifices and subduing his senses, becomes, tired with (giving) alms and offerings of food, an ascetic, gains bliss after death.

36. Having studied the Vedas in accordance

with the rule, having begat sons according to the sacred law, and having offered sacrifices according to his ability, he may direct his mind to (the attainment of) final liberation.

37. A twice-born man who seeks final liberation, without having studied the Vedas, without having begotten sons, and without having offered sacrifices, sinks downwards.

38. Having performed the *Iṣṭi*, sacred to the Lord of creatures (Prajāpati), where (he gives) all his property as a sacrificial fee, having reposited the sacred fires in himself, a *brāhmin* may depart from his house (as an ascetic).

41. Departing from his house fully provided with the means of purification, let him wander about absolutely silent, and caring nothing for enjoyments that may be offered (to him).

42. Let him always wander alone, without any companion, in order to attain (final liberation), fully understanding that the solitary (man, who) neither forsakes nor is forsaken, gains his end.

43. He shall neither possess a fire, nor a dwelling, he may go to a village for his food, (he shall be) indifferent to everything, firm of purpose, meditating (and) concentrating his mind on *Brahman*.

45. Let him not desire to die, let him not desire to live; let him wait for (his appointed) time, as a servant (waits) for the payment of his wages.

49. Delighting in what refers to the Self, sitting (in the postures prescribed by the Yoga), independent (of external help), entirely abstaining from sensual enjoyments, with himself for his only companion, he shall live in this world, desiring the bliss (of final liberation).

65. By deep meditation let him recognise the subtle nature of the supreme Self, and its presence in all organisms, . . .

73. Let him recognise by the practise of meditation the progress of the individual soul through beings of various kinds, (a progress) hard to understand for unregenerate men.

74. He who possesses the true insight (into the nature of the world), is not fettered by his deeds; but he who is destitute of that insight, is drawn into the circle of births and deaths.

75. By not injuring any creatures, by detaching the senses (from objects of enjoyment), by the rites prescribed in the Veda, and by rigorously practising austerities, (men) gain that state (even) in this (world).

80. When by the disposition (of his heart) he becomes indifferent to all objects, he obtains eternal happiness both in this world and after death.

81. He who has in this manner gradually given up all attachments and is freed from all the pairs (of opposites), reposes in *Brahman* alone.

83. Let him constantly recite (those texts of) the Veda which refer to the sacrifice, (those) referring to the deities, and (those) which treat of the Self and are contained in the concluding portions of the Veda (Vedānta).

85. A twice-born man who becomes an ascetic, after the successive performance of the above-mentioned acts, shakes off sin here below and reaches the highest *Brahman*.

Study Questions

C.4.2 *The Laws of Manu*, The Four Stages and Duties of the Hindu Life

1. Explain and critique the four stages of Hindu life and explain the relationship between them.
2. Explain and critique the main duties to be performed during each stage.
3. Explain whether we should organize our human life into four stages. If "Yes," what modifications of the model offered in the *Laws of Manu*, are necessary?
4. Compare this Hindu philosophy of life with other Eastern philosophies of life (Buddhist, Confucianist, and Taoist).

C.4.3

Freedom and Renunciation

The Bhagavad Gita

Arjuna:

O Krishna, destroyer of evil, please explain to me sannyasa and tyaga and how one kind of renunciation differs from another.

Sri Krishna:

To refrain from selfish acts is one kind of renunciation, called sannyasa; to renounce the fruit of action is another, called tyaga.

Among the wise, some say that all action should be renounced as evil. Others say that certain kinds of action—self-sacrifice, giving, and self-discipline—should be continued. Listen, Arjuna, and I will explain three kinds of tyaga and my conclusions concerning them.

Self-sacrifice, giving, and self-discipline should not be renounced, for they purify the thoughtful. Yet even these, Arjuna, should be performed without desire for selfish rewards. This is essential.

To renounce one's responsibilities is not fitting. The wise call such deluded renunciation tamasic. To avoid action from fear of difficulty or physical discomfort is rajasic. There is no reward in such renunciation. But to fulfill your responsibilities knowing that they are obligatory, while at the same time desiring nothing for yourself—this is sattvic renunciation. Those endowed with sattva clearly understand the meaning of renunciation and do not waver. They are not intimidated by unpleasant work, nor do they seek a job because it is pleasant.

As long as one has a body, one cannot renounce action altogether. True renunciation is giving up all desire for personal reward.

Those who are attached to personal reward will reap the consequences of their actions: some pleasant, some unpleasant, some mixed. But those who renounce every desire for personal reward go beyond the reach of karma.

Listen, Arjuna, and I will explain the five elements necessary for the accomplishment of every action, as taught by the wisdom of Sankhya. The body, the means, the ego, the performance of the act, and the divine will: these are the five factors in all actions, right or wrong, in thought, word, or deed.

Those who do not understand this think of themselves as separate agents. With their crude intellects they fail to see the truth.

From *The Bhagavad Gita*, trans. Eknath Easwaran, found of the Blue Mountain Center of Meditation, copyright 1985; reprinted by permission of Nilgiri Press, www.nilgiri.org

The person who is free from ego, who has attained purity of heart, though he slays these people, he does not slay and is not bound by his action.

Knowledge, the thing to be known, and the knower: these three promote action. The means, the act itself, and the doer: these three are the totality of action. Knowledge, action, and the doer can be described according to the gunas. Listen, and I will explain their distinctions to you.

Sattvic knowledge sees the one indestructible Being in all beings, the unity underlying the multiplicity of creation. Rajasic knowledge sees all things and creatures as separate and distinct. Tamasic knowledge, lacking any sense of perspective, sees one small part and mistakes it for the whole.

Work performed to fulfill one's obligations, without thought of personal reward or of whether the job is pleasant or unpleasant, is sattvic. Work prompted by selfish desire or self-will, full of stress, is rajasic. Work that is undertaken blindly, without any consideration of consequences, waste, injury to others, or one's own capacities, is tamasic.

A sattvic worker is free from egotism and selfish attachments, full of enthusiasm and fortitude in success and failure alike. A rajasic worker has strong personal desires and craves rewards for his actions. Covetous, impure, and destructive, he is easily swept away by fortune, good or bad. The tamasic worker is undisciplined, vulgar, stubborn, deceitful, dishonest, and lazy. He is easily depressed and prone to procrastination.

Listen, Arjuna, as I describe the three types of understanding and will.

To know when to act and when to refrain from action, what is right action and what is wrong, what brings security and what insecurity, what brings freedom and what bondage: these are the signs of a sattvic intellect.

The rajasic intellect confuses right and wrong actions, and cannot distinguish what is to be done from what should not be done. The tamasic intellect is shrouded in darkness, utterly reversing right and wrong wherever it turns.

The sattvic will, developed through meditation, keeps prana, mind, and senses in vital harmony. The rajasic will, conditioned by selfish desire, pursues wealth, pleasure, and respectability. The tamasic will shows itself in obstinate ignorance, sloth, fear, grief, depression, and conceit.

Now listen, Arjuna: there are also three kinds of happiness. By sustained effort, one comes to the end of sorrow.

That which seems like poison at first, but tastes like nectar in the end—this is the joy of sattva, born of a mind at peace with itself.

Pleasure from the senses seems like nectar at first, but it is bitter as poison in the end. This is the kind of happiness that comes to the rajasic. Those who are tamasic draw their pleasures from sleep, indolence, and intoxication. Both in the beginning and in the end, this happiness is a delusion.

No creature, whether born on earth or among the gods in heaven, is free from the conditioning of the three gunas. The different responsibilities found in the social order—distinguishing brahmin, kshatriya, vaishya, and shudra—have their roots in this conditioning.

The responsibilities to which a brahmin is born, based on his nature, are self-control, tranquility, purity of heart, patience, humility, learning, austerity, wisdom, and faith.

The qualities of a kshatriya, based on his nature, are courage, strength, fortitude, dexterity, generosity, leadership, and the firm resolve never to retreat from battle. The occupations suitable for a vaishya are agriculture, dairying, and trade. The proper work of a shudra is service.

By devotion to one's own particular duty, everyone can attain perfection. Let me tell you how. By performing his own work, one worships the Creator who dwells in every creature. Such worship brings that person to fulfillment.

It is better to perform one's own duties imperfectly than to master the duties of another. By fulfilling the obligations he is born with, a person never comes to grief. No one should abandon duties because he sees defects in them. Every action, every activity, is surrounded by defects as a fire is surrounded by smoke.

He who is free from selfish attachments, who has mastered himself and his passions, attains the supreme perfection of freedom from action. Listen and I shall explain now, Arjuna, how one who has attained perfection also attains Brahman, the supreme consummation of wisdom.

Unerring in his discrimination, sovereign of his senses and passions, free from the clamor of likes and dislikes, he leads a simple, self-reliant life based on meditation, controlling his speech, body, and mind.

Free from self-will, aggressiveness, arrogance, anger, and the lust to possess people or things, he is at peace with himself and others and enters into the unitive state. United with Brahman, ever joyful, beyond the reach of desire and sorrow, he has equal regard for every living creature and attains supreme devotion to me. By loving me he comes to know me truly; then he knows my glory and enters into my boundless being. All his acts are performed in my service, and through my grace he wins eternal life.

Make every act an offering to me; regard me as your only protector. Relying on interior discipline, meditate on me always. Remembering me, you shall overcome all difficulties through my grace. But if you will not heed me in your self-will, nothing will avail you.

If you egotistically say, "I will not fight this battle," your resolve will be useless; your own nature will drive you into it. Your own karma, born of your own nature, will drive you to do even that which you do not wish to do, because of your delusion.

The Lord dwells in the hearts of all creatures and whirls them round upon the wheel of maya. Run to him for refuge with all your strength, and peace profound will be yours through his grace.

I give you these precious words of wisdom; reflect on them and then do as you choose.

These are the last words I shall speak to you, dear one, for your spiritual fulfillment. You are very dear to me.

Be aware of me always, adore me, make every act an offering to me, and you shall come to me; this I promise; for you are dear to me. Abandon all supports and look to me for protection. I shall purify you from the sins of the past; do not grieve.

Do not share this wisdom with anyone who lacks in devotion or self-control, lacks the desire to learn, or scoffs at me. Those who teach this supreme mystery of the Gita to all who love me perform the greatest act of love; they will come to me without doubt. No one can render me more devoted service; no one on earth can be more dear to me.

Those who meditate on these holy words worship me with wisdom and devotion. Even those who listen to them with faith, free from doubts, will find a happier world where good people dwell.

Have you listened with attention? Are you now free from your doubts and confusion?

Arjuna:

You have dispelled my doubts and delusions, and I understand through your grace. My faith is firm now, and I will do your will.

Sanjaya:

This is the dialogue I heard between Krishna, the son of Vasudeva, and Arjuna, the great-hearted son of Pritha. The wonder of it makes my hair stand on end! Through Vyasa's grace, I have heard the supreme secret of spiritual union directly from the Lord of Yoga, Krishna himself.

Whenever I remember these wonderful, holy words between Krishna and Arjuna, I am filled with joy. And when I remember the breathtaking form of Krishna, I am filled with wonder and my joy overflows.

Wherever the divine Krishna and the mighty Arjuna are, there will be prosperity, victory, happiness, and sound judgment. Of this I am sure!

Study Questions

C.4.3 *The Bhagavad Gita*, Freedom and Renunciation

1. Explain the two kinds of renunciation and three forms of tyaga according to Krishna.
2. Explain the reasons why Krishna argues that one should renounce "all desire for personal reward" when one acts. Critically respond to the Bhagavadgitaian doctrine of true renunciation as argued by Krishna concerning the question of whether we should or should we not renounce our desire for reward in mind.
3. Discuss whether or not there is a biological connection between the "three gunas" and the Hindu caste system (brahmin, kshatriya, vaishya, shudra) as assumed in the *Bhagavad Gita.*
4. Explain whether or not "true renunciation" lead to freedom and happiness as advocated in the *Bhagavad Gita.*

CHAPTER 5

The Buddhist Philosophy of Life

C.5.1

How you figure out nature of the Buddha of middle way of think.

The First Sermon for Self-Mastery

The Buddha

The Introduction

The "Buddha" is the most famous title of the "founder" of Buddhism, even though, it is one of his many titles used by his faithful disciples. Some other titles are "Shakyamuni" (Sage of the Shakya tribe), "Tathāgata" (One who has reached complete thusness), the "Blessed One." For more background information on the Buddha and his "First Sermon," please see A.1.7.

Having thus spoken, the Blessed One arose and went into his own cell.

The Lord had not been gone long when the reverent Sāriputta proceeded to the exposition of the Truth-finder's Four Noble Truths, as follows:

What, reverend sirs, is the Noble Truth of suffering? —Birth is a suffering; decay is a suffering; death is a suffering; grief and lamentation, pain, misery and tribulation are sufferings; it is a suffering not to get what is desired;—in brief all the factors of the fivefold grip on existence are suffering.

Birth is, for living creatures of each several class, the being born or produced, the issue, the arising or the re-arising, the appearance of the impressions, the growth of faculties.

Decay, for living creatures of each several class, is the decay and decaying, loss of teeth, grey hair, wrinkles, a dwindling term of life, sere faculties.

Death, for living creatures of each several class, is the passage and passing hence, the dissolution, disappearance, dying, death, decease, the dissolution of the impressions, the discarding of the dead body.

Grief is the grief, grieving, and grievousness, the inward grief and inward anguish of anyone who suffers under some misfortune or is in the grip of some type of suffering.

Lamentation is the lament and lamentation, the wailing and the lamenting of anyone who

From *Further Dialogues of the Buddha, II, Sacred Books of the East, VI* by Lord Chalmers, trans. Copyright © 1927 by Lord Chalmers. Reprinted by permission.

suffers under some misfortune or is in the grip of some type of suffering.

Pain is any bodily suffering or bodily evil, and suffering bred of bodily contact, any evil feeling.

Misery is mental suffering and evil, any evil feeling of the mind.

Tribulation is the tribulation of heart and mind, the state to which tribulation brings them, in anyone who suffers under some misfortune or is in the grip of some type of suffering.

There remains not to get what is desired. In creatures subject to birth—or decay—or death—or grief and lamentation, pain, misery, and tribulation—the desire arises not to be subject thereto but to escape them. But escape is not to be won merely by desiring it; and failure to win it is another suffering.

What are in brief all the factors of the fivefold grip on existence which are sufferings?—They are: the factors of form, feeling, perception, impressions, and consciousness.

The foregoing, sirs, constitutes the Noble Truth of suffering.

What now is the Noble Truth of the origin of suffering? It is any craving that makes for re-birth and is tied up with passion's delights and culls satisfaction now here now there—such as the craving for sensual pleasure, the craving for continuing existence, and the craving for annihilation.

Next, what is the Noble Truth of the cessation of suffering?—It is the utter and passionless cessation of this same craving,—the abandonment and rejection of craving, deliverance from craving, and aversion from craving.

Lastly, what is the Noble Truth of the Path that leads to the cessation of suffering?—It is just the Noble Eightfold Path, consisting of right outlook, right resolves, right speech, right acts, right livelihood, right endeavour, right mindfulness and right rapture of concentration.

Right outlook is to know suffering, the origin of suffering, the cessation of suffering, and the path that leads to the cessation of suffering.

Right resolves are the resolve to renounce the world and to do no hurt or harm.

Right speech is to abstain from lies and slander, from reviling, and from tattle.

Right acts are to abstain from taking life, from stealing, and from lechery.

Right livelihood is that by which the disciple of the Noble One supports himself, to the exclusion of wrong modes of livelihood.

Right endeavour is when an almsman brings his will to bear, puts forth endeavour and energy, struggles and strives with all his heart, to stop bad and wrong qualities which have not yet arisen from ever arising, to renounce those which have already arisen, to foster good qualities which have not yet arisen, and, finally, to establish, clarify, multiply, enlarge, develop, and perfect those good qualities which are there already.

Right mindfulness is when realizing what the body is—what feelings are—what the heart is—and what the mental states are—an almsman dwells ardent, alert, and mindful, in freedom from the wants and discontents attendant on any of these things.

Right rapture of concentration is when, divested of lusts and divested of wrong dispositions, an almsman develops, and dwells in, the first ecstasy with all its zest and satisfaction, a state bred of aloofness and not divorced from observation and reflection. By laying to rest observation and reflection, he develops and dwells in inward serenity, in [the] focussing of heart, in the zest and satisfaction of the second ecstasy, which is divorced from observation and reflection and is bred of concentration—passing thence to the third and fourth ecstasies.

This, sirs, constitutes the Noble Truth of the Path that leads to the cessation of suffering. . . .

2 ways of life.
(1) self indulence
(2) self mortication

Study Questions

C.5.1 The Buddha, The Four Noble Truths and Noble Eightfold Path for Self-Mastery

1. Explain and critique the Buddhaian doctrine of life ("Four Noble Truths").
2. Explain the "Noble Eightfold Path" and whether or not its faithful practice can lead to the morally good and happy life (Nirvana) as claimed by the Buddha.
3. Critically discuss whether or not the Buddha violates the principle of his "Middle Way" when he introduces his "Four Noble Truths" and "Noble Eightfold Path."

Knowledge of Death Leads to Self-Enlightenment: The Case of Kisa Gotami

Gotami was her family name, but because she tired easily, she was called Kisa Gotami, or Frail Gotami. She was reborn at Savatthi in a poverty-stricken house. When she grew up, she married, going to the house of her husband's family to live. There, because she was the daughter of a poverty-stricken house, they treated her with contempt. After a time she gave birth to a son. Then they accorded her respect.

But when that boy of hers was old enough to play and run hither and about, he died. Sorrow sprang up within her. Thought she: Since the birth of my son, I, who was once denied honor and respect in this very house, have received respect. These folk may even seek to cast my son away. Taking her son on her hip, she went about from one house door to another, saying: "Give me medicine for my son!"

Wherever people encountered her, they said, Where did you ever meet with medicine for the dead? So saying, they clapped their hands and laughed in derision. She had not the slightest idea what they meant.

Now a certain wise man saw her and thought: This woman must have been driven out of her mind by sorrow for her son. But medicine for her, no one else is likely to know—the Possessor of the Ten Forces alone is likely to know. Said he: "Woman, as for medicine for your son—there is no one else who knows—the Possessor of the Ten Forces, the foremost individual in the world of men and the worlds of the gods, resides at a neighboring monastery. Go to him and ask."

The man speaks the truth, thought she. Taking her son on her hip, when the Tathagata sat down in the Seat of the Buddhas, she took her stand in the outer circle of the congregation and said: "O Exalted One, give me medicine for my son!"

The Teacher, seeing that she was ripe for conversion, said: "You did well, Gotami, in coming hither for medicine. Go enter the city, make the rounds of the entire city, beginning at the beginning, and in whatever house no one has ever died, from that house fetch tiny grains of mustard seed."

"Very well, reverend sir," said she. Delighted in heart, she entered within the city, and at the

From *The Teachings of the Compassionate Buddha* by Edwin A. Burtt. Copyright © 1955 by Estate of Edwin A. Burtt. Reprinted by permission.

very first house said: "The Possessor of the Ten Forces bids me fetch tiny grains of mustard seed for medicine for my son. Give me tiny grains of mustard seed."

"Alas! Gotami," said they, and brought and gave to her.

"This particular seed I cannot take. In this house some one has died!"

"What say you, Gotami! Here it is impossible to count the dead!"

"Well then, enough! I'll not take it. The Possessor of the Ten Forces did not tell me to take mustard seed from a house where any one has ever died."

In this same way she went to the second house, and to the third. Thought she: In the entire city this must be the way! This the Buddha, full of compassion for the welfare of mankind, must have seen! Overcome with emotion, she went outside of the city, carried her son to the burning-ground, and holding him in her arms, said: "Dear little son, I thought that you alone had been overtaken by this thing which men call death. But you are not the only one death has overtaken. This is a law common to all mankind." So saying, she cast her son away in the burning-ground. Then she uttered the following stanza:

> No village law, no law of market town,
> No law of a single house is this—
> Of all the world and all the worlds of gods
> This only is the Law, that all things are impermanent.

Now when she had so said, she went to the Teacher. Said the Teacher to her: "Gotami, did you get the tiny grains of mustard seed?"

"Done, reverend sir, is the business of the mustard seed! Only give me a refuge!" Then the Teacher recited to her the following stanzas:

> That man who delights in children and cattle,
> That man whose heart adheres thereto,
> Death takes that man and goes his way,
> As sweeps away a mighty flood a sleeping village. . . .
> Though one should live a hundred years,
> Not seeing the Region of the Deathless,
> Better were it for one to live a single day,
> The Region of the Deathless seeing. . . .

Study Questions

C.5.2 Knowledge of Death Leads to Self-Enlightenment: The Case of Kisa Gotami

1. Analyze the reasons why Gotami's knowledge of death leads to her knowledge of life, which results in her happiness and devotion.
2. Does the knowledge of death lead to the knowledge of life and happiness? Explain.
3. Explore the applicability of the Buddha's method of teaching to your own life.

C.5.3

The Worldly Life as a Big Illusion:
The Case of a Stonecutter

A Chinese Story

There was once a stonecutter, who was dissatisfied with himself and with his position in life. One day, he passed a wealthy merchant's house, and through the open gateway, saw many fine possessions and important visitors. "How powerful that merchant must be!" thought the stonecutter. He became very envious, and wished that he could be like the merchant. Then he would no longer have to live the life of a mere stonecutter.

To his great surprise, he suddenly became the merchant, enjoying more luxuries and power than he had ever dreamed of, envied and detested by those less wealthy than himself. But soon a high official passed by, carried in a sedan chair, accompanied by attendants, and escorted by soldiers beating gongs. Everyone, no matter how wealthy, had to bow low before the procession. "How powerful that official is" he thought. "I wish that I could be a high official!"

Then he became the high official, carried everywhere in his embroidered sedan chair, feared and hated by the people all around, who had to bow down before him as he passed. It was a hot summer day, and the official felt very uncomfortable in the sticky sedan chair. He looked up at the sun. It shone proudly in the sky, unaffected by his presence. "How powerful the sun is!" he thought. "I wish that I could be the sun!"

Then he became the sun, shining fiercely down on everyone, scorching the fields, cursed by the farmers and laborers. But a huge black cloud moved between him and the earth, so that his light could no longer shine on everything below. "How powerful that storm cloud is!" he thought. "I wish that I could be a cloud!"

Then he became the cloud, flooding the fields and the villages, shouted at by everyone. But soon he found that he was being pushed away by some great force, and realized that it was the wind. "How powerful it is!" he thought. "I wish that I could be the wind!"

Then he became the wind, blowing tiles off the roofs of houses, uprooting trees, hated and feared by all below him. But after a while, he ran up against something that would not move, no

[Source: Taken from "The Stonecutter," in Benjamin Hoff, *The Tao of Pooh* (New York: Penguin Books, 1983), pp. 118–119].

matter how forcefully he blew against it—a huge, towering stone. "How powerful that stone is!" he thought. "I wish that I could be a stone!"

Then he became the stone, more powerful than anything else on earth. But as he stood there, he heard the sound of a hammer pounding a chisel into the solid rock, and felt himself being changed. "What could be more powerful than I, the stone?" he thought. He looked down and saw far below him the figure of a stonecutter.

Study Questions

C.5.3 The Worldly Life as a Big Illusion: The Case of a Stonecutter

1. What does the "stonecutter" represent?
2. Why does he desire to have many things?
3. Critically discuss the reasons why wealth, power, sex, and other material objects cannot produce the good life as symbolized by the "Story of a Stonecutter."

The Eight Awarenesses of Great People

Dogen

The Introduction

Dogen (1200–253 CE) was one of the most original and brilliant thinkers of traditional Japan. He was perhaps Japan's greatest Zen thinker. He is revered by most Japanese buddhists as a *bodhisattva*, an honor that monks of Indian Buddhism enjoyed. He is known as the "founder" of the Soto School of Japanese Zen Buddhism.

While in China, like his beloved Master Myozen, the young Dogen received the teaching of Master Ju Ching (1163–1268), who adhered to a strict *ascetic* form of Chinese Ch'an Buddhism. Dogen is said to have attained his sudden "*satori*" (enlightenment) while overhearing Master Ju Ching admonished a student during a meditation session: "In Zen, body and mind are cast off. Why do you sleep?" Dogen's self-realization of sudden *satori* may not be as "sudden" as it seemed. Dogen had been preoccupied with the true nature of the relationship between the truth of our intrinsic Buddha-nature and the need for the attainment of self-enlightenment through the protracted practice of meditation. When Dogen *suddenly* realized that all is *empty* (*shunya*), his preoccupation with that most plaguing philosophical question just vanished!

The famous work that has earned Dogen his esteemed status in Japanese Zen Buddhism is the *Shobogenzo*, which is rendered into English as "*Treasury of the Eye of True Teaching*" [Koller and Koller 1991:345] or "*Treasury of Knowledge Regarding the True Dharma*" [Brannigan 2000:45]. It is a classic treatise on *zazen* (sitting meditation), through which, one can achieve self-enlightenment (satori).

The Eight Awarnesses of Great People

The Buddhas are great people. As these are what is realized by great people, they are called the awareness of great people. Realizing these principles is the basis of nirvana. This was the final teaching of our original teacher, Shakyamuni Buddha, on the night he passed away into final extinction.

1. Having few desires

Not extensively seeking objects of desire not yet attained is called having few desires.

Buddha said, "You monks should know that people with many desires seek to gain a lot, and therefore their afflictions are also many. Those with few desires have no seeking and no craving, so they don't have this problem. You should cultivate having few desires even for this reason alone, to say nothing of the fact that having few desires can produce virtues. People with few desires are free from flattery and deviousness whereby they might seek to curry people's favor, and they also are not under the compulsion of their senses. Those who act with few desires are calm, without worry or fear. Whatever the situation, there is more than enough—there is never insufficiency. Those who have few desires have nirvana."

2. Being content

To take what one has got within bounds is called being content.

Buddha said, "O monks, if you want to shed afflictions, you should observe contentment. The state of contentment is the abode of prosperity and happiness, peace and tranquility. Those who are content may sleep on the ground and still consider it comfortable; those who are not content would be dissatisfied even in heaven. Those who are not content are always caught up in sensual desires; they are pitied by those who are content."

3. Enjoying quietude

Leaving the clamor and staying alone in deserted places is called enjoying quietude.

Buddha said, "O monks, if you wish to seek the peace and happiness of quietude and nonstriving, you should leave the clamor and live without clutter in a solitary place. People in quiet places are honored by the gods. Therefore you should leave your own group as well as other groups, stay alone in a deserted place, and think about extirpating the root of suffering. Those who like crowds suffer the vexations of crowds, just as a big tree will suffer withering and breakage when flocks of birds gather on it. Worldly ties and clinging sink you into a multitude of pains, like an old elephant sunk in the mud, unable to get itself out."

4. Diligence

Diligently cultivating virtues without interruption is called diligence, pure and unalloyed, advancing without regression.

Buddha said, "O monks, if you make diligent efforts, nothing is hard. Therefore you should be diligent. It is like even a small stream being able to pierce rock if it continually flows. If the practitioner's mind flags and gives up time and gain, that is like drilling for fire but stopping before heat is produced—though you want to get fire, fire can hardly be gotten this way."

5. Unfailing recollection

This is also called keeping right mindfulness; keeping the teachings without loss is called right mindfulness, and also called unfailing recollection.

Buddha said, "O monks, if you seek a good companion and seek a good protector and helper, nothing compares to unfailing recollection. Those who have unfailing recollection cannot be invaded by the thieving afflictions. Therefore you should concentrate your thoughts and keep mindful. One who loses mindfulness loses virtues. If one's power of mindfulness is strong, even if one enters among the thieving desires one will not be harmed by them. It is like going to the front lines wearing armor—then one has nothing to fear."

6. Cultivating meditation concentration

Dwelling on the teaching without distraction is called meditation concentration.

Buddha said, "O monks, if you concentrate the mind, it will be in a state of stability and you will be able to know the characteristics of the phenomena arising and perishing in the world. Therefore you should energetically cultivate and learn the concentrations. If you attain concentration, your mind will not be distracted. Just as a household careful of water builds a dam, so does the practitioner, for the sake of the water of knowledge and wisdom, cultivate meditation concentration well, to prevent them from leaking."

7. Cultivating wisdom

Developing learning, thinking, and application, the realization is wisdom.

Buddha said, "O monks, if you have wisdom, you will have no greedy attachment. Always examine yourselves and do not allow any heedlessness. Then you will be able to attain liberation from ego and things. Otherwise, you are neither people of the Way nor laypeople—there is no way to refer to you. True wisdom is a secure ship to cross the sea of aging, sickness, and death. It is also a bright lamp in the darkness of ignorance, good medicine for all the ailing, a sharp axe to fell the trees of afflictions. Therefore you should use the wisdom of learning, thinking, and application, and increase it yourself. If anyone has the illumination of wisdom, this is a person with clear eyes, even though it be the mortal eye."

8. Not engaging in vain talk

Realizing detachment from arbitrary discrimination is called not engaging in vain talk; when one has fully comprehended the character of reality, one will not engage in vain talk.

Buddha said, "O monks, if you indulge in various kinds of vain talk, your mind will be disturbed. Even if you leave society you will still not attain liberation. Therefore you should immediately give up vain talk which disturbs the mind. If you want to attain bliss of tranquility and dispassion, you should extinguish the affliction of vain talk."

Study Questions

C.5.4 Dogen, The Eight Awarenesses of Great People

1. Analyze the four conditions that produce the good life according to Dogen.
2. Discuss the possible reasons why the state of having few desires combined with diligence may lead to contentment and quietude (inner qualities of the good life).

CHAPTER 6

The Ancient Confucianist and Taoist Philosophies of Life

Perfect Happiness

Chuang Tzu (v. Trang Tử)

The Introduction

"Happiness" appears to be the ultimate end that all human beings have sought. The search for happiness has remained unfulfilled and probably will never be fulfilled due to the very nature of the human psychology and spirit. Failure to achieve ultimate happiness may also be due to the failure of philosophers to resolve two questions of the philosophy of life: what happiness is, and how happiness can be achieved.

Happiness is a shared existential goal of Asian philosophies: Hindus seek "*moksha*," Buddhists seek "*nirvana*," Confucianists seek "*wu fu*" (v. *ngũ phúc* [five good fortunes]), and "*wu wei*" (v. vô vi [non-action]) is treasured by Taoists. To be spiritually near or one with the Brahman is the final state of happiness for Hindus. To be completely empty, from within and from without, is the ultimate state of happiness for Buddhists. To be successful in worldly endeavors is the continuing state of real happiness for Confucianists. To be totally free from all bondages and in harmony with Nature is the ultimate condition of happiness for Taoists.

What follows is one ancient East Asian Taoist view of happiness offered by Chuang Tzu (v. Trang Tử).

Is there such a thing as perfect happiness in the world or isn't there? Is there some way to keep yourself alive or isn't there? What to do, what to rely on, what to avoid, what to stick by, what to follow, what to leave alone, what to find happiness in, what to hate?

This is what the world honors: wealth, eminence, long life, a good name. This is what the world finds happiness in: a life of ease, rich food, fine clothes, beautiful sights, sweet sounds. This is what it looks down on: poverty, meanness, early death, a bad name. This is what it finds bitter: a life that knows no rest, a mouth that gets no rich food, no fine clothes for the body, no beautiful sights for the eye, no sweet sounds for the ear.

People who can't get these things fret a great deal and are afraid—this is a stupid way to treat the body. People who are rich wear themselves out rushing around on business, piling up more wealth than they could ever use—this is a superficial way to treat the body. People who are eminent spend night and day scheming and wondering if they are doing right—this is a shoddy way to treat the body. Man lives his life in company with worry, and if he lives a long while, till he's dull and doddering, then he has spent that much time worrying instead of dying, a bitter lot indeed! This is a callous way to treat the body.

Men of ardor are regarded by the world as good, but their goodness doesn't succeed in keeping them alive. So I don't know whether their goodness is really good or not. Perhaps I think it's good—but not good enough to save their lives. Perhaps I think it's no good—but still good enough to save the lives of others. So I say, if your loyal advice isn't heeded, give way and do not wrangle. Tzu-hsü wrangled and lost his body.[1] But if he hadn't wrangled, he wouldn't have made a name. Is there really such a thing as goodness or isn't there?

What ordinary people do and what they find happiness in—I don't know whether such happiness is in the end really happiness or not. I look at what ordinary people find happiness in, what they all make a mad dash for, racing around as though they couldn't stop—they all say they're happy with it. I'm not happy with it and I'm not unhappy with it. In the end is there really happiness or isn't there?

I take inaction to be true happiness, but ordinary people think it is a bitter thing. I say: perfect happiness knows no happiness, perfect praise knows no praise. The world can't decide what is right and what is wrong. And yet inaction can decide this. Perfect happiness, keeping alive—only inaction gets you close to this!

Let me try putting it this way. The inaction of Heaven is its purity, the inaction of earth is its peace. So the two inactions combine and all things are transformed and brought to birth. Wonderfully, mysteriously, there is no place they come out of. Mysteriously, wonderfully, they have no sign. Each thing minds its business and all grow up out of inaction. So I say, Heaven and earth do nothing and there is nothing that is not done. Among men, who can get hold of this inaction?

Chuang Tzu's wife died. When Hui Tzu went to convey his condolences, he found Chuang Tzu sitting with his legs sprawled out, pounding on a tub and singing. "You lived with her, she brought up your children and grew old," said Hui Tzu. "It should be enough simply not to weep at her death. But pounding on a tub and singing—this is going too far, isn't it?"

Chuang Tzu said, "You're wrong. When she first died, do you think I didn't grieve like anyone else? But I looked back to her beginning and the time before she was born. Not only the time before she was born, but the time before she had a body. Not only the time before she had a body, but the time before she had a spirit. In the midst of the jumble of wonder and mystery a change took place and she had a spirit. Another change and she had a body. Another change and she was born. Now there's been another change and she's dead. It's just like the progression of the four seasons, spring, summer, fall, winter.

"Now she's going to lie down peacefully in a vast room. If I were to follow after her bawling and sobbing, it would show that I don't understand anything about fate. So I stopped."

Uncle Lack-Limb and Uncle Lame-Gait were seeing the sights at Dark Lord Hill and the wastes of K'un-lun, the place where the Yellow Emperor rested.[2] Suddenly a willow sprouted out of Uncle

---

[1] Wu Tzu-hsü, minister to the king of Wu, repeatedly warned the king of the danger of attack from the state of Yüeh. He finally aroused the king's ire and suspicion and was forced to commit suicide in 484 B.C.

[2] These are all places or persons associated in Chinese legend with immortality. The Yellow Emporer, as we have seen above, p. 82, did not die but ascended to Heaven.

Lame-Gait's left elbow.[3] He looked very startled and seemed to be annoyed.

"Do you resent it?" said Uncle Lack-Limb.

"No—what is there to resent?" said Uncle Lame-Gait. "To live is to borrow. And if we borrow to live, then life must be a pile of trash. Life and death are day and night. You and I came to watch the process of change, and now change has caught up with me. Why would I have anything to resent?"

When Chuang Tzu went to Ch'u, he saw an old skull, all dry and parched. He poked it with his carriage whip and then asked, "Sir, were you greedy for life and forgetful of reason, and so came to this? Was your state overthrown and did you bow beneath the ax, and so came to this? Did you do some evil deed and were you ashamed to bring disgrace upon your parents and family, and so came to this? Was it through the pangs of cold and hunger that you came to this? Or did your springs and autumns pile up until they brought you to this?"

When he had finished speaking, he dragged the skull over and, using it for a pillow, lay down to sleep.

In the middle of the night, the skull came to him in a dream and said, "You chatter like a rhetorician and all your words betray the entanglements of a living man. The dead know nothing of these! Would you like to hear a lecture on the dead?"

"Indeed," said Chuang Tzu.

The skull said, "Among the dead there are no rulers above, no subjects below, and no chores of the four seasons. With nothing to do, our springs and autumns are as endless as heaven and earth. A king facing south on his throne could have no more happiness than this!"

Chuang Tzu couldn't believe this and said, "If I got the Arbiter of Fate to give you a body again, make you some bones and flesh, return you to your parents and family and your old home and friends, you would want that, wouldn't you?"

The skull frowned severely, wrinkling up its brow. "Why would I throw away more happiness than that of a king on a throne and take on the troubles of a human being again?" it said.

When Yen Yüan went east to Ch'i, Confucius had a very worried look on his face.[4] Tzu-kung got off his mat and asked, "May I be so bold as to inquire why the Master has such a worried expression now that Hui has gone east to Ch'i?"

"Excellent—this question of yours," said Confucius. "Kuan Tzu[5] had a saying that I much approve of: 'Small bags won't hold big things; short well ropes won't dip up deep water.' In the same way I believe that fate has certain forms and the body certain appropriate uses. You can't add to or take away from these. I'm afraid that when Hui gets to Ch'i he will start telling the marquis of Ch'i about the ways of Yao, Shun, and the Yellow Emperor, and then will go on to speak about Sui Jen and Shen Nung.[6] The marquis will then look for similar greatness within himself and fail to find it. Failing to find it, he will become distraught, and when a man becomes distraught, he kills.

"Haven't you heard this story? Once a sea bird alighted in the suburbs of the Lu capital. The marquis of Lu escorted it to the ancestral temple, where he entertained it, performing the Nine Shao music for it to listen to and presenting it with the meat of the T'ai-lao sacrifice to feast on. But the bird only looked dazed and forlorn, refusing to eat a single slice of meat or drink a cup of wine, and in three days it was dead. This is to try to nourish a bird with what would nourish you instead of what would nourish a bird. If you want to nourish a bird with what nourishes a bird, then you should let it roost in the deep forest, play among the banks and islands, float on the rivers and lakes, eat mudfish and minnows, follow the

---

[3] According to the more prosaic interpretation of Li Tz'u-ming, the character for "willow" is a loan for the word "tumor."

[4] Yen Yüan or Yen Hui, who has appeared earlier, was Confucius' favorite disciple.

[5] Kuan Chung, a 7th-century statesman of Ch'i whom Confucius, judging from the Analects, admired, though with reservations.

[6] Sui Jen and Shen Nung are mythical culture heroes, the discoverers of fire and agriculture respectively.

rest of the flock in flight and rest, and live any way it chooses. A bird hates to hear even the sound of human voices, much less all that hubbub and to-do. Try performing the Hsien-ch'ih and Nine Shao music in the wilds around Lake Tung-t'ing—when the birds hear it they will fly off, when the animals hear it they will run away, when the fish hear it they will dive to the bottom. Only the people who hear it will gather around to listen. Fish live in water and thrive, but if men tried to live in water they would die. Creatures differ because they have different likes and dislikes. Therefore the former sages never required the same ability from all creatures or made them all do the same thing.

Names should stop when they have expressed reality, concepts of right should be founded on what is suitable. This is what it means to have command of reason, and good fortune to support you."

Lieh Tzu was on a trip and was eating by the roadside when he saw a hundred-year-old skull. Pulling away the weeds and pointing his finger, he said, "Only you and I know that you have never died and you have never lived. Are you really unhappy?[7] Am I really enjoying myself?

[7] Following the interpretation of Yü Yüeh.

Study Questions

C.6.1 Chuang Tzu (v. Trang Tử), Perfect Happiness

1. "Is there such a thing as perfect happiness in the world or isn't there?"
    a. Identify the things that "the world finds happiness in" according to Chuang Tzu (v. Trang Tử).
    b. Explain the reason why he rejects each thing to be the condition for happiness.
2. "Perfect happiness knows no happiness."
    a. Offer your interpretation of this apparently paradoxical proposition.
    b. Discuss the *means* that Chuang Tzu (v. Trang Tử) proposes for the self-realization of perfect happiness (the end of life).
    c. Discuss your philosophical response to both the end and the means of the good life that Chuang Tzu (v. Trang Tử) proposes.
        (Do not forget to incorporate the stories of "an old skull" and "a sea bird" in your critical analysis).
3. "Chuang Tzu's wife died. When Hui Tzu went to convey his condolences, he found Chuang Tzu sitting with his legs sprawled out, pounding on a tub and singing."
    a. Does one's philosophical knowledge of the life cycle determine the character of one's emotion?
    b. If "Yes," then, explain the philosophical reasons that lie behind the second reaction of Chuang Tzu (v. Trang Tử) to the death of his wife, and compare it with his first reaction.
    c. Compare the Buddha's view of death (C.5.2) with that of Chuang Tzu (v. Trang Tử) and respond to both.

C.6.2

An Ancient East Asian Confucianist Pursuit of Self-Perfection

The Great Learning

The Introduction

The *Great Learning* (*Ta Hsueh* [v. *Đại Học*]) is one of the "Four Books" (Ssu Shu [v. *Tứ Thư*]). Also included in the "Four Books" are the *Lun Yu* (v. *Luận Ngữ* [*Analects*]), the *Meng Tzu* (v. *Mạnh Tử* [*Mencius*]), and the *Chung Yung* (v. *Trung Dung* [*Doctrine of the Mean*]).

Originally, the *Great Learning* was chapter 42 of the *Li Chi* (v. *Lễ Ký* [*Classic of Rites*]. Like other Chinese Confucianist scholars, Chu Hsi (1130–1200 CE) rearranged the *Great Learning* into two parts, the "text" and the "commentary." The "text" corresponds with paragraphs 1–7 in our selection and chapters VI–X in our selection belong to the "supplement." To authenticate its Confucianisticity, Chu Hsi claims that the "text" belongs to the words of Confucius handed down by his disciple Tseng Tzu (v. Tăng Tử) (ca. 505–436 BCE) and the "commentary" constitutes Tseng Tzu's interpretation compiled by his disciples. Professor Wing-Tsit Chan is correct to have noted: "There is no evidence for this contention." [Chan 1963:85] The *Great Learning* is also credited to the authorship of Tzu Ssu (v. *Tử Tư*), the grandson of Confucius! This is characteristic of the ideology of Chinese Confucianist scholarship.

Most modern scholars have dismissed these claims and dated the work around 200 BCE. The authorship and date of the *Great Learning* have remained unresolved and will never be resolved unless Chinese archaeology can come up with an archaeological find. It may be multiculturally safe to speculate that the "text" might have been written by an ancient East Asian *Ju* (v. *Nho*) scholar and the "commentary" authored by many Confucianist scholars of Han times.

1. What the Great Learning teaches, is—to illustrate illustrious virtue; to renovate the people; and to rest in the highest excellence.

2. The point where to rest being known, the object of pursuit is then determined; and, that being determined, a calm unperturbedness may be

[Source: Taken from the *Great Learning*, printed in James Legge, trans., *The Chinese Classics*, vols. I–II (London: Oxford University Press, 1893), paragraphs and chapters cited].

attained to. To that calmness there will succeed a tranquil repose. In that repose there may be careful deliberation, and that deliberation will be followed by the attainment *of the desired end.*

3. Things have their root and their branches. Affairs have their end and their beginning. To know what is first and what is last will lead near to what is taught *in the Great Learning.*

4. The ancients who wished to illustrate illustrious virtue throughout the kingdom, first ordered well their own States. Wishing to order well their States, they first regulated their families. Wishing to regulate their families, they first cultivated their persons.

Wishing to cultivate their persons, they first rectified their hearts. Wishing to rectify their hearts, they first sought to be sincere in their thoughts. Wishing to be sincere in their thoughts, they first extended to the utmost their knowledge. Such extension of knowledge lay in the investigation of things.

5. Things being investigated, knowledge became complete. Their knowledge being complete, their thoughts were sincere. Their thoughts being sincere, their hearts were then rectified. Their hearts being rectified, their persons were cultivated. Their persons being cultivated, their families were regulated. Their families being regulated, their States were rightly governed. Their States being rightly governed, the whole kingdom was made tranquil and happy.

6. From the Son of Heaven down to the mass of the people, all must consider the cultivation of the person the root of *everything besides.*

7. It cannot be, when the root is neglected, that what should spring from it will be well ordered. It never has been the case that what was of great importance has been slightly cared for, and, at the same time, that what was of slight importance has been greatly cared for.

CHAP. VI. 1. What is meant by 'making the thoughts sincere,' is the allowing no self-deception, as *when* we hate a bad smell, and as *when* we love what is beautiful. This is called self-enjoyment. Therefore, the superior man must be watchful over himself when he is alone.

2. There is no evil to which the mean man, dwelling retired, will not proceed, but when he sees a superior man, he instantly tries to disguise himself, concealing his evil, and displaying what is good. The other beholds him, as if he saw his heart and reins;—of what use *is his disguise?* This is an instance of the saying—'What truly is within will be manifested without.' Therefore, the superior man must be watchful over himself when he is alone.

3. The disciple Tsăng said, 'What ten eyes behold, what ten hands point to, is to be regarded with reverence!'

4. Riches adorn a house, and virtue adorns the person. The mind is expanded, and the body is at ease. Therefore, the superior man must make his thoughts sincere.

CHAP. VII. 1. What is meant by, 'The cultivation of the person depends on rectifying the mind,' *may be thus illustrated*:—If a man be under the influence of passion, he will be incorrect in his conduct. He will be the same, if he is under the influence of terror, or under the influence of fond regard, or under that of sorrow and distress.

2. When the mind is not present, we look and do not see; we hear and do not understand; we eat and do not know the taste of what we eat.

3. This is what is meant by saying that the cultivation of the person depends on the rectifying of the mind.

CHAP. VIII. 1. What is meant by 'The regulation of one's family depends on the cultivation of his person,' is this:—Men are partial where they feel affection and love; partial where they despise and dislike; partial where they stand in awe and reverence; partial where they feel sorrow and compassion; partial where they are arrogant and rude. Thus it is that there are few men in the world, who love and at the same time know the bad qualities of *the object of their love,* or who hate and yet know the excellences of *the object of their hatred.*

2. Hence it is said, in the common adage, 'A man does not know the wickedness of his son; he does not know the richness of his growing corn.'

3. This is what is meant by saying that if the person be not cultivated, a man cannot regulate his family.

CHAP. IX. 1. What is meant by 'In order rightly to govern the State, it is necessary first to regulate the family,' is this:—It is not possible for one to teach others, while he cannot teach his own family. Therefore, the ruler, without going beyond his family, completes the lessons for the State. There is filial piety:—therewith the sovereign should be served. There is fraternal submission:—therewith elders and superiors should be served. There is kindness:—therewith the multitude should be treated.

while, from the ambition and perverseness of the One man, the whole State may be led to rebellious disorder;—such is the nature of the influence. This verifies the saying, 'Affairs may be ruined by a single sentence; a kingdom may be settled by its One man.'

4. Yâo and Shun led on the kingdom with benevolence, and the people followed them. Chieh and Châu led on the kingdom with violence, and the people followed them. The orders which these issued were contrary to the practices which they loved, and so the people did not follow them. On this account, the ruler must himself be possessed of the *good* qualities, and then he may require them in the people. He must not have *the bad qualities* in himself, and then he may require that they shall not be in the people. Never has there been a man, who, not having reference to his own character and wishes in dealing with others, was able effectually to instruct them.

5. Thus we see how the government of the State depends on the regulation of the family.

CHAP. X. 1. What is meant by 'The making the whole kingdom peaceful and happy depends on the government of his State,' is this:—When the sovereign behaves to his aged, as the aged should be behaved to, the people become filial; when the sovereign behaves to his elders, as the elders should be behaved to, the people learn brotherly submission; when the sovereign treats compassionately the young and helpless, the

people do the same. Thus the ruler has a principle with which, as with a measuring-square, he may regulate his conduct.

2. What a man dislikes in his superiors, let him not display in the treatment of his inferiors; what he dislikes in inferiors, let him not display in the service of his superiors; what he hates in those who are before him, let him not therewith precede those who are behind him; what he hates in those who are behind him, let him not therewith follow those who are before him; what he hates to receive on the right, let him not bestow on the left; what he hates to receive on the left, let him not bestow on the right:—this is what is called 'The principle with which, as with a measuring-square, to regulate one's conduct.'

3. In the Book of Poetry, it is said, 'How much to be rejoiced in are these princes, the parents of the people!' When *a prince* loves what the people love, and hates what the people hate, then is he what is called the parent of the people.

5. In the Book of Poetry, it is said. 'Before the sovereigns of the Yin *dynasty* had lost the *hearts of the* people, they could appear before God. Take warning from *the house of* Yin. The great decree is not easily *preserved.*' This shows that, by gaining the people, the kingdom is gained, and, by losing the people, the kingdom is lost.

6. On this account, the ruler will first take pains about his own virtue. Possessing virtue will give him the people. Possessing the people will give him the territory. Possessing the territory will give him its wealth. Possessing the wealth, he will have resources for expenditure.

7. Virtue is the root; wealth is the result.

8. If he make the root his secondary object, and the result his primary, he will *only* wrangle with his people, and teach them rapine.

9. Hence, the accumulation of wealth is the way to scatter the people; and the letting it be scattered among them is the way to collect the people.

10. And hence, the ruler's words going forth contrary to right, will come back to him in the

same way, and wealth, gotten by improper ways, will take its departure by the same.

11. In the Announcement to K'ang, it is said, 'The decree indeed may not always rest on *us*;' that is, goodness obtains the decree, and the want of goodness loses it.

12. In the Book of Ch'û, it is said, 'The kingdom of Ch'û does not consider that to be valuable. It values, *instead*, its good men.'

Study Questions

C.6.2 The Great Learning: An Ancient East Asian Confucianist Pursuit of Self-Perfection

1. Explain the aims of the "Great Learning" and offer your philosophical response regarding whether they are the good aims of education.
2. "From the Son of Heaven down to the mass of the people, all must consider the cultivation of the person the root of *everything besides*."
    a. Explain how "the cultivation of the person" is proposed to be learned and practiced in the *Great Learning*.
    a. Analyze each step of self-cultivation that is explained in the *Great Learning*.
    b. Should we cultivate all the steps as prescribed? Critically make your philosophical response.
    c. Should we or should we not follow *faithfully* the functionally progressive sequence of self-cultivation (step-by-step, low to high, simple to complex, easy to difficult) as prescribed? Offer your philosophical response.

C.6.3

A Taoist Critique of K'ung Fu Tzu (v. Khổng Phu Tử)

The Old Fisherman

Chuang Tzu (v. Trang Tử)

The Introduction

It may be prudent to consider the possibility that the story of "The Old Fisherman" might have been written either by Chuang Tzu (v. Trang Tử) himself or by later Taoist scholars. Their purpose can be interpreted to have been aimed at (1) reconstructing those ancient encounters between Confucius and Taoist masters, (2) questioning the supposed wisdom and knowledge of the founder of Confucianism, and (3) propagating their own Taoist Way.

Confucius, after strolling through the Black Curtain Forest, sat down to rest on the Apricot Altar.[1] While his disciples turned to their books, he strummed his lute and sang. He had not gotten halfway through the piece he was playing when an old fisherman appeared, stepped out of his boat, and came forward. His beard and eyebrows were pure white, his hair hung down over his shoulders, and his sleeves flapped at his sides. He walked up the embankment, stopped when he reached the higher ground, rested his left hand on his knee,

propped his chin with his right, and listened until the piece was ended. Then he beckoned to Tzu-kung and Tzu-lu, both of whom came forward at his call. The stranger pointed to Confucius and said, "What does he do?"

"He is a gentleman of Lu," replied Tzu-lu.

The stranger then asked what family he belonged to, and Tzu-lu replied, "The K'ung family."

"This man of the K'ung family," said the stranger, "what's his occupation?"

Tzu-lu was still framing his reply when Tzu-kung answered, "This man of the K'ung family in his inborn nature adheres to loyalty and

[1] The word "altar" here refers to a mesa or flat-topped hill rising out of the lowland.

good faith, in his person practices benevolence and righteousness; he brings a beautiful order to rites and music and selects what is proper in human relationships. Above, he pays allegiance to the sovereign of the age; below, he transforms the ordinary people through education, and in this way brings profit to the world. Such is the occupation of this man of the K'ung family!"

"Does he have any territory that he rules over?" asked the stranger, pursuing the inquiry.

"No," said Tzu-kung.

"Is he the counselor to some king or feudal lord?"

"No," said Tzu-kung.

The stranger then laughed and turned to go, saying as he walked away, "As far as benevolence goes, he is benevolent all right. But I'm afraid he will not escape unharmed. To weary the mind and wear out the body, putting the Truth in peril like this—alas, I'm afraid he is separated from the Great Way by a vast distance indeed!"

Tzu-kung returned and reported to Confucius what had happened. Confucius pushed aside his lute, rose to his feet and said, "Perhaps this man is a sage!" Then he started down the embankment after him, reaching the edge of the lake just as the fisherman was about to take up his punting pole and drag his boat into the water. Glancing back and catching sight of Confucius, he turned and stood facing him. Confucius hastily stepped back a few paces, bowed twice, and then came forward.

"What do you want?" asked the stranger.

"A moment ago, Sir," said Confucius, "you made a few cryptic remarks and then left. Unworthy as I am, I'm afraid I do not understand what they mean. If I might he permitted to wait upon you with all due humility and be favored with the sound of your august words, my ignorance might in time be remedied."

"Goodness!" exclaimed the stranger. "Your love of learning is great indeed!"[2]

Confucius bowed twice and then, straightening up, said, "Ever since childhood I have cultivated learning, until at last I have reached the age of sixty-nine. But I have never yet succeeded in hearing the Perfect Teaching. Dare I do anything, then, but wait with an open mind?"

"Creatures follow their own kind, a voice will answer to the voice that is like itself," said the stranger; "this has been the rule of Heaven since time began. With your permission, therefore, I will set aside for the moment my own ways and try applying myself to the things that you are concerned about.[3] What you are concerned about are the affairs of men. The Son of Heaven, the feudal lords, the high ministers, the common people—when these four are of themselves upright, this is the most admirable state of order. But if they depart from their proper stations, there is no greater disorder. When officials attend to their duties and men worry about their undertakings, there is no overstepping of the mark.

"Fields gone to waste, rooms unroofed, clothing and food that are not enough, taxes and labor services that you can't keep up with, wives and concubines never in harmony, senior and junior out of order—these are the worries of the common man. Ability that does not suffice for the task, official business that doesn't go right, conduct that is not spotless and pure, underlings who are lazy and slipshod, success and praise that never come your way, titles and stipends that you can't hold on to—these are the worries of the high minister. A court lacking in loyal ministers, a state and its great families in darkness and disorder, craftsmen and artisans who have no skill, articles of tribute that won't pass the test, inferior ranking at the spring and autumn levees at court, failure to ingratiate himself with the Son of Heaven—these are the worries of a feudal lord. The yin and yang out of harmony, cold and heat so untimely that they bring injury to all things, feudal lords violent and unruly, wantonly attacking one another till they all but destroy the common people, rites and

[2] A jocular reference to Confucius' remark that, in any village of ten houses, one might find a person as loyal and true to his word as he, but none with such a great love of learning. *Analects* V, 27.

[3] Another possible interpretation would be, "I will explain my own ways and try applying them to the things" etc.

music improperly performed, funds and resources that are forever giving out, human relationships that are not ordered as they should be, the hundred clans contumacious and depraved—these are the worries of the Son of Heaven and his chancellors. Now on the higher level you do not hold the position of a ruler, a feudal lord, or a chancellor, and on the lower level you have not been assigned to the office of a high minister with its tasks and duties. Yet you presume to 'bring a beautiful order to rites and music, to select what is proper in human relationships,' and in this way to 'transform the ordinary people.' This is undertaking rather a lot, isn't it?

"Moreover, there are eight faults that men may possess, and four evils that beset their undertakings—you must not fail to examine these carefully. To do what it is not your business to do is called officiousness. To rush forward when no one has nodded in your direction is called obsequiousness. To echo a man's opinions and try to draw him out in speech is called sycophancy. To speak without regard for what is right or wrong is called flattery. To delight in talking about other men's failings is called calumny. To break up friendships and set kinfolk at odds is called maliciousness. To praise falsely and hypocritically so as to cause injury and evil to others is called wickedness. Without thought for right or wrong, to try to face in two directions at once so as to steal a glimpse of the other party's wishes is called treachery. These eight faults inflict chaos on others and injury on the possessor. A gentleman will not befriend the man who possesses them, an enlightened ruler will not have him for his minister.

"As for the four evils which I spoke of, to be fond of plunging into great undertakings, altering and departing from the old accepted ways, hoping thereby to enhance your merit and fame—this is called avidity. To insist that you know it all, that everything be done your way, snatching from others and appropriating for your own use—this is called avarice. To see your errors but refuse to change, to listen to remonstrance but go on behaving worse than before—this is called

obstinacy. When men agree with you, to commend them; when they disagree with you, to refuse to see any goodness in them even when it is there— this is called bigotry. These are the four evils. If you do away with the eight faults and avoid committing the four evils, then and only then will you become capable of being taught!"

Confucius looked chagrined and gave a sigh. Then he bowed twice, straightened up, and said, "Twice I have been exiled from Lu; they wiped away my footprints in Wei, chopped down a tree on me in Sung, and besieged me between Ch'en and Ts'ai. I am aware of no error of my own, and yet why did I fall victim to these four persecutions?"

A pained expression came over the stranger's face and he said, "How hard it is to make you understand! Once there was a man who was afraid of his shadow and who hated his footprints, and so he tried to get way from them by running. But the more he lifted his feet and put them down again, the more footprints he made. And no matter how fast he ran, his shadow never left him, and so, thinking that he was still going too slowly, he ran faster and faster without a stop until his strength gave out and he fell down dead. He didn't understand that by lolling in the shade he could have gotten rid of his shadow and by resting in quietude he could have put an end to his footprints. How could he have been so stupid!

"Now you scrutinize the realm of benevolence and righteousness, examine the borders of sameness and difference, observe the alternations of stillness and movement, lay down the rules for giving and receiving, regulate the emotions of love and hate, harmonize the seasons of joy and anger—and yet you barely manage to escape harm. If you were diligent in improving yourself, careful to hold fast to the Truth, and would hand over external things to other men, you could avoid these entanglements. But now, without improving yourself, you make demands on others—that is surely no way to go about the thing, is it?"

Confucius looked shamefaced and said, "Please, may I ask what you mean by 'the Truth'?"

The stranger said, "By 'the Truth' I mean purity and sincerity in their highest degree. He who lacks purity and sincerity cannot move others. Therefore he who forces himself to lament, though he may sound sad, will awaken no grief. He who forces himself to be angry, though he may sound fierce, will arouse no awe. And he who forces himself to be affectionate, though he may smile, will create no air of harmony. True sadness need make no sound to awaken grief; true anger need not show itself to arouse awe; true affection need not smile to create harmony. When a man has the Truth within himself, his spirit may move among external things. That is why the Truth is to be prized!

"It may be applied to human relationships in the following ways. In the service of parents, it is love and filial piety; in the service of the ruler, it is loyalty and integrity; in festive wine drinking, it is merriment and joy; in periods of mourning, it is sadness and grief. In loyalty and integrity, service is the important thing; in festive drinking, merriment is the important thing; in periods of mourning, grief is the important thing; in the service of parents, their comfort is the important thing. In seeking to perform the finest kind of service, one does not always try to go about it in the same way. In assuring comfort in the serving of one's parents, one does not question the means to be employed. In seeking the merriment that comes with festive drinking, one does not fuss over what cups and dishes are to be selected. In expressing the grief that is appropriate to periods of mourning, one does not quibble over the exact ritual to be followed.

"Rites are something created by the vulgar men of the world; the Truth is that which is received from Heaven. By nature it is the way it is and cannot be changed. Therefore the sage patterns himself on Heaven, prizes the Truth, and does not allow himself to be cramped by the vulgar. The stupid man does the opposite of this. He is unable to pattern himself on Heaven and instead frets over human concerns. He does not know enough to prize the Truth but instead, plodding along with the crowd, he allows himself to be changed by vulgar ways, and so is never content. Alas, that you fell into the slough of human hypocrisy at such an early age, and have been so late in hearing of the Great Way!"

Confucius once more bowed twice, straightened up, and said, "Now that I have succeeded in meeting you, it would seem as though Heaven has blessed me. If, Master, you would not consider it a disgrace for one like myself to enter the ranks of those who wait upon you, and to be taught by you in person, then may I be so bold as to inquire where your lodgings are? I would like to be allowed to go there, receive instruction, and at last learn the Great Way!"

The stranger replied, "I have heard it said, If it is someone you can go with, then go with him to the very end of the mysterious Way; but if it is someone you cannot go with, someone who does not understand the Way, then take care and have nothing to do with him—only then may you avoid danger to yourself. Keep working at it! Now I will leave you, I will leave you." So saying, he poled away in his boat, threading a path through the reeds.

Yen Yüan brought the carriage around, Tzu-lu held out the strap for pulling oneself up, but Confucius, without turning in their direction, waited until the ripples on the water were stilled and he could no longer hear the sound of the pole before he ventured to mount.

Tzu-lu, following by the side of the carriage, said, "I have been permitted to serve you for a long time, Master, but I have never seen you encounter anyone who filled you with such awe. The rulers of ten thousand chariots, the lords of a thousand chariots, when they receive you, invariably seat you on the same level as themselves and treat you with the etiquette due to an equal, and still you maintain a stiff and haughty air. But now this old fisherman, pole in hand, presents himself in front of you, and you double up at the waist, as bent as a chiming-stone,[4] and bow every time you reply to his words—this is going too far,

---

[4] Chiming-stones were shaped like an inverted "V."

isn't it? Your disciples all are wondering about it. Why should a fisherman deserve such treatment?"

Confucius leaned forward on the crossbar, sighed, and said, "You certainly are hard to change! All this time you have been immersed in the study of ritual principles and you still haven't gotten rid of your mean and servile ways of thinking. Come closer and I will explain to you. To meet an elder and fail to treat him with respect is a breach of etiquette. To see a worthy man and fail to honor him is to lack benevolence. If the fisherman were not a Perfect Man, he would not be able to make other men humble themselves before him. And if men, in humbling themselves before him, lack purity of intention, then they will never attain the Truth. As a result, they will go on forever bringing injury upon themselves. Alas! There is no greater misfortune than for a man to lack benevolence. And yet you alone dare to invite such misfortune!

"Moreover, the Way is the path by which the ten thousand things proceed. All things that lose it, die; all that get it, live. To go against it in one's undertakings is to fail; to comply with it is to succeed. Hence, wherever the Way is to be found, the sage will pay homage there. As far as the Way is concerned, this old fisherman may certainly be said to possess it. How, then, would I dare fail to show respect to him!"

Study Questions

C.6.3 A Taoist Critique of K'ung Fu Tzu (Khổng Phu Tử)

Chuang Tzu (v. Trang Tử), The Old Fisherman

1. Explain how Tzu-kung (v. Tử Cống) describes "the occupation" of his Master?
2. Analyze why and how Khổng Phu Tử (c. K'ung Fu Tzu) is being criticized by the stranger.
3. Explain the stranger's teaching and how it differs from the teaching of Khổng Phu Tử (c. K'ung Fu Tzu).

Part D

Eastern Ethics and Political Thoughts

CHAPTER 7

The Hindu Ethics and Vision of the Good Life

An Upanishadic Dharma of the Truthful Life

The Taittiriya Upanishad

The Introduction

The *Taittiriya Upanishad* is recognized for its moral teachings as presented in the form of a discourse between the teacher and his pupils, sometimes called a "Convocation Address." Also famous is its doctrine of the "Five Sheaths" of the self, namely, the sheath of food, the sheath of mind, the sheath of intellect, and the sheath of bliss. The scripture is so named because it is a part of the *Taittiriya Aranyaka*.

Eleventh Anuvāka

Practical Precepts to a Student

1. Having taught the Veda, a teacher further instructs a pupil:—

> Speak the truth.
> Practise virtue (*dharma*).
> Neglect not study [of the Vedas].
> Having brought an acceptable gift to the teacher, cut not off the line of progeny.
> One should not be negligent of truth.
> One should not be negligent of virtue.
> One should not be negligent of welfare.
> One should not be negligent of prosperity.
> One should not be negligent of study and teaching.

2. One should not be negligent of duties to the gods and to the fathers.

> Be one to whom a mother is as a god.
> Be one to whom a father is as a god.
> Be one to whom a teacher is as a god.
> Be one to whom a guest is as a god.

Those acts which are irreproachable should be practised, and no others.

[Source: Taken from the *Taittiriya Upanishad* I.11.1–2, printed in R. E. Hume, trans., *The Thirteen Principal Upanishads* (London: Oxford University Press, 1921), pp. 281–82].

Those things which among us are good deeds should be revered by you, [3] and no others.

Whatever Brahmans (*brāhmaṇa*) are superior to us, for them refreshment should be procured by you with a seat.[1]

> One should give with faith (*śraddhā*).
> One should not give without faith.
> One should give with plenty (*śrī*)[2]
> One should give with modesty.
> One should give with fear.

One should give with sympathy (*sam-vid*).[3]

Now, if you should have doubt concerning an act, or doubt concerning conduct, [4] if there should be there Brahmans competent to judge, apt, devoted, not harsh, lovers of virtue (*dharma*)—as they may behave themselves in such a case, so should you behave yourself in such a case.

Now, with regard to [people] spoken against, if there should be there Brahmans competent to judge, apt, devoted, not harsh, lovers of virtue— as they may behave themselves with regard to such, so should you behave yourself with regard to such.

This is the teaching. This is the admonition. This is the mystic doctrine of the Veda (*veda-upaniṣad*). This is the instruction. Thus should one worship. Thus, indeed, should one worship.

---

[1] That is, 'I am the feller of the tree of world-delusion (*saṁsāra*)' according to Śaṅkara. He also proposes, as a synonym for 'mover,' *antaryāmin*, 'inner controller'—which suggests to Deussen the (less likely) interpretation: 'I am the moving (or, animating) spirit of the tree of life.'

[2] Literally 'courser'; a reference here perhaps to the 'honey in the sun' of Chand. 3.1.—So Śaṅkara divides the words, *vājinī 'va sv-amṛtaṁ*. But if *vājinīvasv amṛtaṁ*, as *BR*. suggests, then 'the Immortal, possessing [possibly, 'bestowing'— according to *BR*.] power.'

[3] *amṛto'kṣitaḥ*. If *amṛtokṣitaḥ*, then 'sprinkled with immortality (or, with nectar).'

Study Questions

D.7.1 *The Taittiriya Upanishad*, An Upanishadic Dharma of the Truthful Life

1. Identify the main virtues that are taught by the Upanishadic guru to his disciple. Critically explain how they are related to each other and whether or not they are important for the young to learn.
2. "Speak the truth. Practice virtue (dharma)."
    Explain your own philosophical view regarding why one should do these.
3. List all the five noble spirits that one should have when one gives.
    Explain your own philosophical view of the virtue of giving.

D.7.2

The Moral Logic of Karma

The Laws of Manu

The Introduction

Essential to Hindu ethics is its doctrine of karma and doctrine of samsara. "*Karma*" is a Sanskrit term that signifies the three main types of human action and the *karmically* accumulative results that they produce whenever they are consciously performed. One of the *karmically* accumulative consequences is one's *samsara* (cycle of rebirth) as stated in the selection.

81. ...with whatever disposition of mind (a man) performs any act, he reaps its result in a (future) body endowed with the same quality. (XII.81)

3. Action, which springs from the mind, from speech, and from the body, produces either good or evil results; by action are caused the (various) conditions of men, the highest, the middling, and the lowest.

4. Know that the mind is the instigator here below, even to that (action) which is connected with the body, (and) which is of three kinds, has three locations, and falls under ten heads.

5. Coveting the property of others, thinking in one's heart of what is undesirable, and adherence to false (doctrines), are the three kinds of (sinful) mental action.

6. Abusing (others, speaking) untruth, detracting from the merits of all men, and talking idly, shall be the four kinds of (evil) verbal action.

7. Taking what has not been given, injuring (creatures) without the sanction of the law, and holding criminal intercourse with another man's wife, are declared to be the three kinds of (wicked) bodily action.

8. (A man) obtains (the result of) a good or evil mental (act) in his mind, (that of) a verbal (act) in his speech, (that of) a bodily (act) in his body.

9. In consequence of (many) sinful acts committed with his body, a man becomes (in the next birth) something inanimate, in consequence (of sins) committed by speech, a bird, or a beast,

[Source: Taken from Manu, *Manu Smrti* (IV.155–8, 172–5, 238–40; XII.3–9, 11, 40, 50, 81, 95, 104), printed in G. Buhler, trans., *The Laws of Manu, The Sacred Books of the East*, vol. 25 (Oxford: The Clarendon Press, 1886), chapters and verses cited].

and in consequence of mental (sins he is re-born in) a low caste.

11. That man who keeps this threefold control (over himself) with respect to all created beings and wholly subdues desire and wrath, thereby assuredly gains complete success. (XII.3–9, 11)

104. Austerity and sacred learning are the best means by which a *brāhmin* secures supreme bliss; by austerities he destroys guilt, by sacred learning he obtains the cessation of (births and) deaths. (XII.104)

95. All those traditions (*smṛti*) and all those despicable systems of philosophy, which are not based on the Veda, produce no reward after death; for they are declared to be founded on darkness. (XII.95)

238. Giving no pain to any creature, let him slowly accumulate spiritual merit, for the sake (of acquiring) a companion to the next world, . . .

239. For in the next world neither father, nor mother, nor wife, nor sons, nor relations stay to be his companions; spiritual merit alone remains (with him).

240. Single is each being born; single it dies; single it enjoys (the reward of its) virtue; single (it suffers the punishment of its) sin. (IV.238–40)

155. Let him, untired, follow the conduct of virtuous men, connected with his occupations, which has been fully declared in the revealed texts and in the sacred tradition (*smṛti*) and is the root of the sacred law.

156. Through virtuous conduct he obtains long life, through virtuous conduct desirable offspring, through virtuous conduct imperishable wealth; virtuous conduct destroys (the effect of) inauspicious marks.

157. For a man of bad conduct is blamed among people, constantly suffers misfortunes, is afflicted with diseases, and [is] short-lived.

158. A man who follows the conduct of the virtuous, has faith and is free from envy, lives a hundred years, though he be entirely destitute of auspicious marks.

172. Unrighteousness, practised in this world, does not at once produce its fruit, like a cow; but, advancing slowly, it cuts off the roots of him who committed it.

173. If (the punishment falls) not on (the offender) himself, (it falls) on his sons, if not on the sons, (at least) on his grandsons; but an iniquity (once) committed, never fails to produce to him who wrought it.

174. He prospers for a while through unrighteousness, then he gains great good fortune, next he conquers his enemies, but (at last) he perishes (branch and) root.

175. Let him always delight in truthfulness, (obedience to) the sacred law, conduct worthy of an Āryan, and purity; . . . (IV.155–8, 172–5)

40. Those endowed with Goodness reach the state of gods, those endowed with Activity the state of men, and those endowed with Darkness ever sink to the condition of beasts; that is the threefold course of transmigrations.

50. The sages declare *Brahman*, the creators of the universe, the law, the Great One, and the Undiscernible One (to constitute) the highest order of beings produced by Goodness. (XII.40, 50)

Study Questions

D.7.2 *The Laws of Manu*, The Moral Logic of Karma

1. List all the numerated passages that belong either to the category of positive karma, or the category of negative karma.
2. Introduce the main concept for each type of karma and write it down in the space given. Then, identify any numerated passage that reflects the best meaning for each type of karma and organize it by type. (Clue: the concept of "Verbal Karma").
3. Identify the type of rebirth (reincarnation) that each type of karma produces. Critically discuss whether there is a logically causal connection between karma and rebirth as claimed by Manu. Address also, the Marxist critique that the Hindu and Buddhist doctrines of karma and samsara are essentially a *metaethical strategy* used for the religious control of the masses in order to prevent political rebellion against social injustice.
4. Discuss why humans should be moral rather than immoral according to Manu. Make a philosophical response.

D.7.3

The Status and Role of Hindu Women

The Laws of Manu

The Introduction

Women have not received any philosophical treatment in any of the Eastern philosophies. Historically, women have been mistreated and exploited in strongly patriarchal societies, such as China, Japan, Korea, and India. Women have enjoyed a much better social status and played a more influential role in Việt-Nam and many other countries of South East Asia. Many Việtnamese women, like the Trưng Sisters and Lady Triệu Ẫu, were national heroes because they were revolutionary leaders of anti-Chinese liberation wars. In contrast to the Chinese Confucianist tradition, most Việtnamese role models of high morality are women rather than men. Two socioeconomic reasons can explain the high status of Việtnamese and Southeast Asian women. First, the practice of wet-rice agriculture favors the extensive role of women in the various aspects of social life. Second, many culturally embedded features of the old matriarchy have survived despite the penetration of the Chinese Confucianist patriarchal value system.

Hindu women are apparently given a "high place" in the *Laws of Manu* as indicated by the first passage of the selection. This passage has been quoted often as an example of a positive Hindu attitude towards women. This positive Hindu attitude towards women is not philosophically grounded but is pragmatically considered.

55. Women must be honoured and adorned by their fathers, brothers, husbands, and brothers-in-law, who desire (their own) welfare.

56. Where women are honoured, there the gods are pleased; but where they are not honoured, no sacred rite yields rewards.

57. Where the female relations live in grief, the family soon wholly perishes; but that family where they are not unhappy ever prospers.

58. The houses on which female relations, not being duly honoured, pronounce a curse, perish completely, as if destroyed by magic.

[Source: Taken from Manu, *Manu Smrti* (III.55–59, V.146–66), printed in G. Buhler, trans., *The Laws of Manu*, *Sacred Books of the East*, vol. 25 (Oxford: The Clarendon Press, 1886), chapters and verses cited].

59. Hence men who seek (their own) welfare, should always honour women on holidays and festivals with (gifts of) ornaments, clothes, and (dainty) food.

146. Thus the rules of personal purification for men of all castes, and those for cleaning (inanimate) things, have been fully declared to you: hear now the duties of women.

147. By a girl, by a young woman, or even by an aged one, nothing must be done independently, even in her own house.

148. In childhood a female must be subject to her father, in youth to her husband, when her lord is dead to her sons; a woman must never be independent.

149. She must not seek to separate herself from her father, husband, or sons; by leaving them she would make both (her own and her husband's) families contemptible.

150. She must always be cheerful, clever in (the management of her) household affairs, careful in cleaning her utensils, and economical in expenditure.

151. Him to whom her father may give her, or her brother with the father's permission, she shall obey as long as he lives, and when he is dead, she must not insult (his memory).

152. For the sake of procuring good fortune to (brides), the recitation of benedictory texts (svastyayana), and the sacrifice to the Lord of creatures (Pragâpati) are used at weddings; (but) the betrothal (by the father or guardian) is the cause of (the husband's) dominion (over his wife).

153. The husband who wedded her with sacred texts, always gives happiness to his wife, both in season and out of season, in this world and in the next.

154. Though destitute of virtue, or seeking pleasure (elsewhere), or devoid of good qualities, (yet) a husband must be constantly worshipped as a god by a faithful wife.

155. No sacrifice, no vow, no fast must be performed by women apart (from their husbands); if a wife obeys her husband, she will for that (reason alone) be exalted in heaven.

156. A faithful wife, who desires to dwell (after death) with her husband, must never do anything that might displease him who took her hand, whether he be alive or dead.

157. At her pleasure let her emaciate her body by (living on) pure flowers, roots, and fruit; but she must never even mention the name of another man after her husband has died.

158. Until death let her be patient (of hardships), self-controlled, and chaste, and strive (to fulfil) that most excellent duty which (is prescribed) for wives who have one husband only.

159. Many thousands of Brâhma*n*as who were chaste from their youth, have gone to heaven without continuing their race.

160. A virtuous wife who after the death of her husband constantly remains chaste, reaches heaven, though she have no son, just like those chaste men.

161. But a woman who from a desire to have offspring violates her duty towards her (deceased) husband, brings on herself disgrace in this world, and loses her place with her husband (in heaven).

162. Offspring begotten by another man is here not (considered lawful), nor (does offspring begotten) on another man's wife (belong to the begetter), nor is a second husband anywhere prescribed for virtuous women.

163. She who cohabits with a man of higher caste, forsaking her own husband who belongs to a lower one, will become contemptible in this world, and is called a remarried woman (parapûrvâ).

164. By violating her duty towards her husband, a wife is disgraced in this world, (after death) she enters the womb of a jackal, and is tormented by diseases (the punishment of) her sin.

165. She who, controlling her thoughts, words, and deeds, never slights her lord, resides (after death) with her husband (in heaven), and is called a virtuous (wife).

166. In reward of such conduct, a female who controls her thoughts, speech, and actions, gains in this (life) highest renown, and in the next (world) a place near her husband.

Study Questions

D.7.3 *The Laws of Manu*, The Status and Role of Hindu Women

1. List all the reasons why women must be honored according to Manu. Critically discuss whether women would be still honored, as they should if these reasons were removed. If not, what is the *real problem* with these reasons and how can it be resolved?
2. List all the duties of women according to their own functional categories. Critique Manu's view on the role and status of women in relation to men.
3. Critically discuss the main sociological and theo-philosophical reasons that might have produced the *extremely* low attitude of Hindu men towards women as stated in the *Laws of Manu*.

CHAPTER 8

The Buddhist Ethics and
the Compassionate Life

The Wounded Swan

Thich Nhat Hanh

The Introduction

Thich Nhat Hanh (v. Thích Nhất Hạnh) was born in central Việt-Nam in the mid-1920's, and at the age of 16 (1942), he entered monkhood. An official introduction of Thich Nhat Hanh on the back page of his book *Being Peace*, published by the Parallax Press in 1987, reads: "Thich Nhat Hanh, poet, Zen master, and chairman of the Việtnamese Buddhist Peace delegation during the war, was nominated by Dr. Martin Luther King, Jr. for the Nobel Peace Prize. Thomas Merton described him as "more my brother than many who are nearer to me in race and nationality, because he and I see things in exactly the same way." He has authored many books on Buddhism in both English and Việtnamese. Most recent is his *Thả Một Bè Lau* (*Floating a Batch of Reeds*), a scholarly work on the *Truyện Kiều* (*Story of Kiều*), the all-time masterpiece of Việtnamese literature. He offers an interesting Zen interpretation of the main theme of this greatest and most beloved poem of Việt-Nam.

Early the next morning, Svasti led his buffaloes to graze. By noon he had cut enough grass to fill two baskets. Svasti liked to let the buffaloes graze on the side of the river which bordered the forest. That way, when he finished gathering grass, he could stretch out in the cool breeze and not worry about the buffaloes wandering into someone's rice fields. He carried only his sickle, the tool by which he earned his living. Svasti opened the small fistful of rice Bala had wrapped in a banana leaf for his lunch, but as he was about to eat, his thoughts turned to Siddhartha.

"I could take this rice to the hermit, Siddhartha," he thought. "Surely he won't find my rice too humble." Svasti wrapped the rice, and, leaving the buffaloes at the forest's edge, followed the path to where he had met Siddhartha the day before.

From a distance he saw his new friend sitting beneath the great pippala tree. But Siddhartha was not alone. Before him sat a girl just about Svasti's age, dressed in a fine white sari. There was food already placed before him, and Svasti stopped abruptly. But Siddhartha looked up and called to

Reprinted from *Old Path White Clouds: Walking in the Footsteps of the Buddha* (1991) by Thich Nhat Hanh with permission of Parallaz Press, Berkeley, California.

him, "Svasti!" He motioned for the boy to join them.

The girl in the white sari looked up, and Svasti recognized her as someone he had often passed on the village road. As Svasti approached, she moved to her left to make a place for him, and Siddhartha gestured him to sit down. In front of Siddhartha was a banana leaf which held a fistful of rice and a small amount of sesame salt. Siddhartha divided the rice into two portions.

"Have you eaten yet, child?"

"No, Mister, I haven't."

"Well then, let's share this."

Siddhartha handed Svasti half the rice, and Svasti joined his palms together in thanks, but refused the rice. He took out his own humble rice and said, "I've also brought some."

He opened his banana leaf to reveal coarse grains of brown rice, unlike the soft, white grains on Siddhartha's leaf. He had no sesame salt. Siddhartha smiled at the two children and said, "Shall we put all our rice together and share it?"

He took half the white rice, dipped it in sesame salt and handed it to Svasti. Then he broke off half of Svasti's rice ball and began to eat it with obvious delight. Svasti felt awkward, but seeing Siddhartha's naturalness, he began to eat as well.

"Your rice is so fragrant, Mister."

"Sujata brought it," answered Siddhartha.

"So her name is Sujata," thought Svasti. She looked a bit older than Svasti, perhaps a year or two. Her large black eyes twinkled. Svasti stopped eating and said, "I've seen you before on the village road, but I didn't know your name was Sujata."

"Yes, I am the daughter of the village chief of Uruvela. Your name is Svasti, isn't it? Teacher Siddhartha was just telling me about you," she said, adding gently, "Svasti, it is more correct to call a monk, 'Teacher,' than 'Mister.'"

Svasti nodded.

Siddhartha smiled. "Well then, I don't need to introduce you two. Do you know, children, why I eat in silence? These grains of rice and sesame are so precious, I like to eat silently so that I can appreciate them fully. Sujata, have you ever had a chance to taste brown rice? Even if you've already eaten, please taste a bit of Svasti's rice. It is quite delicious.

Now then, we can eat together in silence, and when we've finished, I'll tell you a story."

Siddhartha broke off a piece of brown rice and handed it to Sujata. She joined her palms like a lotus and respectfully accepted it. The three of them ate quietly in the deep calm of the forest.

When the rice and sesame were gone, Sujata gathered the banana leaves. She took a jug of fresh water from her side and poured some into the only cup she had brought. She lifted the cup to offer water to Siddhartha. He took it in his two hands and offered it to Svasti. Flustered, Svasti blurted, "Please, Mister, I mean, Teacher, please, you take the first drink."

Siddhartha answered in a soft voice, "You drink first, child. I want you to have the first drink." Again he lifted and offered the cup to Svasti.

Svasti felt confused but didn't know how to refuse such an unaccustomed honor. He joined his palms in thanks and took the cup. He drank all the water in one long gulp. He handed the cup back to Siddhartha. Siddhartha asked Sujata to pour a second cup. When it was full he raised it to his lips and sipped the water slowly, with reverence and deep enjoyment. Sujata's eyes did not stray from Siddhartha and Svasti during this exchange. When Siddhartha finished drinking, he asked Sujata to pour a third cup. This one he offered to her. She put down the water jug, joined her palms, and accepted the cup of water. She lifted it to her lips and drank in slow, small sips, just as Siddhartha had done. She was aware that this was the first time she had ever drunk from the same cup as an untouchable. But Siddhartha was her Teacher, and if he had done so, why shouldn't she? And she noticed that she had no feeling whatsoever of being polluted. Spontaneously, she reached out and touched the buffalo boy's hair. It was such a surprise, Svasti didn't have a moment to move out of the way. Then Sujata finished drinking her water. She placed the empty cup on the ground and smiled at her two companions.

Siddhartha nodded. "You children have understood. People are not born with caste. Everyone's tears are salty, and everyone's blood is red. It is wrong to divide people into castes and create division and prejudice among them. This has become very clear to me during my meditation."

Sujata looked thoughtful and she spoke, "We are your disciples and we believe your teaching. But there does not seem to be anyone else like you in this world. Everyone else believes that the sudras and the untouchables came forth from the Creator's feet. Even the scriptures say so. No one dares to think differently."

"Yes, I know. But the truth is the truth whether anyone believes it or not. Though a million people may believe a lie, it is still a lie. You must have great courage to live according to the truth. Let me tell you a story about when I was a boy.

"One day, when I was nine years old and strolling alone in the garden, a swan suddenly dropped from the sky and writhed on the ground in front of me in great pain. I ran to pick it up, and I discovered that an arrow had deeply penetrated one of its wings. I clasped my hand firmly around the arrow's shaft and yanked it out, and the bird cried as blood oozed from its wound. I applied pressure to the wound with my finger to stop the bleeding, and took the bird inside the palace to find princess Sundari, the lady in waiting. She agreed to pick a handful of medicinal leaves and make a poultice for the bird's wound. The swan shivered, so I took off my jacket and wrapped it around her. Then I placed her close to the royal fireplace."

Siddhartha paused for a moment to look at Svasti. "Svasti, I did not tell you yet, but when I was young I was a prince, the son of King Suddhodana in the city of Kapilavatthu. Sujata knows this already. I was about to go find some rice for the swan when my eight-year-old cousin, Devadatta, burst into the room. He was clutching his bow and arrows, and he asked excitedly,

'Siddhartha, did you see a white swan fall down near here?'

"Before I could answer, Devadatta saw the swan resting by the fireplace. He ran towards it, but I stopped him.

"'You may not take the bird.'

"My cousin protested, 'That bird is mine. I shot it myself.'

"I stood between Devadatta and the swan, determined not to let him have it. I told him, 'This bird is wounded. I'm protecting it. It needs to stay here.'

"Devadatta was quite stubborn and not about to give in. He argued, 'Now listen, cousin, when this bird was flying in the sky, it didn't belong to anyone. As I'm the one who shot it out of the sky, it rightfully belongs to me.'

"His argument sounded logical, but his words made me angry. I knew there was something wrong with his reasoning, but I couldn't quite put my finger on it. So I just stood there, speechless, becoming more upset. I felt like punching him. Why I didn't, I don't know. Then, I saw a way to answer him.

"'Listen, cousin,' I told him, 'Those who love each other live together, and those who are enemies live apart. You tried to kill the swan, so you and she are enemies. The bird cannot live with you. I saved her, bandaged her wound, warmed her, and was on my way to find food for her when you arrived. The bird and I love each other, and we can live together. The bird needs me, not you.'"

Sujata clapped her hands together, "That's right! You were right!"

Siddhartha looked at Svasti. "And what do you think, child, of my statement?"

Svasti thought for a moment and then answered slowly, "I think you were right. But not many people would agree. Most people would side with Devadatta."

Siddhartha nodded. "You are right. Most people do follow Devadatta's view.

"Let me tell you what happened next. As we couldn't agree on our own, we decided to take our concern to the adults. That day there was a meeting of the government in the palace, so we scurried to the hall of justice, where they were meeting. I held the swan and Devadatta clasped his bow and arrows. We presented our problem to the ministers and asked them to render judgment. The affairs of state came to a halt as the men listened, first to Devadatta and then to me. They discussed the matter at length, but they also were unable to agree. The majority seemed to be leaning towards Devadatta, when my father, the king, suddenly cleared his throat and coughed a few times. All the ministers suddenly stopped speaking, and—tell me if you don't think this is odd—with total accord, they agreed that my argument was correct and that the bird should be given to me. Devadatta was beside himself with anger, but of course, there was nothing he could do.

"I had the bird, but I wasn't really happy. Even though I was still young, I knew that my victory had been less than honorable. I was given the bird because the ministers wanted to please my father, not because they saw the truth of what I said."

"That's sad," Sujata said and frowned.

"Yes, it was. But turning my thoughts to the bird, I took comfort in the fact that she was safe. Otherwise she surely would have ended up in a cooking pot.

"In this world, few people look with the eyes of compassion, and so we are cruel and merciless toward each other. The weak are always oppressed by the strong. I still see that my reasoning that day was correct, for it arose from love and understanding. Love and understanding can ease the suffering of all beings. The truth is the truth, whether or not it is accepted by the majority. Therefore, I tell you children, it takes great courage to stand up for and protect what is right."

"What happened to the swan, Teacher?" asked Sujata.

"For four days, I cared for her. When I saw that her wound had healed, I released her, after warning her to fly far away lest she be shot again."

Siddhartha looked at the two children, their faces quiet and serious. "Sujata, you must return home before your mother begins to worry. Svasti, isn't it time for you to return to your buffaloes and cut more grass? The armful of kusa grass you gave me yesterday made a perfect cushion for meditation. Last night and this morning, I sat upon it and my meditation was very peaceful. I saw many things clearly. You have been a great help, Svasti. As my understanding deepens, I shall share the fruit of my meditation with both you children. Now I will continue sitting."

Svasti looked down at the grass which Siddhartha had shaped into a cushion. Though the grasses were packed firm, Svasti knew they were still fragrant and soft. He would bring his teacher a fresh armful of grass every three days to make a new cushion. Svasti stood up and, with Sujata, joined his palms and bowed to Siddhartha. Sujata set out for home and Svasti led his buffaloes to graze further along the riverbank.

Study Questions

D.8.1 Thich Nhat Hanh, The Wounded Swan

1. Explain the presupposition behind Devadatta's argument that he should have the swan. Critique his argument and its presupposition according to Thich Nhat Hanh's reconstruction.
2. Explain Siddhartha's argument that he should keep the wounded swan according to the reconstruction by Thich Nhat Hanh (v. Thích Nhất Hạnh).
3. Explain whether there is *a moral connection* between Siddhartha's caring act of saving the wounded swan and his later "Four Noble Truths." In light of his "Four Noble Truths," explain all the possible reasons why the Buddha would not hurt, harm, or kill animals.

Treading the Theravadin
Path to Moral Goodness

The Dhammapada

The Introduction

By 300 years after the death of the Buddha (483 BCE), the Buddhist movement was split into twenty Buddhist schools. Of these schools, four were most influential: the Sthaviravada, the Mahasanghika, the Sarvastivada, and the Sammatiya. Out of the Sthaviravada, the "Theravada" (teachings of the Elders) Buddhism emerged, around 4th century BCE. It is also known as "Southern Buddhism," because it has flourished in South Asia (Sri Lanka) and Southeast Asia (Burma, Kampuchea, Laos, Thailand, and southern Việt-Nam). Sri Lanka was the first country that received Theravada Buddhism, when a delegate headed by Mahinda, the son of the Buddhist King Ashoka, was sent there. Sri Lanka can be considered as the country that best represents the tradition of Theravada Buddhism.

Out of the Mahasanghika, the Mahayana (Great Vehicle) Buddhism emerged, around the first century BCE. It is known also as "Eastern Buddhism," because, it has flourished in East Asia (China, Korea, Japan, Taiwan, and northern Việt-Nam).

Theravada Buddhism reflects an orthodox interpretation of the teachings of the Buddha (Buddhaian Dharma). After the "*paranirvana*" (complete extinction) of the Buddha, his teachings, which had been memorized by his close disciples, were eventually compiled into "*nikyayas*" (collections). It was from these collections, after many modifications and textual alterations, that the *Pali Canon* was textually finalized in the form of the "*Tripitaka*" (*Three Baskets*). After the Fourth Buddhist Council (ca. 100 BCE), the *Tripitaka* was committed to writing in Pali, because, its Theravadin compilers claimed that the Buddha taught his Dharma in the Pali language rather than in the Sanskrit language of the Aryan Hindus.

All that we are is the result of what we have thought: it is founded on our thoughts, it is made up of our thoughts. If a man speaks or acts with an evil thought, pain follows him, as the wheel follows the foot of the ox that draws the carriage.

All that we are is the result of what we have thought: it is founded on our thoughts, it is made up of our thoughts. If a man speaks or acts with a pure thought, happiness follows him, like a shadow that never leaves him.

"He abused me, he beat me, he defeated me, he robbed me"— in those who harbor such thoughts hatred will never cease.

"He abused me, he beat me, be defeated me, he robbed me"— in those who do not harbor such thoughts hatred will cease.

For hatred does not cease by hatred at any time; hatred ceases by love—this is an eternal law.

The world does not know that we must all come to an end here; but those who know it, their quarrels cease at once.

He who lives looking for pleasures only, his senses uncontrolled, immoderate in his food, idle, and weak, Mara[1] will certainly overthrow him, as the wind throws down a weak tree.

He who lives without looking for pleasures, his senses well-controlled, moderate in his food, faithful, and strong, him Mara will certainly not overthrow, any more than the wind throws down a rocky mountain.

He who wishes to put on the yellow robe[2] without having cleansed himself from sin, who disregards also temperance and truth, is unworthy of the yellow robe.

But he who has cleansed himself from sin, is well-grounded in all virtues, and endowed also with temperance and truth: he is indeed worthy of the yellow robe.

They who imagine truth in untruth, and see untruth in truth, never arrive at truth, but follow vain desires.

They who know truth in truth, and untruth in untruth, arrive at truth and follow true desires.

As rain breaks through an ill-thatched house, passion will break through an unreflecting mind.

As rain does not break through a well-thatched house, passion will not break through a well-reflecting mind.

The evildoer mourns in this world, and he mourns in the next; he mourns in both. He mourns and suffers when he sees the evil result of his own acts.

The virtuous man delights in this world, and he delights in the next; he delights in both. He delights and rejoices, when he sees the purity of his own work.

The evildoer suffers in this world, and he suffers in the next; he suffers in both. He suffers when he thinks of the evil he has done; he suffers even more when going on the evil path.

The virtuous man is happy in this world, and he is happy in the next; he is happy in both. He is happy when he thinks of the good he has done; he is still more happy when advancing on the good path.

[1] The great tempter.
[2] The garb of the Buddhist monk.

Study Questions

D.8.2 *The Dhammapada*, Treading the Theravadin Path of Moral Goodness

1. Explain the reasons why humans should be moral and avoid evils according to "The Twin Verses." Make your critical philosophical response.
2. "All that we are is the result of what we have thought: it is founded on our thoughts, it is made up of our thoughts." Explain this statement and make your critical philosophical response.
3. "For hatred does not cease by hatred at any time; hatred ceases by love—this is the eternal law." Explain this statement and make a critical philosophical response.

D.8.3

The Bodhisattva Path of Infinite Compassion

The Introduction

One of the hallmarks of Mahayana Buddhism is the moral idealism of its new type of monks, the *"bodhisattva"* ("a being headed for Buddhahood"), who distinguishes himself from the Theravadin *"arhat"* by his infinite compassion (*mahakaruna*) and transcendental wisdom (*prajnaparamita*). In early Buddhism, the term *"arhat"* means the highest state of being to be achieved; and in Theravada Buddhism, it means the ideal *bhikku* who already acquired complete wisdom and enlightenment. What truly distinguishes the bodhisattva from the arhat is his willingness to postpone his *nirvana* enjoyment until all sentient beings are totally liberated as a result of his selfless and wise actions. Rather than seeking nirvana as the primary aim to overcome dukkha, as arhats have done, "this new Buddhist hero," note John Koller and Patricia Koller, "out of compassion, willingly takes on the suffering of all beings. Guided by wisdom acquired through moral cultivation and deep meditation, he patiently and energetically gives himself completely, without thought of gain or reward, to the task of rescuing others from the sea of suffering." [Koller and Koller 1991:247] The enlightenment of the historical Buddha was thus interpreted in the *Prajnaparamita sutras* of Mahayana Buddhism as the condition for helping all sentient beings to overcome their suffering rather than the means of overcoming his own *dukkha*.

A Bodhisattva resolves: I take upon myself the burden of all suffering, I am resolved to do so, I will endure it. I do not turn or run away, do not tremble, am not terrified, nor afraid, do not turn back or despond.

And why? At all costs I must bear the burdens of all beings, In that I do not follow my own inclinations. I have made the vow to save all beings. All beings I must set free. The whole world of living beings I must rescue, from the terrors of birth, of old age, of sickness, of death and rebirth, of all kinds of moral offence, of all states of woe, of the whole cycle of birth-and-death, of the jungle of false views, of the loss of wholesome dharmas, of the concomitants of ignorance,—from all these terrors I must rescue all beings. . . . I walk so that the kingdom of unsurpassed cognition is built up for all beings. My endeavours do not merely aim at my own deliverance. For with the help of the boat of the thought of all-knowledge, I must rescue all these beings from the stream of Samsara, which is so difficult to cross, I must pull them back from the great precipice, I must free them from all calamities, I must ferry them across the stream of Samsara. I myself must grapple with the whole mass of suffering of all beings. To the limit of my endurance I will experience in all the states of woe, found in any world system, all the abodes of suffering. And I must not cheat all beings out of my store of merit. I am resolved to abide in each single state of woe for numberless aeons; and so I will help all beings to freedom, in all the states of woe that may be found in any world system whatsoever.

And why? Because it is surely better that I alone should be in pain than that all these beings should fall into the states of woe. There I must give myself away as a pawn through which the whole world is redeemed from the terrors of the hells, of animal birth, of the world of Yama, and with this my own body I must experience, for the sake of all beings, the whole mass of all painful feelings. And on behalf of all beings I give surety for all beings, and in doing so I speak truthfully, am trustworthy, and do not go back on my word. I must not abandon all beings.

And why? There has arisen in me the will to win all-knowledge, with all beings for its object, that is to say, for the purpose of setting free the entire world of beings. And I have not set out for the supreme enlightenment from a desire for delights, not because I hope to experience the delights of the five sense-qualities, or because I wish to indulge in the pleasures of the senses. And I do not pursue the course of a Bodhisattva in order to achieve the array of delights that can be found in the various worlds of sense-desire.

And why? Truly no delights are all these delights of the world. All this indulging in the pleasures of the senses belongs to the sphere of Mara.

Study Questions

D.8.3 The Bodhisattva Path of Infinite Compassion

1. "A Bodhisattva resolves: I take upon myself the burden of all suffering, I am resolved to do so, I will endure it. I do not turn or run away, do not tremble, am not terrified, nor afraid, do not turn back or despond."
    Critically discuss all the reasons why a Bodhisattva resolves to "save all beings" and consider whether they are inherently moral reasons or instrumentally missionary.
2. Discuss the Buddhist ethics of caring and whether its daily practice, like that of Vimalakirti, or of a bodhisattva, can transform the basic character of its practitioner into a truly good moral person.

The Status and Role of Buddhist Nuns

The Introduction

The Buddha was reluctant in giving his female followers the formal status of nunhood in his growing *sangha* (monastic order of monks). But under the relentless pressures from his innermost circle, Mahaprajapati Gautami (the one who had nursed him) and Noble Ananda (the Buddha's closest disciple), the Buddha gave in to their repeated demands for formal nunhood! He gave in, but he did so with conditions: "So the Blessed One proclaimed to the Venerable Ananda: 'Ananda, [I am willing to allow Mahaprajapati Gautami to be initiated and ordained, but first] I wish to make known the eight cardinal rules for nuns, which should respect, esteem, honor, and venerate for as long as they live." Of these "eight cardinal rules," the third and fourth rules place nuns under the formal authority of monks, making nuns and women inferior to monks and men.

But his historic decision to establish a monastic order of nuns made the Buddha a social revolutionary or a women's liberator in the ancient South Asian subcontinent that none of the sages of the ancient East had ever done before and after him. The Buddha gave women of the ancient East and modern Asia historically unprecedented high status, the high status of spiritual teachers, that no woman has ever formally enjoyed in Confucianism, Hinduism, Taoism, and others. Thanks to the Buddha's egalitarianistic perspective that traditional and modern Asian women can choose Buddhist nunhood to demonstrate their leadership skills by managing their own monasteries and teaching others to become self-enlightened and self-liberated beings.

Now at that time the Blessed Buddha was staying among the Sakyas in Kapilavatthu, in the Nigrodharama. And Maha-pajapati the Gotami[1] went to the place where the Blessed One was.

[1] *the Gotami:* a relative of Gotama, and his nurse when he was an infant.

When she arrived there, she bowed down before the Blessed One, and remained standing to one side. She said to the Blessed One, "It would be well, Lord, if women should be allowed to renounce their homes and enter the homeless state under the doctrine and discipline proclaimed by the Tathagata."

[Source: Taken, with editing, from T. W. Rhys Davids and Hermann Oldenberg, trans., *Vinaya Texts*, part III, *Sacred Books of the East*, vol. 20 (Oxford: University Press, 1885), pp. 320–26)].

The Buddha replied, "Enough, O Gotami! Let it not please you that women should be allowed to do so." A second and a third time Maha-pajapati made the same request in the same words, and received the same reply. Then Maha-pajapati, sad and sorrowful that the Blessed One would not allow women to enter the homeless state, bowed down before the Blessed One. Keeping him on her right hand as she passed him, she departed weeping and in tears.

Now when the Blessed One had remained at Kapilavatthu as long as he thought fit, he set out on his journey towards Vesali. Travelling straight on, in due course he arrived there. The Blessed One stayed there in the Mahavana, in the Kutagara Hall.

Maha-pajapati cut off her hair, and put on orange-colored robes. She set out, with several women of the Sakya clan, towards Vesali. In due course she arrived at Vesali, at the Mahavana, at the Kutagara Hall. And Maha-pajapati, with swollen feet and covered with dust, sad and sorrowful, weeping and in tears, took her stand outside under the entrance porch.

The venerable Ananda saw her standing there, and on seeing her so, he said to Maha-pajapati, "Why do you stand there, outside the porch, with swollen feet and covered with dust, sad and sorrowful, weeping and in tears?"

"Because, Ananda, the Lord and Blessed One does not allow women to renounce their homes and enter the homeless state under the doctrine and discipline proclaimed by the Tathagata."

Then the venerable Ananda went up to the place where the Blessed One was. Bowing down before the Blessed One, he took his seat on one side. And, so sitting, the venerable Ananda said to the Blessed One:

"Behold, Lord, Maha-pajapati is standing outside under the entrance porch. She has swollen feet and is covered with dust. She is sad and sorrowful, weeping and in tears, because the Blessed One does not allow women to renounce their homes and enter the homeless state under the doctrine and discipline proclaimed by the

Blessed One. It would be well, Lord, if women were to have permission granted to them to do as she desires."

The Buddha replied, "Enough, Ananda! Let it not please you that women should be allowed to do so." A second and a third time Ananda made the same request, in the same words, and received the same reply.

Then the venerable Ananda thought, "The Blessed One does not give his permission. I will now ask the Blessed One on another ground." And the venerable Ananda said to the Blessed One, "Lord, can women—when they have gone forth from the household life and entered the homeless state, under the doctrine and discipline proclaimed by the Blessed One—can they gain the fruit of conversion, or of the second Path, or of the third Path, or of Arhatship?"

"They are capable, Ananda."

"Lord, Maha-pajapati has proved herself of great service to the Blessed One, when as aunt and nurse she nourished him and gave him milk, and on the death of his mother she nursed the Blessed One at her own breast. It would be well, Lord, that women should have permission to go forth from the household life and enter the homeless state, under the doctrine and discipline proclaimed by the Tathagata."

"Ananda, if Maha-pajapati takes upon herself the Eight Chief Rules, let that be reckoned as her initiation. (1) Even if a woman has been a nun for a hundred years, she shall make salutation to, shall rise in the presence of, shall bow down before, and shall perform all proper duties towards a monk, even if he is only just initiated. (2) A nun is not to spend the rainy season in a district in which there is no monk. (3) Every half month a nun is to await from the monks two things, the request about the date of the Uposatha ceremony, and the time when the monk will come to give the Exhortation. (4) After keeping the rainy season, the nun is to enquire whether any fault can be laid to her charge before both Samghas—of monks and of nuns—with respect to three matters: what has been seen, what has been heard, and what has been suspected.

(5) A nun who has been guilty of a serious offence is to undergo the Manatta discipline towards both the Samghas. (6) When a nun, as novice, has been trained for two years in the Six Rules, she is to ask permission for the upasampada initiation from both Samghas. (7) A nun is never to revile or abuse a monk. (8) From this time on, nuns are forbidden to admonish monks, but the official admonition of nuns by monks is not forbidden.

"Ananda, if Maha-pajapati takes upon herself these Eight Chief Rules, let that be reckoned to her as her initiation."

[5] Then the venerable Ananda, when he had learned from the Blessed One these Eight Chief Rules, went to Maha-pajapati and told her all that the Blessed One had said. She replied, "A man or a woman, when young and of tender years, accustomed to adorn himself, would bathe his head and receive with both hands a garland of lotus or jasmine or atimuttaka flowers, and place it on the top of his head. In the same way, I take upon myself these Eight Chief Rules, never to be transgressed my life long."

Then the venerable Ananda returned to the Blessed One, and bowed down before him, and took his seat on one side. So sitting, the venerable Ananda said to the Blessed One, "Lord, Maha-pajapati has taken upon herself the Eight Chief Rules; the aunt of the Blessed One has received the upasampada initiation."

Then the Buddha said, "Ananda, if women had not received permission to go out from the household life and enter the homeless state under the doctrine and discipline proclaimed by the Tathagata, then the pure religion would have lasted long; the good law would have stood fast for a thousand years. But since women have now received that permission, the pure religion will not now last so long, and the good law will now stand fast for only five hundred years. Houses in which there are many women but only a few men are easily violated by robber burglars. In the same way, Ananda, under whatever doctrine and discipline women are allowed to go out from the household life into the homeless state, that religion will not last long. So, Ananda, in anticipation I have laid down these Eight Chief Rules for the nuns, never to be transgressed for their whole life."

Study Questions

D.8.6 The Status and Role of Buddhist Nuns

1. List the number of times that the Buddha refused to accept women into nunhood and discuss the specific settings. How did Gotami and Ananda make their appeals?
2. Discuss the power relationship between monks and nuns as determined by the Buddha. Evaluate and critique the Buddha's policy (speculate also on the reasons why the Buddha first refused and later yielded).
3. Critically compare and contrast the status and role of women, in relation to men, as determined by Manu and the Buddha.

CHAPTER 9

Confucianist and Moist Ethics
and the Harmonious Life

The Tao (v. Đạo) of the Superior Man

K'ung Fu Tzu (v. Khổng Phu Tử)

The Introduction

Traditionally, K'ung Fu Tzu (v. Khổng Phu Tử[551–479 BCE]) was credited by the Han-Chinese scholars to have written or edited all the "Five Classics." Modern scholars have maintained Confucius' status of being the "founder" of Confucianism but rejected his authorship or editorship of the Five Classics. They have now agreed that the only book that contains the thoughts of K'ung Fu Tzu (Master K'ung) is the *Analects*, which is one of the Four Books. The *Analects* was not written by Master K'ung (v. Khổng Tử) himself but compiled by his close disciples when they recollected his "sayings" after his death.

The *Analects* is, therefore, not a philosophical treatise but a collection of the "sayings" of Confucius as recollected by his close disciples. How many of these compiled sayings contained the "thoughts" of Confucius himself? How many of these sayings were actually made by his close disciples but attributed to their Master? No one knows! To maintain one's scholarly skepticism on this matter is a good trait of an intellectually healthy mind.

The *Analects* can be interpreted to have contained, essentially, a philosophy of life, which maintains that the "rectification" of the basic human moral values and behaviors is the fundamental prerequisite for the creation and maintenance of a socially harmonious society. At the foundation of the basic moral values that Confucius recommends is the moral concept of *"jen"* (v. *nhân*), which is variously rendered into English as *"benevolence"* or *"humaneness"* or *"humanity."* The utmost importance that Confucius assigns to this moral virtue is testified by the fact that fifty-eight of the 499 chapters of the *Analects* are devoted to the discussion of *jen* (v. *nhân*) and the word appears 105 times. Morally and theoretically important as it is for Confucius, but, unfortunately, he provides no philosophical grounding for the concept itself, due probably to his failure to work out a theory of human nature. This philosophical task was later taken up by ancient East Asian Confucianist thinkers like Mencius (*ca.* 371–289 BCE) and Hsun Tzu (v. Tuân Tử [*ca.* 298–238 BCE]) and Chinese philosophers like the Ch'eng Hao (1032–1085 CE) and Chu Hsi (1130–1200 CE).

The knowledge and personal cultivation of moral values are to become socially operational as the basic moral virtues of a person, if and only if, one's behavior is to be conditioned by the *"li"* (v. *lễ*) as Confucius demands it. As a cultural and behavioral concept, *li* (v. *lễ*) includes "everything from grand state ceremonies to the proper way to sit or fasten one's lapel" [Slingerland 2001:1]. As one enters into an interactional relationship with others, one has to act and behave properly according to the *li* (v. *lễ*) understood ritualistically as "a refined system of manners designed to regulate the personal interactions arising in the various social relationships." [Bresnan 1999:132]

Unlike Lao Tzu, who prefers personal freedom over political command, Confucius believes in the transforming power of moral charisma and role modeling. The restoration of human morality (moral *tao* [v. *đạo*]) under the self-decaying political framework of Chou feudalism rests with the new type of political leaders, the *chun tzu* (v. *quân tử* [*superior men*]), whom Confucius teaches for the political and moral tasks that his reform program demands.

Text

1. The Master said, "If the people be led by laws, and uniformity sought to be given them by punishments, they will try to avoid the *punishment*, but have no sense of shame. If they be led by virtue, and uniformity sought to be given them by the rules of propriety, they will have the sense of shame, and moreover will become good." [II.3.1]

2. The Master said, "At fifteen, I had my mind bent on learning. At thirty, I stood firm. At forty, I had no doubts. At fifty, I knew the decrees of Heaven. At sixty, my ear was an obedient organ *for the reception of truth.* At seventy, I could follow what my heart desired, without transgressing what was right." [II.4.1–6]

3. Tsze-kung asked what constituted the superior man. The Master said, "He acts before he speaks, and afterwards speaks according to his actions." [II.13]

4. The Master said, "When I walk along with two others, they may serve me as my teachers. I will select their good qualities and follow them, their bad qualities and avoid them." [VII.21]

5. The Master said, "A transmitter and not a maker, believing in and loving the ancients, I venture to compare myself with our old P'ăng." [VI.1]

Dao

6. The Master said, "If a man in the morning hear the right way, he may die in the evening without regret." [IV.8]

7. The Master said, "The mind of the superior man is conversant with righteousness; the mind of the mean man is conversant with gain." [IV.16]

8. The Master said, "Those who are without virtue cannot abide long either in a condition of poverty and hardship, or in a condition of enjoyment. The virtuous rest in virtue; the wise desire virtue." [IV.2]

9. The Master said, "Riches and honours are what men desire. If it cannot be obtained in the proper way, they should not be held. Poverty and meanness are what men dislike. If it cannot be obtained in the proper way, they should not be avoided." [IV.5.1]

10. [The Master said,] "If a superior man abandons virtue, how can he fulfill the requirements of that name?" [IV.5.2]

11. [The Master said,] "The superior man does not, even for the space of a single meal, act contrary to virtue. In moments of haste, he cleaves to it. In seasons of danger, he cleaves to it." [IV.5.3]

12. The Master said, "The superior man thinks of virtue; the small man thinks of comfort. The superior man thinks of the sanctions of law; the small man thinks of favours *which he may receive.*" [IV.11]

[Source: Taken from *Confucian Analects*, printed in James Legge, trans., *The Chinese Classics*, vols. I–II (London: Oxford University Press, 1893), chapters cited].

what confucian love 人 ?

13. The Master said, "Shăn, my doctrine is that of an all-pervading unity." The disciple Tsăng replied, "Yes." The Master went out, and the other disciples asked, saying, "What do his words mean?" Tsăng said, "The doctrine of our master is to be true to the principles of our nature and the benevolent exercise of them to others—this and nothing more." [IV.15.1–2]

14. [The Master said,] "Now the man of perfect virtue, wishing to be established himself, seeks also to establish others; wishing to be enlarged himself, he seeks also to enlarge others. " [VI.28.2]

15. The Master said, "Respectfulness, without the rules of propriety [v. lẽ (c. li)-ccp], becomes laborious bustle; carefulness, without the rules of propriety, becomes timidity; boldness, without the rules of propriety, becomes rudeness." [VIII.2.1]

16. The Master said, "The superior man *seeks to* perfect the admirable qualities of men, and does not *seek to* perfect their bad qualities. The mean man does the opposite of this." [XII.16]

17. The Master said, "The way of the superior man is threefold, but I am not equal to it. Virtuous [v. nhân (c. jen)-ccp], he is free from anxieties; wise, he is free from perplexities; bold, he is free from fear." [XIV.30]

18. The Master said, "What the superior man seeks, is in himself. What the mean man seeks, is in others." [XV.20]

19. Tsze-kung asked, saying, "Is there one word which may serve as a rule of practice for all one's life?" The Master said, "Is not Reciprocity such a word? What you do not want done to yourself, do not do to others." [XV.23]

20. Fan Ch'ih asked about benevolence. The Master said, "It is to love *all* men." He asked about knowledge. The Master said, "It is to know *all* men." [XII.12.1]

21. When the Master went to Wei, Zan Yu acted as driver of his carriage. The Master observed, "How numerous are the people!" Yu said, "Since they are thus numerous, what more shall be done for them?" "Enrich them," was the reply. "And when they have been enriched, what more shall be done?" The Master said, "Teach them." [XIII.9.1–4]

22. Tze-chang asked Confucius about perfect virtue [v. nhân (c. jen)-ccp]. Confucius said, "To be able to practice five things everywhere under heaven constitutes perfect virtue." He begged to ask what they were, and was told, "Gravity, generosity of soul, sincerity, earnestness, and kindness. If you are grave, you will not be treated with disrespect. If you are generous, you will win all. If you are sincere, people will repose trust in you. If you are earnest, you will accomplish much. If you are kind, this will enable you to employ the services of others." [XVII.6]

Study Questions

D.9.1 K'ung Fu Tzu (v. Khổng Phu Tử), The Tao (v. Đạo) of the Superior Man

1. Explain what K'ung Fu Tzu (v. Khổng Phu Tử) means by "benevolence" (jen [v. nhân]) and his reasons why humans should be benevolent.
2. Critically compare and contrast the two types of men, the "superior man," and the "mean [inferior-ccp] man," that K'ung Fu Tzu (v. Khổng Phu Tử) praises and condemns respectively. Using the Yiian (v. Dịchian) doctrine of Yin-Yang (v. Âm-Dương) bipolarity (in the Yin, the Yang is hidden; and in the Yang, the Yin is hidden) as your theoretical resource, critically discuss whether Confucius' dualistic characterization of people is true.
3. Discuss the three main tasks of a Confucian government and make your critical response.
4. [The Master said,] "Now the man of perfect virtue, wishing to be established himself, seeks also to establish others; wishing to be enlarged himself, he seeks also to enlarge others." [VI.28.2]
   Discuss the advantages and disadvantages of this Confucian ethic (tao [đạo]) and consider whether we should practice it.
5. Critically compare and contrast the Confucian tao (v. đạo) of the superior man with the Hindu and Buddhist ethics. Consider also which ethics would produce a more genuine human morality.

The Politics of Filiality in Traditional China

Tan Fu as a Chinese Role Model of Filiality (Hsaio)

Lo Kuan-Chung

The Introduction

Filiality or Filial Piety (Hsiao [v. Hiếu]) has historically been the moral cornerstone of all East Asian families, ancient, traditional, and modern. Being the basic building blocks of society, the family is characterized by its three fundamental bonds, namely, the husband-wife bond, the parent-child bond, and the child-child bond, which are governed by their respective family tao (v. đạo [family ethics]). Filiality is the moral tao (v. đạo) of children (ethics of children) to be cultivated and *religiously* fulfilled by each child to one's parents. Otherwise, the child could be judged or even condemned to be *"unfilial"* (*pu hsiao* [v. *bất hiếu*]), which means "immoral," to one's parent while still alive and deceased. The sin of unfiliality is not simply a matter of immorality but metaphysically dangerous, because, the *hun* (v. hồn [soul]) of one's parent may suffer and punish the "unfilial" child.

It was the Confucianist philosophers, beginning with Confucius, who turned this moral tao (v. đạo) of the family into the political tao (v. đạo) of the state, because, they saw the politically exploitable vital connection between family loyalty and political loyalty. So, Yu Tzu (v. Hữu Tử), one of Confucius' disciples, is recollected in the *Analects* to have said, "Few of those who are filial sons and respectful brothers will show disrespect to superiors, and there has never been a man who is not disrespectful to superiors and yet creates disorder. A superior man is devoted to the fundamentals (the root). When the root is firmly established, the moral law (Tao) will grow. Filial piety and brotherly respect are the root of humanity (*jen*)." (Chan 1963:19–20)

The politicization of filiality led to the politics of filiality and fateful family destructions as illustrated in the case of the Confucianist scholar-strategist Tan Fu of the Three Kingdoms China (220–280 CE) and other numerous cases in the histories of China, Japan, and Việt-Nam. On the politics of filiality in the traditional Việtnamese and Chinese societies, see Nguyên Du, *The Tale of Kiêù*, trans. Huỳnh Sanh Thống (New Haven: Yale University Press, 1983).

Ts'ao Jen, having mobilized local Fan troops, struck out across the river Ch'ing, meaning to trample Hsin Yeh flat.

In Hsin Yeh meanwhile, Tan Fu said to Liu Pei: "When Ts'ao Jen discovers that his two generals have been put to death, he will raise a massive army and come to do battle."

Liu Pei asked how he should respond. Tan Fu: "If they come in full force, Fan will stand vacant and vulnerable and can be captured in the interim." Liu Pei asked for specific tactics, and Tan Fu whispered certain strategies in his ear.

The outposts reported Ts'ao Jen's approach, as Tan Fu had predicted, and Liu Pei put his forces into the field against them. The opposed ranks were drawn up. Chao Yün issued the challenge to the opposing generals. Ts'ao Jen ordered Li Tien to go forth from the ranks and begin combat. They had crossed weapons some dozen times when Li Tien judged that he could not overcome Chao Yün and wheeled back to his own line. Yün charged after him, but from both wings there was a sustained firing of arrows. The two combatants held their weapons and returned to camp.

Li Tien said to Ts'ao Jen: "Their army is spirited and keen and may not be recklessly engaged. We would do better to return to Fan."

Ts'ao Jen: "You! Even before the campaign you were already wearing down our morale. And now again you betray the ranks to save yourself— a crime that merits beheading." Only the most strenuous appeals by the assembled commandants prevented him from putting Li Tien to death.

Ts'ao Jen led the front unit himself, and the next day the drums sounded the army on to Hsin Yeh. There it deployed in formation, and Jen sent a messenger to Liu Pei to ask if he recognized the particular pattern. Tan Fu, having surveyed the enemy from a hilltop, told Liu Pei: "This is the 'eight gates iron-sealed formation.' First, 'refrain'; second, 'alive'; third, 'wounded'; fourth, 'blocked'; fifth, 'high ground'; sixth, 'death';

seventh, 'panic'; and eighth, 'open up.' If you enter through 'alive,' 'high ground,' or 'open up,' things will go in your favor. If you take 'wounded,' 'panic,' or 'refrain,' you will be wounded. If you take 'blocked' or 'death,' you are lost. Now, these 'gates' are deployed in perfect order, and yet the central mainstay or axis is missing. Surprise them at 'alive' on the southeast corner, move due west and out at 'high ground,' and their ranks will be dislocated."

Liu Pei ordered his men to maintain the "horn points" of their formation and commanded Chao Yün to take five hundred men and carry out Tan Fu's recommendation. As Yün cut his way in, Ts'ao Jen retreated to the north. Instead of pursuing him, Yün broke through the west gate and swung around to the southeast again. Ts'ao Jen's army was in complete disarray. Liu Pei signaled his force to advance at full speed, and Ts'ao Jen's men retreated in total ruin. Tan Fu halted the pursuit, regathered his force, and returned.

Ts'ao Jen, now beginning to have some respect for Li Tien's views, said to him: "In Liu Pei's army there must be someone very capable, as my formations were utterly destroyed."

Li Tien: "While we are here, I am especially worried about Fan." Ts'ao Jen returned to Fan, and from the city walls he heard a volley of drums as a general rode forward and shouted: "I took Fan some time ago." Ts'ao Jen's host looked awestruck at the general: it was Kuan Yü. Jen wheeled his horse around and fled back to Ts'ao Ts'ao in Hsü. On his way he learned that the military strategist proposing plans and stipulating tactics for Pei's army was Tan Fu.

In Hsü, the capital, Ts'ao Jen and Li Tien saw Ts'ao Ts'ao. Tearfully they prostrated themselves and confessed their offense.

"Victory and defeat," said Ts'ao Ts'ao, "are commonplaces to a military man. But I wonder who drafted the plans for Liu Pei."

From *Three Kingdoms: China's Epic Drama* by Lo Kuan-Chung, Moss Roberts, translator. Copyright © 1976 by Moss Roberts. Reprinted by permission of University of California Press.

When Ts'ao Jen mentioned Tan Fu's name, Ch'eng Yü identified him as Hsü Shu from Ying Ch'uan, a man whose majority name was Yüan-chih. He was an expert swordsman who became a fugitive after avenging someone who had been wronged. Tan Fu had then mended his ways and pursued his studies, often in the company of Ssuma Hui.

Ts'ao asked Ch'eng Yü to evaluate Tan Fu's ability. "Ten times mine," replied Ch'eng Yü.

Ts'ao: "It is unfortunate that worthy and capable scholars are opting for Liu Pei. Once his wings are fully formed, what then?"

Ch'eng Yü: "Although Tan Fu is with the other side, if the Chancellor is determined to employ him, there is an easy way to achieve it. He is devoted to his mother, his father having died when he was young. If his mother can be enticed here and then induced to write her son to come, Tan Fu cannot refuse."

The mother, Madam Hsü, was brought to the capital, and Ts'ao treated her royally. Ts'ao: They say your excellent heir is actually one of the extraordinary talents of the empire. Now he is in Hsin Yeh assisting the disobedient subject Liu Pei, traitor to the Court. That so precious a jewel has fallen into the mud is truly unfortunate! We would prevail upon you to write and call him back to the capital. I will guarantee him before the Emperor, who will reward him amply." Ts'ao ordered the instruments for writing brought to them.

The matron Hsü asked: "What manner of man is Liu Pei?"

Ts'ao: "A low-class sort, making preposterous claims to being an 'Imperial Uncle'—utterly without credibility or righteous commitment—a perfect example of 'a noble man outside, it base man inside.'"

The matron Hsü in a strident voice said: "You! what fraudulent fabrication! I have known for many many years that Liu Pei is of the royal House of Han, a man who humbles himself before scholars, who treats others with heartfelt respect, and who has a peerless reputation for humanity.

Why, callow youths and grey old men, flock-tenders and wood-gatherers—all know his name. He is one of the true heroes of this age. And if my son serves him, then he has found himself the right master. As for you, though you claim the name of Chancellor of the Hall, you are in reality a traitor. And when you so perversely take Liu Pei to be the 'disobedient subject' and would have my son forsake the light and elect the dark, are you without *any* shame?" She took an inkstone to strike Ts'ao Ts'ao.

In a fury, Ts'ao ordered armed guards to march the matron out and behead her. But Ch'eng Yü swiftly checked him: "The matron antagonized you *in order* to die. If you kill her you will earn yourself a vicious name even as you raise high the matron's virtue. For once she is dead, Tan Fu will be committed unto death to assist Liu Pei as a means to vengeance. You'd be better off detaining her so that the son's body will be in one place and his heart in another. That way, even if we are letting him assist Liu Pei, he will not give his utmost. Second, by keeping the woman alive, we give ourselves the means of inducing Tan Fu to come here and assist the Chancellor!"

Ts'ao agreed and spared the woman. She was detained and cared for.

Ch'eng Yü visited her regularly and, pretending that he had once sealed a pact of brotherhood with her son, attended her as his own mother. He regularly honored her with gifts which always included a personal note, and the matron would answer in her own hand. Having coaxed this sample of her script out of her, Ch'eng Yü proceeded to imitate it. Then he forged a letter and sent it to Tan Fu in Hsin Yeh. It said:

> The recent death of your younger brother
> has left me without kin wherever I turn.
> In the midst of my sorrow and isolation I
> never dreamed Chancellor Ts'ao would
> entice me to the capital, to protest your
> betrayal and revolt and put me in chains.
> My life has been spared only through
> Ch'eng Yü. Only if we can get you to
> give yourself up will my life be saved.

When you read this do not forget the hardships of your parents, but come with all speed to keep intact the principle of filial piety. Afterwards we can plan at our leisure to go home and till our former gardens, lest we incur some major calamity. My life hangs by a thread, and you are my sole hope of salvation. Need I implore you further?

Tan Fu's tears rose freely within him as he went to Liu Pei to acknowledge his identity and his reasons for joining Pei. Fu: "Water-mirror took me severely to task for not recognizing my true lord; he urged me to serve you. So I made that mad song in the market to interest your lordship. I was favored with your gracious acceptance and was given grave responsibilities. But what am I to do, now that my mother has been tricked and taken by Ts'ao and threatened with harm? She has herself written to summon me, and I cannot fail her. It is not that I am loth to toil for my lordship, but having my tender mother seized is more than I can bear, and I cannot give my utmost. Permit the therefore to announce my departure, giving ourselves time to plan to meet again."

Liu Pei cried out at this. But he said: "Between the son and the mother is the kinship of ordained nature, and there is nothing that need occupy you on our account. We can wait until you have met with your mother for another opportunity to profit from your instruction." However, Liu Pei prevailed upon him to remain for the night rather than leaving at once.

Sun Ch'ien took Liu Pei aside. "This extraordinary genius has been in Hsin Yeh so long that he is thoroughly familiar with our military strengths and weaknesses. If you let him transfer his allegiance to Ts'ao Ts'ao, he will be used at the highest levels, putting us in danger. My sovereign lord should keep him at all costs. Then Ts'ao will execute the mother, and when Tan Fu finds out, he will fight even more fiercely against Ts'ao Ts'ao to avenge her."

Liu Pei: "Unacceptable; to let them kill the mother while we use the son would be inhumane.

To hold him back and sever the link of son to mother is unethical. I would rather die than do it." Moved, the assembled officials all sighed.

Liu Pei invited Tan Fu to drink. But Tan Fu said: "Knowing my mother is imprisoned, I could not force the most precious potion, the most exquisite liquor down my throat."

As they parted outside the city, Liu Pei proposed a last toast: "My meager lot, my paltry destiny keep us from remaining together. I hope you will serve your new master well and achieve a reputation for meritorious work."

Shu: "Someone like me, of insignificant talent and superficial knowledge, was charged by your lordship with the gravest responsibility. Now adversity separates us midway, truly on my old mother's account. But however Ts'ao Ts'ao may compel me, I will not propose a single strategy for him to my dying day."

Liu Pei: "Once you have gone, master, Liu Pei himself will also withdraw to the mountain forest."

Fu: "When I lay plans with my lordship for the royal cause, this paltry intelligence is all I count on. Now, because of my mother, I cannot think clearly. Even were I to remain, I would be of no use. My lordship would be advised to seek elsewhere some high-minded worthy to support and assist you in conceiving your great enterprise. Consume yourself no more on my account."

Liu Pei: "None surpasses you."

Fu: "How can my useless commonplace qualities deserve such high praise?"

When Ts'ao Ts'ao learned of Tan Fu's arrival, he ordered Hsün Yü, Ch'eng Yü, and other advisers to go out and receive him. Tan Fu then entered the Chancellor's headquarters and offered his respects.

Ts'ao: "Sir, how could such a noble and enlightened scholar as you lower himself to serve a Liu Pei?"

Fu: "In my youth I got into trouble and ran away, floating through all sorts of places. By chance I came to Hsin Yeh, where I formed a strong friendship with Liu Pei. But now that my dear mother, whose maternal kindness has been my blessing, lives here, I have been overcome with a sense of my negligence."

Ts'ao: "Now, sir, you are here precisely so that you may tend and care for this honored relation at all times. I too may be able to listen to your lucid clarifications."

Fu, respectfully declining the compliment, left and rushed to see his mother. Tearfully he prostrated himself before his home. His mother said in amazement: "What brings *you* here?"

"I have been serving Liu Pei," he said. "Your letter came, and I rushed here."

The matron Hsü exploded in rage and swore as she struck the table: "You disgrace! Flitting around hither and thither for so many years! I thought you were making progress with your studies. How can someone who started well turn out so badly? At least you have read enough to know that loyalty and filial piety do not always complement each other. How could you *not* realize that Ts'ao Ts'ao is a traitor who has abused and ruined his sovereign? And that Liu Pei is known far and wide for his humanity and his ethics? Not only that, but once you were in the service of a Liu, the patronym of the Han, you had found yourself a proper master. But now, trusting a forged scrap of paper (which you never verified), you have abandoned the light and elected the darkness and earned yourself a contemptible name. How gross! With what kind of self-respect am I supposed to receive you, now that you have shamed the spirit of your ancestors and uselessly wasted your own life?"

She swore so furiously that Tan Fu cowered on the ground, hands clasped above his head, not daring to look up. And with that the matron wheeled around and vanished behind the screens. Moments later a handmaiden screamed: "Our mistress has hanged herself from the rafters!" Crazed, Tan Fu rushed in, but her breath had ceased.

Later someone wrote "In Praise of Mother Hsü":

> Mother Hsü's integrity
> Will savor for eternity . . .
> A model lesson for her son:
> Self-execution, martyrdom.
> An aura like a sacred hill,
> Allegiance sprung from depth of will . . .
> In life her proper designation,
> In death her proper destination:
> Mother Hsü's integrity
> Will savor for eternity.

Seeing his mother already dead, Tan Fu lay broken on the ground. Much time passed before he revived. Ts'ao Ts'ao sent a representative to the ceremonial presentations and the vigil over the body, and he personally attended the sacrificial offering. Tan Fu interred the coffin at the Southern Font of the capital, abided the mourning, and guarded the grave site. Every gift Ts'ao Ts'ao proffered he declined.

At the time, Ts'ao was considering launching his southern expedition. But he was persuaded to await the spring thaw. He then diverted water from the river Chang to make a lake, on which he began naval maneuvers in preparation for the southern expedition.

Study Questions

D.9.2 The Politics of Filiality in Traditional China

1. Should children be filial to their fathers (Confucianist-Chinese ethics) or to their parents (Việtnamese ethics)?
2. Comparatively discuss the importance of the ethics of filiality and its politics as portrayed in the case of Tan Fu (Chinese role model of filiality) and in the case of Kiều (Việtnamese role model).
3. Taking the eight Confucianist virtues for men as your theoretical resources, critique the course of action that Tan Fu deliberated and took. (Clue: which of the Confucianist virtues did Tan Fu violate and why was his filiality also negated?).

A Moist (v. Mặcian) Alternative Ethics

Universal Love

Mo Tzu (v. Mặc Tử)

The Introduction

Mo Tzu (v. Mặc Tử [fl. 479–438 BCE]) is the founder of Moism. Up to the beginning of the Han Dynasty (206 BCE –220 CE), Confucianism and Moism were the greatest schools of philosophy that dominated the intellectual landscape of the northern region of the mainland of ancient East Asia from the fifth to at least the third century BCE. And they were antagonistic to each other, because, their philosophical thoughts and political positions were diametrically opposed.

Scholars are not sure of the cultural and ethnic background of Mo Tzu. He may have been a native of either the Kingdom of Sung or the Kingdom of Lu (Confucius' native state). This attribution is not supported by the cultural orientation of Mo Tzu in relation to that of Confucius. Instead looking to the Western Chou (v. Tây Chu [1111–770 BCE]) as the ideal political system model and making his holy mission to restore it as Confucius did, Mo Tzu (v. Mặc Tử) took the Hsia (v. Hạ [ca. 2183–1752 BCE]) to be the Golden Age state model, to which, the non-Chou Kingdom of Yueh (v. Việt) traced its cultural origin. Mo Tzu (v. Mặc Tử) also "strongly condemn ceremonies, music, elaborate funerals, and the belief in fate (ming, destiny), all of which were promoted by Confucius and his followers." [Chan 1963:211].

But the most important difference between Moism and Confucianism is the issue of human relation. Instead of advocating for graded love as Confucius did, Mo Tzu calls for universal love. The Confucianist orientation has politically tended to lead to familism and nationalism rather than humanism as it could if the Moist doctrine of universal love were practiced. Moist humanism was philosophically too progressive for its time and now deserves our serious consideration.

Mo Tzu said: Humane men are concerned about providing benefits for the world and eliminating its calamities. Now among all the current calamities, which are the worst? I say that the attacking of small states by large states, the making of inroads on small houses by large houses, the plundering of the weak by the strong, the oppression of the few by the many, the deception of the simple by the cunning, the disdain of the noble towards the humble—these are some of the calamities in the world. Again, the want of kindness on the part of the ruler, the want of loyalty on the part of the ruled, the want of affection on the part of the father, the want of filial piety on the part of the son—these are some further calamities in the world. Added to these, the mutual injury and harm which the vulgar people do to one another with weapons, poison, water, and fire is still another kind of calamity in the world.

When we come to inquire about the cause of all these calamities, whence have they arisen? Is it out of people's loving others and benefiting others? We must reply that it is not so. We should say that it is out of people's hating others and injuring others. If we should classify one by one all those who hate others and injure others, should we find them to be universal or partial in their love? Of course, we should say they are partial. Now, since partiality among one another is the cause of the major calamities in the world, then partiality is wrong.

Mo Tzu continued: He who criticizes others must have something to offer in replacement. Criticism without an alternative proposal is like trying to stop flood with flood and put out fire with fire. It will surely be worthless.

Therefore Mo Tzu said: Partiality is to be replaced by universality. But how is partiality to be replaced by universality? Now, when everyone regards the states of others as he regards his own, who would attack the other's state? One would regard others as one's self. When everyone regards the cities of others as he regards his own, who would seize the others' cities? One would regard others as one's self. When everyone regards the houses of others as he regards his own, who would disturb the others' houses? One would regard others as one's self. Now when the states and cities do not attack and seize each other, and when the clans and individuals do not disturb and harm one another—is this a calamity or a benefit to the world? Of course it is a benefit.

When we come to inquire about the cause of all these benefits, whence have they arisen? Is it out of men's hating and injuring others? We must reply that it is not so. We should say that it is out of men's loving and benefiting others. If we should classify one by one all those who love others and benefit others, should we find them to be partial or universal in their love? Of course we should say they are universal. Now, since universal love is the cause of the major benefits in the world, therefore Mo Tzu proclaims that universal love is right. . . .

Yet the objections from the gentlemen of the world are never exhausted. It is asked: It may be a good thing, but can it be of any use?

Mo Tzu replies: If it were not useful, I myself would disapprove of it. But how can there be anything that is good but not useful? Let us consider the matter from both sides. Suppose there are two men. Let one of them hold to partiality and the other universality. Then the advocate of partiality would say to himself: "How could I be expected to take care of my friend as I do of myself, how could I be expected to take care of his parents as my own?" Therefore when he finds his friend hungry he would not feed him, and when he finds him cold he would not clothe him. In his illness he would not minister to him, and when he is dead he would not bury him. Such is the word and such is the deed of the advocate of partiality. The advocate of universality is quite unlike this either in word or in deed. He would say to himself: "I have heard that to be a superior man one should take care of his friend as he does of himself, and take care of his friend's parents as he does his own." Therefore when he finds his friend hungry he would feed him, and when he finds him cold he would clothe him. In his sickness he would minister to him, and when he is dead he would bury him. Such is the word and such is the deed of the advocate of universality.

These two persons, then, are opposed to each other in word and also in deed. Suppose both of them are sincere in word and decisive in deed so that their word and deed are made to agree like the two parts of a tally, every word being expressed in deed. Then let us ask: Suppose here is a battlefield, and one is in armor and helmet, ready to go into combat, and life and death hang in the balance. Or suppose one is sent as an emissary by the ruler to such far countries as Pa, Yüeh, Ch'i, and Ching, and one cannot be certain as to one's safe arrival and return. Now let us inquire, upon whom would one (under such circumstances) lay the trust of one's family and parents, wife, and children? Would it be upon the friend whose code of conduct is universality, or upon him whose code is partiality? It seems to me, on occasions like these, there are no fools in the world. Even though he be a person who objects to universal love himself, he would lay the trust upon the friend believing in universal love all the same. This is rejection of the principle in word but acceptance of it in actually making a choice—this is contradiction between one's word and deed. It is incomprehensible, then, why the gentlemen of the world should object to universal love when they hear of it.

Yet the objections from the gentlemen of the world are never exhausted. It is objected: Perhaps it is a good criterion by which one may choose among ordinary men, but it would not apply to the choice of rulers.

Let us again consider the matter from both sides. Suppose there are two rulers. Let one of them hold to partiality and the other universality. Then the "partial" ruler would say to himself: "How could I be expected to take care of the people as I do of myself? This would be quite contrary to the nature of things. A man's life on earth is of short duration; it is like a galloping horse rushing past a crack in the wall." Therefore when he finds his people hungry he would not feed them, and when he finds them cold he would not clothe them. When they are sick he would not minister to them, and upon their death he would not bury them. Such is the word and such is the deed of the "partial" ruler. The "universal" ruler is quite unlike this either in word or in deed. He would say to himself: "I have heard that to be an intelligent ruler of the empire one should attend to his people before he attends to himself." Therefore when he finds his people hungry he would feed them, and when he finds them cold he would clothe them. In their sickness he would minister to them, and upon their death he would bury them. Such is the word and such is the deed of the "universal" ruler.

These two rulers, then, are opposed to each other in word and also in deed. Suppose both of them are sincere in word and decisive in deed so that their word and deed are made to agree like the two parts of a tally, every word being expressed in deed. Then let us ask: Suppose, now, that there is a disastrous pestilence, that most people are in misery and privation, and that many lie dead in ditches. Now, let us inquire, if a person could choose between the two rulers, which would he prefer? It seems to me on such occasions as these there are no fools in the world. Even though he be a person who objects to universal love himself, he would choose the "universal" ruler. This is rejection of the principle in word but acceptance of it in actually making a choice—this is contradiction between one's word and deed. It is incomprehensible, then, why the gentlemen of the world should object to universal love when they hear of it.

Yet the objections from the gentlemen of the world are never exhausted. It is pointed out that universal love may be humane and righteous, but is it meant to be put into practice? Universal love is as possible as picking up Mount T'ai and leaping over rivers with it. So, then, universal love is but a pious wish, and how can anyone expect it to be materialized? Mo Tzu replied: To pick up Mount T'ai and leap over the rivers is a feat that has never been accomplished since the existence of man. But universal love and mutual aid have been personally practiced by the great ancient sage-kings.

How do we know that they have practiced it?

Mo Tzu said: I am no contemporary of theirs; neither have I heard their voices nor seen their countenances. The sources of our knowledge lie in what is written on bamboo and silk, what is engraved in metal and stone, and what is cut in the vessels that have been handed down to posterity. . . .

Yet the objections from the gentlemen of the world are never exhausted. The question is raised: When one does not pay special attention to the welfare of one's parents, is not harm done to the virtue of filial piety?

Mo Tzu replied: Now let us inquire into the way the filial sons take care of their parents. I may ask, in caring for their parents, whether they desire to have others love their parents, or hate them? Judging from the whole doctrine [of filial piety], it is certain that they desire to have others love their parents. Now, then, what should I do first in order to attain this? Should I first love others' parents in order that they would love my parents in return, or should I first hate others' parents in order that they would love my parents in return? Assuredly I should first love others' parents in order that they would love my parents in return. Hence, is it not evident that those who desire to see others filial to their own parents, had best proceed first by loving and benefiting others' parents? . . . It is then quite incomprehensible why the gentlemen of the world should object to universal love when they hear of it.

Is it because they deem it so difficult and inpracticable? But there have been instances of much harder tasks that have been accomplished. Formerly, Lord Ling of the state of Ching was fond of slender waists. During his life time, the Ching people ate not more than once a day. They could not stand up without support, and could not walk without leaning against the wall. Now, limited diet is quite hard to endure, and yet it was endured, because Lord Ling encouraged it. . . .

Now, as to universal love and mutual aid, they are incalculably more beneficial and less difficult. It seems to me that the only trouble is that there is no ruler who will encourage them. If there were a ruler who would encourage them, bringing to bear the lure of reward and the threat of punishment, I believe the people would tend toward universal love and mutual aid like fire tending upward and water downwards—nothing in the world could stop them.

Chapter 28: The Will of Heaven (Part III)

Mo Tzu said: What is the reason for the disorder in the world? It is that the gentlemen of the world understand only trifles but not things of importance. How do we know they understand trifles but not things of importance? Because they do not understand the will of Heaven. How do we know they do not understand the will of Heaven? By observing the way people conduct themselves in the family. When a man commits an offense in the family, he might still escape to some other family for refuge. Yet, father reminds son, elder brother reminds younger brother, saying: "Beware, be careful! If one is not cautious and careful in his conduct in the family, how is he to get along in the state?" When a man commits an offense in the state, he might still escape to some other state for refuge. Yet father reminds son and elder brother reminds younger brother, saying: "Beware, be careful! One cannot get along in a state if he is not cautious and careful." Now all men live in the world and serve Heaven. When a man sins against Heaven he has nowhere to escape for refuge. On this point, however, people fail to caution and warn each other. Thus I know that they do not understand things of importance.

And Mo Tzu said: Beware, be careful! Be sure to do what Heaven desires and forsake what Heaven abominates. Now, what does Heaven desire and what does Heaven abominate? Heaven desires righteousness and abominates unrighteousness. How do we know that this is so? Because righteousness is the proper standard. How do we know righteousness is the proper standard? Because when righteousness prevails in the world, there is order; when righteousness ceases to prevail in the world, there is chaos. So, I know righteousness is the proper standard.

Now a standard is never given by a subordinate to a superior, it is always given by the superior to the subordinate. Hence the common people may not take any standard they please; there are the scholars to give them the standard. The scholars may not take any standard they please; there are the ministers to give them the standard. The ministers may not take any standard they please; there are the feudal lords to give them the standard. The feudal lords may not take any standard they please; there are the three ministers to give them the standard. The three ministers may not take any standard they please; there is the Son of Heaven to give them the standard. The Son of Heaven may not take any standard he pleases; there is Heaven to give him the standard. The gentlemen of the world all can see that the Son of Heaven gives the standard to the empire, but they fail to see that Heaven gives the standard to the Son of Heaven. The sages of old, explaining this, said: "When the Son of Heaven has done good, Heaven rewards him. When the Son of Heaven has committed wrong, Heaven punishes him. When the Son of Heaven is unfair in dispensing reward and punishment and not impartial in judging lawsuits, the empire is visited with disease and calamity, and frost and dew will be untimely." Thereupon the Son of Heaven will have to fatten the oxen and sheep and dogs and pigs, and prepare clean cakes and wine to offer prayer to Heaven and invoke its blessing. I have not yet heard of Heaven praying and invoking the Son of Heaven for blessing. Thus I know that Heaven is more honorable and wise than the Son of Heaven.

Therefore, righteousness does not issue from the ignorant and humble, but from the honorable and wise. Who is the most honorable? Heaven is the most honorable. Who is the most wise? Heaven is the most wise. And so righteousness assuredly issues from Heaven. Then the gentlemen of the world who desire to do righteousness cannot but obey the will of Heaven.

Study Questions

D.9.3 The Moist (v. Măcian) Alternative Ethics
Mo Tzu (v. Mặc Tử), Universal Love

1. Identify the "worst" calamities that have inflicted sufferings upon the peoples of the Central Plains (Chung Yung [v. Trung Nguyên]) kingdoms as condemned by Mặc Tử (c. Mo Tzu).
2. Critically discuss the "cause" of these human calamities and the ultimate solution that Mo Tzu (v. Mặc Tử) proposes for their removal. Discuss the arguments he makes in support of his proposal.
3. Even though the Măcian call for "universal love" was dismissed as politically unrealistic by the ruling elites of the powerful kingdoms in the Central Plains (Chung Yung [v. Trung Nguyên]) region, could it be *the new humanistic cry* for modern humans to make it the new universal human reality?

CHAPTER 10

Eastern Ethics and Wisdom of Political Vô Vi (c. Wu Wei)

The Hindu Varna System:
A Closed Social Class Model

The Laws of Manu

The Introduction

The "*varna*" system has provided the most stable social class model for the early Vedic and later Indian societies over the past three thousand years or so. The word "varna" literally means "color" which had probably referred to the darker skin color of the ancient South Asian (indigenous) Dravidian population whom the invading "Aryans" ("Noble Ones") conquered and enslaved.

The author of the *Laws of Manu* cites the *Rig Veda* 10.90 as the divine basis for the organization of the population of the Vedic society (ca. 1500–400 BCE) into four basic varnas (four classes). The social classes of the late Vedic society were believed to be created from the four parts of the cosmic being Purusha. The *brahmana* (class of priests) was his mouth. The *rajanya* (class of warriors) was from his two arms. The *vaishya* (class of traders and farmers) was from his thighs. The *shudra* (class of servants) was from his feet.

The Aryans might have been ranked into only three main classes before they settled in the northern region of the ancient South Asian subcontinent after 1500 BCE [Fenton *et al* 1988:62]. But after their conquest, the Aryan rulers turned the vanquished Dravidians into the shudras. The result was the creation of the four basic varnas. Another change was also made: "In Aryan societies of the Middle East and Europe, the warrior class always occupied the highest level of leadership, but in India the priesthood has from this time onward been supreme and has been the model for much that is distinctive in the standards of Hindu civilization." [*Ibid*].

(a) Brāhmin (Priest or Teacher)

97. It is better (to discharge) one's own (appointed) duty incompletely than to perform completely that of another; for he who lives according to the law of another (caste) is instantly excluded from his own. (X.97)

[Source: Taken from G. Buhler, trans., *The Laws of Manu, Sacred Books of the East*, volume XXV (Oxford: The Clarendon Press, 1886), chapters cited)].

74. *Brāhmins* who are intent on the means (of gaining union with) *Brahman* and firm in (discharging) their duties, shall live by duly performing the following six acts (which are enumerated) in their (proper) order.

75. Teaching, studying, sacrificing for himself, sacrificing for others, making gifts and receiving them are the six acts (prescribed) for a *brāhmin.*

76. But among the six acts (ordained) for him three are his means of subsistence, (viz.,) sacrificing for others, teaching, and accepting gifts from pure men. (X. 74–6)

77. (Passing) from the *brāhmin* to the *kṣatriya*, three acts (incumbent on the former) are forbidden, (viz.,) teaching, sacrificing for others, and, thirdly, the acceptance of gifts.

78. The same are likewise forbidden to a *vaiśya*, that is a settled rule; for Manu, the lord of creatures (Prajāpati), has not prescribed them for (men of) those two (castes).

79. To carry arms for striking and for throwing (is prescribed) for *kṣatriyas* as a means of subsistence; to trade, (to rear) cattle, and agriculture for *vaiśyas*; but their duties are liberality, the study of the Veda, and the performance of sacrifices.

80. Among the several occupations the most commendable are, teaching the Veda for a *brāhmin*, protecting (the people) for a *kṣatriya*, and trade for a *vaiśya*.

81. But a *brāhmin*, unable to subsist by his peculiar occupations just mentioned, may live according to the law applicable to *kṣatriyas*; for the latter is next to him in rank.

82. If it be asked, "How shall it be, if he cannot maintain himself by either (of these occupations?" the answer is), he may adopt a *vaiśya's* mode of life, employing himself in agriculture and rearing cattle.

83. But a *brāhmin*, or a *kṣatriya*, living by a *vaiśya's* mode of subsistence, shall carefully avoid (the pursuit of) agriculture, (which causes) injury to many beings and depends on others.

85. But he who, through a want of means of subsistence, gives up the strictness with respect

to his duties, may sell, in order to increase his wealth, the commodities sold by *vaiśyas*, making (however,) the (following) exceptions.

92. By (selling) flesh, salt, and lac a *brāhmin* at once becomes an outcaste; by selling milk he becomes (equal to) a *śūdra* in three days.

93. But by willingly selling in this world other (forbidden) commodities, a *brāhmin* assumes after seven nights the character of a *vaiśya.*

95. A *kṣatriya* who has fallen into distress, may subsist by all these (means); but he must never arrogantly adopt the mode of life (prescribed for his) betters.

98. A *vaiśya* who is unable to subsist by his own duties, may even maintain himself by a *śūdra's* mode of life, avoiding (however) acts forbidden (to him), and he should give it up, when he is able (to do so).

99. But a *śūdra*, being unable to find service with the twice-born and threatened with the loss of his sons and wife (through hunger), may maintain himself by handicrafts.

101. A *brāhmin* who is distressed through a want of means of subsistence and pines (with hunger), (but) unwilling to adopt a *vaiśya's* mode of life and resolved to follow his own (prescribed) path, may act in the following manner.

102. A *brāhmin* who has fallen into distress may accept (gifts) from anybody; for according to the law it is not possible (to assert) that anything pure can be sullied.

103. By teaching, by sacrificing for, and by accepting gifts from despicable (men) *brāhmins* (in distress) commit not sin; for they (are as pure) as fire and water.

104. He who, when in danger of losing his life, accepts food from any person whatsoever, is no more tainted by sin than the sky by mud. (X.77–83, 85, 92–3, 95, 98–9, 101–4)

(b) Kṣatriya (King or Prince or Warrior)

1. I will declare the duties of kings, (and) show how a king should conduct himself,. . . and how (he can obtain) highest success.

2. A *kṣatriya* who has received according to the rule the sacrament prescribed by the Veda, must duly protect this whole (world).

3. For, when these creatures, being without a king, through fear dispersed in all directions, the Lord created a king for the protection of this whole (creation),

8. Even an infant king must not be despised, (from an idea) that he is a (mere) mortal; for he is a great deity in human form.

13. Let no (man), therefore, transgress that law which the king decrees with respect to his favourites, nor (his orders) which inflict pain on those in disfavour.

14. For the (king's) sake the Lord formerly created his own son, Punishment, the protector of all creatures, (an incarnation of) the law, formed of *Brahman's* glory.

18. Punishment alone governs all created beings, punishment alone protects them, punishment watches over them while they sleep; the wise declare punishment (to be identical with) the law.

19. If (punishment) is properly inflicted after (due) consideration, it makes all people happy; but inflicted without consideration, it destroys everything.

20. If the king did not, without tiring, inflict punishment on those worthy to be punished, the stronger would roast the weaker, like fish on a spit;

22. The whole world is kept in order by punishment, for a guiltless man is hard to find; through fear of punishment the whole world yields the enjoyments (which it owes).

24. All castes would be corrupted (by intermixture), all barriers would be broken through, and all men would rage (against each other) in consequence of mistakes with respect to punishment.

26. They declare that king to be a just inflicter of punishment, who is truthful, who acts after due consideration, who is wise, and who knows (the respective value of) virtue, pleasure, and wealth.

35. The king has been created (to be) the protector of the castes and orders, who, all

according to their rank, discharge their several duties.

87. A king who, while he protects his people, is defied by (foes), be they equal in strength, or stronger, or weaker, must not shrink from battle, remembering the duty of *kṣatriyas*.

88. Not to turn back in battle, to protect the people, to honour the *brāhmins*, is the best means for a king to secure happiness.

89. Those kings who, seeking to slay each other in battle, fight with the utmost exertion and do not turn back, go to heaven.

99. Let him strive to gain what he has not yet gained; what he has gained let him carefully preserve; let him augment what he preserves, and what he has augmented let him bestow on worthy men.

100. Let him know that these are the four means for securing the aims of human (existence); let him, without ever tiring, properly employ them.

144. The highest duty of a *kṣatriya* is to protect his subjects, for the king who enjoys the rewards, just mentioned, is bound to (discharge that) duty.

198. He should (however) try to conquer his foes by conciliation, by (well-applied) gifts, and by creating dissension, used either separately or conjointly, never by fighting, (if it can be avoided).

199. For when two (princes) fight, victory and defeat in the battle are, as experience teaches, uncertain; let him therefore avoid an engagement.

205. All undertakings (in) this (world) depend both on the ordering of fate and on human exertion; but among these two (the ways of) fate are unfathomable; in the case of man's work action is possible. (VII.1–3, 8, 13–14, 18–20, 22, 24, 26, 35, 87–89, 99–100, 144, 198–9, 205)

410. (The king) should order a *vaiśya* to trade, to lend money, to cultivate the land, or to tend cattle, and a *śūdra* to serve the twice-born castes.

418. (The king) should carefully compel *vaiśyas* and *śūdra* to perform the work (prescribed) for them; for if these two (castes) swerved from their duties, they would throw this (whole) world into confusion.

420. A king who thus brings to a conclusion all the legal business enumerated above, and removes all sin, reaches the highest state (of bliss). (VIII.410, 418, 420)

(c) Vaiśya (Tradesman)

326. After a *vaiśya* has received the sacraments and has taken a wife, he shall be always attentive to the business whereby he may subsist and to (that of) tending cattle.

327. For when the Lord of creatures (Prajāpati) created cattle, he made them over to the *vaiśya*; to the *brāhmins* and to the king he entrusted all created beings.

328. A *vaiśya* must never (conceive this) wish, "I will not keep cattle"; and if a *vaiśya* is willing (to keep them), they must never be kept by (men of) other (castes).

329. (A *vaiśya*) must know the respective value of gems, of pearls, of coral, of metals, of (cloth) made of thread, of perfumes, and of condiments.

330. He must be acquainted with the (manner of) sowing of seeds, and of the good and bad qualities of fields, and he must perfectly know all measures and weights.

331. Moreover, the excellence and defects of commodities, the advantages and disadvantages of (different) countries, the (probable) profit and loss on merchandise, and the means of properly rearing, cattle.

332. He must be acquainted with the (proper) wages of servants, with the various languages of men, with the manner of keeping goods, and (the rules of) purchase and sale.

333. Let him exert himself to the utmost in order to increase his property in a righteous manner, and let him zealously give food to all created beings. (IX.326–33)

(d) Śūdras (Workers)

334. ... to serve *brāhmins* (who are) learned in the Vedas, householders, and famous (for virtue)

is the highest duty of a *śūdra*, which leads to beatitude.

335. (A *śūdra* who is) pure, the servant of his betters, gentle in his speech, and free from pride, and always seeks a refuge with *brāhmins*, attains (in his next life) a higher caste. (IX.334–5)

413. But a *śūdra*, whether bought or unbought, he may compel to do servile work; for he was created by the Self-existent (*Svayambhū*) to be the slave of a *brāhmin*.

414. A *śūdra*, though emancipated by his master, is not released from servitude; since that is innate in him, who can set him free from it? (VIII.413–14)

121. If a *śūdra*, (unable to subsist by serving *brāhmins*), seeks a livelihood, he may serve *kṣatriyas*, or he may also seek to maintain himself by attending on a wealthy *vaiśya*.

122. But let a (*śūdra*) serve *brāhmins*, either for the sake of heaven, or with a view to both (this life and the next); for he who is called the servant of a *brāhmin* thereby gains all his ends.

123. The service of *brāhmins* alone is declared (to be) an excellent occupation for a *śūdra*; for whatever else besides this he may perform will bear him no fruit.

126. A *śūdra* cannot commit an offence, causing loss of caste, and he is not worthy to receive the sacraments; he has no right to (fulfill) the sacred law (of the Āryans, yet) there is no prohibition against (his fulfilling certain portions of) the law.

127. (*Śūdras*) who are desirous to gain merit, and know (their) duty, commit no sin, but gain praise, if they imitate the practice of virtuous men without reciting sacred texts.

128. The more a (*śūdra*), keeping himself free from envy, imitates the behaviour of the virtuous, the more he gains, without being censured, (exaltation in) this world and the next. (X.121–3, 126–8)

Study Questions

D.10.1 *The Laws of Manu*, The Hindu Varna System

1. Discuss the four varna system and its division of labor.
2. Discuss the advantages and disadvantages of the varna system.
3. Write your philosophical response to this "political philosophy" question: Should society be organized into *closed classes* like the Hindu varna system or into *open classes* like most industrial societies, or remain "*classless*" as Karl Marx advocates?

D.10.2

The Yoga of Political Renunciation

The Bhagavad Gita

The Introduction

The supreme Lord Krishna recommends *"karma yoga"* to Arjuna as the highest end of political practice and the best means of perfect self-mastery.

The essence of karma yoga is true freedom. True freedom is the state of being free from within and from without. To be free from within and from without is the attainment of complete self-mastery. Thus the author of the *Bhagavad Gita* says: "When one does not get attached to the object of sense or to works, and has renounced all purposes, then, he is said to have attained to yoga."

To be driven by the gratification of one's own interests and pleasures means to be enslaved from within. Subjective slavery always necessitates objective slavery. True freedom negates both. So it is stated in the *Gita*: "When one has conquered his [lower] self and has attained to the calm of self-mastery, his Supreme Self abides ever concentrate: he is at peace in cold and heat, in pleasure and pain, in honour and dishonour."

Renunciation and Action Are One

The Blessed Lord [Krishna] said:

1. He who does the work which he ought to do without seeking its fruit he is the samnyasin, he is the yogin, not he who does not light the sacred fire, and performs no rites.
2. What they call renunciation, that known to be disciplined activity, O Pandava [Arjuna], for no one becomes a yogin who has not renounced his [selfish] purpose.

The Pathway and the Goal

3. Work is said to be the means of the sage who wishes to attain to yoga; when he has attained to yoga, serenity is said to be the means.
4. When one does not get attached to the object of sense or to works, and has renounced all purposes, then, he is said to have attained to yoga.
5. Let a man lift himself by himself; let him not degrade himself; for the Self alone is the

friend of the self and the Self alone is the enemy of the self.

6. For him who has conquered his [lower] self by the [higher] Self his Self is a friend but for him who has not possessed his [higher] Self, his very Self will act in enmity, like an enemy.

7. When one has conquered one's self [lower] and has attained to the calm of self-mastery, his Supreme Self abides ever concentrate, he is at peace in cold and heat, in pleasure and pain, in honour and dishonour.

8. The ascetic [yogi] whose soul is satisfied with wisdom and knowledge, who is unchanging and master of his senses, to whom a clod, a stone and a piece of gold are the same, is said to be controlled [in yoga].

9. He who is equal-minded among friends, companions and foes, among those who are neutral and impartial, among those who are hateful and related, among saints and sinners, he excels.

Eternal Vigilance over Body and Mind Is Essential

10. Let the yogin try constantly to concentrate his mind [on the Supreme Self] remaining in solitude and alone, self-controlled, free from desires and (longing for) possessions.

11. Having set in a clean place his firm seat, neither too high nor too low, covered with sacred grass, a deerskin, and a cloth, one over the other.

12. There taking his place on the seat, making his mind one-pointed and controlling his thought and sense, let him practice yoga for the purification of the soul.

13. Holding the body, head and neck, erect and still, looking fixedly at the tip of his nose, without looking around [without allowing his eyes to wander].

14. Serene and fearless, firm in the vow of celibacy, subdued in mind, let him sit, harmonized, his mind turned to Me and intent on Me alone.

15. The yogin of subdued mind, ever keeping himself thus harmonized, attains to peace, the supreme nirvana, which abides in Me.

16. Verily, yoga is not for him who eats too much or abstains too much from eating. It is not for him, O Arjuna, who sleeps too much or keeps awake too much.

17. For the man who is temperate in food and recreation, who is restrained in his actions, whose sleep and waking are regulated, there ensues discipline [yoga] which destroys all sorrow.

The Perfect Yogi

18. When the disciplined mind is established in the Self alone, liberated from all desires, then is he said to be harmonized [in yoga].

19. As a lamp in a windless place flickered not, to such is likened the yogi of subdued thought who practices union with the Self [or discipline of himself].

20. That in which thought is at rest, restrained by the practice of concentration, that in which he beholds the Self through the self and rejoices in the Self.

21. That in which he finds this supreme delight, perceived by the intelligence and beyond the reach of the senses, wherein established, he no longer falls away from the truth.

22. That, on gaining which he thinks that there is no greater gain beyond it, wherein established he is not shaken even by the heaviest sorrow.

23. Let that be known by the name of yoga, this disconnection from union with pain. This yoga should be practiced with determination, with heart undismayed.

24. Abandoning without exception all desires born of [selfish] will, restraining with the mind all the senses on every side.

25. Let him gain little by little tranquillity by means of reason controlled by steadiness and having fixed the mind on the Self, let him not think of anything [else].

26. Whatsoever makes the wavering and unsteady mind wander away let him restrain and bring it back to the control of the Self alone.

27. For supreme happiness comes to the yogin whose mind is peaceful, whose passions are at rest, who is stainless and has become one with God.

28. Thus making the self ever harmonized, the yogin, who has put away sin, experiences easily the infinite bliss of contact with the Eternal.

29. He whose self is harmonized by yoga seeth the Self abiding in all beings and all beings in the Self; everywhere he sees the same.

30. He who sees Me everywhere and sees all in Me; I am not lost to him nor is he lost to Me.

31. The yogin who established in oneness, worships Me abiding in all beings lives in Me, however he may be active.

32. He, O Arjuna, who sees with equality everything, in the image of his own self, whether in pleasure or in pain, he is considered a perfect yogi.

Control of Mind Is Difficult but Possible

Arjuna said:

33. This yoga declared by you to be of the nature of equality [eveness of mind], O Madhusudana [Krishna], I see no stable foundation for, on account of restlessness.

34. For the mind is verily fickle, O Krishna, it is impetuous, strong and obstinate. I think it is as difficult to control as the wind.

35. Without doubt, O Mighty-armed [Arjuna], the mind is difficult to curb and restless but it can be controlled, O Son of Kunti [Arjuna], by constant practice and non-attachment.

36. Yoga is hard to attain, I agree, by one who is not self-controlled; but by the self-controlled it is attainable by striving through proper means.

37. He who cannot control himself though he has faith, with the mind wandering away from yoga, failing to attain perfection in yoga, what way does he go, O Krishna?

38. Does he not perish like a rent cloud, O Mighty-armed [Krishna], fallen from both and without any hold and bewildered in the path that leads to the Eternal?

39. Thou shouldst despel completely this, my doubt, O Krishna, for there is none else than Thyself who can destroy this doubt.

40. O, Partha [Arjuna], neither in this life nor hereafter is there destruction for him; for never does any one who do good, dear friend, tread the path of woe.

41. Having attained to the world of the righteous and dwelt there for very many years, the man who has fallen away from yoga is again born in the house of such as are pure and prosperous.

42. Or he may be born in the family of yogins who are endowed with wisdom. For such a birth as this is more difficult to obtain in the world.

43. There he regains the [mental] impressions [of union with the Divine] which he had developed in his previous life and with this [as the starting point] he strives again for perfection, O Joy of the Kurus [Arjuna].

44. By his former practice, he is carried on irresistibly. Even the seeker after the knowledge of yoga goes beyond the Vedic rule.

45. But the yogi who strives with assiduity, cleansed of all sins, perfecting himself through many lives, then attains to the highest goal.

46. The yogin is greater than the ascetic; he is considered to be greater than the man of knowledge, greater than the man of ritual works, therefore do thou become a yogin, O Arjuna.

47. And of all yogins, he who full of faith worship Me, with his inner self abiding in Me, him, I hold to be the most attuned [to me in Yoga].

Study Questions

D.10.2 *The Bhagavad Gita*, The Yoga of Political Renunciation

1. Discuss the method of doing yoga and practicing it.
2. Discuss the reasons why one has to renounce the fruits of one's action. Offer your critical response.

D.10.3

Discoursing on the Sword

Chuang Tzu (v. Trang Tử)

The Introduction

"*Wu wei*" (v. *Vô vi*) is one of the main doctrines in the *Tao Te Ching* (v. *Đạo Đúc Kinh*) of Lao Tzu (v. Lão Tử) and the *Nan Hua Ching* (v. Nam Hoa Kinh) of Chuang Tzu (v. Trang Tử). "Wu wei" (v. Vô vi) is normally rendered into English as "nonaction" or "actionless action" or "not-action."

"Wu wei" (v. Vô vi) is one of the most difficult and least understood doctrines of Lao Tzu (v. Lão Tử) in particular and of Taoism (v. Đạoism) in general. Lao Tzu (v. Lão Tử) says that the ontological Tao (v. Đạo) is "wu wei" (v. vô vi) and recommends that humans should practice "wu wei" (non-action). What is "wu wei" (v. vô vi)? This is probably the best statement that Lao Tzu makes on "wu wei" (v. vô vi): "[The] Tao invariably takes no action, and yet there is nothing left undone." [Lao Tzu:37]. This statement sounds very paradoxical and almost meaningless. The first part of the statement says that the Tao does nothing. The second part of the statement says that everything is done. How is this practically possible? Practically speaking, if no action is taken, then, nothing is done. How should we then interpret the above cited statement of Lao Tzu in particular and Lao Tzu's doctrine of wu wei (v. vô vi) in general?

One of the interpretive ways that we can contemplate is found in Chuang Tzu's "Discoursing on the Sword."

In ancient times King Wen of Chao was fond of swords. Expert swordsmen flocked to his gate, and over three thousand of them were supported as guests in his household, day and night engaging in bouts in his presence till the dead and wounded numbered more than a hundred men a year. Yet the king's delight never seemed to wane and things went on in this way for three years, while the state sank into decline and the other feudal lords conspired against it.

The crown prince K'uei, distressed at this, summoned his retainers about him and said, "I will bestow a thousand pieces of gold upon any

[1] The title may also be interpreted to mean "Delighting in Swords." Why both meanings are appropriate will be apparent.

man who can reason with the king and make him give up these sword fights!"

"Chuang Tzu is the one who can do it," said his retainers.

The crown prince thereupon sent an envoy with a thousand pieces of gold to present to Chuang Tzu, but Chuang Tzu refused to accept the gift. Instead he accompanied the envoy on his return and went to call on the crown prince. "What instructions do you have for me, that you present me with a thousand pieces of gold?" he asked.

"I had heard, Sir," said the crown prince, "that you are an enlightened sage, and I wished in all due respect to offer this thousand in gold as a gift to your attendants. But if you refuse to accept it, then I dare say no more about the matter."

Chuang Tzu said, "I have heard that the crown prince wishes to employ me because he hopes I can rid the king of this passion of his. Now if, in attempting to persuade His Majesty, I should arouse his anger and fail to satisfy your hopes, then I would be sentenced to execution. In that case, what use could I make of the gold? And if I should be able to persuade His Majesty and satisfy your hopes, then what could I ask for in the whole kingdom of Chao that would not be granted me?"

"The trouble is," said the crown prince, "that my father, the king, refuses to see anyone but swordsmen."

"Fine!" said Chuang Tzu. "I am quite able to handle a sword."

"But the kind of swordsmen my father receives," said the crown prince, "all have tousled heads and bristling beards, wear slouching caps tied with plain, coarse tassels, and robes that are cut short behind; they glare fiercely and have difficulty getting out their words. Men like that he is delighted with! Now, Sir, if you should insist upon going to see him in scholarly garb, the whole affair would go completely wrong from the start."

"Then allow me to get together the garb of a swordsman," said Chuang Tzu. After three days, he had his swordsman's costume ready and went to call on the crown prince. The crown prince and he then went to see the king. The king, drawing his sword, waited with bare blade in hand. Chuang Tzu entered the door of the hall with unhurried steps, looked at the king but made no bow.

The king said, "Now that you have gotten the crown prince to prepare the way for you, what kind of instruction is it you intend to give me?"

"I have heard that Your Majesty is fond of swords, and so I have come with my sword to present myself before you."

"And what sort of authority does your sword command?" asked the king.

"My sword cuts down one man every ten paces, and for a thousand li it never ceases its flailing!"

The king, greatly pleased, exclaimed, "You must have no rival in the whole world!"

Chuang Tzu said, "The wielder of the sword makes a display of emptiness, draws one out with hopes of advantage, is behind-time in setting out, but beforehand in arriving.[2] May I be allowed to try what I can do?"

The king said, "You may leave now, Sir, and go to your quarters to await my command. When I am ready to hold the bout, I will request your presence again."

The king then spent seven days testing the skill of his swordsmen. Over sixty were wounded or died in the process, leaving five or six survivors who were ordered to present themselves with their swords outside the king's hall. Then the king sent for Chuang Tzu, saying, "Today let us see what happens when you cross swords with these gentlemen."

Chuang Tzu said, "It is what I have long wished for."

"What weapon will you use, Sir," asked the king, "a long sword or a short one?"

"I am prepared to use any type at all. It happens that I have three swords—Your Majesty has only to indicate which you wish me to use. If I may, I will first explain them, and then put them to the test."

---

[2] The sentence is deliberately cryptic and capable of interpretation on a variety of levels.

"Let me hear about your three swords," said the king.

"There is the sword of the Son of Heaven, the sword of the feudal lord, and the sword of the commoner."

"What is the sword of the Son of Heaven like?" asked the king.

"The sword of the Son of Heaven? The Valley of Yen and the Stone Wall are its point, Ch'i and Tai its blade, Chin and Wey its spine, Chou and Sung its sword guard, Han and Wei its hilt.[3] The four barbarian tribes enwrap it, the four seasons enfold it, the seas of Po surround it, the mountains of Ch'ang girdle it. The five elements govern it, the demands of punishment and favor direct it. It is brought forth in accordance with the yin and yang, held in readiness in spring and summer, wielded in autumn and winter. Thrust it forward and there is nothing that will stand before it; raise it on high and there is nothing above it; press it down and there is nothing beneath it; whirl it about and there is nothing surrounding it. Above, it cleaves the drifting clouds; below, it severs the sinews of the earth. When this sword is once put to use, the feudal lords return to their former obedience and the whole world submits. This is the sword of the Son of Heaven."

King Wen, dumbounded, appeared to be at an utter loss. Then he said, "What is the sword of the feudal lord like?"

"The sword of the feudal lord? It has wise and brave men for its point, men of purity and integrity for its blade, men of worth and goodness for its spine, men of loyalty and sageliness for its swordguard, heroes and prodigies for its hilt. This sword too, thrust forward, meets nothing before it; raised, it encounters nothing above; pressed down, it encounters nothing beneath it; whirled about, it meets nothing surrounding it. Above, it takes its model from the roundness of heaven, following along with the three luminous bodies of the sky.[4] Below, it takes its model from the

squareness of earth, following along with the four seasons. In the middle realm, it brings harmony to the wills of the people and peace to the four directions. This sword, once put into use, is like the crash of a thunderbolt: none within the four borders of the state will fail to bow down in submission, none will fail to heed and obey the commands of the ruler. This is the sword of the feudal lord."

The king said, "What is the sword of the commoner like?"

"The sword of the commoner? It is used by men with tousled heads and bristling beards, with slouching caps tied with plain, coarse tassels and robes cut short behind, who glare fiercely and speak with great difficulty, who slash at one another in Your Majesty's presence. Above, it lops off heads and necks; below, it splits open livers and lungs. Those who wield this sword of the commoner are no different from fighting cocks— any morning their lives may be cut off. They are of no use in the administration of the state.

"Now Your Majesty occupies the position of a Son of Heaven, and yet you show this fondness for the sword of the commoner.[5] If I may be so bold, I think it rather unworthy of you!"

The king thereupon led Chuang Tzu up into his hall, where the royal butler came forward with trays of food, but the king merely paced round and round the room.

"Your Majesty should seat yourself at ease and calm your spirits," said Chuang Tzu. "The affair of the sword is all over and finished!"

After this, King Wen did not emerge from his palace for three months, and his swordsmen all committed suicide in their quarters.

---

[3] These are all feudal states or strategic places of northern China surrounding the state of Chao.

[4] The stars collectively make up the third luminous body.

[5] The state of Chao, situated in north central China, was never very powerful, and its king, only one among many feudal rulers of the time, in no sense occupied anything that could be called "the position of a Son of Heaven." If the writer has not abandoned all pretense at historicity, he must mean that the king of Chao, if he were to rule wisely, might in time gain sufficient power and prestige to become a contender for the position of Son of Heaven.

Study Questions

D.10.3 Chuang Tzu (v. Trang Tử), Discoursing on Swords

1. Explain your characterization of the action that Chuang Tzu (v. Trang Tử) took: Is it "yu wei (v. hữu vi [action]) or "wu wei (v. vô vi [non-action]) or another form?
2. Critically discuss whether the approach that Chuang Tzu (v. Trang Tử) took is wise.
3. Explain how Chuang Tzu (v. Trang Tử) did not fight not but won a complete victory in light of the Laoian definition of "wu wei" (v. vô vi [non-action]) as "doing nothing but nothing is left undone." Address the possible reasons why all the swordsmen committed suicide.

D.10.4

Thánh Gióng: The Việtnamese Ideal Sage of Political Vô Vi (c. Wu Wei)

The Introduction

"*Vô vi*" (c. *Wu wei* [*non-action*]) as a doctrine can be applied in many ways to solve practical problems of life. One of its practical applications is found in the world of politics, as we have seen in the reading on "Discoursing on the Sword" by Chuang Tzu (v. Trang Tử). The form of vô vi (c. wu wei) that is practiced in the world of practical politics can be called political vô vi (c. wu wei).

Unlike Chuang Tzu (v. Trang Tử), who does not really care much about practical politics or statecraft, Lao Tzu (v. Lão Tử) teaches the wisdom of political wu wei (v. vô vi) like Krishna trains the Aryan warrior Arjuna the art of karma yoga. Concerning the deep political concern of Lao Tzu (v. Lão Tử), A. C. Graham writes: "Certainly the audience to which *Lao-tzu* (unlike *Chuang-tzu*) is directly addressed is the ruler of a state—a small state, one might guess, which has to bend with the wind to survive among stronger states. Its strategy of retreating before a rising power until it overstretches itself and passes the point of decline has very practical applications in government, military strategy and wrestling—Japanese Judo ('the Way of Weakness') is named straight from the terminology of *Lao-tzu*." [Graham 1989:234] This may be true as far as the political interests of the rulers of small states are concerned, but Lao Tzu (v. Lão Tử) is indeed concerned with *the art of statecraft* in general. State size is not the real question of political wu wei (v. vô vi).

But there is one thing that is true about Lao Tzu (v. Lão Tử) the man. That is the fact that Lao Tzu is *not* known as a successful practitioner of political wu wei but *only* its pure theorist. Of successful practitioners of political vô vi (c. wu wei), we can recognize Chiang Liang (v. Trương Lương) from the ancient East Asian Kingdom of Han (v. Hàn), the Zen master Vạn Hạnh of traditional Việt-Nam, and Thánh Gióng (The Sage in a Bamboo Cradle) or Phù Đổng Thiên Vương (the Heavenly King from [the village of] Phù Đổng) of the ancient Văn Lang Quốc.

All the peoples of the Văn Lang Quốc (Kingdom of Civilized Peoples) were enjoying peace and prosperity. Using the pretext that Hùng Vương (King Hùng) of the Sixth Branch[1] failed to make the proper state tributes to the Ân (c. Yin) Dynasty as expected,[2] the Ân Vương (Yin King) planned his invasion against the Văn Lang Quốc (Kingdom of Civilized Peoples).[3]

Informed of the grave news, Hùng Vương summoned his officials to discuss the best possible strategy for national defense. One official in charge of divination offered this suggestion: "Should we pray for our Long Vương (Dragon King),[4] so that, He may use his yin forces (âm binh) against the invaders in our defense?" Following this suggestion, Hùng Vương ordered the construction of an altar, where, his Majesty and his officials fasted and prayed solemnly for three days. Then heavy rains and powerful storms swept the sky, and, suddenly, there appeared a very Old Man, nine meters in height, having a golden face, a long white beard, and a big belly. He sat at a three-way intersection, talking, laughing, and dancing at times.

Recognizing that the Old Man was not just an ordinary person but a divine being, King Hùng was informed of his strange presence. The King went out to greet him in person and escorted him to the altar. But the Old Man remained silent and composed, neither eating nor talking. The King finally made his sincere inquiry about the future of his kingdom:

"It is known that the Northerners are planning an invasion. What will the outcome be, defeat or victory? Do you have any advice for me, Sir?"

While maintaining his silence, the Old Man took out his oracle stalks, divined, and told the King these words:

"In three years the Northerners will come. Prepare the weapons and train the soldiers to defend the country, and also search for those persons of extraordinary abilities and good virtues among the peoples and reward those who could destroy the enemy with appropriate titles and benefits. If persons of great talents and good virtues were found, then, the invaders could be defeated."

Upon his last word, the Old Man took leave of him, flying away into the air, and disappeared behind the clouds. He was then believed to be but Long Quân (Dragon King) himself.

Three years later, it was reported from the frontier that the Ân (c. Yin) invading forces were crossing the frontier in great numbers. Following the instructions of the Old Man, the King dispatched his messengers to all the corners of the kingdom to call on all those persons of wisdom, goodness, and talents (bâc hiên tài) to come to the defense of their country.

In the village of Phù-Đổng, district of Tiên-Du, province of Vũ-Ninh, there was a child, who was born to his 60 year old parents on the 7th of January. Being already three years old, but, strangely, he could not talk, not even a single word or a single sound. He always lay flat on his back, because, he was incapable of sitting up at all. Learning of the arrival of the King's messenger in the village, the poor mother teased at her son by saying:

Oh, my little boy whom I gave birth to! But he knew only how to eat rather than to fight the invaders for the Court's good rewards, so that, he could repay the debts he owed to his mother's nurturing labor and loving care. What a pity!

Upon hearing his mother's words, suddenly, the boy spoke to her: "Mother, please call up the King's Messenger for me!" Being overtaken by joy and amazement, the mother went out to tell her neighbors the great miracle. Welcoming the

[Source: Translated from "Truyện Phù Đổng Thiên Vương" (The Story of Phù Đổng Thiên Vương) in Lê Hữu Mục, trans., *Lĩnh Nam Chích Quái (The Fabulous Stories of Lĩnh Nan)* (Sài-Gòn: Khai Trí, 1962), pp. 55–57.]

miracle with great joys they did, and, they sent for the King's Messenger immediately.

Upon seeing the little boy, the Messenger said: "Hey, you are just a little baby, hardly knowing how to talk, what do you call me here for?" The boy rose up from his bed and told the Messenger these words:

> "Go quickly and tell the King to make an iron horse of 18 meters in height, an iron sword of 7 meters in length, an iron whip, and an iron helmet. I shall ride the horse, wear the helmet, and fight to defeat the invaders. The King should have nothing to worry about."

Upon learning the news that apparently reflected the long-expected message of the Old Man, the King declared: "I now indeed have nothing to worry about!" But his officials had this question to ask him in disbelief: "Your Majesty, how could one person defeat the invaders?" In response to their concern, the King assured them: "The past words of Long Quân (Dragon King) were not so empty after all. Have no doubts, my dear officials. Hurry and find 50 tons of iron and make the horse, the sword, the whip, and the helmet."

When the King's Messenger returned with all the items requested, the mother became apprehended and warned her son that he might have just asked for trouble. But her child warmly smiled at her and said:

> Dear mother, please feed me a lot of rice and wine, and, don't worry!

The child grew up miraculously fast and ate so much that his mother soon ran out of food. To her rescue, the villagers brought in great quantities of meat, rice, wine, and cakes, but the child was still hungry. There was also not enough clothing around, so, flowers and leaves were used to cover up his growing body.

As the Ân (c. Yin) forces arrived in great numbers and took up positions all over and around the edges of the Trâu-Sơn (Water Buffalo

Mountains), the child stretched out his legs, and in a sudden, he transformed into a giant of 10 *trượng* in height. Opening his nostrils, taking 10 deep breaths, putting on his iron helmet, pulling out his iron sword, and pointing it to the sky, and with a thundering voice, he declared:

> "Here, I, the Celestial General (Thiên Tướng) come!"

Then mounting his iron horse, which whinnied an earth-shaking neigh, and to the front he galloped. And in seconds, he made his appearance in front of King Hùng's army, already in its war formation. In lightning action, as he engaged himself in battle, the invading forces fell apart, many surrendered, others fled in disarray, and the Ân King (Yin King) was rightly killed.

After the battle was victoriously won, to the Sóc-Sơn Mountains, away and alone, the Celestial General galloped. It was there he flew deep into the heaven and disappeared in the clouds on high, leaving behind his uniform and weapons. This was on the 9th of April.

During the 644 years of its reign, the Ân (c. Yin) Dynasty never dared to attack the Văn Lang Quốc again. Honoring his great deed and gracious virtue, King Hùng named Him, "Phù Đổng Thiên Vương" (The Celestial King from Phù-Đổng), ordering the construction of a temple in his home village, and granted one thousand *mẫu* of land to be used for His worship. But for the people of Phù-Đổng, he is honored as their beloved "Thánh Gióng" (the Sage in a Bamboo Cradle).

Notes

[1] "Hùng Vương (King Hùng) is the name of the leadership line of the Hồng Bàng Dynasty that governed the Văn Lang Quốc from 2879 to 258 BCE. There were either "18 Generations" or "18 Branches" of the Hùng Vương leadership line. According to Đào Duy Anh, a modern Việtnamese encyclopedian, the Sino-Việtnamese character "*hùng*" means the "male bird" of the "*Hồng*" bird species as it is used in the dynastic title "Hồng Bàng Thị" and as its totemic animal. The "hồng" is also used as the philosophical symbol of the

cosmogonic state of primal chaos before cosmic evolution.

[2] Was the Sino-Vietnamese character "Ân Dynasty" or "Ân King" referred to the historical "Yin Dynasty" or "Yin King" that ruled the northern region of the ancient East Asian Mainland (now North China) or not? No one is sure of the true meaning of the "Ân Dynasty" or "Ân King" as narrated in the story. This historical question has not been properly studied and resolved. Any TrPuPong new study, based on both mythological and archaeological evidence, is desirable.

[3] "Văn Lang Quốc" is believed by the Vietnamese to be the name of the second kingdom that had marked the "Golden Age" of ancient Việt-Nam. It is presently established by Vietnamese archaeologists to correspond with the so-called "Đôngsơhian Civilizaton" of Bronze Age Việt-Nam and Southeast Asia.

[4] In the "Truyện Hồng Bàng," which can be translated either as "The Story of the Hồng Bàng Dynasty" or "The Story of Great Vermillion Immensity," one of the most important Vănlangian world genesis stories, "Long Vương" (Dragon King) and his lovely wife "Âu Cơ" (Authentic Foundation) are said to be the primal world parents of the "Bách Việt" (Hundred Việts, i.e., humanity as a whole).

Study Questions

D.10.4 Thánh Gióng: The Vietnamese Ideal Sage of Political Vô Vi (c. Wu Wei)

1. Characterize the theoretical nature of the form of political action that the "Old Man" and Thánh Gióng (the Sage in a Bamboo Cradle) took and provide your philosophical analysis of their form of political action.

2. Compare and contrast the form of political action that the "Old Man" and Thánh Gióng took with that of Chuang Tzu as well as with the Laoian doctrine of vô vi (c. wu wei [non-action]) as theoretized in the *Đạo Đức Kinh* (c. *Tao Te Ching*).

3. What was the strategy by which the practice of political vô vi (c. wu wei [non-action]) was carried out? This question can be asked differently: How was the đạo of political vô vi practiced by the Old Man and the Baby?

4. What was the đức (c. te) of political vô vi as revealed in the đạo of political vô vi that the Old Man the Baby practiced?

5. How would Lão Tử (c. Lao Tzu) respond to the đạo đức (tao te) of political vô vi as practiced by the Old Man and the Baby?

Buddhist Economics

E. F. Schumacher

The Introduction

The teachings of Buddhism and Buddhist vegetarianism should have encouraged Buddhist monks, nuns, and scholars to develop a "Buddhist economics" which may lead to a true "Buddhist economy" as a foundation of a true "Buddhist state." But no Buddhist economics is yet established as an alternative scholarly discipline in relation to capitalist and socialist economics. A Buddhist economics still remains a scholarly need to be realized. But I believe the development of a Buddhist political economy is philosophically more appropriate than just a Buddhist economics because the latter is too narrow. Schumacher offers some basic principles of a Buddhist economics. This is really a good start.

"Right Livelihood" is one of the requirements of the Buddha's Noble Eightfold Path. It is clear, therefore, that there must be such a thing as Buddhist economics.

Buddhist countries have often stated that they wish to remain faithful to their heritage. So Burma: "The New Burma sees no conflict between religious values and economic progress. Spiritual health and material well-being are not enemies: they are natural allies." Or: "We can blend successfully the religious and spiritual values of our heritage with the benefits of modern technology." Or: "We Burmans have a sacred duty to conform both our dreams and our acts to our faith. This we shall ever do."

All the same, such countries invariably assume that they can model their economic development plans in accordance with modern economics, and they call upon modern economists from so-called advanced countries to advise them, to formulate the policies to be pursued, and to construct the grand design for development, the Five-Year Plan or whatever it may be called. No one seems to think that a Buddhist way of life would call for Buddhist economics, just as the modern materialist way of life has brought forth modern economics.

Economists themselves, like most specialists, normally suffer from a kind of metaphysical blindness, assuming that theirs is a science of absolute and invariable truths, without any presuppositions. Some go as far as to claim that economic laws are as free from "metaphysics" or "values" as the law of gravitation. We need not, however, get involved in arguments of methodology. Instead, let us take some fundamentals and see what they look like when viewed by a modern economist and a Buddhist economist.

There is universal agreement that a fundamental source of wealth is human labour. Now, the modern economist has been brought up to consider "labour" or work as little more than a necessary evil. From the point of view of the employer, it is in any case simply an item of cost, to be reduced to a minimum if it cannot be eliminated altogether, say, by automation. From the point of view of the workman, it is a "disutility"; to work is to make a sacrifice of one's leisure and comfort, and wages are a kind of compensation for the sacrifice. Hence the ideal from the point of view of the employer is to have output without employees, and the ideal from the point of view of the employee is to have income without employment.

The consequences of these attitudes both in theory and in practice are, of course, extremely far-reaching. If the ideal with regard to work is to get rid of it, every method that "reduces the work load" is a good thing. The most potent method, short of automation, is the so-called "division of labour" and the classical example is the pin factory eulogised in Adam Smith's *Wealth of Nations*. Here it is not a matter of ordinary specialisation, which mankind has practised from time immemorial, but of dividing up every complete process of production into minute parts, so that the final product can be produced at great speed without anyone having had to contribute more than a totally insignificant and, in most cases, unskilled movement of his limbs.

The Buddhist point of view takes the function of work to be at least threefold: to give a man a chance to utilise and develop his faculties; to enable him to overcome his ego-centredness by joining with other people in a common task; and to bring forth the goods and services needed for a becoming existence. Again, the consequences that flow from this view are endless. To organise work in such a manner that it becomes meaningless, boring, stultifying, or nerve-racking for the worker would be little short of criminal; it would indicate a greater concern with goods than with people, an evil lack of compassion and a soul-destroying degree of attachment to the most primitive side of this worldly existence. Equally, to strive for leisure as an alternative to work would be considered a complete misunderstanding of one of the basic truths of human existence, namely that work and leisure are complementary parts of the same living process and cannot be separated without destroying the joy of work and the bliss of leisure.

From the Buddhist point of view, there are therefore two types of mechanisation which must be clearly distinguished: one that enhances a man's skill and power and one that turns the work of man over to a mechanical slave, leaving man in a position of having to serve the slave. How to tell the one from the other? "The craftsman himself," says Ananda Coomaraswamy, a man equally competent to talk about the modern West as the ancient East, "can always, if allowed to, draw the delicate distinction between the machine and the tool. The carpet loom is a tool, a contrivance for holding warp threads at a stretch for the pile to be woven round them by the craftsmen's fngers; but the power loom is a machine, and its significance as a destroyer of culture lies in the fact that it does the essentially human part of the work." It is clear, therefore, that Buddhist economics must be very different from the economics of modern materialism, since the Buddhist sees the essence of civilisation not in a multiplication of wants but in the purification of human character. Character, at the same time, is formed primarily by a man's work. And work, properly conducted in conditions of human dignity and freedom, blesses those who do it and equally their products. The Indian philosopher and economist J. C. Kumarappa sums the matter up as follows:

> If the nature of the work is properly appreciated and applied, it will stand in the same relation to the higher faculties as food is to the physical body. It nourishes and enlivens the higher man and urges him to produce the best he is capable of. It directs his free will along the proper course and disciplines the animal in him into progressive channels. It furnishes an excellent background for man to display his scale of values and develop his personality.

If a man has no chance of obtaining work he is in a desperate position, not simply because he lacks an income but because he lacks this nourishing and enlivening factor of disciplined work which nothing can replace. A modern economist may engage in highly sophisticated calculations on whether full employment "pays" or whether it might be more "economic" to run an economy at less than full employment so as to ensure a greater mobility of labour, a better stability of wages, and so forth. His fundamental criterion of success is simply the total quantity of goods produced during a given period of time. "If the marginal urgency of goods is low," says Professor Galbraith in *The Affluent Society*, "then so is the urgency of employing the last man or the last million men in the labour force." And again: "If . . . we can afford some unemployment in the interest of stability—a proposition, incidentally, of impeccably conservative antecedents—then we can afford to give those who are unemployed the goods that enable them to sustain their accustomed standard of living."

From a Buddhist point of view, this is standing the truth on its head by considering goods as more important than people and consumption as more important than creative activity. It means shifting the emphasis from the worker to the product of work, that is, from the human to the subhuman, a surrender to the forces of evil. The very start of Buddhist economic planning would be a planning for full employment, and the primary purpose of this would in fact be employment for everyone who needs an "outside" job: it would not be the maximisation of employment nor the maximisation of production. Women, on the whole, do not need an "outside" job, and the large-scale employment of women in offices or factories would be considered a sign of serious economic failure. In particular, to let mothers of young children work in factories while the children run wild would be as uneconomic in the eyes of a Buddhist economist as the employment of a skilled worker as a soldier in the eyes of a modern economist.

While the materialist is mainly interested in goods, the Buddhist is mainly interested in liberation. But Buddhism is "The Middle Way" and therefore in no way antagonistic to physical well-being. It is not wealth that stands in the way of liberation but the attachment to wealth; not the enjoyment of pleasurable things but the craving for them. The keynote of Buddhist economics, therefore, is simplicity and non-violence. From an economist's point of view, the marvel of the Buddhist way of life is the utter rationality of its pattern—amazingly small means leading to extraordinarily satisfactory results.

For the modern economist this is very difficult to understand. He is used to measuring the "standard of living" by the amount of annual consumption, assuming all the time that a man who consumes more is "better off" than a man who consumes less. A Buddhist economist would consider this approach excessively irrational: since consumption is merely a means to human well-being, the aim should be to obtain the maximum of well-being with the minimum of consumption. Thus, if the purpose of clothing is a certain amount of temperature comfort and an attractive appearance, the task is to attain this purpose with the smallest possible effort, that is, with the smallest annual destruction of cloth and with the help of designs that involve the smallest possible input of toil. The less toil there is, the more time and strength is left for artistic creativity. It would be highly uneconomic, for instance, to go in for complicated tailoring, like the modern West, when a much more beautiful effect can be achieved by the skilful draping of uncut material. It would be the height of folly to make material so that it should wear out quickly and the height of barbarity to make anything ugly, shabby or mean. What has just been said about clothing applies equally to all other human requirements. The ownership and the consumption of goods is a means to an end, and Buddhist economics is the systematic study of how to attain given ends with the minimum means.

Modern economics, on the other hand, considers consumption to be the sole end and purpose of all economic activity, taking the factors of production—land, labour, and capital—as the means. The former, in short, tries to maximise human satisfactions by the optimal pattern of consumption, while the latter tries to maximise consumption by the optimal pattern of productive effort. It is easy to see that the effort needed to sustain a way of life which seeks to attain the optimal pattern of consumption is likely to be much smaller than the effort needed to sustain a drive for maximum consumption. We need not be surprised, therefore, that the pressure and strain of living is very much less in, say, Burma than it is in the United States, in spite of the fact that the amount of labour-saving machinery used in the former country is only a minute fraction of the amount used in the latter.

Simplicity and non-violence are obviously closely related. The optimal pattern of consumption, producing a high degree of human satisfaction by means of a relatively low rate of consumption, allows people to live without great pressure and strain and to fulfil the primary injunction of Buddhist teaching: "Cease to do evil; try to do good." As physical resources are everywhere limited, people satisfying their needs by means of a modest use of resources are obviously less likely to be at each other's throats than people depending upon a high rate of use. Equally, people who live in highly self-sufficient local communities are less likely to get involved in large-scale violence than people whose existence depends on world wide systems of trade.

Front the point of view of Buddhist economics, therefore, production from local resources for local needs is the most rational way of economic life, while dependence on imports from afar and the consequent need to produce for export to unknown and distant peoples is highly uneconomic and justifiable only in exceptional cases and on a small scale. Just as the modern economist would admit that a high rate of consumption of transport services between a man's home and his place of work signifies a misfortune and not a high standard of life, so the Buddhist economist would hold that to satisfy human wants from faraway sources rather than from sources nearby signifies failure rather than success. The former tends to take statistics showing an increase in the number of ton/miles per head of the population carried by a country's transport system as proof of economic progress, while to the latter—the Buddhist economist—the same statistics would indicate a highly undesirable deterioration in the *pattern* of consumption.

Another striking difference between modern economics and Buddhist economics arises over the use of natural resources. Bertrand de Jouvenel, the eminent French political philosopher, has characterised "Western man" in words which may be taken as a fair description of the modern economist:

> He tends to count nothing as an expenditure, other than human effort; he does not seem to mind how much mineral matter he wastes and, far worse, how much living matter he destroys. He does not seem to realise at all that human life is a dependent part of an ecosystem of many different forms of life. As the world

is ruled from towns where men are cut off from any form of life other than human, the feeling of belonging to an ecosystem is not revived. This results in a harsh and improvident treatment of things upon which we ultimately depend, such as water and trees.

The teaching of the Buddha, on the other hand, enjoins a reverent and non-violent attitude not only to all sentient beings but also, with great emphasis, to trees. Every follower of the Buddha ought to plant a tree every few years and look after it until it is safely established, and the Buddhist economist can demonstrate without difficulty that the universal observation of this rule would result in a high rate of genuine economic development independent of any foreign aid. Much of the economic decay of southeast Asia (as of many other parts of the world) is undoubtedly due to a heedless and shameful neglect of trees.

Modern economics does not distinguish between renewable and non-renewable materials, as its very method is to equalise and quantify everything by means of a money price. Thus, taking various alternative fuels, like coal, oil, wood, or water-power: the only difference between them recognised by modern economics is relative cost per equivalent unit. The cheapest is automatically the one to be preferred, as to do otherwise would be irrational and "uneconomic." From a Buddhist point of view, of course, this will not do; the essential difference between non-renewable fuels like coal and oil on the one hand and renewable fuels like wood and water-power on the other cannot be simply overlooked. Non-renewable goods must be used only if they are indispensable, and then only with the greatest care and the most meticulous concern for conservation. To use them heedlessly or extravagantly is an act of violence, and while complete non-violence may not be attainable on this earth, there is nonetheless an ineluctable duty on man to aim at the ideal of non-violence in all he does.

Just as a modern European economist would not consider it a great economic achievement if all European art treasures were sold to America at attractive prices, so the Buddhist economist would insist that a population basing its economic life on non-renewable fuels is living parasitically, on capital instead of income. Such a way of life could have no permanence and could therefore be justified only as a purely temporary expedient. As the world's resources of non-renewable fuels—coal, oil and natural gas—are exceedingly unevenly distributed over the globe and undoubtedly limited in quantity, it is clear that their exploitation at an ever-increasing rate is an act of violence against nature which must almost inevitably lead to violence between men.

This fact alone might give food for thought even to those people in Buddhist countries who care nothing for the religious and spiritual values of their heritage and ardently desire to embrace the materialism of modern economics at the fastest possible speed. Before they dismiss Buddhist economics as nothing better than a nostalgic dream, they might wish to consider whether the path of economic development outlined by modern economics is likely to lead them to places where they really want to be. Towards the end of his courageous book *The Challenge of Man's Future*, Professor Harrison Brown of the California Institute of Technology gives the following appraisal:

> Thus we see that, just as industrial society is fundamentally unstable and subject to reversion to agrarian existence, so within it the conditions which offer individual freedom are unstable in their ability to avoid the conditions which impose rigid organisation and totalitarian control. Indeed, when we examine all of the foreseeable difficulties which threaten the survival of industrial civilisation, it is difficult to see how the achievement of stability and the maintenance of individual liberty can be made compatible.

Even if this were dismissed as a long-term view there is the immediate question of whether "modernisation," as currently practised without regard to religious and spiritual values, is actually producing agreeable results. As far as the masses are concerned, the results appear to be disastrous—a collapse of the rural economy, a rising tide of unemployment in town and country, and the growth of a city proletariat without nourishment for either body or soul.

It is in the light of both immediate experience and long-term prospects that the study of Buddhist economics could be recommended even to those who believe that economic growth is more important than any spiritual or religious values. For it is not a question of choosing between "modern growth" and "traditional stagnation." It is a question of finding the right path of development, the Middle Way between materialist heedlessness and traditionalist immobility, in short, of finding "Right Livelihood."

Study Questions

D.10.5 E. F. Schumacher, Buddhist Economics

1. Explain what Schumacher mean by "economics" and the reasons he thinks there is a Buddhist economics.
2. Discuss the differences between modern economics and Buddhist economics as explained by Schumacher.
3. Offer your modifications of Schumacher's version of the "Buddhist economics", if you think that his version is a good start but remains theoretically and practically inadequate.

Part E

Eastern Cosmological Traditions and Universal Equality

CHAPTER 11

Ancient South Asian and Hindu Cosmological Traditions

Vedic Cosmological Thoughts
(ca. 800 or 500–300 BCE)

The Introduction

The early Vedic cosmological thoughts paved the way for the emergence of Upanishadic Brahmanism during the late Vedic Period of Hinduism (800 BCE at the earliest or 500 BCE at the latest). One of the main features of Upanishadic Brahmanism (the first philosophy of Hinduism) is its cosmological thoughts.

The cosmological thoughts of Upanishadic Brahmanism are of two main theoretical orientations. The first one can be characterized as *creationistic*, as represented by the selection from the *Brihadāranyaka Upanishad*, and the other as *evolutionistic*, as represented by the selection from the *Taittiriya Upanishad*.

The *Taittiriya Upanishad*, which is so named because it is a part of the *Taittiriya Āranyaka*, is famous for its doctrine of the "Five Sheaths" of the human self. The "five sheaths" of the human self are one's food, breath, mind, intellect, and bliss. The sheath of bliss contains also the "calculus of bliss," leading to the ultimate bliss of the Brahman.

The *Brihadāranyaka Upanishad*, which means "great forest-book," is the longest and oldest of the *Upanishads*. Most philosophically significant about this *Upanishad* is the discourse between Yājnavalkya ("the greatest of the Upanishadic sages") and his wife Maitreyi: "Nowhere else is the notion of the transcendental *Atman* as universal and undifferentiated consciousness better portrayed." [Radhakrishnan and Moore 1957:77]

E.II.1.a

The Hymn of Creation (X.129)

1. Non-being then existed not nor being:
   There was no air, nor sky that is beyond it.
   What was concealed? Wherein? In whose protection?
   And was there deep unfathomable water?
2. Death then existed not nor life immortal;
   Of neither night nor day was any token.
   By its inherent force the One breathed windless:
   No other thing than that beyond existed.
3. Darkness there was at first by darkness hidden;
   Without distinctive marks, this all was water.
   That which, becoming, by the void was covered,
   That One by force of heat came into being.
4. Desire entered the One in the beginning:
   It was the earliest seed, of thought the product.
   The sages searching in their hearts with wisdom,
   Found out the bond of being in non-being.
5. Their ray extended light across the darkness:
   But was the One above or was it under?
   Creative force was there, and fertile power:
   Below was energy, above was impulse.
6. Who knows for certain? Who shall here declare it?
   Whence was it born, and whence came this creation?

[Source: Taken from *Hymns from the Rigveda*, trans. A. A. Macdonell (London: Oxford University Press; Calcutta: Association Press, 1922), pp. 19–20].

The gods were born after this world's creation:
Then who can know from whence it has arisen?

7. None knoweth whence creation has arisen;
And whether he has or has not produced it:
He who surveys it in the highest heaven,
He only knows, or haply he may know not.

E.11.1.b

The Hymn to Purusha (X.90)

1. Thousand-headed was the Puruṣa, thousand-eyed, thousand-footed. He embraced the earth on all sides, and stood beyond the breadth of ten fingers.

2. The Puruṣa is this all, that which was and which shall be. He is Lord of immortality, which he grows beyond through (sacrificial) food.

3. Such is his greatness, and still greater than that is the Puruṣa. One fourth of him is all beings. The three fourths of him is the immortal in Heaven.

4. Three fourths on high rose the Puruṣa. One fourth of him arose again here (on the earth). Thence in all directions he spread abroad, as that which eats and that which eats not.

5. From him Virāj was born, from Virāj the Puruṣa. He when born reached beyond the earth behind as well as before.

6. When the Gods spread out the sacrifice with the Puruṣa as oblation, spring was its ghee, summer the fuel, autumn the oblation.

7. As the sacrifice on the strewn grass they besprinkled the Puruṣa, born in the beginning. With him the Gods sacrificed, the Sādhyas and the sages.

8. From that sacrifice completely offered was the sprinkled ghee collected. He made it the beasts of the air, of the forest, and those of the village.

9. From that sacrifice completely offered were born the Verses (*Ṛg Veda*) and the *Sāman*-melodies (*Sāma Veda*). The metres were born from it. From it was born the Sacrificial formula (*Yajur Veda*).

10. From it were born horses, and they that have two rows of teeth. Cattle were born from it. From it were born goats and sheep.

11. When they divided the Puruṣa, into how many parts did they arrange him? What was his mouth? What his two arms? What are his thighs and feet called?

12. The *brāhmin* was his mouth, his two arms were made the *rājanya* (warrior), his two thighs the *vaiśya* (trader and agriculturist), from his feet the *śūdra* (servile class) was born.

13. The moon was born from his spirit (*manas*), from his eye was born the sun, from his mouth Indra and Agni, from his breath Vāyu (wind) was born.

[Source: Taken from *Vedic Hymns*, trans. Edward J. Thomas (London: HWV, Ltd., 1923), pp. 120–22].

14. From his navel arose the middle sky, from his head the heaven originated, from his feet the earth, the quarters from his ear. Thus did they fashion the worlds.
15. Seven were his sticks that enclose (the fire), thrice seven were made the faggots. When the Gods spread out the sacrifice, they bound the Puruṣa as a victim.
16. With the sacrifice the Gods sacrificed the sacrifice. These were the first ordinances. These great powers reached to the firmament, where are the ancient Sādhyas, the Gods.

Study Questions

E.11.1 Vedic Cosmological Thoughts (ca. 800 or 500–300 BCE)

1. Identify and discuss the pre-cosmological thesis concerning the origin of the universe that is stated in the "Hymn of Creation" in comparison to the Laoian thesis as advanced in the *Đạo Đúc Kinh* (c. *Tao Te Ching*).
2. Explain the spirit of skepticism and relativism as revealed in the "Hymn of Creation." Compare it with the "Genesis" (in the *Bible*).
3. Critically discuss the cosmogonic thought of the "Hymn of Creation" in comparison to that of the "Hymn To Purusha."
4. Explain the "divine" origin of the Hindu varna system and critique its "divinity" or "biology," as the legitimate basis for the construction of any closed class system.

E.11.2.a

Upanishadic Cosmological Thoughts
(ca. 600–200 BCE)

The Creation of the Manifold World

The Brihadāranyaka Upanishad

1. In the beginning this world was Self (*Ātman*) alone in the form of a Person. Looking around, he saw nothing else than himself. He said first: "I am." Thence arose the name "I." Therefore even today, when one is addressed, he says first just "It is I" and then speaks whatever name he has. Since before all this world he burned up (√ *uṣ*) all evils, therefore he is a person (*pur-uṣ-a*). He who knows this, verily, burns up him who desires to be ahead of him.

2. He was afraid. Therefore one who is alone is afraid. This one then thought to himself: "Since there is nothing else than myself, of what am I afraid?" Thereupon, verily, his fear departed, for of what should he have been afraid? Assuredly it is from a second that fear arises.

3. Verily, he had no delight. Therefore one alone has no delight. He desired a second. He was, indeed, as large as a woman and a man closely embraced. He caused that self to fall into two pieces. Therefrom arose a husband and a wife. Therefore this [is true]: "Oneself is like a half-fragment,". . . Therefore this space is filled by a wife. He copulated with her. Therefrom human beings were produced.

4. [She changed herself into the forms of various animals; he did likewise.] . . . Thus, indeed, he created all. . . .

5. He knew: "I, indeed, am this creation, for I emitted it all from myself." Thence arose creation. Verily, he who has this knowledge comes to be in that creation of his.

7. Verily, at that time the world was undifferentiated. It became differentiated just by name and form, as the saying is: "He has such a name, such a form.". . .

He entered in here, even to the fingernail-tips, as a razor would be hidden in a razor-case, or fire in a fire-holder. Him they see not, for [as seen] he is incomplete. When

[Source: (The Creation of the Manifold World). Taken from the *BrihadāranyakaI Upanishad* (I.i.v.1–5, 10–14, 17), printed in R. E. Hume, trans., *The Thirteen Principal Upanishads* (London: Oxford University Press, 1921), chapters and verses cited].

breathing, he becomes breath by name; when speaking, voice; when seeing, the eye; when hearing, the ear; when thinking, the mind: these are merely the names of his acts. Whoever worships one or another of these—he knows not; for he is incomplete with one or another of these. One should worship with the thought that he is just one's self, for therein all these become one. That same thing, namely, this self, is the trace of this All, for by it one knows this All. . . . He finds fame and praise who knows this. . . .

10. Verily, in the beginning this world was *Brahman*.

    It knew only itself: "I am *Brahman*!" Therefore it became the All. Whoever of the gods became awakened to this, he indeed became it; likewise in the case of seers, likewise in the case of men. . . .

    . . . Whoever thus knows "I am *Brahman*!" becomes this All; even the gods have not power to prevent his becoming thus, for he becomes their self. . . .

11. Verily, in the beginning this world was *Brahman*, one only. Being one, he was not developed. He created still further a superior form, the *kṣātra*hood, even those who are *kṣātras* (rulers) among the gods: Indra, Varuṇa, Soma, Rudra, Parjanya, Yama, Mṛtyu, Īśāna. . . .

12. He was not yet developed. He created the *viś* (the commonalty), those kinds of gods that are mentioned in numbers: the Vasus, the Rudras, the Ādityas, the Viśvedevas, the Maruts.

13. He was not yet developed. He created the *śūdra* caste, Pūṣan. Verily, this [earth] is Pūṣan, for she nourishes (√ *puṣ*) everything that is.

14. He was not yet developed. He created still further a better form, Law (*dharma*). This is the power of the *kṣatriya* class; viz., Law. Therefore there is nothing higher than Law. So a weak man controls a strong man by Law, just as if by a king. Verily, that which is Law is truth. . . .

17. In the beginning this world was just the Self, one only. He wished: "Would that I had a wife; then I would procreate. Would that I had wealth; then I would offer sacrifice." So far as he does not obtain any one of these, he thinks that he is, assuredly, incomplete. Now his completeness is as follows: his mind truly is his self (*ātman*); his voice is his wife; his breath is his offspring; his eye is his worldly wealth, for with his eye he finds; his ear is his heavenly [wealth], for with his ear he hears it; his body (*ātman*), indeed, is his work, for with his body he performs work. . . .

E.11.2.b

The Cosmic Self-Evolution of Atman

The Taittiriya Upanishad

Together with the intelligent (*vipaścit*) Brahma

The course of evolution from the primal Ātman through the five elements to the human person

From this Soul (*Ātman*), verily, space (*ākāśa*) arose; from space, wind (*vāyu*); from wind, fire; from fire, water; from water, the earth; from the earth, herbs; from herbs, food; from food, semen; from semen, the person (*puruṣa*).

The person consisting of food

This, verily, is the person that consists of the essence of food. This, indeed, is his head; this, the right side; this, the left side; this, the body (*ātman*); this, the lower part, the foundation.

As to that there is also this verse:—

Second Anuvāka

Food the supporting, yet consuming, substance of all life; a phase of Brahma

From food, verily, creatures are produced Whatsoever [creatures] dwell on the earth.

Moreover by food, in truth, they live.

Moreover into it also they finally pass.[1]

For truly, food is the chief of beings;

Therefore it is called a panacea.[2]

Verily, they obtain all food

Who worship Brahma as food.

For truly, food is the chief of beings;

Therefore it is called a panacea.

From food created things are born.

By food, when born, do they grow up.

It both is eaten and eats things.

Because of that it is called food.[3]

The person consisting of breath

Verily, other than and within that one that consists of the essence of food is the self that consists of breath. By that this is filled. This, verily, has the form of a person. According to that one's personal form is this one with the form of a person. The in-breath (*prāṇa*) is its head; the diffused breath (*vyāna*), the right wing; the out-breath

[1] These first four lines are quoted in Maitri 6.11.
[2] *sarvausadham,* literally 'consisting of all sorts of herbs.'
[3] The last four lines recur at Maitri 6.12.

[Source: (The Evolution of Atman). Taken from the *Taittiriya Upanishad* (II.2), printed in R. E. Hume, trans. . . . Chapter and verse cited].

(*apāna*), the left wing; space, the body (*ātman*); the earth, the lower part, the foundation.

As to that there is also this verse:—

Third Anuvāka

Breath, the life of all living beings; a phase of Brahma

The gods do breathe along with breath (*prāṇa*),
As also men and beasts.
For truly, breath is the life (*āyus*) of beings
Therefore it is called the Life-of-all (*sarvāyuṣa*).
To a full life (*sarvam āyus*) go they
Who worship Brahma as breath.
For truly, breath is the life of beings;
Therefore it is called Life-of-all.

This, indeed, is its bodily self (*śarīra-ātman*), as of the former.

The person consisting of mind

Verily, other than and within that one that consists of breath is a self that consists of mind (*mano-maya*). By that this is filled. This, verily, has the form of a person. According to that one's personal form is this one with the form of a person. The Yajur-Veda is its head; the Rig-Veda, the right side; the Sāma-Veda, the left side; teaching,[4] the

[4] Possibly referring to the Brāhmanas, which contain 'teaching' concerning the sacrifices.

body (*ātman*); the Hymns of the Atharvans and Angirases, the lower part, the foundation.

As to that there is also this verse:—

Fourth Anuvāka

Inexpressible, fearless bliss; a phase of Brahma

Wherefrom words turn back,
Together with the mind, not having attained—
The bliss of Brahma he who knows,
Fears not at any time at all.

This, indeed, is its bodily self (*śarīra-ātman*), as of the former.

The person consisting of understanding

Verily, other than and within that one that consists of mind is a self that consists of understanding (*vijñāna-maya*). By that this is filled. This, verily, has the form of a person. According to that one's personal form is this one with the form of a person. Faith (*śraddhā*) is its head; the right (*ṛta*), the right side; the true (*satya*), the left side; contemplation (*yoga*), the body (*ātman*); might (*mahas*), the lower part, the foundation.

Study Questions

E.11.2 Upanishadic Cosmological Thoughts (ca. 800 or 500–300 BCE)

1. Explain who Atman was and the reason why he was motivated to create.
2. Explain *how* and *what* Atman created and His relationship to his creations.
3. Characterize and explain the *theoretical* nature of the Upanishadic cosmological thoughts as expounded in the *Brihad-Aranyaka Upanishad* and the *Taittiriya Upanishad* (clues: is it monotheistic or pantheistic or creationistic or evolutionistic?).

E. 11.3

A Jain Critique of Creationism

The Introduction

The Jains look back to Vardhamana Mahavira ("Great Hero") as their great teacher and the twenty-fourth and last Tirthankara ("Ford-maker") of the present age of cosmic life. Mahavira (599–527 BCE) was a contemporary of the Buddha (563–483 BCE), coming from the same region as the Buddha, often mentioned in the Buddhist sutras under the name "Nigantha Nataputta" ("the naked ascetic of the clan of the Jnatrikas").

Mahavira is said to have left home when he was thirty and wandered for twelve years within the Ganges valley in search of enlightenment. He achieved his full enlightenment at the age of forty-two and became a "'completed soul" (*kevalin*) and a "conqueror" (*jina*). It is from a derivative form of the title "*jina*" that the Jains took their name. After teaching for some thirty years and founding a disciplined order of naked monks, Mahavira died at the age of 72 at Pava, a village at a good distance from Patna, which is still one of the most sacred sites of Jain pilgrimage.

The Jain doctrine of reality is essentially dualistic, because the whole universe is traced back to the two everlasting, uncreated, and independent substances, the "*jiva*" (life or the conscious) and the "*ajiva*" (not-soul or the unconscious). All things, organic and inorganic, are composed of soul (jiva) and matter (ajiva), and, thus, equal and sacred. For the Jains, dualism is not just a matter of theory but also a matter of moral practice. They practice five fundamental virtues: (1) *ahimsa* (non-violence), (2) truth-speaking, (3) non-stealing, (4) chastity, and (5) non-attachment to worldly things. The ultimate end of life is to realize total self-liberation: "The phenomenal individual consists of a soul closely enmeshed in matter, and his salvation is to be found by freeing the soul from matter so that it may regain its pristine purity and enjoy omniscient self-sufficient bliss for all eternity." [Embree 1988:52]

The selection focuses on the Jain critique of creationism, which reveals also another significant aspect of the Jain philosophy, namely, the Jain dialectic. Jainism is essentially atheistic, even though, the existence of superhuman beings is not denied. It makes no philosophical compromise with theism as Mahāyāna Buddhism does.

Some foolish men declare that Creator made the world.

The doctrine that the world was created is ill-advised, and should be rejected.

If God created the world, where was he before creation?

If you say he was transcendent then, and needed no support, where is he now?

No single being had the skill to make this world—

For how can an immaterial god create that which is material?

How could God have made the world without any raw material?

If you say he made this first, and then the world, you are faced with an endless regression.

If you declare that this raw material arose naturally you fall into another fallacy,

For the whole universe might thus have been its own creator, and have arisen equally naturally.

If God created the world by an act of his own will, without any raw material,

Then it is just his will and nothing else—and who will believe this silly stuff?

If he is ever perfect and complete, how could the will to create have arisen in him?

If, on the other hand, he is not perfect, he could no more create the universe than a potter could.

If he is formless, actionless, and all-embracing, how could he have created the world?

Such a soul, devoid of all modality, would have no desire to create anything.

If he is perfect, he does not strive for the three aims of man,

So what advantage would be gained by creating the universe?

If you say that he created to no purpose, because it was his nature to do so, then God is pointless.

If he created in some kind of sport, it was the sport of a foolish child, leading to trouble.

If he created because of the karma of embodied beings [acquired in a previous creation]

He is not the Almighty Lord, but subordinate to something else. . . .

If out of love for living things and need of them he made the world,

Why did he not make creation wholly blissful, free from misfortune?

If he were transcendent he would not create, for he would be free;

Nor if involved in transmigration, for then he would not be almighty.

Thus the doctrine that the world was created by God

Makes no sense at all.

And God commits great sin in slaying the children whom he himself created.

If you say that he slays only to destroy evil beings, why did he create such beings in the first place? . . . .

Good men should combat the believer in divine creation, maddened by an evil doctrine.

Know that the world is uncreated, as time itself is, without beginning and end,

And is based on the principles, life and the rest.

Uncreated and indestructible, it endures under the compulsion of its own nature,

Divided into three sections—hell, earth, and heaven.

Study Questions

E.11.3 A Jain Critique of Creationism

1. Identify all the arguments and classify them into separate types.
2. Explain each argument and critically respond to it.
3. Critically respond to Jain anti-creationism and the Jain position on the *cosmological* nature of the universe.

CHAPTER 12

Ancient East Asian Taoist and Chinese Cosmological Traditions

The Taoist (v. Đạoist) Cosmological Thoughts of Ancient East Asia

The Cosmic Self-Evolution of the Tao (v. Đạo)

Lao Tzu (v. Lão Tử)

The Introduction

Those ideas that are of cosmological in nature in the *Tao Te Ching* (v. *Đạo Đức Kinh*) can be determined to have attained to the theoretical status of "cosmological thoughts" rather than that of a "cosmological theory." Less than ten passages that are found scattered in the text contain cosmological thoughts. A similar case is observed in the *Chou Yi Ching* (v. *Chu Dịch Kinh* [*Classic of Universal Change*]). It should be noted also that the theoretical contents of the cosmological thoughts in the two texts of ancient East Asian cultures are of the same cosmological nature.

Two explanations are possible. First, the authors of both texts did not develop their cosmological theories as textually self-evident. Second, they did develop their cosmological theories but were textually lost. Either new archaeological discoveries or new interpretative studies of all discovered archaeological finds may provide the final judgment. The Heger Type I bronze drums of the Vănlangian Civilization ("Đôngsơnian Civilization") may hold the key to a new direction of studies of this "origins" question. On this possibility, I am working on an article "The theoretical Relationships between the *Chou Yi Ching* (v. *Chu Dịch Kinh*) and the Heger Type I Bronze Drums."

[01] The Tao that can be told of is not the eternal Tao;
The name that can be named is not the eternal name.
The Nameless is the origin of Heaven and Earth;

The Named is the mother of all things [10,000 Things-ccp].
Therefore let there always be non-being so we may see their subtlety,
And let there always be being so we may see their outcome.

The two are the same,

But after they are produced, they have different names.

They both may be called deep and profound [v. *huyền*-ccp].

Deeper and more profound,

The door of all subtleties [v. *diệu*-ccp]!

[*TTC*:1 (which refers to *The Tao Te Ching* [v. *Đạo Đức Kinh*], chapter 1)]

[02] We look at it and do not see it;

Its name is The Invisible.

We listen to it and do not hear it;

Its name is The Inaudbile.

We touch it and do not find it;

Its name is The Subtle (formless).

These three cannot be further inquired into,

and hence merge into one.

Going up high, it is not bright, and coming down low, it is not dark.

Infinite and boundless, it cannot be given any name;

It reverts to nothingness.

This is called shape without shape,

Form [v. *tượng*-ccp] without object.

It is the Vague and Elusive.

Meet it and you will not see its head.

Follow it and you will not see its back.

Hold on to the Tao of old in order to master the things of the present.

From this one may know the primeval beginning [of the universe].

This is called the bond of [the-ccp] Tao. [*TTC*:14]

[03] Attain complete vacuity.

Maintain steadfast quietude.

All things come into being,

And I see thereby their return.

All things flourish,

But each one returns to its root.

This return to its root means tranquility.

It is called returning to its destiny.

To return to destiny is called the eternal (Tao).

To know the eternal is called enlightenment.

Not to know the eternal is to act blindly to result in disaster.

He who knows the eternal is all-embracing.

Being all-embracing, he is impartial.

Being impartial, he is kingly (universal).

Being kingly, he is one with Nature [Heaven-ccp].

Being one with Nature, he is in accord with [the-ccp] Tao.

Being in accord with [the-ccp] Tao, he is everlasting.

And is free from danger throughout his lifetime. [*TTC*:16]

[04] The all-embracing quality of the great virtue (*Te* [v. *Đức*]) follows

alone from the Tao.

The thing that is called [the-ccp] Tao is eluding and vague.

Vague and eluding, there is in it the form [v. *tượng*-ccp].

Eluding and vague, in it are things [v. *vật*-ccp].

Deep and obscure, in it is the essence [v. *tính*-ccp].

The essence is very real; in it are evidences [*tín*-ccp].

From the time of old until now, its name (manifestations) ever remains,

By which we may see the beginning of all things.

How do I know that the beginnings of all things are so?

Through this (Tao). [*TTC*:21]

[05] There was something [vật-ccp] undifferentiated and yet complete,

Which existed before heaven and earth.

Soundless and formless, it depends on nothing and does not change [constantly moving without self-exhaustion-ccp].

It operates everywhere and is free from danger.

It may be considered the mother of the universe.

I do not know its name; it is called Tao [It is known by the word "Tao" (v. Đạo)-ccp]

If forced to give it a name, I shall call it Great.

Now being great means functioning everywhere.

Functioning everywhere means far-reaching.

Being far-reaching means returning to the original point.

Therefore [the-ccp] Tao is great.

Heaven is great.

Earth is great.

And the king is also great.

There are four great things in the universe, and the king is one of them.

Man models himself after Earth.

Earth models itself after Heaven.

Heaven models itself after Tao.

And Tao models itself after Nature [v. *tự nhiên* (that which is natural)-ccp]. [*TTC*:25]

[06] The Great Tao flows everywhere.

It may go left or right.

All things depend on it for life, and it does not turn away from them.

It accomplishes its task, but does not claim credit for it.

It clothes and feeds all things but does not claim to be master over them.

Always without desires, it may be called The Small.

All things come to it and it does not master them; it may be called The Great.

Therefore (the sage) never strive himself for the great, and thereby the great is achieved. [*TTC*:34]

[07] [The-ccp] Tao invariably takes no action, and yet there is nothing left undone.

If kings and barons can keep it, all things will transform spontaneously.

If, after transformation, they should desire to be active,

I would restrain them with simplicity, which has no name.

Simplicity, which has no name, is free of desires.

Being free of desires, it is tranquil.

And the world will be at peace of its own accord. [*TTC*:37]

[08] Of old those that obtained the One:

Heaven obtained the One and became clear.

Earth obtained the One and became tranquil.

The spiritual beings obtained the One and became divine.

The valley obtained the One and became full.

The myriad things obtained the One and lived and grew.

Kings and barons obtained the One and became rulers of the empire.

What made them so is the One. [*TTC*:39]

[09] Reversion is the action of [the-cep] Tao.

Weakness is the function of [the ccp] Tao.

All things in the world come from being.

And being comes from non-being. [*TTC*:40]

[10] [The-ccp] Tao produces them (the ten thousand things).

Virtue [*Te* (v. *Đức*)-ccp] fosters them.

Matter gives them physical form.

The circumstances and tendencies complete them.

Therefore the ten thousand things esteem [the-ccp] Tao and honor virtue.

[The-ccp] Tao is esteemed and virtue [*Te* [v. *Đức*]-ccp] is honored without anyone's order.

They always come spontaneously.

Therefore [the-ccp] Tao produces them and virtue fosters them.

They rear them and develop them.

They give them security and give them peace.

They nurture them and protect them.

([The-ccp] Tao) produces them but does not take possession of them.

It acts, but does not rely on its own ability.

It leads them but does not master them.

This is called profound and secret virtue [*hsüan Te* (v. *huyền Đức*)-ccp]. [*TTC*:51]

[11] There was a beginning of the universe

Which may he called the Mother of the universe.

He who has found the mother (Tao)

And thereby understands her sons (things),

And having understood the sons,

Still keeps to its mother,

Will be free from danger throughout his lifetime. [*TTC*:52]

[12] [The-ccp] Tao is the storehouse of all things.

It is the good man's treasure and the bad man's refuge. [*TTC*:62]

Study Questions

E.12.1.a Lao Tzu (v. Lão Tử), The Cosmic Self-Evolution of the Tao (v. Đạo)

1. Reconstruct the two methods that Lao Tzu (v. Lão Tử) uses in his effort to discover the ontological Tao (v. Đạo) as the "beginning of Heaven and Earth" and the "Mother of the 10,000 Beings." One can be called "the phenomenological method" (ch. 16) and the other the "method of cause-effect analysis" (ch. 52, 40, 25).
2. Explain the Laoian (v. Lãoian) conception of the ontological Tao (v. Đạo) in its precosmological state of non-being and characterize its theoretical nature (ch. 25).
3. Explain the *cosmogonic* principles by which the Tao (v. Đạo) transforms itself from its precosmological state of Non-Being into its cosmological state of Being (ch. 42).
4. Where did Heaven, Earth, and the 10,000 Entities come from according to Lao Tzu (v. Lão Tử)? Explain and critique the Laoian (v. Lãoian) view of the cosmic evolution of the Tao (v. Đạo).

The "Great Form" of One, Two and Three

N. J. Girardot

The Introduction

The theoretical essence of Laoian cosmological thought is found in chapter 42. Lao Tzu (v. Lão Tử) begins the chapter "with an incredibly terse and numerically coded account of the Tao in relation to the process of creation" as stated by Girardot.

It is also one of the most famous passages in the *Tao Te Ching* (v. *Đạo Đức Kinh*). One of the reasons that make it famous is the ambiguity or unintelligibility of its "cosmogonic" meanings. What did Lao Tzu (v. Lão Tử) really mean? To solve the theoretical problematics of the numerology of Laoian cosmological thought, Professor Girardot offers his textually oriented interpretation. His carefully crafted method of textual analysis (hermeneutics) is recommended for students to use as the model for their textual interpretations and writings.

Chapter 42 opens with an incredibly terse and numerically coded account of the Tao in relation to the process of creation:

> The Tao gave birth to the one.
> The one gave birth to the two.
> The two gave birth to the three,
> And the three gave birth to the Ten Thousand Things.
> The Ten Thousand Things carry *yin*,
> And embrace *yang*;
> And achieve harmony by the mixing of *ch'i* [*ch'ung ch'i i wei ho*][1]

While the precise terminology of *hun-tun* is not present,[2] scholars have often called attention to the fact that in this chapter there is "a conception of origins still very close to mythology: the Heaven and Earth are conceived as the Father and Mother of creatures. The One is clearly an abstract designation of Chaos which is itself generally described as an undifferentiated unitary condition of the 'primordial breath'."[3] In Chapter 42, in other words, mythological images have been reduced to numerical cyphers but, possibly as Lévi-Strauss would have it, content has revealed its deep structure of binary opposition and a mythological "logic" of resolution. One and two are resolved by a third term of synthesis that suggests a certain kind of mythological intentionality.

An initial problem in dealing with this passage is that there appear to be several corruptions and possible anachronisms. The terns *yin* and *yang*, for example, did not come into technical use until a somewhat later period. Moreover, the first verse is possibly garbled because of the reference to the "Tao giving birth to the one." Throughout the rest of the *Tao Te Ching* the Tao is ordinarily identified with the one (cf. chapters 10, 14, 22, 39).[4] Also relevant, although by no means decisive, is that the *Huai Nan Tzu*, in quoting this passage, omits the opening verse.[5]

Despite these considerations, it is important to recognize that there is a long Chinese tradition of commentary concerning this passage and that it is very often seen to be the very crux of early Taoist ideology and cosmology.[6] Furthermore, the cosmological theory found in this chapter is "common to nearly all Chinese philosophical schools" including the early cosmological speculations of the *I Ching* down to Chu Hsi and the formulations of Neo-Confucianism.[7] What is more important here, however, is not that this theory, which is already abstract and philosophical in nature, forms a backdrop for nearly all of early Chinese cosmological thought but that it is used by the Taoists, both in the early texts and in the *Tao Tsang*, in a specific context of interpretation and application. It is especially in the Taoist tradition that the mythological and religiously relevant character of this passage is preserved and emphasized.[8]

By way of a preliminary analysis, the puzzling issue of the meaning of the "one, two, and three" must be addressed. This is more difficult than it might seem since traditional commentarial opinion holds that the "one" refers to the Tao or the *t'ai-shih* (the "Great Beginning"), the "two" to the heaven and earth (or *yin* and *yang*, *wu*[b] and *yu*[a]), and the "three" to the basic triad of heaven, earth, and man.[9] In the light of later Chinese philosophical speculation these identifications are

generally understandable and meaningful. In fact, they already indicate a certain indebtedness to mythological thought. But an approach more in harmony with the mystical "naturalism" of the *Tao Te Ching* suggests an even broader range of archaic mythological associations and images, especially in relation to the meaning of the ideas of "one" and "three."

Based on the cosmological context found throughout the *Tao Te Ching*, the idea of the "one" can be identified with the chaotic condition at the beginning that is variously called *hun-ch'eng*, *ch'ang-Tao*, "mother," or what the *Chuang Tzu* refers to as the "great unity" (*ta-t'ung*[a]). It is that which gave birth to the separate dual principles classically called either heaven and earth or *yin* and *yang*. In fact, the theme of "one" is specifically linked to the term *hun*[d] in chapter 14 of the *Tao Te Ching* where it is said that the "three things" of the mysterious Tao (its "dimness [*i*[c]]", and its "soundless [*hsi*[c]]", and "formless [*wei*[a]]" qualities) are "chaotically fused into the one [*hun erh wei i*]."[10] Chiang Hsi-ch'ang comments on this passage to the effect that the reference to the chaotic "oneness" of the Tao goes back to the cosmogonic theme of the great beginning (the *t'ai-ch'u*). This was the creation time before heaven and earth were separated, the period when there was only an undifferentiated condition of wholeness (*t'ung*[a]) without any particular sound, form, or substance.

Throughout the *Tao Te Ching*, this is known as the "great form" (*ta-hsiang*) of the "hidden" Tao, which is without any name (*wu-ming*) or shape (*wu-hsing*)—the amorphous, faceless condition of the mythological Emperor Hun-tun in chapter 7 of the *Chuang Tzu*.[11] According to the passage from chapter 41 that immediately precedes the creation scenario from chapter 42;

> Great form has no shape.
> Tao is hidden and nameless.
> Yet it is Tao alone that skillfully
> provides for all and brings them to
> perfection.[12]

Another technical use of the idea of "one" is found in the expression *pao-i*[a]—"embracing the one" or to return to an identity with the Tao as the source of life. The term *pao-i*[a] is found in chapter 10 where it has the initiatory connotation of returning to the condition of the child. In chapter 19 there is found the similar term of *pao-p'u*, and in chapter 39 the related term *te-i*. In chapter 22, it is said that the "sage embraces the one" (*pao-i*[a]) and in this case it indicates the condition of being identified with the Tao.[13]

This interpretation of "one" is in keeping with the traditional understanding, but the real problem is to decide the nature of the "three" or the "third term" that is said to give rise to the phenomenal universe of the Ten Thousand Things.[14] In distinction to the orthodox interpretation of this as "man" (man-king-emperor being the mediating factor between the hierarchical structure of the universe constituted by heaven and earth or the dual principles of *yin* and *yang*), the early Taoists maintained a less humanistically inclined and more ultimately cosmocentric interpretation.[15] Consequently, in this passage from chapter 42, it is probably wrong to attribute any particularly human characteristic to the idea of the "three."[16]

Granting that in the sequence of creation presented here it is not until after the creation of the "three" that there is the final creation of the phenomenal world, it would seem legitimate to consider the state of the "three" as a phase of creation still in some manner partaking of the original condition of primordial unity represented by the "one." The implication is that throughout the cosmogonic process of movement from one to two to three there is a paradise condition that returns to and duplicates the harmony of absolute unity. In a mythological sense the one, two, and three are all part of a precosmological period of development best designated by the idea of *hun-ch'eng* or *hun-tun*. The passage from three to the Ten Thousand Things represents a moment of rupture with, or fall from, the creation time. With the transition from the condition of three the paradise condition of unity is ended and the human world is created.

During the period of the "three" there is still the "chaos" condition of *hun-tun*, but it is a

condition that has its own internal principles of organization, change, order, and life. "Three" in this sense is the "paradise form" or "great form" (*ta-hsiang*, chap. 41) of cosmological unity that possesses the principles of duality in harmonious union and communication. There are "two" things present, but these two are mysteriously balanced by a third term that unites them perfectly. This condition of the three can at the same time be associated with the undifferentiated or embryonic condition of wholeness at the beginning, the time of "one" or *hun-ch'eng*, since in chapter 25 *hun*[d] is related to the time before the birth of heaven and earth and in chapter 14 it is the union of the "three." Here it is necessary to speak of the paradoxical idea of an "ordered chaos" since the idea of *hun*[d] (*hun-ch'eng* potentially or *hun-tun* in actuality) is not presented as an absolute chaos, disorder, or confusion. Rather, as seems to be manifest in these passages, there is a harmonious "order" of life and time inherent in the Taoist idea of the "chaos" period of creation.

Aside from the general associations with the theme of the chaos time of the Tao, the idea of the "three" or the "third term" can also be related to the idea of *ch'i*[a]—the mysterious life breath, ether-mist, fluidlike vapour, matter-energy, life force—that is said to pervade all things and constitute the connective matrix of microcosmic-macrocosmic solidarity.[17] This is suggested by the rest of the passage from chapter 42 that says that the working of the phenomenal universe is a cyclic interaction of the dual principles of *yin* and *yang* and that their interaction is achieved through a return to the mediation (blending, mixing—*ch'ung*[a]) of the *ch'i*[a]. *Ch'i*[a] is the active force or power of the empty center that links the "two" into a form that is equivalent to the original state of unity.

It can also be noted that the term *ch'ung*[a] is especially evocative of the chaotic watery void or "emptiness" (cf: chaps. 3, 4, 5) at the beginning of time. *Ch'ung*[a] connotes the idea of a "watery, bubbling" condition, "to clash or dash against," an "empty void" (such as the compound *ch'ung-hsü*), or "blended and complaisant" (i.e., the compound *ch'ung-ning* meaning "melted and congealed, blended together"). The terms *ch'ung*[a], *hsü*[a], and *ning*[a] are all specifically linked to the *hun-tun* theme in the early Taoist texts. Chapter 7 of the *Chuang Tzu*, for example, refers to the *t'ai-ch'ung*, which is said to be a particular stage of the process of returning to an identification with the Tao. In chapter 4 of the *Tao Te Ching*, *ch'ung*[a] (in the sense of an empty container) is used in relation to the terms *yüan*[c] ("bottomless pool") and *chan* ("deep" or "clear as water") and suggests an allusion to the watery, chaotic condition of the primordial Tao or the "ancestor [origin]" of the Ten Thousand Things (see below). Furthermore, terms like *hun-yüan*, *hun-lun*, and *hun-hun*[c] suggest the revolving motion of flowing water (especially in the sense of a whirlpool) or the turning of a wheel (cf. *yun*).[18]

In a comparative context there is a suggestion here that corresponds to some of the early Greek cosmogonies whereby the original seed, egg, or substance of creation experiences an internal precosmic process of organization and change— especially the motif of "swelling" to a point where its center is a "hollow" or "empty gap" infused with the invisible breath (*pneuma*) that is the source and basis of life.[19] Then comes the moment in the process when the cosmic embryo, sack, seed, gourd, or egg shapes itself into two constituent dual principles of the world and a perfect cosmos is formed. For the *Tao Te Ching* this perfect cosmos is the paradise condition of the "three" that still reflects the condition at the absolute beginning of creation. The "two" are separated by a chaotic void or hollow emptiness, but this void is alive with the invisible life-force of *ch'i*[a]. This is a paradise condition of total harmony cyclically ordering the interaction and synthesis of the dual principles through a continual process of going out (expansion, swelling, rising) and returning (contraction, coagulation, lowering) mediated by the "emptiness" of the center, that third term or primordial principle (frequently called the *yüan-ch'i* or *hun-yüan* in later Taoist texts) that constantly connects all phenomenal

forms, images, things with the Mother.[20] It is the empty gap of the center that allows for the original movement, sound, or flow of the life-principle.

The mythological underpinning of this passage and its technical association with the theme of *hun-tun* is brought out in chapter 7 of the *Huai Nan Tzu*, which offers an explicit reworking of the creation sequence of one, two, and three.[21] This chapter is really the earliest Chinese commentary on the creation paradigm presented by chapter 42 of the *Tao Te Ching*, and it is significant that it opens with the following cosmogonic refrain: "In the primeval period, before the time of heaven and earth, there was neither shape or form [*wu-hsing*]." These introductory verses are then followed with characteristically reduplicated terminology referring to the idea of the *hun-ch'eng* or *hun-tun* condition of unity before the appearance of the "two." The terms used are "*yao-yao ming-ming . . . mang wen mo min*," which are suggestive of the darkness, obscurity, and formlessness of this stage of the creation process.

That these terms may be identified with the theme of *hun-tun* is asserted by the next verse where this stage (or mythological god) of the creation time is called "*hung meng hung tung*." Aside from the possible homophonic identification of *hung-tung* with *hun-tun*, the use of the expression *hung-meng* is also mythologically relevant since it refers to a figure or deity that was identified with the mythic figure of Hun-tun.[22] The *Chuang Tzu*, for example, has a passage that expressly connects a certain Hung-meng with the theme of *hun-tun*.[23] More important, however, is that all of these terms for "chaos" are rooted in a congruent cosmogonic narrative related to the numerological sequence found in the *Tao Te Ching*.

A rather enigmatic verse follows the above lines saying that "no one knows its opening(s) [or gates]" (cf. *Chuang Tzu*, chap. 25), which might be taken as a mythic allusion to a condition resembling a closed, egglike unity internally harboring all of the fertile stirrings and sounds of creation. This passage continues by saying that "two spirits" (*erh shen*) were born but these "two" are still "one" by virtue of the fact that they are "born chaotically blended [*hun sheng*]."[24] There is now a "center" present that orders the "two" back into a condition that is equivalent with the "one" and gives a preliminary organization to the heaven and earth. In other words, the condition of "three" spoken of in the *Tao Te Ching* has been established as the paradise condition of the harmonious unity of the one and the two.

There is some repetitious garbling in the next few verses but the meaning seems relatively clear. Thus, the passage goes on to say that the two spirits that were previously a chaotic oneness now "separated and became *yin* and *yang* [*pieh wei yin-yang*]." These two opposite principles (the "hard and the soft") through their alternate separation and fusion then produced the Ten Thousand Things of the phenomenal world. As in chapter 42 of the *Tao Te Ching*, the condition of the three is necessary in order to give birth to the phenomenal world. This world was still a part of the paradise time since everything in it naturally reflected the oneness of the two things working together through the dialectical mediation of the *ch'i*[a].

The microcosm and macrocosm of reality were one solidarity and man's body reflects the sacred "order" of the universe: "the head is round, the shape of heaven, and the feet are square, the shape of earth." Man is linked with the source of life at the beginning of time since "heaven is his father and earth is his mother." It is at this point in the cosmogonic narrative that, in distinction to the *Tao Te Ching*, "man" can be equated with the idea of "three." Man's life is the creative product of the synthesis of "two" things and human nature basically reflects the threeness of the creation time since there must always be a blending of the two, or a return to the beginning, to maintain the fullness of life. Paraphrasing chapter 42 of the *Tao Te Ching*, this passage continues by saying that as the "two spirits" were originally blended and harmonized during the chaos time, so also do the

Ten Thousand Things bear *yin* and embrace *yang*. And the mixing [*ch'ung*[a]] of the *ch'i*[a] causes harmonious unity [*ho*]." This is the *creatio continua* principle of "Heaven's Constancy" (see *Tao Te Ching*, chap. 14).

Life itself is based on the alternation and commingling of the dualities through the circulation of the third term of *ch'i*[a]. This is the ruling principle or "bond" (*kang* and *ch'i*[a] of the Tao—see *Tao Te Ching*, chap. 14) that binds the sage to the sacred time of the beginning. The Tao is that which "dwells" always in the order of *hun-tun*, that realm of "empty nothingness" at the center of all things. The Tao, then, is the root of life, the original seed or egg of all creation, and all creative processes are a replication of the cosmogony. Embryological development inside the womb is but a miniature recreation of the world. This is indicated by the fact that after invoking the *Tao Te Ching's* creation paradigm of one, two, three, the *Huai Nan Tzu* goes on to discuss the "ten stages" of embryological development leading to birth, stating that in the seventh month the fetus is complete and whole. As will be shown in the next chapter, creation is completed in seven (or nine) stages of "boring" in the *Chuang Tzu's* story of Emperor Hun-tun.

For the *Huai Nan Tzu* the art of the Tao is specifically related to the art of nourishing or prolonging life, which seems to imply a reversal of the ordinary life current back to the original germ plasm of life, a *regressus ad uterum* that is a recapitulation of the cosmogony. Once the return to the absolute beginnings is accomplished, the Taoist can again experience the development of the one to the two to the three, or reach, in a sense, that seventh stage of fetal perfection where all is internally "complete" (*ch'eng*, or more accurately, *hun-ch'eng*). This symbolism has a bearing on the root meaning of other important Taoist expressions such as *pao-i*[a] ("to embrace the one") since the etymological associations for the term *pao*[b] are closely related to the idea of an enfolding, motherly embrace, or a womb/gourd/cocoon-like enclosure.

Based on the more mythologically detailed perspective gained from the *Huai Nan Tzu*, the creation scenario in chapter 42 of the *Tao Te Ching* might not be as corrupt as Duyvendak and others would have it, since the phases of Tao, one, two, and three indicate a particular type of cosmogonic narrative emphasizing a series of interrelated stages in the precosmic development of chaos.[25] Even though the *Huai Nan Tzu* leaves out the verse "the Tao gives birth to the one," it had already established with abundant mythological imagery that there was an "uncreated" stage before "one" appeared. Tao, one, two, and three are, however, all part of the overall centering process of the cosmogonic chaos-order. In this mythological sense, it may be said that the "'one' is born of Tao (chap. 42). . . . As the origin and seed of all things, 'one' still pertains to the dark, it is not yet born, thus it is even weaker than the infant."[26]

The Tao is that absolute mystery of the beginning, the "hidden Tao without name," "great form" (see chap. 41), or great "ancestor" (see chap. 4) that initiates the ordering process of creation. There is an internal development, imagined as a kind of germination process, producing a new state or level or organization that is depicted as a swelling or hollowing out of the original prime matter. This is simultaneously the stages of "one" and "three" (undifferentiated and ordered-chaos), which may be more readily named and numbered since there is now some organized dark form, some vague shape present.

Mythologically speaking, the overall sequence of Tao to three can be named as *hun-ch'eng* or *hun-tun*. *Hun-tun* is a mythological symbol of the paradisical creation time (the time of Tao, one, two, three before the creation of the profane human world, before the "fall") having primarily feminine characteristics in the *Tao Te Ching*. It is "chaotically whole," and as "one" it is identified with the Tao as the primordial source and ground of all life. As "three" it displays an organic "order" and internal process of gestation, which is manifested by the creative power of its "emptiness" or "nothingness."

As a final observation on chapter 42, I want to note that in a mythological sense *hun-tun* must be identified both with the symbolism of a female creatress (Hun-tun as the "Divine Bird" in the *Shan Hai Ching*?) and, at the same time, with her spawn (i.e., the analogous symbolism of embryo, egg, seed, gourd, drum, cocoon, sack, bellows, etc.).[27] In this way, Erkes's interpretation of chapter 42 as really meaning "the primal female laid the cosmic egg" is not entirely correct when applied to the overall implications of the *hun-tun* theme in the early Taoist texts.[28] To be sure, some primitive mythologies do require the existence of a primal mother or creature that gives birth to the cosmic egg; but this is not always the case, or even the most typical case, with cosmic egg mythologies when incorporated into mystical thought.[29] More commonly, cosmic egg myths answer the classic puzzle of the "chicken and egg" in favor of the priority of the egg and, in a very general way, this might also be said to be the answer given by early Taoism (especially in the *Chuang Tzu* and later texts) in its espousal of the *hun-tun* theme. The imagery of "mother," "dark female," "divine bird," "primal ancestor," and also the primordial couple, primal giant, and "mass of flesh" imagery, is all relevant to the development of early Taoist thought; but the essential mystical intentionality seems to favor the idea of creation always lacking any creator separate from the creation. It is better, then, to see the idea of "chicken" as inherent in the primordial "nothingness" of the egg. Or, perhaps in keeping with the *creatio continua* idea and Stoppard's observation, it is really the case of chickens and eggs "succeeding each other in one form or another literally for ever." This is the mystery of the "three," that "great form without shape" (chap. 41).

Notes

1. *LTCK* [Lao Tzu Chiao Ku-ccp], pp. 278–280 (including relevant Chinese commentaries); and Chan, pp. 176–177.
2. In the *Tao Te Ching* the terms *hun* and *tun* are used six times (see chaps. 14, 15, 20, 25, and 49).

3. Max Kaltenmark, "La naissance du monde en Chine," in *La Naissance du monde* (Paris: Editions du seuil, 1959), p. 464; see also Erkes, "Spüren," pp. 16–35; and Needham, *SCC*, 2:78.

4. For a discussion of Tao in relation to the idea of "one" see Chen, "Origin and Development of Being from Non-Being," pp. 409–410; and Robinet, *Commentaires*, passim. See also *LTCK*, p. 252, where Chiang Hsi-ch'ang specifically identifies the "one" of chapter 39 with the cosmogonic idea of the Tao and one found in chapter 42.

5. *HNTCS*, p. 99; and below.

6. See *LTCK*, pp. 278–280 and Erkes's discussion of relevant commentary, *"Spüren,"* pp. 16–28.

7. Chan, p. 176.

8. Erkes, "Spüren," p. 28; and below, chap. 9.

9. *LTCK*, p. 279. See also Fu's discussion, "Lao Tzu's Conception of Tao," pp. 376–379; and W. T. Chan, "Chu Hsi's Appraisal of Lao Tzu," *Philosophy East and West* 25 (1975): 132–141.

10. *LTCK*, pp. 76–78; and Chan, pp. 124–125. See below.

11. *LTCK*, p. 78; and Lo, "Primeval State," pp. 20 ff.

12. *LTCK*, p. 277; and Chan, p. 174.

13. For a discussion of some of the significance of these terms see M. Kaltenmark, "Ling-Pao: Note sur un term du Taoisme religieux," *Mélanges publiés par l'institute des hautes études chinoises* (Paris: University of France, 1960), pp. 581–582, 585–586.

14. Fung originally identified the one with *Chuang Tzu's ta-t'ung*[a,b], the two with heaven and earth, and the three with *yin* and *yang* and their harmonious interaction *(History* 1:178–179— originally written in the 1930s); but more recently he has put forth a more Marxian "dialectical" interpretation. See also Fu's discussion, "Lao Tzu's Conception of Tao," p. 376.

15. Within the context of imperial ideology Tung Chung-shu writes in his *Ch'un Ch'iu Fan Lu:* "Those who in ancient times invented writing drew three lines and connected them through the middle, calling the character 'king' [*wang*]. The three lines are heaven, earth, and man, and that which passes through the middle joins the principles of all three. Occupying the center of heaven, earth, and man, passing through and joining all three—if he is not a king, who can do this?"—Quoted from W. T. de

Bary, ed., *Sources of Chinese Tradition* (New York: Columbia University Press, 1960), vol. 1, p. 163. See also H. Wilhelm, "The Interaction of Heaven, Earth, and Man," in *Heaven, Earth and Man in the Book of Changes* (Seattle: University of Washington Press, 1977), pp. 126–163.

16. See, for example, Munro, *Concept of Man*, pp. 121 ff. By the time of the *Huai Nan Tzu*, however, the idea of "man" for "three" is a factor in the Taoist interpretation—see below.

17. See Jan Yün-hua's discussion in his "Problems of Tao," pp. 213–216. On the general concept of *ch'i*[a] see M. Yosida, "The Chinese Concept of Nature," in *Chinese Science,* ed. Shigeru Nakayama and Nathan Sivin (Cambridge: Massachusetts Institute of Technology Press, 1973), pp. 71–89.

18. See the *Tz'u Hai* on these terms, pp. 1741–1742, 1756–1757; and below, chapter 8.

19. The etymology of the Greek term for "chaos" is related to the idea of a "yawning gulf or gap," a "hollow," or "space." See above, "Introduction."

20. On the Taoist idea of the "original" or primordial *ch'i*[a], the *yüan-ch'i*, see H. Maspero, "Les Procedes de 'nourir de principe vital' dans la religion taoiste ancienne," *Journal Asiatique* 228 (1937): 206 ff. Maspero states that in later Taoism "this interior breath, personal to each man, is the Original Breath (*yüan-ch'i*). In man this Original Breath corresponds to the primordial breaths which before the creation formed the Heaven and Earth" (pp. 206–207).

21. *HNTCS*, pp. 99–100; and see below, chapter 5.

22. Mythologically, Hung-meng is related to Ti Hung (or Ti Chiang) who was said to be the father of Hun-tun (see the *Tso Chuan* in Legge, *Chinese Classics* 5: 279–283). The terms *hung*[b,c,d] mean "flood waters," "cinnabar" (the metallurgical theme is frequently a factor with all of these terms) or, as in the compound *tung-hung*, suggest the idea of "communication"—see F. S. Couvreur, *Dictionnaire classique* (reprint ed., Taipei: Kuangchi Press, 1966), p. 537.

23. See below, chapter 3.

24. As Kaltentnark suggests, this may be a reference to a cosmogony involving a primordial couple— see "Naissance du monde," p. 466. Cf. *Tao Te Ching,* chapter 14; and see below.

25. Duyvendak, p. 99.

26. Chen, "Development of Being from Non-Being," p. 409, n. 12.

27. See the following: Granet, *DL*, pp. 537–548 (sack, drum, owl, and bellows symbolism associated with *hun-tun*); Stein, "Jardins en miniature," pp. 42–80 (calabash gourd); Eberhard, *LC*, pp. 438–446 (egg, sack, thunder); and Lo, "Primeval State," pp. 287 ff. (gourd and cocoon). See also David Yu, "Creation Myth and Symbolism in Classical Taoism," pp. 492–495 (discussion of Lo's views).

28. Erkes, "Spüren," p. 35.

29. See below, chapter 6; and Long, *Alpha: The Myths of Creation* (New York: George Braziller, 1963). pp. 109 ff.

Study Questions

E.12.1.b N. J. Girardot, The "Great Form" of One, Two and Three

1. Describe the initial "considerations" that Girardot makes in preparation for his textual analysis of the passage from chapter 42 of the *Tao Te Ching* (v. *Đạo Đức Kinh*).
2. Discuss Girardot's explanation of the traditional Chinese interpretation of the meaning of "one, two and three."
3. Explain Girardot's interpretation of the meaning of "one, two and three" and compare it with the traditional Chinese interpretation.
4. Critique both the traditional Chinese interpretation and Girardot's interpretation of the Lãoian cosmogonic numerology of the one, the two, and the three, and offer your own interpretation.
5. Discuss Girardot's method of textual analysis as a model for your textual analysis of any text of Eastern philosophy that you examine.

An Explanation of the Diagram
of the Great Ultimate

Chou Tun-I (v. Châu Đôn Di)

The Introduction

Chou Tun-I (1017–1073 CE) is generally considered as the pioneer of Chinese Confucianism because in two short treatises, "the *T'ai-chi-t'u shuo* (An Explanation of the Diagram of the Great Ultimate) and the *T'ung-shu* (Penetrating the Book of Changes), he laid the pattern of metaphysics and ethics for later Neo-Confucianism." [Chan 1963:460]

The theoretical contents of "An Explanation of the Diagram of the Great Ultimate" point back to philosophical sources that Chou Tun-I takes as the origins of his cosmology and ontology. The first source is the Yi Li (v. Dịch Lý [Philosophy of Change]) of the *Chou Yi Ching* (v. *Chu Dịch Kinh*) as he reinterprets it in his *T'ung-shu*. Of the Yiian (v. Dịchian) concepts, he employs the concept of "Yi" (v. Dịch [Change]), the concept of "Great Ultimate" (T'ai Chi [v. Thái Cực]), the concept of Ch'ien (v. Kiền [the Powerful]), the concept of K'un (v. Khôn [the Wise]), and the concept of "Wu Hsing" [v. Ngũ Hành [Five Agents]). The second philosophical source that Chou uses for his cosmology is the Taoist concept of "Wu Chi" (v. Vô Cực [Ultimate of Non-Being]) and the "diagram" that he is said to have obtained from a Taoist priest.

By combining these two ancient East Asian philosophies with the moral concepts of ancient East Asian Confucianism, Chou Tun-I came up with a new cosmology, which reveals the creative power of his eclecticism.

It was during the T'ang Dynasty (618–907 CE) that Chinese Buddhism reached its apogee and Chinese Confucianism emerged as the intellectual movement that was to become dominant during the Sung (960–1279 CE) and Ming (1368–1643 CE) dynasties. This new intellectual movement of the Chinese Confucianist scholars, which is today commonly but mistakenly referred as "Neo-Confucianism," was traditionally known as the "Tao Hsueh Chia" (v. Đạo Học Gia [School of the Study of the Tao]). It is more appropriate to call it "Chinese Confucianism" as a notable Chinese revival of the two earlier Confucianist movements, namely, (1) "Han Confucianism" led by Tung Chung-Shu (ca. 179–104 BCE), and (2) "ancient East Asian Confucianism" founded by Confucius and developed further by Mencius and Hsun Tzu (v. Tuân Tử).

The Ultimate of Non-being and also the Great Ultimate (*T'ai-chi*)! The Great Ultimate through movement generates yang. When its activity reaches its limit, it becomes tranquil. Through tranquillity the Great Ultimate generates yin. When tranquillity reaches its limit, activity begins again. So movement and tranquillity alternate and become the root of each other, giving rise to the distinction of yin and yang, and the two modes are thus established.

By the transformation of yang and its union with yin, the Five Agents of Water, Fire, Wood, Metal, and Earth arise. When these five material forces (*ch'i*) are distributed in harmonious order, the four seasons run their course.

The Five Agents constitute one system of yin and yang, and yin and yang constitute one Great Ultimate. The Great Ultimate is fundamentally the Non-ultimate. The Five Agents arise, each with its specific nature.

When the reality of the Ultimate of Non-being and the essence of yin, yang, and the Five Agents come into mysterious union, integration ensues. *Ch'ien* (Heaven) constitutes the male element, and *k'un* (Earth) constitutes the female element. The interaction of these two material forces engenders and transforms the myriad things. The myriad things produce and reproduce, resulting in an unending transformation.

It is man alone who receives (the Five Agents) in their highest excellence, and therefore he is the most intelligent. His physical form appears, and his spirit develops consciousness. The five moral principles of his nature (humanity or *jen*, righteousness, propriety, wisdom, and faithfulness) are aroused by and react to, the external world and engage in activity; good and evil are distinguished; and human affairs take place.

The sage settles these affairs by the principles of the Mean, correctness, humanity, and righteousness (for the way of the sage is none other than these four) regarding tranquillity as fundamental. (Having no desire, there will therefore be tranquillity.) Thus he establishes himself as the ultimate standard for man. Hence the character of the sage is "identical with that of Heaven and Earth; his brilliancy is identical with that of the sun and moon; his order is identical with that of the four seasons; and his good and evil fortunes are identical with those of spiritual beings." The superior man cultivates these moral qualities and enjoys good fortune, where as the inferior man violates then and suffers evil fortune.

Therefore it is said that "yin and yang are established as the way of Heaven, the weak and the strong as the way of Earth, and humanity and righteousness as the way of man." It is also said that "if we investigate the cycle of things, we shall understand the concepts of life and death." Great is the *Book of Changes*! Herein lies its excellence! (*Chou Tzu ch'uan-shu*, chs. 1–2, pp. 4–32).

Study Questions

E.12.2 Chou Tun-I (v. Châu Đôn Di), An Explanation of the Diagram of the Great Ultimate

1. Explain how Heaven, Earth, and all things came into existence according to Chou Tun-I.
2. Identify each stage of the self-transformation of the Great Ultimate and explain the creative forces that were generated in each stage.
3. Concerning the Laoian (v. Laõian) influence over the later Chinese cosmological tradition, Professor Girardot writes: "the cosmological theory found in this chapter [chapter 42 of the *Đạo Đức Kinh*-ccp] is 'common to nearly all Chinese philosophical schools' including the early cosmological speculations of the *I Ching* down to Chu Hsi and the formulations of Neo-Confucianism." Explain whether this is true in the case of Chou Tun-I's theory of world evolution.
4. Explore the possible impact the Laoian and Chouian ontologies and cosmologies may have upon the natural environment and the treatment of animals if people accept them.
5. Characterize the theoretical nature of the Chouian cosmology in comparison with those of the Upanishadic and Laoian (v. Laõian) cosmological thoughts.

Part F

Eastern Views of the Human Self and Self-Knowledge

CHAPTER 13

Hindu Views of the Spiritual Self and the Self-Realization of Moksha

The Upanishadic Doctrines of the Self

The Philosophical Education of God Indra and Demon Virocana

The Chandogya Upanishad

The Introduction

The *Upanishads* contain the first philosophy that had emerged in the northern region of ancient South Asia as a result of the "first paradigm shift" from Vedic religious beliefs to Upanishadic philosophical consciousness.

This first textual selection is from the *Chandogya*, the oldest and most well known of the *Upanishads*. The *Chandogya* is so called because it is derived from "chandoga," the name of certain Upanishadic rishis specializing in the *Sama Veda*. The method that the author(s) of the *Chandogya Upanishad* employs for the metatheological education of Indra and Virocana can be termed *the method of critical thinking*, which is essential for students of philosophy and life.

Seventh Khaṇḍa

The progressive instruction of Indra by Prajāpati concerning the real self

1. 'The Self (Ātman), which is free from evil, ageless, deathless, sorrowless, hungerless, thirstless, whose desire is the Real, whose conception is the Real—He should be searched out, Him one should desire to understand. He obtains all worlds and all desires who has found out and who understands that Self.'—Thus spake Prajāpati.

2. Then both the gods and the devils (*deva-asura*) heard it. Then they said: 'Come! Let us search out that Self, the Self by searching out whom one obtains all worlds and all desires!'

Then Indra from among the gods went forth unto him, and Virocana from among the devils. Then, without communicating with each other, the two came into the presence of Prajāpati, fuel in hand.[1]

[1] In token of discipleship.

[Source: Taken from the *Chandogya Upanishad* (VIII.7–12), printed in R. E. Hume, trans., *The Thirteen Principal Upanishads* (London: Oxford University Press, 1921), pp. 268–72].

3. Then for thirty-two years the two lived the chaste life of a student of sacred knowledge (*brahmacarya*).

Then Prajāpati said to the two: 'Desiring what have you been living?'

Then the two said: '"The Self (Ātman), which is free from evil, ageless, deathless, sorrowless, hungerless, thirstless, whose desire is the Real, whose conception is the Real—He should be searched out, Him one should desire to understand. He obtains all worlds and all desires who has found out and who understands that Self."—Such do people declare to be your words, sir. We have been living desiring Him.'

4. Then Prajāpati said to the two: 'That Person who is seen in the eye—He is the Self (Ātman) of whom I spoke.[2] That is the immortal, the fearless. That is Brahma.'

'But this one, sir, who is observed in water and in a mirror—which one is he?'

'The same one, indeed, is observed in all these,' said he.

Eighth Khaṇḍa

1. 'Look at yourself in a pan of water. Anything that you do not understand of the Self, tell me.'

Then the two looked in a pan of water.

Then Prajāpati said to the two: 'What do you see?'

Then the two said: 'We see everything here, sir, a Self corresponding exactly, even to the hair and fingernails!'

2. Then Prajāpati said to the two: 'Make yourselves well-ornamented, well-dressed, adorned, and look in a pan of water.'

Then the two made themselves well-ornamented, well-dressed, adorned, and looked in a pan of water.

Then Prajāpati said to the two: 'What do you see?'

3. Then the two said: 'Just as we ourselves are here, sir, well-ornamented, well-dressed, adorned—so there, sir, well-ornamented, well-dressed, adorned.'

'That is the Self,' said he. 'That is the immortal, the fearless. That is Brahma.'

Then with tranquil heart (*śānta-hṛdaya*) the two went forth.

4. Then Prajāpati glanced after them, and said: 'They go without having comprehended, without having found the Self (Ātman). Whosoever shall have such a doctrine (*upaniṣad*), be they gods or be they devils, they shall perish.'

Then with tranquil heart Virocana came to the devils. To them he then declared this doctrine (*upaniṣad*): 'Oneself (*atman*)[3] is to be made happy here on earth. Oneself is to be waited upon. He who makes his own self (*ātman*) happy here on earth, who waits upon himself—he obtains both worlds, both this world and the yonder.'

5. Therefore even now here on earth they say of one who is not a giver, who is not a believer (*a-śraddadhāna*), who is not a sacrificer, 'Oh! devilish (*āsura*)!' for such is the doctrine (*upaniṣad*) of the devils. They adorn the body (*śarīra*) of one deceased with what they have begged, with dress, with ornament, as they call it, for they think that thereby they will win yonder world.

Ninth Khaṇḍa

1. But then Indra, even before reaching the gods, saw this danger: 'Just as, indeed, that one [i.e. the bodily self] is well-ornamented when this body (*śarīra*) is well-ornamented, well-dressed when this is well-dressed, adorned when this is adorned, even so that one is blind when this is

---

[2] Or the text might be translated: '"That Person who is seen in the eye—He is the Self," said he. "That is the immortal, the fearless. That is Brahma."' Such quite certainly is the translation of the very same words which have already occurred in 4.15.1.

[3] Besides meaning 'oneself,' as it evidently does both in this paragraph and in the beginning of the following paragraph, the word *ātman* may also have the connotation 'one's body,' which seems to be the meaning in the latter half of the following paragraph.

blind, lame when this is lame, maimed when this is maimed. It perishes immediately upon the perishing of this body. I see nothing enjoyable in this.'

2. Fuel in hand, back again he came. Then Prajāpati said to him: 'Desiring what, O Maghavan ('Munificent One'), have you come back again, since you along with Virocana went forth with tranquil heart?'

Then he said: 'Just as, indeed, that one [i.e. the bodily self] is well-ornamented when this body is well-ornamented, well-dressed when this is well-dressed, adorned when this is adorned, even so it is blind when this is blind, lame when this is lame, maimed when this is maimed. It perishes immediately upon the perishing of this body. I see nothing enjoyable in this.'

3. 'He is even so, O Maghavan,' said he. 'However, I will explain this further to you. Live with me thirty-two years more.'

Then he lived with him thirty-two years more.

To him [i.e. to Indra] he [i.e. Prajāpati] then said:—

Tenth Khaṇḍa

1. 'He who moves about happy in a dream— he is the Self (Ātman),' said he. 'That is the immortal, the fearless. That is Brahma.'

Then with tranquil heart he [i.e. Indra] went forth.

Then, even before reaching the gods, he saw this danger: 'Now, even if this body is blind, that one [i.e. the Self, Ātman] is not blind. If this is lame, he is not lame. Indeed, he does not suffer defect through defect of this. [2] He is not slain with one's murder. He is not lame with one's lameness. Nevertheless, as it were (iva), they kill him; as it were, they unclothe[4] him; as it were, he comes to experience what is unpleasant; as it were, he even weeps. I see nothing enjoyable in this.'

---

[4] Reading vicchādayanti with all the texts, from √ chad. However, the Com. explains as 'they chase.' The parallel passage in Bṛih. 4.3.20 has vicchāyayati 'tear to pieces,' from √ chā.

3. Fuel in hand, back again he came. Then Prajāpati said to him: 'Desiring what, O Maghavan, have you come back again, since you went forth with tranquil heart?'

Then he said: 'Now, sir, even if this body is blind, that one [i.e. the Self] is not blind. If this is lame, he is not lame. Indeed, he does not suffer defect through defect of this. [4] He is not slain with one's murder. He is not lame with one's lameness. Nevertheless, as it were, they kill him; as it were, they unclothe him; as it were, he comes to experience what is unpleasant; as it were, he even weeps. I see nothing enjoyable in this.'

'He is even so, O Maghavan,' said he. 'However, I will explain this further to you. Live with me thirty-two years more.'

Then he lived with him thirty-two years more.

To him [i.e. to Indra] he [i.e. Prajāpati] then said:—

Eleventh Khaṇḍa

1. 'Now, when one is sound asleep, composed, serene, and knows no dream—that is the Self (Ātman),' said he. 'That is the immortal, the fearless. That is Brahma.'

Then with tranquil heart he went forth.

Then, even before reaching the gods, he saw this danger: 'Assuredly, indeed, this one does not exactly know himself (ātmānam) with the thought "I am he," nor indeed the things here. He becomes one who has gone to destruction. I see nothing enjoyable in this.'

2. Fuel in hand, back again he came. Then Prajāpati said to him: 'Desiring what, O Maghavan, have you come back again, since you went forth with tranquil heart?'

Then he [i.e. Indra] said: 'Assuredly, this [self] does not exactly know himself with the thought "I am he," nor indeed the things here. He becomes one who has gone to destruction. I see nothing enjoyable in this.'

3. 'He is even so, O Maghavan,' said he. 'However, I will explain this further to you, and there is nothing else besides this. Live with me five years more.'

Then he lived with him five years more.—That makes one hundred and one years. Thus it is that people say, 'Verily, for one hundred and one years Maghavan lived the chaste life of a student of sacred knowledge (*brahmacarya*) with Prajāpati.'—

To him [i.e. to Indra] he [i.e. Prajāpati] then said:—

Twelfth Khaṇḍa

1. 'O Maghavan, verily, this body (*śarīra*) is mortal. It has been appropriated by Death (Mṛityu). [But] it is the standing-ground of that deathless, bodiless Self (Ātman). Verily, he who is incorporate has been appropriated by pleasure and pain. Verily, there is no freedom from pleasure and pain for one while he is incorporate. Verily, while one is bodiless, pleasure and pain do not touch him.

2. The wind is bodiless. Clouds, lightning, thunder—these are bodiless. Now as these, when they arise from yonder space and reach the highest light, appear each with its own form, [3] even so that serene one (*samprasāda*), when he rises up from this body (*śarīra*) and reaches the highest light, appears with his own form. Such a one is the supreme person (*uttama puruṣa*). There such a one goes around laughing, sporting, having enjoyment with women or chariots or friends, not remembering the appendage of this body. As a draft-animal is yoked in a wagon, even so this spirit (*prāṇa*) is yoked in this body.

4. Now, when the eye is directed thus toward space, that is the seeing person (*cākṣuṣa puruṣa*); the eye is [the instrument] for seeing. Now, he who knows "Let me smell this"—that is the Self (Ātman); the nose is [the instrument] for smelling. Now, he who knows "Let me utter this"—that is the Self; the voice is [the instrument] for utterance. Now, he who knows "Let me hear this"—that is the Self; the ear is [the instrument] for hearing.

5. Now, he who knows "Let me think this"—that is the Self; the mind (*manas*) is his divine eye (*daiva cakṣu*). He, verily, with that divine eye the mind, sees desires here, and experiences enjoyment.

6. Verily, those gods who are in the Brahma-world reverence that Self. Therefore all worlds and all desires have been appropriated by them. He obtains all worlds and all desires who has found out and who understands that Self (Ātman).'

Thus spake Prajāpati—yea, thus spake Prajāpati!

Study Questions

F.13.1.a *The Chandogya Upanishad*, The Philosophical Education of God Indra and Demon Virocana

1. Describe the critical method that Indra uses to discover the flaw of each instruction that he receives from Prajāpati and compare it with Virocana's approach.
2. Discuss each doctrine of the Self that Indra learns and characterize its theoretical nature (clue: materialistic or idealistic).
3. Analyze the final doctrine of the Self that Indra accepts to be true and formulate a philosophical critique.
4. Explain whether it is true that one would become completely desireless and happy having acquired the philosophical knowledge of the Self as claimed by Prajāpati.

F.13.1.b

[handwritten: Sum up of Upanishad ~ Analigy ~ compare of each person.]

The Multiple Coverings of the Person

The Katha Upanishad

The Introduction

The *Katha Upanishad* is called after the name of a school of the *Black Yajur Veda*. It is one of the most philosophical texts of the *Upanishads*. Besides the philosophical dialogue between Naciketas (a young boy) and Yama (the god of hell) on the question of the immortality of the Self and the ultimate end of life that it contains, the *Katha Upanishad* also offers the most interesting doctrine of the person. By using the method of explaining by analogy, the *Katha Upanishad* identifies the five different coverings or layers that constitute the being of a person in comparison with the five parts of a chariot, explains their functional relationships, and the divine status of one's soul.

Third Valli

Parable of the individual soul in a chariot

3. Know thou the soul (*ātman*, self) as riding in a chariot, *[handwritten: soul is a self → Atman]*
The body as the chariot. *[handwritten: Analigy]*
Know thou the intellect (*buddhi*) as the chariot-driver,
And the mind (*manas*) as the reins.

4. The senses (*indriya*), they say, are the horses;
The objects of sense, what they range over.
The self combined with senses and mind
Wise men call 'the enjoyer' (*bhoktṛ*).

[handwritten: need to understand of your sense / compare sense with horses,]

[handwritten: Atman, allow sense to control you]

5. He who has not understanding (*a-vijñāna*),
Whose mind is not constantly held firm—
His senses are uncontrolled,
Like the vicious horses of a chariot-driver.

6. He, however, who has understanding,
Whose mind is constantly held firm—
His senses are under control,
Like the good horses of a chariot-driver:

Intelligent control of the soul's chariot needed to arrive beyond reincarnation

7. He, however, who has not understanding,
Who is unmindful and ever impure,

[Source: Taken from the *Katha Upanishad* (III.2–12), printed in R. E. Hume; trans., *The Thirteen Principal Upanishads* (London: Oxford University Press, 1921), pp. 351–52].

223

Reaches not the goal,
But goes on to reincarnation (*saṃsāra*).

8. He, however, who has understanding,
Who is mindful and ever pure,
Reaches the goal
From which he is born no more.

9. He, however, who has the understanding of a chariot-driver,
A man who reins in his mind—
He reaches the end of his journey,
That highest place of Vishnu. → *most powerful Hindu goal.*

The order of progression to the supreme Person

10. Higher than the senses are the objects of sense.

An alagy

Higher than the objects of sense is the mind (*manas*);
And higher than the mind is the intellect (*buddhi*).
Higher than the intellect is the Great Self (Ātman).

11. Higher than the Great is the Unmanifest (*avyakta*).
Higher than the Unmanifest is the Person.
Higher than the Person there is nothing at all.
That is the goal. That is the highest course.

The subtle perception of the all-pervading Soul

12. Though He is hidden in all things,
That Soul (Ātman, Self) shines not forth.
But he is seen by subtle seers
With superior, subtle intellect.

— way of ball.
— Does not make itself know.

Study Questions

F.13.1.b *The Katha Upanishad*, The Multiple Coverings of the Person

1. Identify the different coverings of a person and discuss their respective function and relationship by the power of the "chariot" analogy.
2. Since the whole person or any other organism came from the Self, is it philosophically justified to accept the *internal duality* between the Self and the Not-Self as conceptualized by the author of the *Katha Upanishad*? Critically explain.
3. "He is hidden in all things"! If this Upanishadic thesis were accepted, how should we treat the natural environment and all non-human species?

F.13.1.c

The Four States of the Self

The Māndukya Upanishad

The Introduction

The *Māndukya Upanishad* is named after the sage-teacher Māndukya. It testifies to the strong monistic orientation since the whole universe is reduced to and derived from one single word "OM!"

Of theoretical significance is the doctrine of the two types of knowledge, a higher (*para*) and a lower (*apara*), and the doctrine of the four states of the Self. The practice of yoga is believed to enable one to realize the highest self-knowledge: "He is the Self (Atman)." That is to say one can know the truth that one's innermost is God and can prove it to be subjectively true. This doctrine has given later Indian philosophy and psychology the famous doctrine of the four states of consciousness.

1. *Om!*—This syllable[1] is this whole world.
    Its further explanation is:—
    The past, the present, the future—everything is just the word *Om.*
    And whatever else that transcends threefold time[2]—that, too, is just the word *Om.*

2. For truly, everything here is Brahma; this self (*ātman*) is Brahma. This same self has four fourths.

3. The waking state (*jāgarita-sthāna*), outwardly cognitive, having seven limbs,[3] having nineteen mouths,[4] enjoying the gross (*sthūla-bhuj*), the Common-to-all-men (*vaiśvānara*), is the first fourth.

[1] Inasmuch as akṣaram means also 'imperishable,' the word may in this connection be used with a double significance, namely, 'This imperishable syllable . . . '
[2] A similar phrase occurs at Śvet. 6.5.b.

[3] Śankara refers to the enumeration of the several parts of the universal (*vaiśvānara*) Self at Chānd. 5.18.2; there, however, the list is longer than seven. The exact significance of the number here is uncertain.
[4] Śankara explains this to mean: the five organs of sense (*buddhīndriya*), namely those of hearing, touch, sight, taste, and smell, the five organs of action (*karmen-driya*), namely those of speech, handling, locomotion, generation, and excretion, the five vital breaths (*prāna*), the sensorium (*manas*), the intellect (*buddhi*), egoism (*ahamkāra*), and thinking (*citta*).

[Source: Taken from the *Māndukya Upanishad*, printed in R. E. Hume, trans., *The Thirteen Principal Upanishads* (London: Oxford University Press, 1921), pp. 391–93].

4. The dreaming state (*svapna-sthāna*), inwardly cognitive, having seven limbs, having nineteen mouths, enjoying the exquisite (*pravivikta-bhuj*), the Brilliant (*taijasa*), is the second fourth.

5. If one asleep desires no desire whatsoever, sees no dream whatsoever,[5] that is deep sleep (*suṣupta*).

   The deep-sleep state (*suṣupta-sthāna*), unified (*ekī-bhūta*),[6] just (*eva*) a cognition-mass (*prajñāna ghana*),[7] consisting of bliss (*ānanda-maya*),[8] enjoying bliss (*ānanda-bhuj*), whose mouth is thought (*cetas-*), the Cognitional (*prājña*), is the third fourth.

6. This is the lord of all (*sarveśvara*).[9] This is the all-knowing (*sarva jña*).[10] This is the inner controller (*antaryāmin*).[11] This is the source (*yoni*)[12] of all, for this is the origin and the end (*prabhavāpyayau*)[13] of beings.

7. Not inwardly cognitive (*antah prajña*), not outwardly cognitive (*bahih prajña*), not both-wise cognitive (*ubhayatah-prajña*), not a cognition-mass (*prajñāna-ghana*), not cognitive (*prajña*), not non-cognitive (*a-prajña*), unseen (*a-dṛṣṭa*), with which there can be no dealing (*a-vyavahārya*), ungraspable (*a-grāhya*), having no distinctive mark (*a-lakṣaṇa*), non-thinkable (*a-cintya*), that cannot be designated (*a-vyapadeśya*), the essence of the assurance of which is the state of being one with the Self[14] (*ekātmya-*

pratyaya-sāra), the cessation of development (*prapañcopasama*), tranquil (*śānta*), benign (*śiva*), without a second (*a-dvaita*)—[such] they think is the fourth.[15] He is the Self (Ātman). He should be discerned.

8. This is the Self with regard to the word *Om*, with regard to its elements. The elements (*mātra*) are the fourths; the fourths, the elements: the letter *a*, the letter *u*, the letter *m*.[16]

9. The waking state, the Common-to-all-men, is the letter *a*, the first element, from *āpti* ('obtaining') or from *ādimatvā* ('being first').

   He obtains, verily, indeed, all desires, he becomes first—he who knows this.

10. The sleeping state, the Brilliant, is the letter *u*, the second element, from *utkarṣa* ('exaltation') or from *ubhayatā* ('intermediateness').

    He exalts, verily, indeed, the continuity of knowledge; and he becomes equal[17] (*samāna*); no one ignorant of Brahma is born in the family of him who knows this.

11. The deep-sleep state, the Cognitional, is the letter *m*, the third element, from *miti* ('erecting') or from *apīti*[18] ('immerging').

---

[5] The part of the sentence up to this point has occurred already in Bṛih. 4.3.19.

[6] A detailed description of the condition of being 'unified' occurs at Bṛih. 4.4.2.

[7] This compound has already occurred in Bṛih. 4.5.13.

[8] A description of the self 'consisting of bliss' occurs in Tait. 2.5. It is declared to be the acme of attainment over every other form of self at Tait. 2.8.1 and 3.10.5.

[9] A phrase in Bṛih. 4.4.22.

[10] A phrase in Muṇḍ. 1.1.9; 2.2.7.

[11] The subject of discourse in Bṛih. 3.7.

[12] Literally, 'womb.'

[13] A phrase in Kaṭha 6.11.

[14] Or, according to the reading *ekātma-*, 'the oneness of the Self' or 'one's own self.'

[15] The designation here used for the 'fourth,' or superconscious, state is *caturtha*, the usual and regular form of the ordinal numeral adjective. In Bṛih. (at 5.14.3, 4, 6, 7) it is named *turiya*, and in Maitri (at 6.19; 7.11.7) *turya*—variant forms of the same ordinal. All later philosophical treatises have the form *turīya*, which came to be the accepted technical term.

[16] In Sanskrit the vowel *o* is constitutionally a diphthong, contracted from *a + u*. *Om* therefore may be analyzed into the elements *a + u + m*.

[17] Either (1) in the sense of 'equable,' i.e. unaffected in the midst of the pairs of opposites (*dvandva*); or (2) in the sense of 'equitable,' i.e. impartial, alike, indifferent to both friend and foe; or (3) in the sense of 'equalized,' i.e. with the universe, which a knower understands exists only as his Self's consciousness; or even (4) in the very common sense of 'same,' i.e. the same as that which he knows.

All these four (and more) are possible interpretations. They evidence how vague (or, how pregnant—it is urged) are some of the statements in the Upanishads, and how capable therefore of various interpretations.

Of each of sections 8–10 there are, similarly, several interpretations.

[18] Possibly as a synonym for another meaning of *miti* (derived from √ *mi*, *mināti*), 'destroying' or 'perishing.'

He, verily, indeed, erects (*minoti*) this whole world,[19] and he becomes its immerging—he who knows this.

12. The fourth is without an element, with which there can be no dealing, the cessation of de-velopment, benign, without a second. Thus *Om* is the Self (Ātman) indeed. He who knows this, with his self enters the Self [20]—yea, he who knows this!

[19] That is, out of his own consciousness—according to the philosophic theory of subjective idealism expounded in the Upanishads.

[20] This is a phrase which has previously occurred at VS. 32.11.

Study Questions

F.13.1.c *The Māndukya Upanishad*, The Four States of the Self

1. Discuss the four states of the Self and how they are related.
2. Discuss whether the Atman can be "discerned" by the method claimed in the *Māndukya Upanishad* 1–12.

F.13.2

The Later Hindu Doctrine of the Self

The Bhagavad Gita

The Introduction

The *Bhagavad Gita* (*Song of the Lord*) is the most beloved poem of the Hindus. It may be considered the most typical expression of Hinduism as a whole and an authoritative bible of the popular cult of Krishna in particular. Its authorship is normally attributed to Vyāsa.

Concerning its theoretical origins, Radhakrishnan and Moore write: "The *Gita* derives its main inspiration from the Upanishads and integrates into a comprehensive synthesis the different elements of the Vedic cult of sacrifice, the Upanishadic teaching of the Absolute Brahman, the Bhagavata theism, the Samkhya dualism, and the Yoga meditation." [Radhakrishnan and Moore 1957:101]

What is most interesting about this eclectic synthesis is the intellectual skills of its author(s) to situate the *discourse* on religion, psychology, philosophy, political philosophy, and war in the context of the great final battle between the two warring camps of the ruling house Mahābhārata. The ultimate end is the realization of self-enlightenment through *political karma yoga* rather than any other path (*marga*). The *Gita* thus differs from the *Upanishads* since the latter takes social escape and the path of knowledge as the best way of life. Instead, the *Gita* teaches that each person has the sacred *dharma* (moral duty) to promote "*lokasangraha*," namely, the stability, security, solidarity, and progress of society.

Sri Krishna:

The body is called a field, Arjuna; he who knows it is called the Knower of the field. This is the knowledge of those who know. I am the Knower of the field in everyone, Arjuna. Knowledge of the field and its Knower is true knowledge.

Listen and I will explain the nature of the field and how change takes place within it. I will also describe the Knower of the field and his power. These truths have been sung by great sages in a variety of ways, and expounded in precise arguments concerning Brahman.

The field, Arjuna, is made up of the following: the five areas of sense perception; the five elements; the five sense organs and the five organs of action; the three components of the mind: *manas*, *buddhi*, and *ahamkara*; and the undifferentiated energy from which all these evolved. In this field arise desire and aversion, pleasure and pain, the body, intelligence, and will.

Those who know truly are free from pride and deceit. They are gentle, forgiving, upright, and pure, devoted to their spiritual teacher, filled with inner strength, and self-controlled. Detached from sense objects and self-will, they have learned the painful lesson of separate birth and suffering, old age, disease, and death.

Free from selfish attachment, they do not get compulsively entangled even in home and family. They are even-minded through good fortune and bad. Their devotion to me is undivided. Enjoying solitude and not following the crowd, they seek only me. This is true knowledge, to seek the Self as the true end of wisdom always. To seek anything else is ignorance.

I will tell you of the wisdom that leads to immortality: the beginningless Brahman, which can be called neither being nor nonbeing.

It dwells in all, in every hand and foot and head, in every mouth and eye and ear in the universe. Without senses itself, it shines through the functioning of the senses. Completely independent, it supports all things. Beyond the gunas, it enjoys their play.

It is both near and far, both within and without every creature; it moves and is unmoving. In its subtlety it is beyond comprehension. It is indivisible, yet appears divided in separate creatures. Know it to be the creator, the preserver, and the destroyer.

Dwelling in every heart, it is beyond darkness. It is called the light of lights, the object and goal of knowledge, and knowledge itself.

I have revealed to you the nature of the field and the meaning and object of true knowledge. Those who are devoted to me, knowing these things, are united with me.

Know that prakriti and Purusha are both without beginning, and that from prakriti come the gunas and all that changes. Prakriti is the agent, cause, and effect of every action, but it is Purusha that seems to experience pleasure and pain.

Purusha, resting in prakriti, witnesses the play of the gunas born of prakriti. But attachment to the gunas leads a person to be born for good or evil.

Within the body the supreme Purusha is called the witness, approver, supporter, enjoyer, the supreme Lord, the highest Self.

Whoever realizes the true nature of Purusha, prakriti, and the gunas, whatever path he or she may follow, is not born separate again.

Some realize the Self within them through the practice of meditation, some by the path of wisdom, and others by selfless service. Others may not know these paths; but hearing and following the instructions of an illumined teacher, they too go beyond death.

Whatever exists, Arjuna, animate or inanimate, is born through the union of the field and its Knower.

He alone sees truly who sees the Lord the same in every creature, who sees the Deathless in the hearts of all that die. Seeing the same Lord everywhere, he does not harm himself or others. Thus he attains the supreme goal.

They alone see truly who see that all actions are performed by prakriti, while the Self remains unmoved. When they see the variety of creation rooted in that unity and growing out of it, they attain fulfillment in Brahman.

This supreme Self is without a beginning, undifferentiated, deathless. Though it dwells in the body, Arjuna, it neither acts nor is touched by action. As akasha pervades the cosmos but remains unstained, the Self can never be tainted though it dwells in every creature.

As the sun lights up the world, the Self dwelling in the field is the source of all light in the field. Those who, with the eye of wisdom, distinguish the field from its Knower and the way to freedom from the bondage of prakriti, attain the supreme goal.

Sri Krishna:

Let me tell you more about the wisdom that transcends all knowledge, through which the saints and sages attained perfection. Those who rely on this wisdom will be united with me. For them there is neither rebirth nor fear of death.

My womb is prakriti; in that I place the seed. Thus all created things are born. Everything born, Arjuna, comes from the womb of prakriti, and I am the seed-giving father.

It is the three gunas born of prakriti—sattva, rajas, and tamas—that bind the immortal Self to the body. Sattva—pure, luminous, and free from sorrow—binds us with attachment to happiness and wisdom. Rajas is passion, arising from selfish desire and attachment. These bind the Self with compulsive action. Tamas, born of ignorance, deludes all creatures through heedlessness, indolence, and sleep.

Sattva binds us to happiness; rajas binds us to action. Tamas, distorting our understanding, binds us to delusion. Sattva predominates when rajas and tamas are transformed. Rajas prevails when sattva is weak and tamas overcome. Tamas prevails when rajas and sattva are dormant.

When sattva predominates, the light of wisdom shines through every gate of the body. When rajas predominates, a person runs about pursuing selfish and greedy ends, driven by restlessness and desire. When tamas is dominant a person lives in darkness—slothful, confused, and easily infatuated.

Those dying in the state of sattva attain the pure worlds of the wise. Those dying in rajas are reborn among people driven by work. But those who die in tamas are conceived in the wombs of the ignorant.

The fruit of good deeds is pure and sattvic. The fruit of rajas is suffering. The fruit of tamas is ignorance and insensitivity.

From sattva comes understanding; from rajas, greed. But the outcome of tamas is confusion, infatuation, and ignorance.

Those who live in sattva go upwards; those in rajas remain where they are. But those immersed in tamas sink downwards.

The wise see clearly that all action is the work of the gunas. Knowing that which is above the gunas, they enter into union with me.

Going beyond the three gunas which form the body, they leave behind the cycle of birth and death, decrepitude and sorrow, and attain to immortality.

Arjuna:

What are the characteristics of those who have gone beyond the gunas, O Lord? How do they act? How have they passed beyond the gunas' hold?

Sri Krishna:

They are unmoved by the harmony of sattva, the activity of rajas, or the delusion of tamas. They feel no aversion when these forces are active, nor do they crave for them when these forces subside.

They remain impartial, undisturbed by the actions of the gunas. Knowing that it is the gunas which act, they abide within themselves and do not vacillate.

Established within themselves, they are equal in pleasure and pain, praise and blame, kindness and unkindness. Clay, a rock, and gold are the same to them. Alike in honor and dishonor, alike to friend and foe, they have given up every selfish pursuit. Such are those who have gone beyond the gunas.

By serving me with steadfast love, a man or woman goes beyond the gunas. Such a one is fit for union with Brahman.

Study Questions

F.13.2 *The Bhagavad Gita*, The Later Hindu Doctrine of the Self

1. What is the Self?
   a. Identify the main concepts that are related to the Self.
   b. Discuss the natures or attributes of the Self.
   c. Analyze the relationship of the Self to each human being and to the world.
   d. Offer your philosophical critique of the Bhagavadgitaian doctrine of the Self.
2. What is the Human Self?
   a. Identify the main concepts that are related to the human self.
   b. Discuss the three types of human beings and determine whether you belong to these types of humanity.
   c. Analyze the theory of human nature and determine whether it has resolved certain problems of human nature (namely, why some are good, some are bad, etc.).
3. Compare and critique both the Upanishadic and Bhagavadgitaian doctrines of the Self.

CHAPTER 14

Buddhist Views of the Selfless Self and the Pursuit of Universal Compassion

Nikaya (Theravadin) Doctrines of the Human Self

The Buddhaian Doctrine of the Human Self

The Buddha's Silence

The Samyutta-Nikaya

The Introduction

Did the Buddha develop any doctrine of the human self? Probably not at the time he achieved his Buddhahood (Enlightenment) as indicated by the theoretical contents of his "First Sermon." The first selection ("The Buddha's Silence") shows the practical need that would have necessitated the Buddha to develop his own doctrine of the human self during the early years of his missionary activities. The Buddha is said to have been asked by Vacchagotta, a wandering ascetic, the following question:

"Well, then, good Gotama, is there a Self?"

The question was asked twice, and, the Buddha "remained silent" each time! In response to Ananda's question why he did not answer Vacchagotta's inquiry, the Buddha said that he would not want to violate his "Middle Way" doctrine. The Buddha's silence may be indicative of a possibility that he did not develop a doctrine of the human self up to that point. And he used his public silence to teach his disciples about the Middle Way doctrine.

Then Vacchagotta, the wandering ascetic, approached the Blessed One, greeted him courteously, sat down to one side, and said: "Well, now, good Gotama, is there a Self?"

The Blessed One remained silent.

"Well, then, good Gotama, is there not a Self?"

Once again, the Blessed One remained silent, and the wandering ascetic Vacchagotta got up and went away.

[Source: Taken from Léon Feer, ed., *The Samyutta-Nikaya* (London: Pali Text Society, 1894), 4:400–401].

Soon thereafter, the Venerable Ānanda said to the Blessed One: "Master, why did you not respond to the wandering ascetic Vacchagotta's question?"

"Ānanda, if in response to Vacchagotta's first question I asserted that there is a Self, that would be associating myself with the renouncers and brahmins who are eternalists. But, Ānanda, if in response to his second question I asserted that there is no Self, that would be associating myself with the renouncers and brahmins who are annihilationists.

"Or again, Ānanda, if in response to the wandering ascetic Vacchagotta's first question I asserted that there is a Self, would that be in accord with the knowledge that all elements of reality are without Self?"

"No, it would not, Master."

"But, Ānanda, if in response to Vacchagotta's second question I asserted that there is no Self, the confused Vacchagotta would have been even more confused, saying, 'Formerly, I had a Self, but now it does not exist.'"

Study Questions

F.14.1.a.1 *The Samyutta-Nikaya*, The Buddhaian Doctrine of the Human Self, The Buddha's Silence

1. Discuss the reasons the Buddha offers for his "silence" concerning Vacchagotta's question about the Self. Consider also if the Buddha intends to maintain his "Middle Way" perspective on the Self.
2. Explain the possible reasons why he who "knows" the Buddhist doctrines of the five *skandhas* and dependent origination (*pratityasamutpada*) "wants to promote the good of the world." Incorporate in your analysis the relationship between the Buddhist theory of reality and Buddhist ethics.
3. Analyze the "chain of causation" by discerning its various stages. How are the stages linked together in the whole chain that binds humans in samsara and how can humans break free?
4. Explore how the doctrines of five skandhas and dependent origination can really provide the *philosophical* foundation for Buddhist monks and nuns to successfully renounce all that needs to be renounced and pursue all of their Buddhist ideals to the end.

The Human Self as an Illusion

Nagasena

This selection from the Pali text records a lively dialogue between the famous monk Nagasena and the Greek King Milinda on the ontological subject *"Anatta"* (No-Self or Selfless Self). The doctrine of Anatta (s. *Anatman*) is one of the hallmarks of Buddhist philosophy. This Buddhist doctrine of Anatta has not only set the Buddha and Buddhist philosophers apart from the Hindu masters but has also created philosophical confusions among many Buddhist masters themselves. It is desirable here to cite Professor John S. Strong's background explanation on the Buddhist debates about the human self. "The notion that there is no abiding entity that can be called the Self (atman) is not an easy one for Westerners to accept, but it caused difficulties for Buddhists as well. Indeed, it was long before there was at least one Nikaya Buddhist sect, the so-called Personalists, who held that even though there was no Self, there was something called a Person (pudgala, Pali: puggala), which was ineffable, neither the same as nor different from the agglomerations of elements (skandhas) that make up human beings and all of reality." [Strong 1995:91].

1. [25] Now Milinda the king went up to where the venerable Nâgasena was, and addressed him with the greetings and compliments of friendship and courtesy, and took his seat respectfully apart. And Nâgasena reciprocated his courtesy, so that the heart of the king was propitiated.

And Milinda began by asking, 'How is your Reverence known, and what, Sir, is your name?'

'I am known as Nâgasena, O king, and it is by that name that my brethren in the faith address me. But although parents, O king, give such a name as Nâgasena, or Sûrasena, or Vîrasena, or Sîhasena, yet this, Sire—Nâgasena and so on—is only a generally understood term, a designation in common use. For there is no permanent individuality (no soul) involved in the matter.'

Then Milinda called upon the Yonakas and the brethren to witness: 'This Nâgasena says there is no permanent individuality (no soul) implied in his name. Is it now even possible to approve him in that?' And turning to Nâgasena, he said: 'If, most reverend Nâgasena, there be no permanent individuality (no soul) involved in the matter, who is it, pray, who gives to you members of the Order

[Source: Taken from the *Milindapanha* II:1.25–8, printed in M. Muller, ed., *Sacred Books of the East*, volume XXXV (London: Oxford University Press, 1886), pp. 40–5].

your robes and food and lodging and necessaries for the sick? Who is it who enjoys such things when given? Who is it who lives a life of righteousness? Who is it who devotes himself to meditation? Who is it who attains to the goal of the Excellent Way, to the Nirvâna of Arahatship? And who is it who destroys living creatures? Who is it who takes what is not his own? Who is it who lives an evil life of worldly lusts, who speaks lies, who drinks strong drink, who (in a word) commits any one of the five sins which work out their bitter fruit even in this life? If that be so there is neither merit nor demerit: there is neither doer nor causer of good or evil deeds; there is neither fruit nor result of good or evil Karma.

[26]—If, most reverend Nâgasena, we are to think that were a man to kill you there would be no murder, then it follows that there are no real masters or teachers in your Order, and that your ordinations are void. —You tell me that your brethren in the Order are in the habit of addressing you as Nâgasena. Now what is that Nâgasena? Do you mean to say that the hair is Nâgasena?'

'I don't say that, great king.'

'Or the hairs on the body, perhaps?'

'Certainly not.'

'Or is it the nails, the teeth, the skin, the flesh, the nerves, the bones, the marrow, the kidneys, the heart, the liver, the abdomen, the spleen, the lungs, the larger intestines, the lower intestines, the stomach, the faeces, the bile, the phlegm, the pus, the blood, the sweat, the fat, the tears, the serum, the saliva, the mucus, the oil that lubricates the joints, the urine, or the brain, or any or all of these, that is Nâgasena?'[1]

And to each of these he answered no.

'Is it the outward form then (Rûpa) that is Nâgasena, or the sensations (Vedanâ), or the ideas (Saññâ), or the confections (the constituent elements of character, Samkhârâ), or the consciousness (Viññâna), that is Nâgasena?'

And to each of these also he answered no.

'Then is it all these Skandhas combined that are Nâgasena?'

'No! great king.'

'But is there anything outside the five Skandhas that is Nâgasena?'

And still he answered no.

'Then thus, ask as I may, I can discover no Nâgasena. Nâgasena is a mere empty sound. Who then is the Nâgasena that we see before us? It is a falsehood that your reverence has spoken, an untruth!'

And the venerable Nâgasena said to Milinda the king: 'You, Sire, have been brought up in great luxury, as beseems your noble birth. If you were to walk this dry weather on the hot and sandy ground, trampling underfoot the gritty, gravelly grains of the hard sand, your feet would hurt you. And as your body would be in pain, your mind would be disturbed, and you would experience a sense of bodily suffering. How then did you come, on foot, or in a chariot?'

'I did not come, Sir, on foot [27]. I came in a carriage.'

'Then if you came, Sire, in a carriage, explain to me what that is. Is it the pole that is the chariot?'

'I did not say that.'

'Is it the axle that is the chariot?'

'Certainly not.'

'Is it the wheels, or the framework, or the ropes, or the yoke, or the spokes of the wheels, or the goad, that are the chariot?'[2]

And to all these he still answered no.

'Then is it all these parts of it that are the chariot?'

'No, Sir.'

'But is there anything outside them that is the chariot?'

And still he answered no.

'Then thus, ask as I may, I can discover no chariot. Chariot is a mere empty sound. What then is the chariot that you say you came in? It is a falsehood that your Majesty has spoken, an

[1] The whole question and answer are repeated in the text for each physical element.

[2] Same remark for each part of the chariot.

untruth! There is no such thing as a chariot! You are king over all India, a mighty monarch. Of whom then are you afraid that you speak untruth?' And he called upon the Yonakas and the brethren to witness, saying: 'Milinda the king here has said that he came by carriage. But when asked in that case to explain what the carriage was, he is unable to establish what he averred. Is it, forsooth, possible to approve him in that?'

When he had thus spoken the five hundred Yonakas shouted their applause, and said to the king: 'Now let your Majesty get out of that if you can.'

And Milinda the king replied to Nâgasena, and said: 'I have spoken no untruth, reverend Sir.

It is on account of its having all these things—the pole, and the axle, the wheels, and the framework, the ropes, the yoke, the spokes, and the goad—that it comes under the generally understood term, the designation in common use, of "chariot".'

'Very good! Your Majesty has rightly grasped the meaning of "chariot". And just even so it is on account of all those things you questioned me about—[28] the thirty-two kinds of organic matter in a human body; and the five constituent elements of being—that I come under the generally understood term, the designation in common use, of "Nâgasena".'

Study Questions

F.14.1.a.2 Nagasena, The Human Self as an Illusion

1. Summarize the context surrounding Nagasena's introduction to his theory of the human self.
2. Identify Nagasena's thesis and explain step by step and point by point how Nagasena argues to validate his own thesis.
3. Evaluate and critique Nagasena's theory of the human self.
a. For your evaluation, consider if the *conditions* are important in the generation of a thing (like a chariot) or an organism (like a person).

For your critique, question the validity of Nagasena's chariot analogy. Use the concepts of part, whole, form, essence, function, and their organic relationships as your theoretical resources. Finally, consider the so-called "soul" of a human being as the *emerging* energy, resulting from biological formation, when all the necessary conditions are functionally in place for the maintenance of one's existence in space-time.

F.14.2

Mahayanist (Yogacara) Doctrine
of the Human Self

The Selflessness of the Human Self

The Lankavatara Sutra

The Introduction

Of all the schools of Buddhist philosophy, the Madhyamika and the Vijnanavada or Yogacara of Mahayana Buddhism are most influential. The Madhyamika (Middle Way School), founded by the most creative philosopher-monk Nagarjuna (first to second centuries CE), maintains that reality is "empty" (*shunya*) or all things are devoid of their self-nature and self-existence. Its key doctrine of reality is "emptiness" (*shunyata*). Thus the human self is empty or selfless. A philosophical important group of Mahayanist sutras that represent the Madhyamika philosophy is the *Prajnaparamita Sutras* (Discourses on the Perfection of Wisdom).

The Yogacara (Yoga Way), founded by Asanga and Vasubandhu (fourth century), can be characterized as a school of absolute idealism like those of Berkeley and Hume. It maintains that all things are mental since they are the projections of one's *alaya vijnana* (store consciousness). For its idealist position, it is also known as the Vijnanavada (School of Consciousness). Its key doctrine is "suchness" (*tathata*) which can be compared with the "emptiness" (*shuynata*) of the Madhyamika and the Brahman of the Vedanta. The *Sandhinirmocana Sutra* and the *Lankavatara Sutra* represent the earlier unsytematic form of Yogacara philosophy, while a more systematic form of theoretical refinement is found the *Vijnaptimatratasiddhi* of Vasubandhu. In particular, the *Lankavatara Sutra* has inspired the developments of Meditative Buddhism (Chan, Zen, Son, and Thiền).

A Bodhisattva, a great being, should become one who is skilful in investigating the mark of the twofold egolessness.

1. There is first the lack of self in *persons*. (*a*) Persons are a conglomeration of skandhas, elements and sense-fields, devoid of a self or anything belonging to a self. (*b*) Consciousness arises from ignorance, karma and craving, and it keeps going by settling down in the grasping at form, etc., by means of the eye, etc. (*c*) Through all the sense-organs a world of objects and bodies is manifested owing to the discrimination that takes place in the world which is of mind itself, that is, in the store-consciousness. (*a*)[1] Like a river, a seed, a lamp, wind, a cloud beings are broken up from moment to moment. (*b*) Always restless like a monkey, like a fly which is ever in search of unclean things and defiled places, like a fire never satisfied, (consciousness persists) by reason of the habit-energy stored up by false imagination since beginningless time. (*c*) (The world) proceeds like a water-drawing wheel or machine, rolling the wheel of Samsara, carrying along various bodies and forms, resuscitating the dead like the demon Vetala, moving beings about as a magician moves puppets. The skill in the cognition of these marks, that is called the cognition of the absence of self in persons.

2. What, then, is the cognition of the absence of self in *dharmas*? It is the recognition that own-being and marks of the skandhas, elements and sense-fields are imagined. Since the skandhas, elements and sense-fields are devoid of a self,—a mere agglomeration of heaps, closely tied to the string of their root cause (i.e. ignorance), karma and craving, proceeding by mutual conditioning, (and therefore) inactive, —therefore the skandhas are also devoid of the special and general marks. The variety of their marks is the result of unreal imagination, and they are distinguished from one another by the fools, but not by the saints.

Study Questions

F.14.2 The Mahayanist (Yogacarin) Doctrine of the Human Self

1. "Through all the sense-organs a world of objects and bodies is manifested owing to the discrimination that takes place in the world which is of mind itself, that is, in the store-consciousness."
   a. Explain why this thesis is "idealistic" given the two arguments concerning "the twofold egolessness" that are given in the selection.
   b. Critically discuss and respond to the two arguments concerning "the twofold egolessness" of the human self.
2. Compare and contrast the Hindu and Buddhist doctrines of the human self and identify how they can help one to attain self-knowledge. Offer your philosophical critique.

CHAPTER 15

The Confucianist Doctrines of the Moral Self and the Quest for Social Harmony

The Ancient East Asian Confucianist Theories of Human Nature

Human Nature Is Good

Meng Tzu (v. Mạnh Tử)

The Introduction

Confucius calls for the restoration of moral human goodness by the self-cultivation of the core moral virtues within the feudalistic political framework of the Chou Dynasty. But Confucian ethics is devoid of an ontological foundation because Confucius develops no theory of human nature as his contemporary Hindu and Buddhist philosophers in the subcontinent of ancient South Asia do.

To remove this theoretical poverty as well as to respond to the challenges of non-Confucianist views of human nature, Meng Tzu (v. Mạnh Tử [Mencius]) offers his positive theory of human nature during his debate with Kao Tzu (v. Cáo Tử) on this important philosophical question. In his critical response to the Mengian (v. Mạnhian) theory, Hsün Tzu (v. Tuân Tử) develops his negative theory of human nature. These two conflicting ancient East Asian theories of human nature pave the way for the developments of Chinese Confucianist theories of human nature to come.

Kao Tzu[1] said: "The nature of man may be likened to the willow tree, whereas righteousness may be likened to wooden cups and wicker baskets. To turn man's nature into humanity and righteousness is like turning a willow tree into cups and baskets."

[1] Kao Tzu was a critic and possibly a former pupil of Mencius. In general, Kao Tzu held human nature to be neutral, while Mencius insisted it was good.

Mencius replied: "Sir, can you follow the nature of the willow tree, and make the cups and baskets? Or must you violate its nature to make the cups and baskets? If you must violate the nature of the willow tree to turn it into cups and baskets, then don't you mean you must also violate the nature of man to turn it into humanity and righteousness? Your words, alas, would incite everyone in the

From *Sources of Chinese Tradition, Vol. 1*, ed. William Theodore de Bary, Wing-Tsit Chan and Burton Watson. © 1960 Columbia University Press. Reprinted by permission of the publisher.

world to regard humanity and righteousness as a curse!" (VI A:1]

Kao Tzu said: "The nature of man may be likened to a swift current of water: you lead it eastward and it will flow to the east; you lead it westward and it will flow to the west. Human nature is neither disposed to good nor to evil, just as water is neither disposed to east nor west." Mencius replied: "It is true that water is neither disposed to east nor west, but is it neither disposed to flowing upward nor downward? The tendency of human nature to do good is like that of water to flow downward. There is no man who does not tend to do good; there is no water that does not flow downward. Now you may strike water and make it splash over your forehead, or you may even force it up the hills. But is this in the nature of water? It is of course due to the force of circumstances. Similarly, man may be brought to do evil, and that is because the same is done to his nature." [VI A:2]

Kao Tzu said: "Nature is what is born in us." Mencius asked: "'Nature is what is born in us'— is it not the same as saying white is white?" "Yes," said Kao Tzu. Mencius asked: "Then the whiteness of a white feather is the same as the whiteness of white snow, and the whiteness of white snow the same as the whiteness of white jade?" "Yes," Kao Tzu replied. Mencius asked: "Well, then, the nature of a dog is the same as the nature of a cow, and the nature of a cow the same as the nature of a man, is it not?"[2] [VI A:3]

Kao Tzu said: "The appetite for food and sex is part of our nature. Humanity comes from within and not from without, whereas righteousness comes from without and not from within." Mencius asked: "What do you mean when you say that humanity comes from within while righteousness comes from without?" Kao Tzu replied: "When I see anyone who is old I regard

him as old. This regard for age is not a part of me. Just as when I see anyone who is white I regard him as white, because I can observe the whiteness externally. For this reason I say righteousness comes from without." Mencius said: "Granted there is no difference between regarding the white horse as white and the white man as white. But is there no difference between one's regard for age in an old horse and one's regard for age in an old man, I wonder? Moreover, is it old age itself or our respectful regard for old age that constitutes a point of righteousness?" Kao Tzu persisted: "My own brother I love; brother of a man of Ch'in I do not love. Here the sanction for the feeling rests in me, and therefore I call it [i.e., humanity] internal. An old man of Ch'u I regard as old, just as an old man among my own people I regard as old. Here the sanction for the feeling lies in old age, and therefore I call it [i.e., righteousness] external." Mencius answered him: "We love the Ch'in people's roast as much as we love our own roast. Here we have a similar situation with respect to things. Would you say, then, that this love of roast is also something external?" [VI A:4]

The disciple Kung-tu Tzu said: "Kao Tzu says that human nature is neither good nor bad. Some say that human nature can be turned to be good or bad. Thus when [sage-kings] Wen and Wu were in power the people loved virtue; when [wicked kings] Yü and Li were in power the people indulged in violence. Some say that some natures are good and some are bad. Thus even while [the sage] Yao was sovereign there was the bad man Hsiang, even a bad father like Ku-sou had a good son like [the sage-king] Shun, and even with [the wicked] Chou for nephew and king there were the men of virtue Ch'i, the Viscount of Wei, and the Prince Pi-kan. Now, you say that human nature is good. Are the others then all wrong?" Mencius replied: "When left to follow its natural feelings human nature will do good. This is why I say it is good. If it becomes evil, it is not the fault of man's original capability. The sense of mercy is found in all men; the sense of shame is found in all men; the sense of respect is found in all men; the sense

[2] Evidently Mencius here considers he has achieved a *reductio ad absurdum* of Kao's original proposition. The point of Mencius' complaint is that Kao Tzu has failed to distinguish between the nature of man and the nature of any other being, which Mencius insists must be made.

of right and wrong is found in all men. The sense of mercy constitutes humanity; the sense of shame constitutes righteousness; the sense of respect constitutes decorum (*li*); the sense of right and wrong constitutes wisdom. Humanity, righteousness, decorum, and wisdom are not something instilled into us from without; they are inherent in our nature. Only we give them no thought. Therefore it is said: `Seek and you will find them, neglect and you will lose them.' Some have these virtues to a much greater degree than others—twice, five times, and incalculably more— and that is because those others have not developed to the fullest extent their original capability. It is said in the *Book of Odes*:

> Heaven so produced the teeming multitudes that
> For everything there is its principle.
> The people will keep to the constant principles,
> And all will love a beautiful character.[3]

Confucius said, regarding this poem: 'The writer of this poem understands indeed the nature of the Way! For wherever there are things and affairs there must be their principles. As the people keep to the constant principles, they will come to love a beautiful character.'" [VI A:6]

Mencius said: "All men have a sense of commiseration. The ancient kings had this commiserating heart and hence a commiserating government. When a commiserating government is conducted from a commiserating heart, one can rule the whole empire as if one were turning it on one's palm. Why I say all men have a sense of commiseration is this: Here is a man who suddenly notices a child about to fall into a well. Invariably he will feel a sense of alarm and compassion. And this is not for the purpose of gaining the favor of the child's parents, or seeking the approbation of his neighbors and friends, or for fear of blame should he fail to rescue it. Thus we see that no man is without a sense of compassion, or a sense of shame, or a sense of courtesy, or a sense of right and wrong. The sense of compassion is the beginning of humanity; the sense of shame is the beginning of righteousness; the sense of courtesy is the beginning of decorum; the sense of right and wrong is the beginning of wisdom. Every man has within himself these four beginnings, just as he has four limbs. Since everyone has these four beginnings within him, the man who considers himself incapable of exercising them is destroying himself. If he considers his sovereign incapable of exercising them, he is likewise destroying his sovereign. Let every man but attend to expanding and developing these four beginnings that are in our very being, and they will issue forth like a conflagration being kindled and a spring being opened up. If they can be fully developed, these virtues are capable of safeguarding all within the four seas; if allowed to remain undeveloped, they will not suffice even for serving one's parents." [II A:6]

Mencius said: "Man's innate ability is the ability possessed by him that is not acquired through learning. Man's innate knowledge is the knowledge possessed by him that is not the result of reflective thinking. Every child knows enough to love his parents, and when he is grown up he knows enough to respect his elder brothers. The love for one's parents is really humanity and the respect for one's elders is really righteousness— all that is necessary is to have these natural feelings applied to all men." [VIIA:15]

---

[3] *Shih ching*, Ta ya: T'ang, Cheng-min.

Study Questions

F.15.1.a Mencius (c. Meng Tzu [v. Mạnh Tử]), Human Nature is Good

1. List all the theories of human nature that are mentioned in the reading.
2. Identify the theses of Kao Tzu (v. Cáo Tử) and Meng Tzu (v. Mạnh Tử) on human nature and explain their debate. If you were Kao Tzu, who seems to have lost the debate, how would you silence Meng Tzu with a new counter-argument (clue: using the modern theory of gravity)?
3. Explain the arguments that Meng Tzu makes in support of his positive theory of human nature.
4. Critique the Mengian (v. Mạnhian) theory of human nature if you find problems with it.

F.15.1.b

Human Nature Is Evil

Hsün Tzu (v. Tuân Tử)

The Introduction

Hsün Tzu (v. Tuân Tử [fl. 298–238 BCE]) came from the northern Kingdom of Chao (v. Triệu), which was annexed by the western "barbarian" Kingdom of Ch'in (v. Tần) in 222 BCE. The *Shih Chi* (v. *Sử Ký* [chapter 74]) says that when Hsün Tzu was fifty, he first came to spread his teachings in the northern Kingdom of Ch'i (v. Tề), where he was regarded as the most eminent learned scholar during the time of King Hsiang of Ch'i (265 BCE). Being slandered in Ch'i (v. Tề), Hsün Tzu went to the southern "barbarian" Kingdom of Ch'u (v. Sở), where Prince Ch'un Shen made him magistrate of Lan Ling and eventually died there.

Both Meng Tzu (v. Manh Tử) and Hsün Tzu (v. Tuân Tử) belong to the school of ancient East Asian Confucianism. But unlike Meng Tzu, who enjoys the honor of being the second sage after Confucius, Hsün Tzu is never being honored in Chinese Confucianism. He is ignored until the nineteenth century CE since no commentaries were written on his work until the ninth century and not much thereafter. His work is not recognized as belonging to the Confucianist corpus as also the case of the *Tao Te Ching* (v. *Đạo Đức Kinh*) of Lao Tzu (v. Lão Tử).

Hsün Tzu exerts more influence upon scholars and princes before and through the Han period than does Meng Tzu. Most famous were his two disciples, Han Fei Tzu (v. Hàn Phi Tử [d. 233 BCE]) and Li Ssu (Lý Tư [d. 208 BCE]), once, the most powerful ministers of the Ch'in (v. Tần).

In line with his rationalist philosophy and political pragmatism, Hsün Tzu (v. Tuân Tử) advances a negative theory of human nature in direct opposition to the positive theory by Meng Tzu (v. Mạnh Tử).

The nature of man is evil; his goodness is acquired.

His nature being what it is, man is born, first, with a desire for gain. If this desire is followed, strife will result and courtesy will disappear.

Second, man is born with envy and hate. If these tendencies are followed, injury and cruelty will abound and loyalty and faithfulness will disappear. Third, man is born with passions of the ear and

From *Sources of Chinese Tradition, Vol. 1*, ed. William Theodore de Bary, Wing-Tsit Chan and Burton Watson. © 1960 Columbia University Press. Reprinted by permission of the publisher.

eye as well as the love of sound and beauty. If these passions are followed, excesses and disorderliness will spring up and decorum and righteousness will disappear. Hence to give rein to man's original nature and to yield to man's emotions will assuredly lead to strife and disorderliness, and he will revert to a state of barbarism. Therefore it is only under the influence of teachers and laws and the guidance of the rules of decorum and righteousness that courtesy will be observed, etiquette respected, and order restored. From all this it is evident that the nature of man is evil and that his goodness is acquired.

Crooked wood needs to undergo steaming and bending by the carpenter's tools; then only is it straight. Blunt metal needs to undergo grinding and whetting; then only is it sharp. Now the original nature of man is evil, so he must submit himself to teachers and laws before he can be just; he must submit himself to the rules of decorum and righteousness before he can be orderly. On the other hand, without teachers and laws, men are biased and unjust; without decorum and righteousness, men are rebellious and disorderly. In ancient times the sage-kings knew that man's nature was evil and therefore biased and unjust, rebellious and disorderly. Thereupon they created the codes of decorum and righteousness and established laws and ordinances in order to bend the nature of man and set it right, and in order to transform his nature and guide it. All men are thus made to conduct themselves in a manner that is orderly and in accordance with the Way. At present, those men who are influenced by teachers and laws, who have accumulated culture and learning, and who are following the paths of decorum and righteousness, are the gentlemen. On the other hand, those who give rein to their nature, who indulge in their willfulness, and who disregard decorum and righteousness, are the inferior men. From all this it is evident that the nature of man is evil and that his goodness is acquired.

Mencius says: "The reason man is ready to learn is that his nature is originally good." I reply:

This is not so. This is due to a lack of knowledge about the original nature of man and of understanding of the distinction between what is natural and what is acquired. Original nature is a heavenly endowment; it cannot be learned, and it cannot be striven after. As to rules of decorum and righteousness, they have been brought forth by the sages, they can be attained by learning, and they can be achieved by striving. That which cannot be learned and cannot be striven after and rests with Heaven is what I call original nature. That which can be attained by learning and achieved by striving and rests with man is what I call acquired character. This is the distinction between original nature and acquired character. Now by the nature of man, the eye has the faculty of seeing and the ear has the faculty of hearing. But the keenness of the faculty of sight is inseparable from the eye, and the keenness of the faculty of hearing is inseparable from the ear. It is evident that keenness of sight and keenness of hearing cannot be learned.

Mencius says: "The original nature of man is good; but because men all ruin it and lose it, it becomes evil." I reply: In this he is gravely mistaken. Regarding the nature of man, as soon as he is born, he tends to depart from its original state and depart from its natural disposition, and he is bent on ruining it and losing it. From all this, it is evident that the nature of man is evil and that his goodness is acquired.

To say that man's original nature is good means that it can become beautiful without leaving its original state and it can become beneficial without leaving its natural disposition. This is to maintain that beauty pertains to the original state and disposition and goodness pertains to the heart and mind in the same way as the keenness of the faculty of sight is inseparable from the eye and the keenness of the faculty of hearing is inseparable from the ear, just as we say that the eye is keen in seeing or the ear is keen in hearing. Now as to the nature of man, when he is hungry he desires to be filled, when he is cold he desires warmth, when he is tired he desires rest. This is man's natural disposition. But now a man may he hungry and yet in the presence of elders he dare not be the first to eat. This is because he has to yield precedence to someone. He may be tired and yet he dare not take a rest. This is because he has to labor in the place of someone. For a son to yield to his father and a younger brother to yield to his older brother, for a son to labor in the place of his father and a younger brother to labor in the place of his older brother—both of these kinds of actions are opposed to man's original nature and contrary to man's feeling. Yet they are the way of the filial son and in accordance with the rules of decorum and righteousness. It appears if a person follows his natural disposition he will show no courtesy, and if he shows courtesy he is acting contrary to his natural disposition. From all this it is evident that the nature of man is evil and that his goodness is acquired.

It may be asked: "If man's original nature is evil, whence do the rules of decorum and righteousness arise" I reply: All rules of decorum and righteousness are the products of the acquired virtue of the sage and not the products of the nature of man. Thus, the potter presses the clay and makes the vessel—but the vessel is the product of the potter's acquired skill and not the product of his original nature. Or again, the craftsman hews pieces of wood and makes utensils—but utensils are the product of the carpenter's acquired skill and not the product of his original nature. The sage gathers many ideas and thoughts and becomes well versed in human affairs, in order to bring forth the rules of decorum and righteousness and establish laws and institutions. So then the rules of decorum and righteousness and laws and institutions are similarly the products of the acquired virtue of the sage and not the products of his original nature. . . .

Man wishes to be good because his nature is evil. If a person is unimportant he wishes to be important, if he is ugly he wishes to be beautiful, if he is confined he wishes to be at large, if he is poor he wishes to be rich, if he is lowly he wishes to be honored—whatever a person does not have within himself, he seeks from without. But the rich

do not wish for wealth and the honorable do not wish for position, for whatever a person has within himself he does not seek from without. From this it may be seen that man wishes to be good because his nature is evil. Now the original nature of man is really without decorum and righteousness, hence he strives to learn and seeks to obtain them. . . .

Straight wood does not require the carpenter's tools to be straight; by nature it is straight. Crooked wood needs to undergo steaming and bending by the carpenter's tools and then only will it be straight; by nature it is not straight. As the nature of man is evil, it must be submitted to the government of the sage-kings and the reforming influence of the rules of decorum and righteousness; then only will everyone issue forth in orderliness and be in accordance with goodness. From all this it is evident that the nature of man is evil and that his goodness is acquired.

It may be objected: "Decorum and righteousness and the accumulation of acquired virtues must be in the nature of man so that the sage could bring them forth." I reply: This is not so. Now the potter pounds and molds the clay and produces earthenware. Are the earthenware and clay then in the nature of the potter? The workman hews a piece of wood and makes utensils. Are furniture and wood then in the nature of the carpenter? So it is with the sage and decorum and righteousness; he produces them in the same way as earthenware is produced. Are decorum and righteousness and the accumulation of acquired virtues then in the original nature of man? As far as the nature of man is concerned, the sage-kings Yao and Shun have the same nature as the wicked King Chieh and robber Chih; the gentleman has the same nature as the inferior man. Should we now regard decorum and righteousness and the accumulation of acquired virtues as being in the nature of man, then why should we prize the sage-kings Yao and Yü and why should we prize the gentlemen? We prize Yao, Yü, and the gentlemen because they were able to transform nature and produce acquired virtue, and from acquired virtue decorum and righteousness issued forth. . . .

There is a saying: "The man on the street can become a Yü." How would you account for that? I reply: All that made Yü what he was was that he instituted humanity and righteousness, laws, and government. However, there are principles by which humanity and righteousness, laws and government can be known and practiced. At the same time any man on the street has the faculty for knowing them and has the capacity for practicing them. Thus it is evident that he can become a Yü. Should we assume there were really no principles by which humanity and righteousness, laws and government could be known and practiced, then even Yü would not be able to know them or practice them. Or, should we assume the man on the street really had no faculty for knowing humanity and righteousness, laws and government, or the capacity for practicing them, then the man cannot know, on the one hand, the proper relation between father and son and, on the other, the proper discipline between sovereign and minister. Thus it is evident that the man on the street does have the faculty for knowing and the capacity for practicing these virtues. Now let the man on the street take his faculty for knowing and his capacity for practicing humanity and righteousness, laws and government, and bring them to bear upon the principles by which these virtues can be known and can be practiced—then it is self-evident that he can become a Yü. Yes, let the man on the street pursue the path of knowledge and devote himself to learning, with concentration of mind and a singleness of purpose; let him think, search, examine, and re-examine, day in and day out, with persistence and patience—let him thus accumulate good works without cease, then he may be counted among the gods and may form a triad with Heaven and earth. Hence sagehood is a state that any man can achieve by cumulative effort. . . .

Study Questions

F.15.1.b Hsün Tzu (v. Tuân Tử), Human Nature Is Evil

1. Identify Hsün Tzu's thesis on human nature and discuss his arguments.
2. Offer your philosophical critique of Hsün Tzu's negative theory of human nature.
3. Discuss and critique Hsün Tzu's theory of human morality and law.

A Chinese (Neo-Confucianist) Theory of Human Nature

The Li Ch'i (v. Lý Khí) of Human Nature

Chu Hsi (v. Chu Hy)

The Introduction

The development of Chinese Confucianism (also so-called "Neo-Confucianism") through the works of Chou Tun-I (v. Chu Đôn Di), Shao Yung (v. Thiệu Ung), Chang Tsai (v. Trương Tái), Ch'eng Hao (v. Trình Hạo), and Ch'eng Yi (v. Trinh Di) paved the way for the emergence of its two major schools. They are known as the "Li Hsüeh" (v. Lý Học ["Study of Principle"]) and the "Hsin Hsüeh" (v. Tâm Học ["Study of Heart"]. Chu Hsi (1130–1200 CE) is the Chinese Confucianist who synthesizes the doctrines of all his predecessors into "one all-embracing system."

By applying the five main Yiian (v. Dịchian) doctrines (Tao, Li, Ch'i, Yin, and Yang) from the *Chou Yi Ching* (v. *Chu Dịch Kinh*) in his philosophical synthesis, Chu Hsi (v. Chu Hy) is able to bring all the previous Confucianist theories of human nature to the highest theoretical level. What is theoretically creative and eclectic about his theory of human nature is the fact that other theories of human nature can find their respective place in his theory. On the one hand, he maintains firm the Confucianist claim that human nature is truly good (the Mengian theory), and on the other hand, he can show why some humans are good and others evil at birth.

63. When we speak of the nature of Heaven and Earth, we refer to principle [li-ccp] alone. When we speak of the physical nature, we refer to principle and material force [ch'i-ccp] combined. Before material force existed, basic nature was already in existence. Material force does not always exist, but nature is eternal. Although nature is implanted in material force, yet material force is still material force and nature is still nature, without being confused or mixed up. As to its

immanence in things and universal existence, regardless of whether material force is refined or coarse, there is nothing without its principle. (43:3a–b)

64. The physical nature is no different from the nature of Heaven and Earth. The point is that the nature of Heaven and Earth runs through the physical nature. For example, the good nature is like water. The physical nature is as though you sprinkled some sauce and salt in it and it then acquired a peculiar flavor. (43:4a)

65. The nature of all men is good, and yet there are those who are good from their birth and those who are evil from their birth. This is because of the difference in material force with which they are endowed. The revolutions of the universe consist of countless variety and are endless. But these may be seen: If the sun and moon are clear and bright, and the climate temperate and reasonable, the man born at such a time and endowed with such material force, which is clear, bright, well-blended, and strong, should be a good man. But if the sun and moon are darkened and gloomy, and the temperature abnormal, all this is evidence of violent material force. There is no doubt that if a man is endowed with such material force, he will be a bad man. The objective of learning is to transform this material endowment. (43:4b)

66. Nature is like water. If it flows in a clean channel, it is clear, if it flows in a dirty channel, it becomes turbid. When physical nature that is clear and balanced is received, it will be preserved in its completeness. This is true of man. When physical nature that is turbid and unbalanced is received, it will be obscured. This is true of animals. Material force may be clear or turbid. That received by men is clear and that received by animals is turbid. Men mostly have clear material force; hence the difference between them and animals. However, there are some whose material force is turbid, and they are not far removed from animals. (43:7a–b)

67. Someone asked about the inequality in the clearness of the material endowment. The Teacher said: The differences in the material endowment are not limited to one kind and are not described only in terms of clearness and turbidity. There are men who are so bright that they know everything. Their material force is clear, but what they do may not all be in accord with principle. The reason is that their material force is not pure. There are others who are respectful, generous, loyal, and faithful. Their material force is pure, but in their knowledge they do not always penetrate principle. The reason is that their material force is not clear. From this you can deduce the rest. (42:8a)

68. Although nature is the same in all men, it is inevitable that [in most cases] the various elements in their material endowment are unbalanced. In some men the material force of Wood predominates. In such cases, the feeling of commiseration is generally uppermost, but the feeling of shame, of deference and compliance, and of right and wrong are impeded by the predominating force and do not emanate into action. In others, the material force of Metal predominates. In such cases, the feeling of shame is generally uppermost, but the other feelings are impeded and do not emanate into action. So with the material forces of Water and Fire. It is only when yin and yang are harmonized and the five moral natures (of humanity, righteousness, propriety, wisdom, and good faith) are all complete that a man has the qualities of the Mean and correctness and becomes a sage. (43:8a–b)

[Master Ch'eng Hao also said,] "What is inborn is called nature. . . . They (nature and material force, ch'i) are both inborn." [His meaning is this]: What is imparted by Heaven (Nature) to all things is called destiny (ming, mandate, fate). What is received by them from Heaven is called nature. But in the carrying out of the Mandate of Heaven, there must first be the interaction, mutual influence, consolidation, and integration of the two material forces (yin and yang) and the Five Agents (of Metal, Wood, Water, Fire, and Earth) before things can be produced. Man's nature and destiny exist before physical form [and are without it], while material force exists after physical form [and is with it]. What exists before physical form is the one principle harmonious and undifferentiated, and is invariably good. What exists after physical form, however, is confused and mixed, and good and evil are thereby differentiated. Therefore when man and things are produced, they have in them this material force, with the endowment of which they are produced. But the nature endowed by Heaven is therein preserved. This is how Master Ch'eng elucidated the doctrine of Kao Tzu that what is inborn is called nature, and expressed his own thought by saying that "One's nature is the same as material force and material force is the same as nature."

[Master Ch'eng also said,] "[According to principle, there are both good and evil] in the material force with which man is endowed at birth. . . . [Nature is of course good], but it cannot be said that evil is not nature." It is the principle of nature that the material force with which man is endowed necessarily has the difference of good and evil. For in the operation of material force, nature is the controlling factor. In accordance with its purity or impurity, material force is differentiated into good and evil. Therefore there are not two distinct things in nature opposing each other. Even the nature of evil material force is good, and therefore evil may not be said to be not a part of nature. The Master further said, "Good and evil in the world are both the Principle of Nature. What is called evil is not original evil. It becomes evil only because of deviation from the mean." For there is nothing in the world which is outside of one's nature. All things are originally good but degenerated into evil, that is all.

[The Master further said,] "For what is inborn is called one's nature. . . . [The fact that whatever issues from the Way is good may be compared to] water always flowing downward." Nature is simply nature. How can it be described in words? Therefore those who excel in talking about nature only do so in terms of the beginning of its emanation and manifestation, and what is involved in the concept of nature may then be understood in silence, as when Mencius spoke of the Four Beginnings (of humanity, righteousness, propriety, and wisdom). By observing the fact that water necessarily flows downward, we know the nature of water is to go downward. Similarly, by observing the fact that the emanation of nature is always good, we know that nature involves goodness.

[The Master further said,] "Water as such is the same in all cases. . . . [Although they differ in being turbid or clear, we cannot say that the turbid water ceases to be water. . . . The original goodness of human nature is like the original clearness of water. Therefore it is not true that two distinct and opposing elements of good and evil exist in human nature and that] each issues from it." This is again using the clearness and turbidity of water as an analogy. The clearness of water is comparable to the goodness of nature.

Study Questions

F.15.2 A Chinese (Neo-Confucianist) Theory of Human Nature

Chu Hsi, The Li and Ch'i (v. Lý Khí) of Human Nature

1. Comparatively discuss the concept of "nature" as used by Mencius (v. Mạnh Tử), Hsün Tzu (v. Tuân Tử), and Chu Hsi (v. Chu Hy).
2. Discuss the evolution of the usages of "water" in the Confucianist theories of human nature in comparison with the Laoian view of water.
3. Identify Chu Hsi's thesis and critically discuss his positive theory of human nature.
4. Compare the Chuian theory of human nature with the Bhagavadgitaian theory. Demonstrate how they have resolved some of the major theoretical problems of most human nature theories.

Part G

Eastern Views of Reality and Philosophic Self-Enlightenment

CHAPTER 16

Hindu Views of Reality
and the Quest for Moksha

G.16.1

The Upanishadic (Early Hindu) Doctrine of Reality and Self-Knowledge

The Introduction

The ultimate end of life for the Upanishadic *rishis* (holy seers) is "*moksha*" (the state of enlightenment and bliss in self-liberation). *Moksha* means the total self-liberation from ignorance (*avidya*), sensual attachments to worldly things, and rebirth (*samsara*). The removal of ignorance begins with the knowledge of reality, which can lead one to one's total *moksha*, if one's knowledge of reality is the true knowledge.

To know what the true knowledge is, the *Mundaka Upanishad* points out that one must make a distinction between the two types of knowledge, the lower (*apara*) and the higher (*para*). What is theoretically most worthy of the *Mundaka Upanishad* is its doctrine of the two types of knowledge, since its general philosophical contents are mostly eclectic and expressed most poetically in style.

To obtain the higher knowledge is to obtain the true knowledge of reality. To obtain the true knowledge of reality is to obtain the knowledge of what the *Mundaka Upanishad* calls the "Imperishable" of all the perishables. The *Kena Upanishad* maintains that the higher knowledge of reality is not only for mortals to obtain but immortals as well. The selection from the *Kena Upanishad* shows that even the three most powerful Vedic Gods (Agni, Indra, Vayu) are ignorant of the true nature of reality. They become enlightened after they receive the education in metatheology from the Goddess Uma.

Why do they fail? Agni, Indra, and Vaya fail to understand the true reality because they fail to make the *ontological distinction* between the two main categories of ontology, which the *Brihadaranyaka Upanishad* calls the "two forms of Brahman," the "formed" and the "formless." The Goddess Uma, who can be interpreted to have been sociologically intended to represent some group of female Upanishadic rishis, has this philosophically advanced form of the higher knowledge of reality that most male Upanishadic rishis might not have, as symbolized by Agni, Indra, and Vayu.

If one does all the things that are taught in the above mentioned *Upanishads*, can one achieve one's philosophic self-enlightenment (moksha)? The author of the selection from the *Chandogya Upanishad* would think that one may not if one does not have the right philosophical method. Abstract knowledge is always theoretically abstract. The truth of reality may not be known without a philosophical method that is experimental, experiential, and dialogical. The selection shows the Upanishadic father, Uddalaka, teaches his son Svetaketu about the Self by employing an experiential method. By performing two experiments (salt experiment and Nyagrodha fruit experiment) and participating in the Socratic-like *dialectic* his father teaches, Svetaketu seems to have comprehended the true nature of reality. But the author of the *Brihadāranyaka Upanishad* may ask this methodological question: Can Svetaketu truly understand reality without the benefit of the doctrine of the two forms of the Brahman?

A note on the *Brihadāranyaka Upanishad* ("Great Forest-Book") is desirable here. The *Brihadāranyaka* is the longest, most famous, and one of the oldest of the *Upanishads*. Another feature of this *Upanishad* is the famous discourse between Yajnavalkya ("the greatest of the Upanishadic sages") and his wife Maitreyi on the transcendental *Atman* as the universal and undifferentiated consciousness.

The Two Types of Knowledge

The Mundaka Upanishad

First Muṇḍaka

Preparation for the knowledge of Brahma

First Khaṇḍa

The line of tradition of this knowledge from Brahmā himself

1. Brahmā arose as the first of the gods—
The maker of all, the protector of the world.
He told the knowledge of Brahmā
(*brahma-vidyā*), the foundation of all knowledge,
To Atharva[n], his eldest son.

2. What Brahmā taught to Atharvan,
Even that knowledge of Brahma, Atharvan
told in ancient time to Aṅgir.
He told it to Bhāradvāja Satyavāha;
Bhāradvāja, to Aṅgiras—both the higher and
the lower [knowledge].

Śaunaka's quest for the clue to an understanding of the world

3. Śaunaka, verily, indeed, a great
householder, approached Aṅgiras according to
rule, and asked: 'Through understanding of what,
pray, does all this world become understood, sir?'[1]

Two kinds of knowledge: the traditions of religion, and the knowledge of the eternal

4. To him then he said: 'There are two
knowledges to be known—as indeed the knowers
of Brahma are wont to say:[2] a higher (*para*) and
also a lower (*apara*).

5. Of these, the lower is the Rig-Veda, the
Yajur-Veda, the Sāma-Veda, the Atharva-Veda,

Pronunciation (*śikṣā*), Ritual (*kalpa*),
Grammar (*vyākaraṇa*),
Definition (*nirukta*), Metrics (*chandas*),
and Astrology (*jyotiṣa*).[1]

Now, the higher is that whereby that
Imperishable (*akṣara*) is apprehended.

The imperishable source of all things

6. That which is invisible, ungraspable,
without family, without caste (*a-varṇa*)—

[1] The very same knowledge which Yājñavalkya declared to
Maitreyī, Bṛih, 2.4.5 (end).
[2] Cf. Maitri 6.22.

[Source: Taken from the *Mundaka Upanishad* (I.1.1–9), R. E. Hume, trans., *The Thirteen Principal Upanishads*
(London: Oxford University Press, Humphrey Milford, 1921), pp. 366–67].

Without sight or hearing is It, without hand or foot,

Eternal, all-pervading, omnipresent, exceedingly subtle;

That is the Imperishable, which the wise perceive as the source of beings.

7. As a spider emits and draws in [its thread],

As herbs arise on the earth,

As the hairs of the head and body from a living person,

So from the Imperishable arises everything here.

8. By austerity (*tapas*) Brahma becomes built up.

From that, food is produced;

From food—life-breath, mind, truth,

The worlds, immortality too in works.

9. He who is all-knowing, all-wise,

Whose austerity consists of knowledge—

From Him are produced the Brahma here,

[Namely] name and form, and food.

Goddess Uma Teaches Metatheology to Vedic Gods

The Kena Upanishad

(Third Khaṇḍa)

Allegory of the Vedic gods' ignorance of Brahma [the Brahman-ccp]¹

14 (1). Now, Brahma won a victory for the gods. Now, in the victory of this Brahma the gods were exulting. They bethought themselves: 'Ours indeed is this victory! Ours indeed is this greatness!'

15 (2). Now, It understood this of them. It appeared to them. They did not understand It. 'What wonderful being (*yakṣa*) is this?' they said.

16 (3). They said to Agni (Fire): 'Jātavedas, find out this—what this wonderful being is.'

'So be it.'

17 (4). He ran unto It.

Unto him It spoke: 'Who are you?'

'Verily, I am Agni,' he said. 'Verily, I am Jātavedas.'

18 (5). 'In such as you what power is there?'

'Indeed, I might burn everything here, whatever there is here in the earth!'

19 (6). It put down a straw before him. 'Burn that!'

He went forth at it with all speed. He was not able to burn it. Thereupon indeed he returned, saying: 'I have not been able to find out this—what this wonderful being is.'

20 (7). Then they said to Vāyu (Wind): 'Vāyu, find out this—what this wonderful being is.'

'So be it.'

21 (8). He ran unto It.

Unto him It spoke: 'Who are you?'

'Verily, I am Vāyu,' he said. 'Verily, I am Mātariśvan.'

22 (9). 'In such as you what power is there?'

'Indeed, I might carry off everything here, whatever there is here in the earth.'

23 (10). It put down a straw before him. 'Carry that off!' He went at it with all speed. He was not able to carry it off. Thereupon indeed he returned, saying: ' I have not been able to find out this—what this wonderful being is.'

24 (11). Then they said to Indra: 'Maghavan ('Liberal'), find out this—what this wonderful being is.'

¹ All the words "Brahma" in this selection should be read "Brahman" please.

[Source: Taken from the *Kena Upanishad* (III.14–25. IV.26–32), printed in R. E. Hume, *op. cit.,* p. 97].

'So be it.'

He ran unto It. It disappeared from him.

25 (12). In that very space he came upon a woman exceedingly beautiful, Umā, daughter of the Snowy Mountain (*Himavat*).

To her he said: 'What is this wonderful being?'

(Fourth Khaṇḍa)

Knowledge of Brahma, the ground of superiority

26 (1). 'It is Brahma,' she said. 'In that victory of Brahma, verily, exult ye.'

Thereupon he knew it was Brahman.

27 (2). Therefore, verily, these gods, namely Agni, Vāyu, and Indra, are above the other gods, as it were; for these touched It nearest, for these and [especially] he [i.e. Indra] first knew It was Brahman.

28 (3). Therefore, verily, Indra is above the other gods, as it were; for he touched It nearest, for he first knew It was Brahma.

Brahma in cosmic and in individual phenomena

29 (4). Of It there is this teaching.—

That in the lightning which flashes forth, which makes one blink, and say 'Ah!'—that 'Ah!' refers to divinity.

30 (5). Now with regard to oneself.—

That which comes, as it were, to the mind, by which one repeatedly remembers—that conception (*saṁkalpa*) [is It]!

Brahma, the great object of desire

31 (6). It is called *Tad-vana* ('It-is-the-desire'). As 'It-is-the-desire' (*Tad-vana*). It should be worshiped. For him who knows it thus, all beings together yearn.

Concluding practical instruction and benefits

32 (7). 'Sir, tell me the mystic doctrine (*upaniṣad*)!'

'The mystic doctrine has been declared to you. Verily, we have told you the mystic doctrine of Brahma (*brāhmī upaniṣad*).'

G.16.1.c

The Two Forms of the Brahman

The Brihadāranyaka Upanishad

Third Brāhmaṇa

The two forms of Brahma [the Brahman-ccp][1]

1. There are, assuredly, two forms of Brahma: the formed (*mūrta*) and the formless[2], the mortal and the immortal, the stationary and the moving, the actual (*sat*) and the yon (*tya*).

2. This is the formed [Brahma]—whatever is different from the wind and the atmosphere. This is mortal; this is stationary; this is actual. The essence of this formed, mortal, stationary, actual [Brahma] is yonder [sun] which gives forth heat, for that is the essence of the actual.

3. Now the formless [Brahma] is the wind and the atmosphere. This is immortal, this is moving, this is the yon. The essence of this unformed, immortal, moving, yonder [Brahma] is the Person in that sun-disk, for he is the essence of the yon. —Thus with reference to the divinities.

4. Now, with reference to the self.—

Just that is the formed [Brahma] which is different from breath (*prāṇa*) and from the space which is within the self (*ātman*). This is mortal, this is stationary, this is actual. The essence of this formed, mortal, stationary, actual [Brahma] is the eye, for it is the essence of the actual.

5. Now the formless [Brahma] is the breath and the space which is within the self. This is immortal, this is moving, this is the yon. The essence of this unformed, immortal, moving, yonder [Brahma] is this Person who is in the right eye, for he is the essence of the yonder.

6. The form of this Person is like a saffron-colored robe, like white wool, like the [red] Indragopa beetle, like a flame of fire, like the [white lotus-flower, like a sudden flash of lightning. Verily, like a sudden lightning-flash is the glory of him who knows this.

Hence, now, there is the teaching 'Not thus! not so!' (*neti, neti*), for there is nothing higher than this, that he is thus. Now the designation for him is 'the Real of the real.' Verily, breathing creatures are the real. He is their Real.

[1] All the words "Brahma" in this selection should be read "Brahman" please.

[2] Thus far the sentence recurs at Maitri 6.3.

[Source: Taken from the *Brihadaranyaka Upanishad* (II.3.1–6), printed in R. E. Hume, *op. cit.*, p. 97].

Study Questions

G.16.1 The Upanishadic (Early Hindu) Doctrine of Reality and Self-Knowledge

1. Discuss the two types of knowledge and the historical context that surrounded the relationship between Vedic religion and the Upanishadic philosophy (Brahmanism). Formulate a philosophical response to this dualistic typology of knowledge.
2. Explain the failure of each Vedic god to use its divine power and the main reason why Agni, Vayu, and Indra fail to know the Brahman *except* Uma (clue: appearance-reality relationship).
3. Explain the historical possibility that the role of Uma portrayed as the divine teacher of the three most powerful Vedic gods in Brahmanic theology might have been a mythologization of female teachers who were philosophically active in the late Vedic society (ca. 500-100 BCE).
4. Identify the two forms of Brahman and discuss the characteristics that each is conceptualized to possess (in relation to each other, to the human self, and to the natural world).
5. Explain whether or not the two aspects of the Brahman as conceptualized in the *Brihadaranyaka Upanishad* 2.3.1–6 can help resolve the internal duality of the Self and the Not-Self as theoretically inherent in the various versions of the Upanishadic doctrine of the Self and reality (ex. G.16.1.d) or the origin of matter as absent in Upanishadic Brahmanism.

G.16.1.d

The Self Is the Subtle Essence of All That Is

The Chandogya Upanishad

First Khaṇḍa

Harih, Om. There lived once Svetaketu Âruneya (the grandson of Aruna). To him his father (Uddâlaka, the son of Aruna) said: 'Svetaketu, go to school; for there is none belonging to our race, darling, who, not having studied (the Veda), is, as it were, a Bráhmana, by birth only.'

Having begun his apprenticeship (with a teacher) when he was twelve years of age, Svetaketu returned to his father, when he was twenty-four, having then studied all the Vedas—conceited, considering himself well-read, and stern.

His father said to him: 'Svetaketu, as you are so conceited, considering yourself so well-read, and so stern, my dear, have you ever asked for that instruction by which we hear what cannot be heard, by which we perceive what cannot be perceived, by which we know what cannot be known?'

'What is that instruction, Sir?' he asked.

The father replied: 'My dear, as by one clod of clay all that is made of clay is known, the difference being only a name, arising from speech, but the truth being that all is clay;

'And as, my dear, by one nugget of gold all that is made of gold is known, the difference being only a name, arising from speech, but the truth being that all is gold;

'And as, my dear, by one pair of nail-scissors all that is made of iron is known, the difference being only a name, arising from speech, but the truth being that, all is iron—thus, my dear, is that instruction.'

The son said: 'Surely those venerable men (my teachers) did not know that. For if they had known it, why should they not have told it me? Do you, Sir, therefore tell me that.' 'Be it so', said the father.

Second Khaṇḍa

'In the beginning, my dear, there was that only which is, one only, without a second. Others say, in the beginning there was that only which is not, one only, without a second; and from that which is not, that which is was born.

'But how could it be thus, my dear?' the father continued. 'How could that which is, be born of that which is not? No, my dear, only that which

[Source: Taken from the *Chandogya Upanishad* (VI.1–2, 7–16), printed in M. Muller, trans., *Sacred Books of the East*, volume XX (London: Oxford University Press, 1879), pp. 92–109].

is, was in the beginning, one only, without a second.

'It thought, may I be many, may I grow forth. It sent forth fire.

'That fire thought, may I be many, may I grow forth. It sent forth water.

'And therefore whenever anybody anywhere is hot and perspires, water is produced on him from fire alone.

'Water thought, may I be many, may I grow forth. It sent forth earth (food).

'Therefore whenever it rains anywhere, most food is then produced. From water alone is eatable food produced.

Seventh Khaṇḍa

'Man, my son, consists of sixteen parts. Abstain from food for fifteen days, but drink as much water as you like, for breath comes from water, and will not be cut off, if you drink water.'

Svetaketu abstained from food for fifteen days. Then he came to his father and said: 'What shall I say?' The father said: 'Repeat the *R̥ig*, *Yajus*, and *Sâman* verses.' He replied: 'They do not occur to me, Sir.'

The father said to him: 'As of a great lighted fire one coal only of the size of a firefly may be left, which would not burn much more than this (i.e. very little), thus, my dear son, one part only of the sixteen parts (of you) is left, and therefore with that one part you do not remember the Vedas. Go and eat!

'Then wilt thou understand me.' Then Svetaketu ate, and afterwards approached his father. And whatever his father asked him, he knew it all by heart. Then his father said to him:

'As of a great lighted fire one coal of the size of a firefly, if left, may be made to blaze up again by putting grass upon it, and will thus burn more than this,

'Thus, my dear son, there was one part of the sixteen parts left to you, and that, lighted up with food, burnt up, and by it you remember now the Vedas.' After that, he understood what his father meant when he said: 'Mind, my son, comes from

food, breath from water, speech from fire.' He understood what he said, yea, he understood it.

Ninth Khaṇḍa

'As the bees, my son, make honey by collecting the juices of distant trees, and reduce the juice into one form.

'And as these juices have no discrimination, so that they might say, I am the juice of this tree or that, in the same manner, my son, all these creatures, when they have become merged in the True (either in deep sleep or in death), know not that they are merged in the True.

'Whatever these creatures are here, whether a lion, or a wolf, or a boar, or a worm, or a midge, or a gnat, or a mosquito, that they become again and again.

'Now that which is that subtle essence, in it all that exists has its self. It is the True. It is the Self, and thou, O Svetaketu, art it.'

'Please, Sir, inform me still more', said the son.

'Be it so, my child', the father replied.

Tenth Khaṇḍa

'These rivers, my son, run, the eastern (like the Gangâ) toward the east, the western (like the Sindhu) toward the west. They go from sea to sea (i.e. the clouds lift up the water from the sea to the sky, and send it back as rain to the sea). They become indeed sea. And as those rivers, when they are in the sea, do not know, I am this or that river,

'In the same manner, my son, all these creatures, when they have come back from the True, know not that they have come back from the True. Whatever these creatures are here, whether a lion, or a wolf, or a bear, or a worm, or a midge, or a gnat, or a mosquito, that they become again and again.

'That which is that subtle essence, in it all that exists has its self. It is the True. It is the Self, and thou, O Svetaketu, art it.'

'Please, Sir, inform me still more' said the son.

'Be it so, my child', the father replied.

Eleventh Khaṇḍa

'If some one were to strike at the root of this large tree here, it would bleed, but live. If he were to strike at its stem, it would bleed, but live. If he were to strike at its top, it would bleed, but live. Pervaded by the living Self that tree stands firm, drinking in its nourishment and rejoicing;

'But if the life (the living Self) leaves one of its branches, that branch withers; if it leaves a second, that branch withers; if it leaves a third, that branch withers. If it leaves the whole tree, the whole tree withers. In exactly the same manner, my son. know this.' Thus he spoke:

'This (body) indeed withers and dies when the living Self has left it; the living Self dies not.

'That which is that subtle essence, in it all that exists has its self. Is is the True. It is the Self, and thou, Svetaketu, art it.'

'Please, Sir, inform me still more', said the son.

'Be it so, my child', the father replied.

Twelfth Khaṇḍa

'Fetch me from thence a fruit of the Nyagrodha tree.'

'Here is one, Sir.'

'Break it.'

'It is broken, Sir.'

'What do you see there?'

'These seeds, almost infinitesimal.'

'Break one of them.'

'It is broken, Sir.'

'What do you see there?'

'Not anything, Sir.'

The father said: 'My son, that subtle essence which you do not perceive there, of that very essence this great Nyagrodha tree exists.

'Believe it, my son. That which is the subtle essence, in it all that exists has its self. It is the True. It is the Self, and thou, O Svetaketu, art it.'

'Please, Sir, inform me still more', said the son.

'Be it so, my child', the father replied.

Thirteenth Khaṇḍa

'Place this salt in water, and then wait on me in the morning.'

The son did as he was commanded.

The father said to him: 'Bring me the salt, which you placed in the water last night.'

The son having looked for it, found it not, for, of course, it was melted.

The father said: 'Taste it from the surface of the water. How is it?'

The son replied: 'It is salt.'

'Taste it from the middle. How is it?'

The son replied: 'It is salt.'

'Taste it from the bottom. How is it?

The son replied: 'It is salt.'

The father said: 'Throw it away and then wait on me.'

He did so; but salt exists for ever.

Then the father said: 'Here also, in this body, forsooth, you do not perceive the True, my son; but there indeed it is.

'That which is the subtle essence, in it all that exists has its self. It is the True. It is the Self, and thou, O Svetaketu, art it.'

'Please, Sir, inform me still more', said the son.

'Be it so, my child', the father replied.

Fourteenth Khaṇḍa

'As one might lead a person with his eyes covered away from the Gandhâras, and leave him then in a place where there are no human beings; and as that person would turn towards the east, or the north, or the west, and shout: "I have been brought here with my eyes covered, I have been left here with my eyes covered",

'And as thereupon some one might loose his bandage and say to him, "Go in that direction, it is Gandhâra, go in that direction"; and as thereupon, having been informed and being able to judge for himself, he would by asking his way from village to village arrive at last at Gandhâra— in exactly the same manner does a man, who meets with a teacher to inform him, obtain the true knowledge. For him there is only delay so long as he is not delivered (from the body); then he will be perfect.

'That which is the subtle essence, in it all that exists has its self. It is the True. It is the Self, and thou, O Svetaketu, art it.'

'Please, Sir, inform me still more', said the son.

'Be it so, my child', the father replied.

Fifteenth Khaṇḍa

'If a man is ill, his relatives assemble round him and ask: "Dost thou know me? Dost thou know me?" Now as long as his speech is not merged in his mind, his mind in breath, breath in heat (fire), heat in the Highest Being, he knows them.

'But when his speech is merged in his mind, his mind in breath, breath in heat (fire), heat in the Highest Being, then he knows them not.

'That which is the subtle essence, in it all that exists has its self. It is the True. It is the Self, and thou, O Svetaketu, art it.'

'Please, Sir, inform me still more', said the son.

'Be it so, my child', the father replied.

Sixteenth Khaṇḍa

'My child, they bring a man hither whom they have taken by the hand, and they say: "He has taken something, he has committed a theft." (When he denies, they say) "Heat the hatchet for him." If he committed the theft, then he makes himself to be what he is not. Then the false-minded, having covered his true Self by a falsehood, grasps the heated hatchet—he is burnt, and he is killed.

'But if he did not commit the theft, then he makes himself to be what he is. Then the true-minded, having covered his true Self by truth, grasps the heated hatchet—he is not burnt, and he is delivered.

As that (truthful) man is not burnt, thus has all that exists its self in That. It is the True. It is the Self, and thou, O Svetaketu, art it.' He understood what he said, yea, he understood it.

Study Questions

G.16.1.d *The Chandogya Upanishad*, The Self Is the Subtle Essence of All That Is

1. "Svetaketu, as you are so conceited, considering yourself so well-read, and so stern, my dear, have you ever asked for that instruction by which we hear what cannot be heard, by which we perceive what cannot be perceived, by which we know what cannot be known?"

    Explain the philosophical method that Uddalaka uses to teach his son Svetaketu about what the Self *is*. Explain also why his method can be viewed as a "philosophical method."
2. "In the beginning, my dear, there was that only which is, one only, without a second."

    Explain Uddalaka's thesis and his argument. Characterize its theoretical nature and respond.
3. What is the Self?
    a. Identify and write down Uddalaka's thesis.
    b. Analyze the first sub-thesis concerning the relationship between the Self and the universe or any concrete thing.
    c. Analyze the second sub-thesis concerning the relationship between the Self and every human being.
    d. Characterize and explain the philosophical method that Uddalaka uses to demonstrate his thesis.

e. Characterize the theoretical nature of Uddalaka's theory of the Self. Using the two concepts (concept of Self and concept of Not-Self) as your theoretical resources, critique Uddalaka's theory of the Self.

f. Using the doctrine of the "Two Forms of the Brahman" (in the *Brihadaranyaka Upanishad*) as your theoretical resource, resolve the theoretical problem of Uddalaka's theory as revealed in your critique.

A Vedantic (Later Hindu) Doctrine of Reality and Self-Knowledge

The Metaphysics of Brahman

Shankara

The Introduction

Shankara (ca. 788–820 CE) is one of the eminent philosophers of India. He traveled extensively, founded four monasteries, and wrote major commentaries on Hindu scriptures. Shankara died young. He is the leading advocate for a school of Indian philosophy known as "Advaita" (non-dual) Vedanta. He builds his philosophy by reinterpreting and reinventing the Brahmanistic philosophy (Brahmanism) of the *Upanishads*. One of the most significant philosophical contributions that Shankara should be credited for is his clear metaphysical reformulation of the nature and relationship between the two most important Upanishadic concepts of Atman and Brahman that are theoretically ambiguous in the *Upanishads*.

Together with Ramanuja (ca. 11th century CE) and Madhva (1197–1276 CE), Shankara championed the philosophical and religious cause of the Vedanta school of Hindu philosophy. But he differs with Ramanuja and Madhva on the *true relationship* between the Supreme Brahman and the empirical universe and the individual selves. Madhva maintains that Brahman, being *identical* with the Supreme God Vishnu, can be understood and worshipped, if, the five fundamental differences are established ([1] between God and each individual self, [2] between God and matter, [3] between individual selves themselves, [4] between selves and matter, and [5] between material substances).

Shankara argues that all is *unreal* except the self-consciousness of the divine identity that one truly is and the absolute morality that one lives one's life accordingly. So declares Shankara in his *Crest-Jewel of Discrimination*: "Know the Atman as the real I. Thus you cross the shoreless ocean of wordliness, whose waves are birth and death. Live always in the knowledge of identity with Brahman, and be blessed."

And unlike Ramanuja, who teaches that all things are real since they constitute one organic body whose "inner ruler" is the Brahman, Shankara remains faithful to his idealism, the idealism of an Upanishadic kind. Inherent in the Shankaraian and Upanishadic forms of idealism is the *internal duality* between one's Atman (soul) and Not-Atman (body, senses, mind, intellect) rather than the *external duality* between one's soul and God as conceptualized in monotheism.

The Mind

With a controlled mind and an intellect which is made pure and tranquil, you must realize the Atman directly, within yourself. Know the Atman as the real I. Thus you cross the shoreless ocean of worldliness, whose waves are birth and death. Live always in the knowledge of identity with Brahman, and be blessed.

Man is in bondage because he mistakes what is non-Atman for his real Self. This is caused by ignorance. Hence follows the misery of birth and death. Through ignorance, man identifies the Atman with the body, taking the perishable for the real. Therefore he nourishes this body, and anoints it, and guards it carefully. He becomes enmeshed in the things of the senses like a caterpillar in the threads of its cocoon.

Deluded by his ignorance, a man mistakes one thing for another. Lack of discernment will cause a man to think that a snake is a piece of rope. When he grasps it in this belief he runs a great risk. The acceptance of the unreal as real constitutes the state of bondage. Pay heed to this, my friend.

The Atman is indivisible, eternal, one without a second. It is eternally made manifest by the power of its own knowledge. Its glories are infinite. The veil of tamas[1] hides the true nature of the Atman, just as an eclipse hides the rays of the sun.

When the pure rays of the Atman are thus concealed, the deluded man identifies himself with his body, which is non-Atman. Then rajas, which has the power of projecting illusory forms, afflicts him sorely. It binds him with chains of lust, anger and the other passions.

His mind becomes perverted. His consciousness of the Atman is swallowed up by the shark of total ignorance. Yielding to the power of rajas, he identifies himself with the many motions and changes of the mind. Therefore he is swept hither and thither, now rising, now sinking, in the boundless ocean of birth and death, whose waters are full of the poison of sense-objects. This is indeed a miserable fate.

The sun's rays bring forth layers of cloud. By them, the sun is concealed; and so it appears that the clouds alone exist. In the same way, the ego, which is brought forth by the Atman, hides the true nature of the Atman; and so it appears that the ego alone exists.

On a stormy day the sun is swallowed up by thick clouds; and these clouds are attacked by sharp, chill blasts of wind. So, when the Atman is enveloped in the thick darkness of tamas, the terrible power of rajas attacks the deluded man with all kinds of sorrows.

Man's bondage is caused by the power of these two—tamas and rajas. Deluded by these, he mistakes the body for the Atman and strays on to the path that leads to death and rebirth.

Man's life in this relative world may be compared to a tree. Tamas is the seed. Identification of the Atman with the body is its sprouting forth. The cravings are its leaves. Work is its sap. The body is its trunk. The vital forces are its branches. The sense-organs are its twigs. The sense-objects are its flowers. Its fruits are the

1 [*Tamas* are one of the three gunas that make up all material things. *Gunas* are qualities. In ancient Hindu cosmology it was thought that everything material is made up of some combination or mixture of the *gunas*. *Tamas* is the quality of stupor, laziness, stupidity, heaviness, and inaction in general. *Rajas*, another *guna*, is the active principle and hence the opposite of *tamas*. *Sattva*, the third *guna*, is associated with the pure, the fine, and the calm. —Ed.]

sufferings caused by various actions. The individual man is the bird who eats the fruit of the tree of life.

The Atman's bondage to the non-Atman springs from ignorance. It has no external cause. It is said to be beginningless. It will continue indefinitely until a man becomes enlightened. As long as a man remains in this bondage it subjects him to a long train of miseries—birth, death, sickness, decrepitude, and so forth.

This bondage cannot be broken by weapons, or by wind, or by fire, or by millions of acts. Nothing but the sharp sword of knowledge can cut through this bondage. It is forged by discrimination and made keen by purity of heart, through divine grace.

A man must faithfully and devotedly fulfill the duties of life as the scriptures prescribe. This purifies his heart. A man whose heart is pure realizes the supreme Atman. Thereby he destroys his bondage to the world, root and all.

Wrapped in its five coverings, beginning with the physical, which are the products of its own Maya, the Atman remains hidden, as the water of a pond is hidden by a veil of scum.

When the scum is removed, the pure water is clearly seen. It takes away a man's thirst, cools him immediately and makes him happy.

When all the five coverings are removed, the pure Atman is revealed. It is revealed as God dwelling within; as unending, unalloyed bliss; as the supreme and self-luminous Being.

The wise man who seeks liberation from bondage must discriminate between Atman and non-Atman. In this way, he can realize the Atman, which is Infinite Being, Infinite Wisdom and Infinite Love. Thus he finds happiness.

The Atman dwells within, free from attachment and beyond all action. A man must separate this Atman from every object of experience, as a stalk of grass is separated from its enveloping sheath. Then he must dissolve into the Atman all those appearances which make up the world of name and form. He is indeed a free soul who can remain thus absorbed in the Atman alone.

The Body

This body is the "physical covering." Food made its birth possible; on food it lives; without food it must die. It consists of cuticle, skin, flesh, blood, bone and water. It cannot be the Atman, the ever-pure, the self-existent.

It did not exist before birth, it will not exist after death. It exists for a short while only, in the interim between them. Its very nature is transient, and subject to change. It is a compound, not an element. Its vitality is only a reflection. It is a sense-object, which can be perceived, like a jar. How can it be the Atman—the experiencer of all experiences?

The body consists of arms, legs and other limbs. It is not the Atman—for when some of these limbs have been cut off, a man may continue to live and function through his remaining organs. The body is controlled by another. It cannot be the Atman, the controller.

The Atman watches the body, with its various characteristics, actions and states of growth. That this Atman, which is the abiding reality, is of another nature than the body, must be self-evident.

The body is a bundle of bones held together by flesh. It is very dirty and full of filth. The body can never be the same as the self-existent Atman, the knower. The nature of the Atman is quite different from that of the body.

It is the ignorant man who identifies himself with the body, which is compounded of skin, flesh, fat, bone and filth. The man of spiritual discrimination knows the Atman, his true being, the one supreme reality, as distinct from the body.

The fool thinks, "I am the body." The intelligent man thinks, "I am an individual soul united with the body." But the wise man, in the greatness of his knowledge and spiritual discrimination, sees the Atman as reality and thinks, "I am Brahman."

O fool, stop identifying yourself with this lump of skin, flesh, fat, bones and filth. Identify yourself with Brahman, the Absolute, the Atman in all beings. That is how you can attain the supreme peace.

The intelligent man may be learned in Vedanta and the moral laws. But there is not the least hope of his liberation until he stops mistakenly identifying himself with the body and the sense-organs. This identification is caused by delusion.

You never identify yourself with the shadow cast by your body, or with its reflection, or with the body you see in a dream or in your imagination. Therefore you should not identify yourself with this living body, either.

Those who live in ignorance identify the body with the Atman. This ignorance is the root-cause of birth, death and rebirth. Therefore you must strive earnestly to destroy it. When your heart is free from this ignorance, there will no longer be any possibility of your rebirth. You will reach immortality.

That covering of the Atman which is called "the vital covering" is made up of the vital force and the five organs of action. The body is called "the physical covering". It comes to life when it is enveloped by the vital covering. It is thus that the body engages in action.

This vital covering is not the Atman—for it is merely composed of the vital airs. Air-like, it enters and leaves the body. It does not know what is good or bad for itself, or for others. It is always dependent upon the Atman.

The Covering of Intellect

The discriminating faculty with its powers of intelligence, together with the organs of perception, is known as the "covering of intellect." To be the doer is its distinguishing characteristic. It is the cause of man's birth, death and rebirth.

The power of intelligence that is in the "covering of intellect" is a reflection of the Atman, the pure consciousness. The "covering of intellect" is an effect of Maya. It possesses the faculty of knowing and acting. It always identifies itself entirely with the body, sense-organs, etc.

It has no beginning. It is characterized by its sense of ego. It constitutes the individual man. It is the initiator of all actions and undertakings. Impelled by the tendencies and impressions formed in previous births, it performs virtuous or sinful actions and experiences their results.

It gathers experiences by wandering through many wombs of higher or lower degree. The states of waking and dreaming belong to this "covering of intellect." It experiences joy and sorrow.

Because of its sense of "I" and "mine," it constantly identifies itself with the body, and the physical states, and with the duties pertaining to the different stages and orders of life. This "covering of intellect" shines with a bright light because of its proximity to the shining Atman. It is a garment of the Atman, but man identifies himself with it and wanders around the circle of birth, death and rebirth because of his delusion.

The Atman, which is pure consciousness, is the light that shines in the shrine of the heart, the center of all vital force. It is immutable, but it becomes the "doer" and "experiencer" when it is mistakenly identified with the "covering of intellect."

The Atman assumes the limitations of the "covering of intellect" because it is mistakenly identified with that covering, which is totally different from itself. This man, who is the Atman, regards himself as being separate from it, and from Brahman, who is the one Atman in all creatures. An ignorant man, likewise, may regard a jar as being different from the clay of which it was made.

By its nature, the Atman is forever unchanging and perfect. But it assumes the character and nature of its coverings because it is mistakenly identified with them. Although fire is formless, it will assume the form of red-hot iron. . . .

Atman Is Brahman

The Disciple: Master, if we reject these five coverings as unreal, it seems to me that nothing remains but the void. How, then, can there be an existence which the wise man may realize as one with his Atman?

The Master: That is a good question, O prudent one. Your argument is clever. Nevertheless, there must be an existence, a reality, which perceives the ego-sense and the coverings and is also aware of the void which is their absence. This reality by itself remains unperceived. Sharpen your discrimination that you may know this Atman, which is the knower.

He who experiences is conscious of himself. Without an experiencer, there can be no self-consciousness.

The Atman is its own witness, since it is conscious of itself. The Atman is no other than Brahman.

The Atman is pure consciousness, clearly manifest as underlying the states of waking, dreaming and dreamless sleep. It is inwardly experienced as unbroken consciousness, the consciousness that I am I. It is the unchanging witness that experiences the ego, the intellect and the rest, with their various forms and changes. It is realized within one's own heart as existence, knowledge and bliss absolute. Realize this Atman within the shrine of your own heart.

The fool sees the reflection of the sun in the water of a jar, and thinks it is the sun. Man in the ignorance of his delusion sees the reflection of Pure Consciousness upon the coverings, and mistakes it for the real I.

In order to look at the sun, you must turn away from the jar, the water, and the sun's reflection in the water. The wise know that these three are only revealed by the reflection of the self-luminous sun. They are not the sun itself.

The body, the covering of intellect, the reflection of consciousness upon it—none of these is the Atman. The Atman is the witness, infinite consciousness, revealer of all things but distinct from all, no matter whether they be gross or subtle. It is the eternal reality, omnipresent, all-pervading, the subtlest of all subtleties. It has neither inside nor outside. It is the real I, hidden in the shrine of the heart. Realize fully the truth of the Atman. Be free from evil and impurity, and you shall pass beyond death.

Know the Atman, transcend all sorrows, and reach the fountain of joy. Be illumined by this knowledge, and you have nothing to fear. If you wish to find liberation, there is no other way of breaking the bonds of rebirth.

What can break the bondage and misery of this world? The knowledge that the Atman is Brahman. Then it is that you realize Him who is one without a second, and who is the absolute bliss.

Realize Brahman, and there will be no more returning to this world—the home of all sorrows. You must realize absolutely that the Atman is Brahman.

Then you will win Brahman for ever. He is the truth. He is existence and knowledge. He is absolute. He is pure and self-existent. He is eternal, unending joy. He is none other than the Atman.

The Atman is one with Brahman: this is the highest truth. Brahman alone is real. There is none but He. When He is known as the supreme reality there is no other existence but Brahman.

The Universe

Brahman is the reality—the one existence, absolutely independent of human thought or idea. Because of the ignorance of our human minds, the universe seems to be composed of diverse forms. It is Brahman alone.

A jar made of clay is not other than clay. It is clay essentially. The form of the jar has no independent existence. What, then, is the jar? Merely an invented name!

The form of the jar can never be perceived apart from the clay. What, then, is the jar? An appearance! The reality is the clay itself.

This universe is an effect of Brahman. It can never be anything else but Brahman. Apart from Brahman, it does not exist. There is nothing beside Him. He who says that this universe has an independent existence is still suffering from delusion. He is like a man talking in his sleep.

"The universe is Brahman"—so says the great seer of the Atharva Veda. The universe, therefore, is nothing but Brahman. It is superimposed upon Him. It has no separate existence, apart from its ground.

If the universe, as we perceive it, were real, knowledge of the Atman would not put an end to our delusion. The scriptures would be untrue. The revelations of the Divine Incarnations would make no sense. These alternatives cannot be considered either desirable or beneficial by any thinking person.

Sri Krishna, the Incarnate Lord, who knows the secret of all truths, says in the Gita: "Although I am not within any creature, all creatures exist within me. I do not mean that they exist within me physically. That is my divine mystery. My Being sustains all creatures and brings them to birth, but has no physical contact with them."

If this universe were real, we should continue to perceive it in deep sleep. But we perceive nothing then. Therefore it is unreal, like our dreams.

The universe does not exist apart from the Atman. Our perception of it as having an independent existence is false, like our perception of blueness in the sky. How can a superimposed attribute have any existence, apart from its substratum? It is only our delusion which causes this misconception of the underlying reality.

No matter what a deluded man may think he is perceiving, he is really seeing Brahman and nothing else but Brahman. He sees mother-of-pearl and imagines that it is silver. He sees Brahman and imagines that it is the universe. But this universe, which is superimposed upon Brahman, is nothing but a name.

I Am Brahman

Brahman is supreme. He is the reality—the one without a second. He is pure consciousness, free from any taint. He is tranquillity itself. He has neither beginning nor end. He does not change. He is joy for ever.

He transcends the appearance of the manifold, created by Maya. He is eternal, for ever beyond reach of pain, not to be divided, not to be measured, without form, without name, undifferentiated, immutable. He shines with His own light. He is everything that can be experienced in this universe.

The illumined seers know Him as the uttermost reality, infinite, absolute, without parts—the pure consciousness. In Him they find that knower, knowledge and known have become one.

They know Him as the reality which can neither be cast aside (since He is ever-present within the human soul) nor grasped (since He is beyond the power of mind and speech). They know Him immeasurable, beginningless, endless, supreme in glory. They realize the truth: "I am Brahman."

Study Questions

G.16.2 Shankara, The Metaphysics of Brahman

1. In your own words, reconstruct Shankara's doctrine of the person and characterize its theoretical nature.
2. Analyze Shankara's conception of the "body" and its relation to other coverings.
3. Critically analyze Shankara's conception of the "mind" and its relation to other coverings.
4. Critically analyze Shankara's conception of the "intellect" and its relation to other coverings.
5. Critically analyze Shankara's doctrine of the Atman.
    a. Its nature.
    b. Its function.
    c. Its relation to the Brahman and other coverings of the person.
6. Critically analyze Shankara's doctrine of the Brahman and its relation to the universe.
7. What is real? Discuss Shankara's answer and critique his doctrine of the Self and reality.

CHAPTER 17

Buddhist Views of Reality and the Quest for Nirvana

G.17.1

The Reality of Prajñāpāramitā

The Heart Sutra

The Introduction

At the moment of his Buddhahood (Enlightenment) attainment, the Buddha recognizes the existence of one single reality. That is the human reality. The true nature of the human reality is "*duhka*" (suffering) and the "Noble Eightfold Path" is its best possible cure. In the course of his missionary activities, the Buddha begins to shift his philosophical attention to the external reality, probably in response to the criticisms from other philosophical and religious movements. The result of this theoretical modification of his humanistic worldview (Buddhaian philosophy of life), the Buddha introduces the doctrine of "three marks" of reality and the doctrine of the "five *skandhas*" (heaps or components). The new reality, which embraces both the human and natural worlds, is viewed as inherently suffering, soulless, and impermanent, since it is essentially the changing manifestation of the five skandhas and their chain of causation (interdependent arising).

But the Buddhaian doctrines of reality and life are theoretically more problematic for Buddhist philosophers to resolve than they appear. For instance, the origins and natures of the five skandhas and their structural and functional relations are left as mere concepts in light of the Middle Way that he teaches as the new alternative lifestyle. These philosophical problematics will be up to the three main branches of Buddhism that eventually emerge to work out, namely, Theravada Buddhism, Vajrayana, and Mahayana Buddhism. Taking the concept of interdependent arising as the starting point, the Sarvastivada of Theravada Buddhism and the Madhyamaka and Yogacara of Mahayana Buddhism work out their own Buddhist doctrines of reality and life. What is most characteristic of the Buddhist doctrines of reality and life is their emphasis on the *conditions* that make up reality rather than the metaphysical *quintessence* of reality as overdetermined in the Upanishadic and Vedantic versions of Brahmanism.

The first two textual selections focus on the two Mahayanist doctrines of reality. The third selection focuses on Thich Nhat Hanh's new interpretation of "emptiness" along with his ontological concept of "interbeing." And the last selection contains the main points of Chu Hsi's attack on Buddhism and defense of Confucianism.

[Source: Translated from "The Prajñāpāramitā-hrdaya-sūtra," ed. Edward Conze, in *Thirty Years of Buddhist Studies* (London: Bruno Cassirer, 1967), pp. 148–67.]

Om! Praise to the Blessed Noble Prajñāpāramitā!

The bodhisattva, Noble Avalokiteśvara, while carrying out his practice in profound transcendent wisdom, contemplated the five aggregates, and he saw that they were empty of inherent self-existence.

Here, O Śāriputra, form is emptiness, and emptiness is form. Form is not other than emptiness, and emptiness not other than form; whatever is form, that is emptiness, and whatever is emptiness, that is form. So it is also for [the four other aggregates]: feelings, perceptions, karmic constituents, and consciousness.

Here, O Śāriputra, all elements of reality are empty, without characteristic; they do not come into being, they do not cease; they are not defiled, not undefiled; not defective, not perfect.

Therefore, O Śāriputra, in emptiness, there are [none of the five aggregates]: no form, no feelings, no perceptions, no karmic constituents, no consciousness; there are [none of the six psychophysical sense organs]: no eye, ear, nose, tongue, body, or mind; there are [none of the six psychophysical sense objects]: no forms, sounds, odors, tastes, touchable, or thinkable things; there are [none of the eighteen psychophysical elements that correspond to the sense organs, the sense objects, and the six consciousnesses that connect them]: no eye-element, and so forth up to no mental consciousness element; there are [none of the links of interdependent origination]: no ignorance or elimination of ignorance, and so forth up to no old age and death or elimination of old age and death; there are [none of the Four Noble Truths]: no suffering, origination of suffering, cessation of suffering, or path to the cessation of suffering; there is no knowledge, no attainment, no nonattainment.

Therefore, O Śāriputra, because of his nonattainment, a bodhisattva relies on the perfection of wisdom and stays free from mental hindrances. And because of this freedom from mental hindrances, he is unafraid, he moves beyond error, and is assured of attaining nirvāṇa. All the various Buddhas of the past, present, and future have attained unsurpassed, complete enlightenment, after relying on the perfection of wisdom.

Therefore, one should know the great mantra of Prajñāpāramitā, the mantra of the great spell, the unsurpassed mantra, the peerless mantra, the mantra that soothes all suffering. Because it is not false, it is true. The mantra of Prajñāpāramitā is spoken as follows: gate, gate, paragate, parasamgate, bodhi svāhā (gone, gone, gone beyond, utterly gone beyond: enlightenment!).

Study Questions

G.17.1 *The Heart Sutra*, The Reality of Prajñāpāramitā

1. Critically discuss and respond to Avalokiteshvara's thesis that "form is emptiness, and emptiness is form." Consider Thich Nhat Hanh's interpretation (G.17.4).
2. Critically discuss what Avalokiteshvara means when he declares that "all elements of reality are empty, without characteristic; they do not come into being, they do not cease; they are not defiled, not undefiled; not defective, not perfect."
3. Is this Mahayanist view of reality the "Prajñāpāramitā" (Perfection of Wisdom or Perfect Wisdom) as claimed by the *Heart Sutra*? Evaluate and critique.

Reality as Mind Only

The Lankavatara Sutra

This passage illustrates the irreality of the world by twelve comparisons, of which only six are given here.

Mahamati, foolish common people do not understand that what is seen is merely their own mind. Being convinced that there exists outside a variety of objects and,—as a result of the habit-energy, acquired in past lives,—being addicted to discriminate between existence and non-existence, oneness and otherness, bothness and non-bothness, permanence and imper-manence, as true to the own-being of things, they produce false imaginings.

1. It is as with animals who imagine in a mirage the existence of water. Scorched by the summer heat, desirous of drinking it, they run towards it. They do not understand that it is an erroneous vision in their own minds, and they do not comprehend that there is no water there. Just so the foolish common people, accustomed as they are since beginningless time to all kinds of discursive ideas and discriminations, their minds burning with the fires of passion, hatred and confusion, coveting a variety of forms and objects, bent on viewing things as produced, breaking up and subsisting, unskilled in understanding the true meaning of within and without, of existence and non-existence, fall into the grasping at oneness and otherness, existence and non-existence.

3. It is as if some man, asleep, dreams of a country, full of women and men, elephants, horses, cars, pedestrians, villages, cities and market towns, cows, buffaloes, woods, parks, and adorned with various mountains, rivers and lakes. In his dream he enters the women's apartments of the king's palace, and then he wakes up. Awake, his memory runs back over the country and the women's apartments. It would not be an intelligent thing to do for this man, to go in his memory through the various unreal experiences which he had in his dream, or would it, Mahamati? In the same way, the foolish common people, bitten by false views and under the influence of the heretics, do not realize that what is seen by their own mind is like a dream, and they rely on notions of oneness and otherness, of being and non-being.

5. It is like people with an eye-disease, who see a hair-net before their eyes, and who exclaim to one another, saying: "This is wonderful, this is wonderful! Look, sirs, just look!" But that hair-net has never been produced. It is not an existent, and not a non-existent, because it is seen, and not seen. Just so those who believe in the discriminations and false views to which the heretics are addicted,—who are convinced that there are the

alternatives of `is' and 'is not', of oneness and otherness, bothness and non-bothness—will oppose the good Dharma, and will destroy themselves and others.

6. It is like a wheel made by a firebrand. Fools imagine that it is a real wheel, but not so intelligent people. Just so, those who have fallen into the false views to which the heretics are addicted will, with regard to the genesis of all existents, imagine oneness and otherness, bothness and non-bothness.

10. Just as an echo is heard, when it occurs caused by the connection between a man, a river and the wind. But it is not an existent, nor a non-existent, because it is heard as a voice and yet not as a voice. Just so, existence and nonexistence, oneness and otherness, bothness and non-bothness, are visions falsely constructed by the habit-energy in one's own mind.

Study Questions

G.17.2 *The Lankavatara Sutra*, Reality as Mind Only

1. In your own words, reformulate the thesis contained in the reading and characterize its theoretical nature (clue: is it idealistic or materialistic or something else?).
2. Explain the arguments that are made and how they are actually made.
3. Make a philosophical critique using *other* Eastern views of reality as your theoretical resources.

Interbeing

Thich Nhat Hanh (v. Thích Nhất Hạnh)

If you are a poet, you will see clearly that there is a cloud floating in this sheet of paper. Without a cloud, there will be no rain; without rain, the trees cannot grow; and without trees, we cannot make paper. The cloud is essential for the paper to exist. If the cloud is not here, the sheet of paper cannot be here either. So we can say that the cloud and the paper *inter-are*. "Interbeing" is a word that is not in the dictionary yet, but if we combine the prefix "inter-" with the verb "to be," we have a new verb, inter-be. Without a cloud, we cannot have paper, so we can say that the cloud and the sheet of paper *inter-are*.

If we look into this sheet of paper even more deeply, we can see the sunshine in it. If the sunshine is not there, the forest cannot grow. In fact, nothing can grow. Even we cannot grow without sunshine. And so, we know that the sunshine is also in this sheet of paper. The paper and the sunshine inter-are. And if we continue to look, we can see the logger who cut the tree and brought it to the mill to be transformed into paper. And we see the wheat. We know that the logger cannot exist without his daily bread, and therefore the wheat that became his bread is also in this sheet of paper. And the logger's father and mother are in it too. When we look in this way, we see that without all of these things, this sheet of paper cannot exist.

Looking even more deeply, we can see we are in it too. This is not difficult to see, because when we look at a sheet of paper, the sheet of paper is part of our perception. Your mind is in here and mine is also. So we can say that everything is in here with this sheet of paper. You cannot point out one thing that is not here—time, space, the earth, the rain, the minerals in the soil, the sunshine, the cloud, the river, the heat. Everything co-exists with this sheet of paper. That is why I think the word inter-be should be in the dictionary. "To be" is to inter-be. You cannot just *be* by yourself alone. You have to inter-be with every other thing. This sheet of paper is, because everything else is.

Suppose we try to return one of the elements to its source. Suppose we return the sunshine to the sun. Do you think that this sheet of paper will be possible? No, without sunshine nothing can be. And if we return the logger to his mother, then we have no sheet of paper either. The fact is that this sheet of paper is made up only of "non-paper elements." And if we return these non-paper

Reprinted from *The Diamond that Cuts through Illusion: Commentaries of the Prajnaparamita Diamond Sutra* (1992) by Thich Nhat Hanh with permission of Parallax Press, Berkeley, California.

elements to their sources, then there can be no paper at all. Without "non-paper elements," like mind, logger, sunshine and so on, there will be no paper. As thin as this sheet of paper is, it contains everything in the universe in it.

But the *Heart Sutra* seems to say the opposite. Avalokitesvara tells us that things are empty. Let us look more closely.

Study Questions

G.17.3.a Thich Nhat Hanh (v. Thích Nhất Hạnh), Interbeing

1. Discuss how Thích Nhất Hạnh explains his doctrine of "interbeing."
2. Explain whether or not Hạnh's doctrine of interbeing is "Buddhist."
3. Offer your ontological critique of Hạnh's doctrine if you can.

Long Live Emptiness

Thich Nhat Hanh (v. Thích Nhất Hạnh)

"Listen, Shariputra, form is emptiness, emptiness is form, form does not differ from emptiness, emptiness does not differ from form. The same is true with feelings, perceptions, mental formations, and consciousness."

Form is the wave and emptiness is the water. You can understand through that image. The Indians speak in a language that can scare us, but we have to understand their way of expression in order to really understand them. In the West, when we draw a circle, we consider it to be zero, nothingness. But in India, a circle means totality, wholeness. The meaning is the opposite. So "form is emptiness, emptiness is form" is like wave is water, water is wave. "Form does not differ from emptiness, emptiness does not differ from form. The same is true with feelings, perceptions, mental formations and consciousness," because these five contain each other. Because one exists, everything exists.

In the Vietnamese literature there are two lines of poetry made by a Zen Master of the Ly Dynasty, Twelfth Century. He said:

If it exists, then one speck of dust exists.
If it doesn't exist, then the whole cosmos doesn't.

He means that the notions of existence and nonexistence are just created by our minds. He also said that, "The entire cosmos can be put on the tip of a hair, and the sun and the moon can be seen in a mustard seed." These are images that show us that one contains everything, and everything is just one. You know that modern science has perceived the truth that not only matter and energy are one, but matter and space are also one. Not only matter and space are one, but matter, space, and mind are one, because mind is in it.

Because form is emptiness, form is possible. In form we find everything else—feelings, perceptions, mental formations, and consciousness. "Emptiness" means empty of a separate self. It is full of everything, full of life. The word emptiness should not scare us. It is a wonderful word. To be empty does not mean non-existent. If the sheet of paper is not empty, how could the sunshine, the logger, and the forest come into it? How could it be a sheet of paper. The cup, in order to be empty, has to be there. Form, feelings, perceptions, mental formations, and consciousness, in order to be empty of a separate self, have to be there.

Reprinted from *The Diamond that Cuts through Illusion: Commentaries of the Prajnaparamita Diamond Sutra* (1992) by Thich Nhat Hanh with permission of Parallax Press, Berkeley, California.

Emptiness is the ground of everything. Thanks to emptiness, everything is possible. That is a declaration made by Nagarjuna, the Buddhist philosopher of the second century. Emptiness is quite an optimistic concept. If I am not empty, I cannot be here. And if you are not empty, you cannot be there. Because you are there, I can be here. This is the true meaning of emptiness. Form does not have a separate existence. Avalokita wants us to understand this point.

If we are not empty, we become a block of matter. We cannot breathe, we cannot think. To be empty means to be alive, to breathe in and to breathe out. We cannot be alive if we are not empty. Emptiness is impermanence, it is change. We should not complain about impermanence, because without impermanence nothing is possible. A Buddhist who came to see me from Great Britain complained that life was empty and impermanent. (He had been a Buddhist for five years and had thought about emptiness and impermanence a great deal.) He told me that one day his fourteen-year-old daughter told him, "Daddy, please don't complain about impermanence. Without impermanence, how can I grow up?" Of course she is right.

When you have a grain of corn, and you entrust it to the soil, you hope that it will become a tall corn plant. If there is no impermanence, the grain of corn will remain a grain of corn forever, and you will never have an ear of corn to eat. Impermanence is crucial to the life of everything. Instead of complaining about impermanence, we might say, "Long live impermanence!" Thanks to impermanence everything is possible. That is a very optimistic note. And it is the same with emptiness. Emptiness is important because without emptiness, nothing is possible. So we should also say, "Long live emptiness!" Emptiness is the basis of everything. Thanks to emptiness, life itself is possible. All the five skandhas follow the same principle.

Study Questions

G.17.3.b Thich Nhat Hanh, Long Live Emptiness

1. Discuss Thich Nhat Hanh's interpretation of the Mahayanist thesis, "form is emptiness, emptiness is form, form does not differ from emptiness, emptiness does not differ from form."
2. Offer your philosophical critique of Thich Nhat Hanh's doctrine of interbeing and his interpretation of the Mahayanist thesis on the nature of reality.

The Mistakes of Buddhism

Chu Hsi (v. Chu Hy)

134. *Question:* What is the difference between Buddhist non-being and Taoist non-being?

Answer: For the Taoists, there is still being after all. For example, the saying, "Let there [always] be non-being so we may see their subtlety, and let there [always] be being so we may see their outcome," is an evidence of this. The Buddhists, however, consider heaven and earth as illusory and erroneous and the Four Elements (Earth, Water, Fire, and Wind) as temporary (unreal) aggregates. This means complete non-being. (60:12b)

135. The mistake of the Buddhists arises from their dislike [of the world] which is the result of their selfishness, and the mistake of the Taoists arises from their trickery which is the result of their selfishness. The mistake of the Buddhists is to dislike and take lightly human affairs and therefore wish completely to turn everything into a void. The mistake of the Taoists is to take advantage of critical situations and opportunities and to resort to tricks and expediency, thus exploiting all kinds of schemes and crafts in the world. That is why military strategy, the art of calculation, and the technique of debate today are mostly based on Taoist ideas. (60:12b–13a)

136. It is not necessary to examine the doctrines of Buddhism and Taoism deeply to understand them. The mere fact that they discard the Three Bonds (between ruler and minister, father and son, and husband and wife) and the Five Constant Virtues (righteousness on the part of the father, deep love on the part of the mother, friendliness on the part of the elder brother, respect on the part of the younger brother, and filial piety on the part of the son) is already a crime of the greatest magnitude. Nothing more need be said about the rest. (60:13a)

137. Where the Buddhists have lofty views, they are really lofty. Someone asked why they only talk about Emptiness. The Teacher said:

They talk about Stubborn Emptiness and also True Emptiness. Stubborn Emptiness means that there is Emptiness without anything, whereas True Emptiness means that there is still something. The latter theory is somewhat similar to our Confucian doctrine. However, the Buddhists ignore the universe completely and only pay attention to the mind, very much like the Taoists, who also merely want to preserve the spirit and power [of the mind]. I-ch'uan (Ch'eng I) said that we can draw a final conclusion [that Buddhism and Confucianism are different] from the manifestations of Buddhism alone. I do not know what use there is for such doctrines as these. (60:13a–b)

138. Someone talked about the harm of Chuang Tzu, Lao Tzu, Zen, and [orthodox] Buddhism. The Teacher said: The doctrines of Zen are the most harmful to the Way. Chuang Tzu and Lao Tzu still did not completely destroy moral principles. In the case of [orthodox] Buddhism, human relations are already destroyed. When it comes to Zen, however, from the very start it wipes out all moral principles completely. Looked at this way, Zen has done the greatest harm.

After a moment he said again: Generally speaking, actually [these schools are all harmful] just the same. In the matter of doing harm, there has never been a case which does not proceed from the smaller to the greater degree. (60:13b)

139. Ts'ao asked how to tell the difference between Confucianism and Buddhism. The Teacher said: Just take the doctrine, "What Heaven imparts to man is called human nature." The Buddhists simply do not understand this, and dogmatically say that nature is empty consciousness. What we Confucianists talk about are concrete principles, and from our point of view they are wrong. They say, "We will not be affected by a single speck of dust [such as distinction of right and wrong or subject and object]. . . . and will not discard a single element of existence (dharma) [such as the minister's loyalty to the ruler or the son's filial piety to the father]." If one is not affected by any speck of dust, how is it possible for him not to discard a single element of existence? When he arrives at what is called the realm of Emptiness, he does not find any solution. Take the human mind, for example. There is necessarily in it the Five Relations between father and son, ruler and minister, old and young, husband and wife, and friends. When the Buddhists are thorough in their action, they will show no affection in these relationships, whereas when we Confucianists are thoroughgoing in our action, there is affection between father and son, righteousness between ruler and minister, order between old and young, attention to their separate functions between husband and wife, and faithfulness between friends. We Confucianists recognize only the moral principles of sincerity and genuineness. Sincerity is the essence of all good deeds. (60:14a)

140. The only difference between the Confucianists and Buddhists in their discourses on the nature is that the Buddhists talk about emptiness whereas the Confucianists talk about concreteness, and whereas the Buddhists talk about non-being, the Confucianists talk about being. (60:14b)

141. The Buddhists are characterized by vacuity, whereas we Confucianists are characterized by concreteness. The Buddhists are characterized by duality (of Absolute Emptiness and the illusory world), whereas we Confucianists are characterized by unity (one principle governing all). The Buddhists consider facts and principles as unimportant and pay no attention to them. (60:14b)

142. With us Confucianists, although the mind is vacuous, principle is concrete. The Buddhists, on the other hand, go straightly to their destination of emptiness and void. (60:14b)

143. We consider the mind and principle as one but they consider the mind and principle as two. It is not that the two groups purposely [differ] like this; it is the result of their different points of view. From their point of view, the mind is empty and is without principle, while from our point of view, although the mind is empty, all the principles are complete in it. However, although [we] say that the mind and principle are one, [we] fail to discern the selfishness resulting from material desires with which man is endowed in their physical nature.

Study Questions

G.17.4 Chu Hsi, The Mistakes of Buddhism

1. Explain and critique Chu Hsi's answer to the question, "What is the difference between Buddhist non-being and Taoist non-being?"
2. Explain the Buddhist mistakes that Chu Hsi attacks and whether his attack is justified.
3. Explain Chu Hsi's discussion of the differences between Buddhism and Confucianism.
4. Offer your critique of Chu Hsi's criticism.

CHAPTER 18

Ancient East Asian and Chinese Doctrines of Reality and Self-Enlightenment

The Tao (v. Đạo) of the Universe

Lao Tzu (v. Lão Tử)

The Introduction

Of all the scriptures of ancient East Asian philosophies, the *Tao Te Ching* (v. *Đạo Đức Kinh*), the *Nan Hua Ching* (v. *Nam Hoa Kinh*), and the "Ten Wings" of the *Chou Yi Ching* (v. *Chu Dịch Kinh*) contain some original and philosophically significant doctrines of reality.

These texts take the "Tao" (v. *Đạo* [Way]) as their theoretically hegemonic concept and offer two doctrines of reality, the Lao-Chuangian (v. Lão-Trangian) vision and the Yiian (v. Dịchian) vision, which are philosophically similar in many respects. Their philosophical similarities suggest a historical possibility that they must have been theoretically and culturally related. More researches are needed to determine their philosophical and cultural relationships. What are the similarities and differences between the two visions? Did the Lao-Chuangian vision of the Tao originate from the Yiian (v. Dịchian) vision or the other way around? Did they both originate from one common philosophical tradition?

Concerning modern studies on the origins of the *Chou Yi Ching* (v. *Chu Dịch Kinh*), see Iulian K. Shchutskii, *Researches on the I Ching* (Princeton: Princeton University Press, 1979).

[01] The Tao ([v. Đạo-ccp] Way) that can be told *Continuing forever, no end* of is not the eternal Tao [v. Đạo-ccp];

The name that can be named is not the eternal name.

The Nameless is the origin of Heaven and Earth;

The Named is the mother of all things [10,000 Species-ccp].

Therefore let there always be non-being so we may see their subtlety,

And let there always be being so we may see their outcome.

The two are the same,

But after they are produced, they have different names.

They both may be called deep and profound (*hsüan* [v. huyền-ccp]).

Deeper and more profound,

[Source: "The Laoian Ontology of the Tao (v. *Đạo*)." Taken from Lao Tzu, *The Tao Te Ching*, printed in Wing-Tsit Chan, trans., *The Way of Lao Tzu: A Translation of the Tao-te ching* (New York: Bobbs-Merrill, 1963), chapters cited, pp. 97, 124, 137, 144, 160, 162, 166, 170, 173–74, 190, 210.]

The door of all subtleties!
[*TTC*:1 (which refers to *The Tao Te Ching* [v. *Đạo Đức Kinh*], chapter 1)]

[02] We look at it and do not see it;
   Its name is The Invisible.
We listen to it and do not hear it;
   Its name is The Inaudible.
We touch it and do not find it;
   Its name is The Subtle (formless).
These three cannot be further inquired into,
   and hence merge into one.
Going up high, it is not bright, and coming down low, it is not dark.
Infinite and boundless, it cannot be given any name;
It reverts to nothingness.
This is called shape without shape,
Form (*hsiang* [v. tượng-ccp]) without object.
It is the Vague and Elusive.
Meet it and you will not see its head.
Follow it and you will not see its back.
Hold on to the Tao of old in order to master the things of the present.
From this one may know the primeval beginning [of the universe].
This is called the bond of [the-ccp] Tao.
[*TTC*:14]

[03] The all-embracing quality of the great virtue (te [v. đức-ccp]) follows alone from the Tao [v. Đạo-ccp].
The thing that is called Tao is eluding and vague.
   Vague and eluding, there is in it the form [v. tượng-ccp].
   Eluding and vague, in it are things [v. vật-ccp].
Deep and obscure, in it is the essence [v. tính-ccp].
The essence is very real; in it are evidences [v. tín-ccp].
From the time of old until now, its name (manifestations) ever remains,
By which we may see the beginning of all things.

How do I know that the beginnings of all things are so?
Through this (Tao).
[*TTC*:21]

[04] There was something [wu (v. vật)-ccp] undifferentiated and yet complete,
Which existed before heaven and earth.
Soundless and formless, it depends on nothing and does not change.
It operates everywhere and is free from danger.
It may be considered the mother of the universe.
I do not know its name; it is called [the] Tao.
If forced to give it a name, I shall call it Great.
Now being great means functioning everywhere.
Functioning everywhere means far-reaching.
Being far-reaching means returning to the original point.
Therefore [the] Tao is great.
Heaven is great.
Earth is great.
And the king is also great.
There are four great things in the universe, and the king is one of them.
Man models himself after Earth.
Earth models itself after Heaven.
Heaven models itself after [the] Tao.
And [the] Tao models itself after Nature [v. *tự nhiên* (that which is natural)-ccp].
[*TTC*:25]

[05] The Great Tao flows everywhere.
It may go left or right.
All things depend on it for life, and it does not turn away from them.
It accomplishes its task, but does not claim credit for it.
It clothes and feeds all things but does not claim to be master over them.
Always without desires, it may be called The Small.
All things come to it and it does not master them; it may be called The Great.

[Source: *Tao Te Ching. The Classic Book of Integrity and the Way. Lao Tzu.* A New Translation by Victor H. Mair Based on the Recently Discovered Ma-Wang-Tui Manuscripts (Bantam Books, 1990), chapter 45 (1), p. 59].

Therefore (the sage) never strive himself for the great, and thereby the great is achieved.
[*TTC*:34]

[06] We look at [the] Tao; it is imperceptible.
We listen to it; it is inaudible.
We use it; it is inexhaustible.
[*TTC*:35]

[07] [The] Tao invariably takes no action, and yet there is nothing left undone.
If kings and barons can keep it, all things will transform spontaneously.
If, after transformation, they should desire to be active,
I would restrain them with simplicity, which has no name.
Simplicity, which has no name, is free of desires.
Being free of desires, it is tranquil.
And the world will be at peace of its own accord.
[*TTC*:37]

[08] Of old those that obtained the One:
Heaven obtained the One and became clear.
Earth obtained the One and became tranquil.
The spiritual beings obtained the One and became divine.
The valley obtained the One and became full.
The myriad things obtained the One and lived and grew.
Kings and barons obtained the One and became rulers of the empire.
What made them so is the One.
[*TTC*:39]

[09] Reversion is the action of [the] Tao.
Weakness is the function of [the] Tao.
All things in the world come from being.
And being comes from non-being.
[*TTC*:40]

[10] When the highest type of men hear [the] Tao
They diligently practice it.
When the average type of men hear [the] Tao,
They half believe in it.

When the lowest type of men hear [the] Tao,
They laugh heartily at it.
If they did not laugh at it, it would not be [the] Tao.
Therefore there is the established saying:
The Tao which is bright appears to be dark.
The Tao which goes forward appears to fall backward.
The Tao which is level appears uneven. . . .
[The] Tao is hidden and nameless.
Yet it is [the] Tao alone that skillfully provides for all and bring them to perfection.
[*TTC*:41]

[11] [The] Tao produces them (the ten thousand things).
Virtue [Te (v. Đức)-ccp] fosters them.
Matter gives them physical form.
The circumstances and tendencies complete them.
Therefore the ten thousand things esteem [the] Tao and honor virtue.
[The] Tao is esteemed and virtue [te [v. đức]-ccp] is honored without anyone's order.
They always come spontaneously.
Therefore [the] Tao produces them and virtue fosters them.
They rear them and develop them.
They give them security and give them peace.
They nurture them and protect them.
([The] Tao) produces them but does not take possession of them.
It acts, but does not rely on its own ability.
It leads them but does not master them.
This is called profound and secret virtue [*hsüan te* (v. huyền đức)-ccp].
[*TTC*:51]

[12] [The] Tao is the storehouse of all things.
It is the good man's treasure and the bad man's refuge.
[*TTC*:62]

[Source: Lao Tzu, *Tao Te Ching* (v. Lão Tử, *Đạo Đức Kinh* [*The Classic of the Way and Its Virtue*], trans. Wing-tsit Chan (Princeton: Princeton University Press, 1973), chapters cited)].

Study Questions

G.18.1. Lao Tzu (v. Lão Tử), The Tao (v. Đạo) of the Universe

1. The first two verses of the *Tao Te Ching* (v. *Đạo Đức Kinh*) say:
    "The Tao that can be told of is not the eternal Tao.
    The name that can be named is not the eternal name." [*TTC*:1]
    a. Explain the philosophical reasons why there is such a theoretico-methodological problem (catch 22).
    b. Explain how Lao Tzu (v. Lão Tử) resolves this theoretico-methodological dilemma.
2. What is the philosophical method that Lao Tzu uses for his discovery of the Tao (v. Đạo)?
    a. Identify and characterize the two techniques of his philosophical method.
    b. Explain the two techniques of his philosophical method and their functional relationship as the *means* to achieve his philosophical objectives.
3. How does Lao Tzu (v. Lão Tử) perceive the natural world?
    a. Identify and explain the four main categories of the natural world.
    b. Critique the Laoian (v. Lãoian) conception of the natural world (universe).
4. What is the Tao (v. Đạo) according to Lao Tzu (v. Lão Tử)?
    a. Critically explain your interpretation of the two aspects (Being [Yu (v. Hữu)] and Non-Being (Wu [v. Vô]) of the Tao (v. Đạo).
    b. Critically explain your interpretation of the inherent attributes of the Tao (v. Đạo) conceptualized in chapter 51 (#11) and how these attributes are related to the properties conceptualized in chapter 21 [#03].
    c. Offer your interpretation of the theoretical status of the properties of the Tao conceptualized in chapter 21: Are they the properties of the pre-ontological Tao (as the "beginning" of Heaven and Earth) or of the ontological Tao (as the Being and Non-being of the universe)?
5. Should the Laoian (v. Lãoian) doctrine of the Tao be characterized as a "metaphysics" or as an "ontology"? Explain and defend your philosophical interpretation.

The Tao of Li Ch'i (v. Đạo Lý Khí)

Chu Hsi (v. Chu Hy)

100. In the universe there has never been any material force [Ch'i (v. Khí)-ccp] without principle [Li (v. Lý)-ccp] or principle without material force. (49:1a)

101. *Question:* Which exists first, principle or material force?

Answer: Principle has never been separated from material force. However, principle "exists before physical form [and is therefore without it]" whereas material force "exists after physical form [and is therefore with it]." Hence when spoken of as being before or after physical form, is there not the difference of priority and posteriority? Principle has no physical form, but material force is coarse and contains impurities. (49:1a–b)

102. Fundamentally principle and material force cannot be spoken of as prior or posterior. But if we must trace their origin, we are obliged to say that principle is prior. However, principle is not a separate entity. It exists right in material force. Without material force, principle would have nothing to adhere to. As material force, there are the Agents (or Elements) of Metal, Wood, Water, and Fire. As principle, there are humanity, righteousness, propriety, and wisdom. (49:1b)

Comment. Much discussion has taken place on the question whether Chu Hsi is a dualist. No one can doubt that principle is a universal, that there is a distinction between what exists before physical form and is therefore without it and what exists after form and is therefore with it, and that principle and material are different in many respects. As already suggested, Ch'eng Hao tended more to the monistic view while Ch'eng I tended more to the dualistic view, but it was also noted that whatever dualism there was, was superficial. What Chu Hsi did was to harmonize the two trends of the Ch'eng brothers. In his system, principle has not only a logical priority. It actually exists before physical form and is without it because it is the principle of being. But it is not something outside of material force that imparts a principle of being into it. This is the reason why he said that principle has never been separate from material force. Thus principle is both immanent and transcendent. In other words, he is neither a monist nor a dualist, or he is both a monist and a dualist.

108. Principle attaches to material force and thus operates. (49:4b)

109. Throughout the universe there are both principle and material force. Principle refers to the Way, which exists before physical form [and is without it] and is the root from which all things are produced. Material force refers to material objects, which exists after physical form [and is with it]; it is the instrument by which things are produced. Therefore in the production of man and things, they must be endowed with principle before they have their nature, and they must be endowed with material force before they have physical form. (49:5b)

> *Comment.* Needham correctly understands Neo-Confucian philosophy, especially as developed by Chu Hsi, as essentially organic. As he aptly summarizes it: "The Neo-Confucians arrive at essentially an organic view of the universe. Composed of matter-energy [material force] and ordered by the universal principle of organization [principle], it was a universe which, though neither created nor governed by any personal deity, was entirely real, and possessed the property of manifesting the highest human values (love, righteousness, sacrifice, etc.) when beings of an integrative level sufficiently high to allow of their appearance, had come into existence." Surely the Neo-Confucian conception of the universe is that of a single organism. All things exist in relations, and all relations follow a definite pattern according to which things are organized on various levels. That the universe is a set of relations goes far back to the *Book of Changes*, for Change itself is but relation. Tao as the principle of being is basically

a principle of relationship. Impressed with this relational character of Chinese philosophy, Needham saw a striking similarity between Chinese organism and that of Whitehead. He also has made a most illuminating study of Chu Hsi's influence on Leibniz and the philosophy of organism. We must remember, however, that in Chu Hsi's philosophy, the world is more than just an organism, for principle is metaphysical. Moreover, while the many similarities between Neo-Confucianism and Whitehead's organism as pointed out by Needham are surprising, there is absent in Neo-Confucianism Whitehead's God, who, as the principle of concretion, is ultimate irrationality.

110. What are called principle and material force are certainly two different entities. But considered from the standpoint of things, the two entities are merged one with the other and cannot be separated with each in a different place. However, this does not destroy the fact that the two entities are each an entity in itself. When considered from the standpoint of principle, before things existed, their principles of being had already existed. Only their principles existed, however, but not yet the things themselves. Whenever one studies these aspects, one should clearly recognize and distinguish them, and consider both principle and material force from the beginning to the end, and then one will be free from error. (49:5b–6a)

111. There is principle before there can be material force. But it is only when there is material force that principle finds a place to settle. This is the process by which all things are produced, whether large as heaven and earth or small as ants. Why should we worry that in the creative process of Heaven and Earth, endowment may be wanting? Fundamentally, principle cannot be interpreted in the senses of existence or nonexistence. Before Heaven and Earth came into being, it already was as it is. (49:6a)

112. Considering the fact that all things come from one source, we see that their principle is the same but their material force different. Looking at their various substances, we see that their material force is similar but their principle utterly different. The difference in material force is due to the inequality of its purity or impurity, whereas the difference in principle is due to its completeness or partiality. If you will please examine thoroughly, there should be no further doubt. (49:7a)

113. The nature of man and things is nothing but principle and cannot be spoken of in terms of integration and disintegration. That which integrates to produce life and disintegrates to produce death is only material force.

Study Questions

G.18.2. A Chinese (Neo-Confucianist) Ontology of the Tao (v. Đạo)

Chu Hsi (v. Chu Hy), The Tao of Li Ch'i (v. Đạo of Lý Khí)

1. What is "Li" (v. Lý)? What is "Ch'i" (v. Khí)? Explain Chu Hsi's doctrine.
2. What is the relationship between the Li and the Ch'i according to Chu Hsi?
3. What is the relationship between the Li Ch'i (v. Lý Khí) and the world and each living being? Explain and respond critically.
4. Compare and contrast Chu Hsi's doctrine of reality with the Laoian doctrine of the Đạo (c. Tao) and the Upanishadic doctrine of the Brahman.

CHAPTER 19

An Emerging Theoretical Synthesis of Eastern and Western Views of Reality

The Unity, Emptiness, and Forms of All Things

Fritjof Capra

Although the spiritual traditions described in the last five chapters differ in many details, their view of the world is essentially the same. It is a view which is based on mystical experience—on a direct non-intellectual experience of reality—and this experience has a number of fundamental characteristics which are independent of the mystic's geographical, historical, or cultural background. A Hindu and a Taoist may stress different aspects of the experience; a Japanese Buddhist may interpret his or her experience in terms which are very different from those used by an Indian Buddhist; but the basic elements of the world view which has been developed in all these traditions are the same. These elements also seem to be the fundamental features of the world view emerging from modern physics.

The most important characteristic of the Eastern world view—one could almost say the essence of it—is the awareness of the unity and mutual interrelation of all things and events, the experience of all phenomena in the world as manifestations of a basic oneness. All things are seen as interdependent and inseparable parts of this cosmic whole; as different manifestations of the same ultimate reality. The Eastern traditions constantly refer to this ultimate, indivisible reality which manifests itself in all things, and of which all things are parts. It is called *Brahman* in Hinduism, *Dharmakaya* in Buddhism, *Tao* in Taoism. Because it transcends all concepts and categories, Buddhists also call it *Tathata*, or Suchness:

> What is meant by the soul as suchness,
> is the oneness of the totality of all things,
> the great all-including whole.

In ordinary life, we are not aware of this unity of all things, but divide the world into separate objects and events. This division is, of course, useful and necessary to cope with our everyday environment, but it is not a fundamental feature of reality. It is an abstraction devised by our discriminating and categorizing intellect. To believe that our abstract concepts of separate 'things' and 'events' are realities of nature is an illusion. Hindus and Buddhists tell us that this illusion is based on *avidya*, or ignorance, produced by a mind under the spell of *maya*. The principal aim of the Eastern mystical traditions is therefore to readjust the mind by centering and quietening it through meditation. The Sanskrit term for meditation—*samadhi*—means literally 'mental equilibrium'. It refers to the balanced and tranquil state of mind in which the basic unity of the universe is experienced:

> Entering into the *samadhi* of purity, (one obtains) all-penetrating insight that enables one to become conscious of the absolute oneness of the universe.

The basic oneness of the universe is not only the central characteristic of the mystical experience, but is also one of the most important revelations of modern physics. It becomes apparent at the atomic level and manifests itself more and more as one penetrates deeper into matter, down into the realm of subatomic particles. The unity of all things and events will be a recurring theme throughout our comparison of modern physics and Eastern philosophy. As we study the various models of subatomic physics we shall see that they express again and again, in different ways, the same insight—that the constituents of matter and the basic phenomena involving them are all interconnected, interrelated and interdependent; that they cannot be understood as isolated entities, but only as integrated parts of the whole.

We may therefore regard matter as being constituted by the regions of space in which the field is extremely intense. . . There is no place in this new kind of physics both for the field and matter, for the field is the only reality.

The conception of physical things and phenomena as transient manifestations of an underlying fundamental entity is not only a basic element of quantum field theory, but also a basic element of the Eastern world view. Like Einstein, the Eastern mystics consider this underlying entity as the only reality: all its phenomenal manifestations are seen as transitory and illusory. This reality of the Eastern mystic cannot be identified with the quantum field of the physicist because it is seen as the essence of *all* phenomena in this world and, consequently, is beyond all concepts and ideas. The quantum field, on the other hand, is a well-defined concept which only accounts for some of the physical phenomena. Nevertheless, the intuition behind the physicist's interpretation of the subatomic world, in terms of the quantum field, is closely paralleled by that of the Eastern mystic who interprets his or her experience of the world in terms of an ultimate underlying reality. Subsequent to the emergence of the field concept, physicists have attempted to unify the various fields into a single fundamental field which would incorporate all physical phenomena. Einstein, in particular, spent the last years of his life searching for such a unified field. The *Brahman* of the Hindus, like the *Dharmakaya* of the Buddhists and the *Tao* of the Taoists, can be seen, perhaps, as the ultimate unified field from which spring not only the phenomena studied in physics, but all other phenomena as well.

In the Eastern view, the reality underlying all phenomena is beyond all forms and defies all description and specification. It is therefore often said to be formless, empty or void. But this emptiness is not to be taken for mere nothingness. It is, on the contrary, the essence of all forms and the source of all life. Thus the *Upanishads* say,

> *Brahman* is life. *Brahman* is joy.
> *Brahman* is the Void. . .
> Joy, verily, that is the same as the Void.
> The Void, verily, that is the same as joy.

Buddhists express the same idea when they call the ultimate reality *Sunyata*—'Emptiness', or 'the Void'—and affirm that it is a living Void which gives birth to all forms in the phenomenal world. The Taoists ascribe a similar infinite and endless creativity to the *Tao* and, again, call it empty. 'The *Tao* of Heaven is empty and formless' says the *Kuan-tzu*, and Lao Tzu uses several metaphors to illustrate this emptiness. He often compares the *Tao* to a hollow valley, or to a vessel which is for ever empty and thus has the potential of containing an infinity of things.

In spite of using terms like empty and void, the Eastern sages make it clear that they do not mean ordinary emptiness when they talk about

Brahman, Sunyata or *Tao*, but, on the contrary, a Void which has an infinite creative potential. Thus, the Void of the Eastern mystics can easily be compared to the quantum field of subatomic physics. Like the quantum field, it gives birth to an infinite variety of forms which it sustains and, eventually, reabsorbs. As the *Upanishads* say,

> Tranquil, let one worship It
> As that from which he came forth,
> As that into which he will be dissolved,
> As that in which he breathes.

The phenomenal manifestations of the mystical Void, like the subatomic particles, are not static and permanent, but dynamic and transitory, coming into being and vanishing in one ceaseless dance of movement and energy. Like the subatomic world of the physicist, the phenomenal world of the Eastern mystic is a world of *samsara*—of continuous birth and death. Being transient manifestations of the Void, the things in this world do not have any fundamental identity. This is especially emphasized in Buddhist philosophy which denies the existence of any material substance and also holds that the idea of a constant 'self' undergoing successive experiences is an illusion. Buddhists have frequently compared this illusion of a material substance and an individual self to the phenomenon of a water wave, in which the up-and-down movement of the water particles makes us believe that a 'piece' of water moves over the surface. It is interesting to note that physicists have used the same analogy in the context of field theory to point out the illusion of a material substance created by a moving particle. Thus Hermann Weyl writes:

> According to the [field theory of matter] a material particle such as an electron is merely a small domain of the electrical field within which the field strength assumes enormously high values, indicating that a comparatively huge field energy is concentrated in a very small space. Such an energy knot, which by

no means is clearly delineated against the remaining field, propagates through empty space like a water wave across the surface of a lake; there is no such thing as one and the same substance of which the electron consists at all times.

In Chinese philosophy, the field idea is not only implicit in the notion of the *Tao* as being empty and formless, and yet producing all forms, but is also expressed explicitly in the concept of *ch'i*. This term played an important role in almost every Chinese school of natural philosophy and was particularly important in Neo-Confucianism; the school which attempted a synthesis of Confucianism, Buddhism and Taoism. The word *ch'i* literally means 'gas' or 'ether', and was used in ancient China to denote the vital breath or energy animating the cosmos. In the human body, the 'pathways of *ch'i*' are the basis of traditional Chinese medicine. The aim of acupuncture is to stimulate the flow of *ch'i* through these channels. The flow of *ch'i* is also the basis of the flowing movements of *T'ai Chi Ch'uan*, the Taoist dance of the warrior.

The field theories of modern physics force us to abandon the classical distinction between material particles and the void. Einstein's field theory of gravity and quantum field theory both show that particles cannot be separated from the space surrounding them. On the one hand, they determine the structure of that space, whilst on the other hand they cannot be regarded as isolated entities, but have to be seen as condensations of a continuous field which is present throughout space. In quantum field theory, this field is seen as the basis of all particles and of their mutual interactions.

> The field exists always and everywhere; it can never be removed. It is the carrier of all material phenomena. It is the 'void' out of which the proton creates the pi-mesons. Being and fading of particles are merely forms of motion of the field.

The distinction between matter and empty space finally had to be abandoned when it became evident that virtual particles can come into being spontaneously out of the void, and vanish again into the void, without any nucleon or other strongly interacting particle being present. Here is a 'vacuum diagram' for such a process: three particles—a proton (p), an antiproton (p̄), and a pion (π)—are formed out of nothing and disappear again into the vacuum. According to field theory, events of that kind happen all the time. The vacuum is far from empty. On the contrary, it contains an unlimited number of particles which come into being and vanish without end.

Here then, is the closest parallel to the Void of Eastern mysticism in modern physics. Like the Eastern Void, the 'physical vacuum'—as it is called in field theory—is not a state of mere nothingness, but contains the potentiality for all forms of the particle world. These forms, in turn, are not independent physical entities but merely transient manifestations of the underlying Void. As the *sutra* says, 'Form is emptiness, and emptiness is indeed form.'

The relation between the virtual particles and the vacuum is an essentially dynamic relation; the vacuum is truly a 'living Void', pulsating in endless rhythms of creation and destruction. The discovery of the dynamic quality of the vacuum is seen by many physicists as one of the most important findings of modern physics. From its role as an empty container of the physical phenomena, the void has emerged as a dynamic quantity of utmost importance. The results of modern physics thus seem to confirm the words of the Chinese sage Chang Tsai:

> When one knows that the Great Void is full of *ch'i*, one realises that there is no such thing as nothingness.

Study Questions

G.19.1 Fritjof Capra, The Unity, Emptiness, and Form of All Things

1. Concerning the similarities between the different Eastern views of reality, Capra writes:
   "A Hindu and a Taoist may stress different aspects of the experience; a Japanese Buddhist interprets his or her experience in terms which are very different from those used by an Indian Buddhist; but the basic elements of the world view which has been developed in all these traditions are the same."
   a. Explain how Capra supports his conclusion.
   b. Critique Capra's conclusion if you can.
2. Identify the main concepts that Capra uses in his comparative analysis. *Critically* show the surprisingly close "parallels" between Eastern views and Western scientific theories of reality as he discusses them.

God and the World

Kitaro Nishida

Granting that facts of pure experience are the sole reality and that God is their unity, we can know God's characteristics and relation to the world from the characteristics of the unity of our pure experience or the unity of consciousness and from the relation of that unity to its content. First, we cannot see or hear our unity of consciousness, and it can in no way become an object of knowledge. Because all things come to exist in accordance with it, it totally transcends them. Although the mind conveys black when it encounters black, the mind is not black, and although it conveys white when it encounters white, it is not white. This characteristic unity of consciousness leads to the use of negation in Buddhism and in the so-called negative theology of thinkers in the medieval line of theology started by Dionysius the Areopagite.[1]

Such thinkers as Nicholas of Cusa stated that God transcends both being and non-being and that while God is being, God is non-being as well.[2] When we reflect deeply on the inner recesses of consciousness, we are struck by a lofty, mysterious feeling and discover profound meaning in Boehme's statements that God is "stillness without anything," bottomless (*Ungrund*), or "will without an object" (*Wille ohne Gegenstand*). In addition, God's eternality, omnipresence, omniscience, and omnipotence must all be interpreted from the character of this unity of consciousness. Because time and space are established by the unity of consciousness, God transcends time and space, is eternal and indestructible, and exists everywhere. And because everything arises from the unity of consciousness, God is omniscient and omnipotent; there is nothing God does not know and nothing God cannot do. In God, knowledge and capability are identical.

If this is so, then what is the relation between such an absolutely infinite God and this world? Non-being separate from being is not true

---

[1] Dionysius the Arcopagite, otherwise known as Pseudo-Dionysius, wrote a series of mystical treatises based on Neoplatonism. His exact identity and life dates are unknown.

[2] Nicholas of Cusa sets forth the principle of *coincidentia oppositorum*, which maintains that in God's being the various polarities holding sway in the world of actuality converge, or more precisely, exist in unity prior to any division.

[Source: Taken from Kitaro Nishida, *An Inquiry into the Good*, trans. Masao Abe and Christopher Ives (New Haven and London: Yale University Press, 1990), pp. 167–72].

non-being; a one apart from all things is not the true one; equality divorced from discrimination is not true equality. Just as there is no world without God, there is no God without the world. What I refer to here as the world of course does not indicate only this world. As Spinoza said, because God's attributes are infinite, God must envelop an infinite world. God's manifestation in the world accords with the essence of God, and it is never a contingent activity. It moreover is not that God at one time in the past created the world; as Hegel wrote, God is its eternal creator.[3] In short, the relation between God and the world is the relation between the unity of consciousness and its content. The content of consciousness is established by unity, and there is no unity apart from the content of consciousness—they are not two separate things, but rather the two sides of a single reality. In direct experience all phenomena of consciousness are one activity—however, by making this single activity the object of knowledge and reflecting upon it, the content is analyzed and distinguished in a variety of ways. In the process of this development, the whole at first appears spontaneously as one activity and then, through contradictions and conflicts, its content is reflected upon and discriminated. Here, too, I recall the words of Boehme, who stated that the God prior to revelation—an objectless will—reflects on Godself, that is, makes Godself a mirror; therefore, subjectivity and objectivity are separated and God and the world develop.

Originally, the differentiation of reality and its unity are one, not two. What is called unity in one respect signifies differentiation in another. Taking a tree for example, a flower's perfect "flowerness" and a leaf's perfect "leafness" express the essence of the tree. The distinction between differentiation and unity derives from thought, not from immediate actuality. Just as Goethe said that nature has neither kernel nor shell but that all is simultaneously kernel and shell,[4] so

in concrete true reality—in each fact of direct experience—are differentiation and unity one and the same activity. In a painting or melody, for instance, there is not one brush stroke or one note that does not directly express the spirit of the whole. For a painter or a musician, a single inspiration instantaneously comes forth and becomes an extremely varied landscape or an exquisite, complex melody. In this way, God is none other than the world and the world is none other than God. As Goethe wrote in his poem "Great is Diana of the Ephesians,"[5] silversmiths who earnestly made silver images of Diana without listening to Paul's teaching are in a certain sense closer to God than those who concern themselves with an abstract God in the brain. And, as Eckhart said, one sees the true God where even God has been lost.[6]

In this state of affairs, heaven and earth are merely one finger, and the myriad things and the self are of one body. Yet as stated before, due to the conflicts of the system of reality, and as the necessary process of its development, the system of reality comes to disintegrate; that is, reflection inevitably arises. By this means, that which was actual becomes conceptual, that which was concrete becomes abstract, and that which was one becomes many. At this point, God stands apart from the world and the self stands apart from other things; each is relative to the other and one thing goes against another. In all likelihood, the account of how our ancestors ate the fruit of the tree of wisdom and were driven out of the Garden of Eden signifies this truth. The fall of humans occurred not only in the distant time of Adam and Eve but is taking place moment by moment in our minds. If we look at this in a different way, however, we see that disintegration or reflection is not a separate activity, for it is simply the development of the activity of differentiation that constitutes one facet of unity. At the back of disintegration and reflection lies the possibility of a more profound

---

[3] Hegel argues that the historical process is the continuing creation and revelation of *Geist* (spirit).

[4] In the text Nishida includes the German: "*Natur hat weder Kern noch Schale, alles ist sie mit einen Male.*"

[5] The German title is "*Gross ist die Diana der Epheser.*"

[6] Eckhart is referring to the Godhead, where even the personal God cannot be found.

unity. Reflection is the route along which we attain a profound unity. (Shinran declares in the *Tannisho*, "If even a good person attains rebirth in the Pure Land, how much more so does an evil person.") For God to manifest God's most profound unity, God must first differentiate Godself. From a certain perspective, humans are directly God's self-realization. In terms of Christian legends, salvation through Christ exists precisely because of Adam's fall, and in all of this the infinite love of God becomes clear.

Considering the relation between the world and God in the above way, how should we explain individuality? If we assume that the countless things in the universe are manifestations of God and that only God is true reality, then must we think of our individuality as merely a false appearance which, like a bubble, has no significance whatsoever? I do not think that we have to view individuality in this way. Although there is probably no independent individuality separate from God, our individuality should not be regarded as a mere phantasm; rather, it is part of God's development, one of God's activities of differentiation. Just as all people are born with a mission given by God, individuality is an offshoot of divinity and each person's development completes God's development. In this sense, our individuality possesses an eternal life and constitutes an eternal development. (See Royce's discussion of the immortality of the soul.) The relation between God and our individual consciousness is the relation between the entirety of consciousness and one part of it. In all mental phenomena, each part stands in the unity of the whole, and at the same time each must be an independent consciousness. (In mental phenomena, each part is an end in itself.) In fact, that all things are the manifestation of a single, peerless God does not necessarily imply the negation of each person's self-aware independence. This situation is like an individual unity holding sway over one's consciousness from moment to moment while each momentary consciousness is an independent consciousness.

Illingworth stated that one personality necessarily seeks another, and that in the other personality the self attains to the satisfaction of the personality as a whole; in other words, love is an indispensable characteristic of personality.[7] To acknowledge another personality is to acknowledge one's own, and the relationship in which people mutually acknowledge their personalities is love. In a certain regard, love is the union of both personalities—that is, in love, two personalities, while independent and respecting each other, join together and constitute one personality. Viewed this way, God can envelop all personalities and acknowledge their independence because God is infinite love.

The criticism of pantheistic ideas—such as the idea that all things are a manifestation of God—is voiced in conjunction with the problem of explaining the origin of evil. To my way of thinking, there is originally nothing absolutely evil; all things are fundamentally good, and reality, just as it is, is the good. Although religious figures forcefully preach the evils of the flesh, physical desire is not evil in an abstract sense; it only becomes evil when it hinders spiritual growth. Also, as asserted by ethicists relying on the theory of evolution, that which we now call sin was morality in a past era. Sin is the legacy of a past morality, which in the present age has become evil because it is now inappropriate. Fundamentally, then, things themselves contain nothing evil. Evil arises from the contradictions and conflicts of the

---

[7] Nishida's note is "Illingworth, *Personality, Human and Divine.*" In this work Illingworth states, "We require to find in other persons an end in which our entire personality may rest. And this is the relationship of love. Its intensity may admit of degrees, but it is distinguished from all other affections or desires, by being the outcome of our whole personality. It is our very self, and not a department of us, that loves. And what we love in others is the personality or self, which makes them what they are. We love them for their own sake. And love may be described as the mutual desire of persons for each other as such; the mode in which the life of desire finds its climax, its adequate and final satisfaction." Illingworth, *Personality, Human and Divine: Being the Bampton Lectures for the Year 1894* (London: Macmillan, 1917), 38.

system of reality. If someone asks about the origin of these conflicts, we can answer that they are based on the differentiating activity of reality and are a necessary condition for the development of reality. Again, reality develops through contradictions and conflicts. Although he constantly sought evil, Mephistopheles professed to be part of the power that constantly creates good. Indeed, evil is an essential element in the construction of the universe.

Because evil is not the activity of the unified advance of the universe, there is of course nothing in it that must be made into a goal. However, a tranquil, uneventful world with no sin and no dissatisfaction would be extremely mundane and shallow. Those who do not know sin cannot truly know the love of God, and those who have no dissatisfaction or anguish cannot comprehend the depths of spirituality. Sin, dissatisfaction, and anguish are necessary conditions for the spiritual advancement of humanity; a true person of religion does not see a divine contradiction in these experiences, but rather feels God's infinite grace. Such things as sin and anguish do not make the world incomplete; on the contrary, they make it rich and profound. If we were to rid the world of them, we would lose the way to spiritual growth and innumerable spiritual enterprises of great beauty would disappear from this world. If we assume the universe as a whole is established according to spiritual meaning, then there is no

imperfection due to the presence of those things— on the contrary, we can know the reason for their necessity and indispensability. Sin is despicable, but there is nothing in the world as beautiful as a sin for which one has repented.

At this point I cannot help recalling a passage in Oscar Wilde's *De Profundis*.[8] Christ loves sinners as people who are closest to human perfection. It was not Christ's aim to transform an interesting thief into a boring honest person. With a method until then unknown in the world, Christ transformed sin and anguish into something beautiful and sacred. A sinner must repent, of course, and his or her repentance perfects the things done in the past. The Greeks believed that a person could not alter the past; they even had an expression to the effect that the gods were also unable to change the past. But Christ showed a way through which even the most ordinary sinner can do so. Wilde wrote that from Christ's perspective, when the prodigal son dropped to his knees and cried, he made the sins and anguish of his past into the most beautiful and sacred events of his life. Wilde himself was a man of sin, so he knew its essence well.

[8] The Irish writer Oscar Wilde (1854–1900) wrote *De Profundis* (published posthumously in 1905) late in his career as a poet, dramatist, and novelist. The work consists of a long letter Wilde wrote to Lord Alfred Douglas while serving a two-year prison sentence in Reading Gaol on charges of sodomy. Benét, *RE*, 264.

Study Questions

G.19.2 Kitaro Nishida, God and the World

1. Explain Nishida's conception of God and make your critical response.
2. Explain Nishida's conception of the God-World relationship.
3. Identify the "criticism" of Nishida's doctrine that he acknowledges. Explain how he responds in his own defense and offer your critique of his doctrine.

Part H

Appendices:
Some Aspects of Vietnamese
Zen and Religion

H. APPENDIX 1

Buddhism and Popular Religion in Medieval Vietnam

J.C. Cleary

This article presents some of the data on the nature of religion in medieval Vietnam preserved in a remarkable thirteenth-century Zen book, the *Truyền Đăng Tập Lục,* the Vietnamese *Record of the Transmission of the Lamp* (hereinafter referred to as TDTL).[1]

The TDTL is a collection of stories and Zen lessons presented as biographies of leading Vietnamese Zen masters. The identity of the compiler or author is unknown. The TDTL bears only a superficial resemblance to the famous eleventh-century Chinese collection of Zen biographies with a similar name, the *Jing De*

Chuan Deng Lu. Unlike the Chinese book, which was edited with notions of Confucian respectability in mind, the Vietnamese *Transmission of the Lamp* is a rich source for the beliefs and practices of folk religion. The Chinese book is a more extensive, loosely knit collection that includes brief notices of little substance on many lesser figures, along with fuller accounts of the famous public champions of the Zen school in China. The Vietnamese work is a carefully crafted whole that skillfully weaves its Zen message into a comprehensive picture of a wide range of Buddhist beliefs and practices and popular images of curing, prophecy, and magic. Never far in the background is the on-going struggle to assert the national identity of Vietnam against Chinese pressure.

The TDTL is a unique source on medieval Vietnamese religion. It also is of general theoretical interest for the study of religion. It shows clearly that the characteristic beliefs of the "folk religion" of Vietnam were held by educated courtiers as well as unlettered commoners. It demonstrates that the Buddhist elite, the

[1] The text consulted in writing this paper is a photocopy of the edition of the TDTL in the archives of the École Francaise d'Extrême Orient, A. 2767, N. 279. A fuller version of the title is *Đại Nam Thiền Uyển Truyền Đăng Tập Lục* [Transmission of the Lamp in the Zen Gardens of Great Vietnam]. The text is divided into sections, each of which gives the story of one Zen teacher. For citations in this paper, I refer to the section cited by the name of the Zen teacher whose story is told there.

An annotated English translation of the entire text by the Vietnamese Buddhist scholar Nguyễn Tự Cường will be forthcoming soon.

Cleary, J. C., "Buddhism and Popular Religion in Medieval Vietnam," *Journal of the American Academy of Religion*, Vol. LIX, No. 1, Spring 1991, pp. 93–118, by permission of Oxford University Press.

enlightened adepts, were not reluctant to express their message within the framework of the beliefs of the folk religion. These facts call into question the validity of the eighteenth-century Enlightenment idea (recycled in the twentieth century as the Great Tradition / little tradition dichotomy) that generally one can expect to find a more intellectual, philosophical version of religion in the higher reaches of the social hierarchy, while the masses hold to a more emotional, superstitious set of beliefs. The interpenetration of "elite" religion and "folk" religion illustrated in the TDTL suggests that there may be a basic flaw in separating the study of folk religion and the study of scriptural religion into distinct specializations.

The Buddhist Spectrum in Old Vietnam

In traditional East Asia, Buddhism (the Buddha Dharma, the teaching of the enlightened ones) existed in many forms. According to the Buddhist conception of how religious teaching ought to be carried out, the principle of *skill in means*, such multiformity was necessary and proper.

Skill in means requires that the presentation of the Buddhist Teaching be adapted to the audience that is being addressed. The Buddhist view is that the totality of truth cannot be captured in words and can only be communicated by the use of provisional expedients that are only partial truths. Since the potentials and capacities of different audiences vary, the form in which the Dharma is communicated must vary accordingly. No particular form is privileged; skill in means is the opposite of dogmatism. The Buddhist criterion for true teaching is effectiveness for the purpose at hand, whether this is the elementary aim of improving the moral level and material welfare of the community and promoting good behavior, or the more advanced aims of deconditioning behavior, restructuring awareness, and liberating enlightened perception.

The TDTL provides evidence that the full spectrum of teachings characteristic of East Asian Buddhism existed in medieval Vietnam, as in contemporary China, Korea, and Japan. This spectrum included scriptural Buddhism in its learned and popular versions, Zen, Pure Land Buddhism, and Tantra.

The TDTL reflects a clear awareness of the Indian origins of Buddhism. In the biography of National Teacher Thông Biện [d. 1134], Thông Biện lectures the Empress Dowager on the history of Buddhism, starting with the story of Śākyamuni Buddha's enlightenment and teaching career. Thông Biện also notes that Buddhism was brought to China and Vietnam from India. The TDTL includes the biography of Vinitaruci [d. 594], by tradition a man from India who studied Zen in China before coming to Vietnam in 580 to start a line of Zen transmission there.

Both Vinitaruci and Thông Biện are shown espousing the central Mahāyāna tenet that all sentient beings have an inherent potential for enlightenment. Thông Biện says: "Fundamentally enlightenment is profoundly clear and eternally present. All beings share this inner truth. Because they are covered over by sentiments and sensory experience, they drift according to their karma and revolve through the various planes of existence."

In the biographies of Ngộ Ấn and Maha, the TDTL notes that certain Zen men in Vietnam knew Sanskrit. The life story of the Zen master and magician Không Lộ relates that Không Lộ and two of his companions travelled from Vietnam to India to seek wisdom and acquire supernatural powers. According to his biography, when Đạo Hạnh wanted to learn magic to avenge his father's murder, he set out for India. The section on Sùng Phạm says that after receiving the mind-seal of his teacher in Vietnam, "Sùng Phạm travelled all over India seeking to broaden his knowledge. After nine years he returned [to Vietnam], clear in both discipline and concentration."

The TDTL has frequent references to the study of the Buddhist sutras. The sutras are the holy scriptures of Buddhism. They generally depict scenes in which Śākyamuni Buddha or other enlightened beings offer teachings to vast arrays of beings. These teachings sometimes take the form of verbal explanations, but Buddha often resorts to direct communication that shows his audiences visions that illustrate aspects of reality as it appears to the enlightened.

The sutras set forth the theoretical framework and worldview of Buddhism. As Buddhism spread outward from India, the sutras were translated into the local languages: in the Far East into written Chinese, the language of literary culture throughout the area. Stories from the sutras were also transmitted orally, and their colorful and memorable scenes penetrated the nonliterate folk culture. Sūtras were often chanted aloud from the texts or memorized and recited. Moreover, the physical texts of the sutras were venerated as holy objects, and copying the sutras was considered a meritorious act of piety.

Several of the most famous Mahāyāna scriptures are mentioned in the TDTL. In the section on Bảo Tính and Minh Tâm, who were companions in the Dharma, we read: "The two masters devoted themselves to chanting the Lotus Sūtra for more than fifteen years without ever neglecting it." Of Thông Biện it is related: "He often taught people to practice by using the Lotus Sūtra, so people spoke of him [with the epithet] Ngộ Pháp Hoa 'Awakened to the Lotus.'" Master Chân Không had his initial insight upon hearing a lecture on the Lotus Sūtra, and later won acclaim in the capital for his own expositions of the Lotus. In the story of Thiện Hội, his teacher Cảm Thành quotes the Vimalakirti Sūtra. Viên Chiếu recited the Complete Enlightenment Sūtra and practiced its meditation perspectives. So did Tín Học. Tĩnh Lực "often lectured on the Complete Enlightenment Sūtra; where [his listeners] were unsure of the meanings and principles, he would set them straight." The ascetic Đại Xả "made it his constant practice to recite the Huayan Sūtra." Ngộ Ấn "concentrated on the Complete Enlightenment Sūtra and the Lotus Sūtra and made a thorough study into their subtlety and beauty."

The TDTL preserves other evidence of the pervasive presence of the sutras among Vietnamese Buddhists. Bảo Giám provided his home temple with copies of the sutras in his own hand. Tín Học came from a family whose trade for generations had been carving the wooden blocks used in printing the sutras. Pháp Dung composed verses of praise for the various scriptures.

Trường Nguyên, a Zen master of a minority race, famous for his asceticism, shunned the patronage of high society, lived in solitude in the mountains, and "devoted himself to chanting scriptures." He gave the gist of the scriptural teaching in these words:

> How strange! How is it that all sentient beings possess the wisdom of the Tathagatas, but are lost in ignorance and delusion and do not see it or know it? I always teach them the Path, so that they can forever leave behind the clinging of false thoughts and witness within their own bodies the vast and great wisdom of the Tathagatas, with its benefits, its peace, and its bliss.

As in the other East Asian countries, in Vietnam it was normal for Zen adepts to know the sutras. For example, Khuông Việt "read widely in the scriptures, and investigated the essential teachings of Zen." Minh Trí studied sutras as well as Zen lore. Huệ Sinh, born in a family of high rank, took time from his Confucian studies as a youth to read "all the sutras and Buddhist philosophical treatises." Later he abandoned conventional society to seek enlightenment as a Zen monk.

Those unfamiliar with Zen from primary sources may be surprised to find Zen masters studying and venerating the Buddhist scriptures. Zen began as a movement that emphasized direct realization of the truth of the Buddhas and criticized the tendency of many Buddhists to study the scriptures at a superficial verbal level without trying to live up to their message. But Zen teachers certainly never rejected the sutras themselves: their quarrel was with those who ignored the sutras' practical intent.

This is reflected in the story of Zen master Maha in the TDTL. Maha, of Champa descent, was the son of a Lê dynasty official learned in Buddhist literature. Maha was very erudite and had studied both Sanskrit and Chinese. "Once when Maha was explaining a sutra, one of the good spirits that protect the Dharma appeared before him and reproached him: 'What is the use of such external learning? You surely cannot use it to comprehend the true principle [of the sutras].' At this, Maha lost his sight." Despondent at being blinded, Maha is saved from suicide by the timely intervention of a Zen teacher. After three years of devoted practice, Maha regains his sight, and goes on to become an adept of formidable powers.

By the time the TDTL was composed, Zen teachers in China and Korea, as well as in Vietnam, were reemphasizing the integral links between Zen and scriptural Buddhism. They insisted that those who see any opposition between Zen and the scriptures, and champion one to the exclusion of the other, misunderstand both.

The biography of Ngộ Ấn contains this dialogue: "Someone asked: 'What is Buddha? What is the Dharma? What is Zen?' Ngộ Ấn said, 'The Supreme Dharma King in his embodiment is Buddha, in his word is the Dharma, and in his mind is Zen. Though they are three, they return to one source. It is like the water in three rivers that is named according to where it is: though the names are not the same, the nature of the water is not different.'"

We also find this metaphoric affirmation of the harmony of Zen and the scriptures in the section on Tịnh Không: "Someone asked, 'Are the meaning of the Zen patriarchs and the meaning of the scriptural teachings the same or different?' Tịnh Không said, 'Sailing the seas for ten thousand miles, all come to the Imperial City.'" (Here the "Imperial City" of course symbolizes enlightenment.)

Basic to the Buddhist teaching is the principle of karmic retribution, which asserts that one receives rewards and punishments according to one's deeds. The corollary is that one's present experience is determined by one's karma, one's actions in this life and past lives. Meritorious actions in past lives can give a person a "karmic link" to Buddhism, the priceless opportunity to come in contact with the Buddha Dharma in the present life. These ideas about karma are amply reflected in the TDTL.

In the TDTL section on Cảm Thành, his teacher Vô Ngôn Thông tells him that their meeting each other "is due to previous karmic links." In the biography of Viên Chiếu it is related that Viên Chiếu became a monk after a physiognomist told him, "You have a karmic connection to the Buddha Dharma. If you leave home [to become a monk] you are sure to become a great bodhisattva among humans." (A bodhisattva is an enlightened person who functions in the world to work for the enlightenment of others.)

The principle of karmic retribution has direct implications for religious practice. The way to advance in the Buddhist Path is to purify one's conduct, to improve one's karma. Conversely, for deluded beings, ignorance generates actions, and these actions create the karmic consciousness that perpetuates delusion and leads to more misguided actions.

In the TDTL the Zen master Đại Xả tells the Emperor Lý Anh Tông [r. 1137–1175]: "If you can keep your karmic consciousness in check until it is quiet and peaceful, then you will cleanse away afflictions. There is no other method to cultivate."

For Buddhist monks and nuns, particularly strict discipline was essential: there were codes of monastic conduct known as *vinaya*. In the biography of Đạo Huệ we read: "When he was twenty-five he became a monk under the guidance of [Thông Biện]. . . . Subsequently he came to Quảng Minh Temple and stayed on there investigating and refining his practice of the vehicle of discipline [*vinaya*]." Of Tĩnh Giới the TDTL relates: "He devoted himself to studying the *vinaya*." Viên Học's biography says: "When he was twenty, upon hearing Chân Không teach, the mind-ground opened through for him. After that his studies of Zen became more and more profound and his observance of the precepts was beyond compare."

Many of the biographies in the TDTL contain accounts of the strenuous austerities practiced by seekers on their way to becoming Zen masters. Austerities represent a dramatic break with the karmic pattern of worldly life, which is based on seeking pleasure and avoiding pain. In popular Buddhist belief, the practice of austerities was one of the hallmarks of the true religious life.

Quảng Trí, from an aristocratic background, "always wore a patched robe and fed himself on pine nuts." Tịnh Không "practiced austerities for five or six years, eating almost nothing, sitting [in meditation] for long periods of time without lying down to sleep. Whenever he went into *samādhi* [deep meditative concentration], he would only come out of it after several days. Donors from all over offered him gifts, which just piled up [unused]." Trường Nguyên, we are told, "went to Mount Từ Sơn and hid his traces. He dressed in straw and lived on chestnuts. His daily companions were the streams and rocks and monkeys. Twenty-four hours a day he gathered in his body and mind and fused them into a single whole."

The purpose of the discipline and austerities undertaken by those who aspired to enlightenment was to break their attachments to the world of sensory experience, to save the energy they would otherwise have expended seeking comfort and pleasure, and to reorient themselves toward the abstract goal of enlightenment. Austerity was taught in Buddhism as a means of empowerment, not as an end in itself. Tales of the austerities practiced by famous adepts figured prominently in the popular religion, to offer proof of the adepts' special dedication and zeal and to explain how they attained their awesome powers.

Another way for Buddhists to improve their karmic prospects was to perform good works and thus accumulate merit. Meritorious works included efforts to promote Buddhism, as well as

acts that served the general public interest. There are many examples of both given in the stories in the TDTL.

Trí Bảo, after living in the mountains as an ascetic, reentered society and dedicated himself to good works "such as repairing roadways and building temples and *stupas*. According to conditions, he gave everyone encouragement [to follow the Dharma]. He never acted for his own profit or to gain support." (*Stupas* were memorial structures where holy relics were interred.) Giới Không served as a curer during a plague. He also was active in restoring old temples in his home area. After twenty years in the mountains, Chân Không was summoned to the imperial court and attracted patronage from some of the leading men in the state: "He used all that he received to repair temples, build *stupas*, and cast great bells, in order to safeguard the Dharma for posterity." Chân Không's disciple Viên Học "regularly took the lead in projects such as repairing bridges, building roads, and so on." Y Sơn "travelled everywhere teaching, intent on benefiting people. All the money he received as donations he used to support Buddhist activities."

Y Sơn described the motives of the genuine Zen adept in attracting patronage in these terms: "Fishing for fame, longing for profit—these are like bubbles floating on the water. Planting merit, sowing the seeds of good causal conditions—these are the truly precious jewels in our hearts."

A major branch of Buddhism in East Asia was the Pure Land teaching. Pure Land believers put their faith in the power of Amitābha Buddha, the Buddha of Infinite Life and Infinite Light. Long ago Amitābha vowed to deliver all those who invoke his name, promising them rebirth in his Pure Land in the West. Amitābha's Pure Land is a paradise, where there is no suffering, disease, or death, where the environment is beautiful and pleasing, and where food and clothing are provided ready-made. Once reborn in the Pure Land, people can continue the quest for complete enlightenment in the direct presence of Amitābha Buddha, unhindered by the sufferings of this world.

The Pure Land teaching was devised and propagated as an easy way, open to all. Even sinners could achieve birth in the Pure Land, if they had faith in Amitābha and invoked his name sincerely. The fundamental Pure Land practice was recitation of the name of Amitābha, reinforced by vows to seek rebirth in the Pure Land.

Many Zen teachers from the tenth century on made room for Pure Land practice, encouraging certain students to recite the buddha-name as a means of concentrating and focusing their minds. Combining Zen and Pure Land practice became a common trend. In the Zen interpretation, Amitābha Buddha is the inherent enlightenment of our true nature, and the Pure Land is its fundamental purity. Reciting the buddha-name is efficacious when it becomes real mindfulness of buddha, unmixed with worldly concerns.

The TDTL contains only a few references to Pure Land Buddhism. When the Empress Dowager questions National Teacher Thông Biện, she asks him about reaching the mind of the Zen patriarchs through reciting the buddha-name. This question implies an acquaintance with the combined practice of Zen and Pure Land. According to his biography, the Zen master Không Lộ cast a large image of Amitābha Buddha at Quỳnh Lâm Temple. The TDTL relates that after an illustrious public career spanning seventy-five years as a magician, exorcist, and healer, Không Lộ returned to the Western Paradise. While living in a reed hut in the mountains, Tĩnh Lực "had deep attainment in the *samādhi* of buddha-remembrance through reciting the buddha-name." This is an example of using the Pure Land practice of reciting the name of Amitābha to attain a state of stable meditative concentration (*samādhi*). Tĩnh Lực told his students: "Use your minds to be mindful [of Buddha] and your mouths to recite [the buddha-name] until you achieve decisive faith and understanding."

Very much in evidence in the TDTL is the use of *mantra* or *dhāranī*, a practice derived from Tantric Buddhism. Tantric theory views the physical world, with its interplay of matter and energy, as an expression of absolute reality. Tantric practice involves elaborate rituals and intricate visualizations, which use sound and form to align the mind of the participants with larger cosmic energies, often conceptualized as deities. Mantras (or *dhāranīs*) are specific sequences of sounds that are linked to cosmic energy patterns; by reciting the mantra, the practitioners can attune their minds to these forces and achieve a deeper communion with the total reality.

Because Tantric forms invited misuse by those seeking sensory stimulation or self-aggrandizing magic powers, Tantra was an esoteric tradition. Its advanced practices were open only to those who had been properly initiated after undergoing a long process of purification and discipline. Nevertheless, Tantric influences diffused into popular Buddhism, where mantras were conceived of along the lines of magical spells. People sought power through the chanting of mantras and saw in the interplay of cosmic deities in Tantric mandalas a pattern for myths and exoteric rituals.

Throughout the TDTL, the use of mantras is closely associated with the possession of supernatural powers. It is related that Không Lộ, the great Zen master and magician, concentrated on the Great Compassion mantra when he first returned from his journey to India. Đại Xả, besides reciting the Huayan Sutra, chanted the Samantabhadra mantra, and was able to resist severe torture without showing any sign of fear. Nguyện Học "always recited the *dhāranī* of the Fragrant Ocean of Great Compassion, and so he always got results when he treated sicknesses or prayed for rain." Vạn Hạnh, who could foretell the future, had devoted himself in his youth to the practice of *dhāranī-samādhi*, the attainment of meditative concentration through reciting *dhāranī*. Dao Hanh acquired a spirit-protector and magical powers by diligently reciting the Mind of Great Compassion mantra.

In all these stories of the use of mantras by famous adepts, great prominence is given to the popular idea of reciting mantras as a route to magical powers. But the author of the TDTL also includes a view of *dhāraṇī* from the perspective of the Zen school, in the section on Thông Thiền. "A monk asked, 'What is buddha?' Thông *Thiền* said, 'The original mind is buddha. That's why Xuanzang said, "Just comprehend the mind-ground: this is called *dhāraṇī*, total command."'"

Buddhism and National Identity

Vietnamese national identity has been shaped in part by a centuries-long struggle against Chinese hegemony. Despite a millennium of Chinese suzerainty and strong Chinese influence on their elite culture, the Vietnamese were able to resist the assimilation into China that was the fate of the coastal peoples immediately north of them. Chinese control was shaken off in the tenth century, but the Vietnamese still had to repel several more rounds of Chinese invasion to preserve their independence. The TDTL adroitly reflects on this enduring theme in Vietnam's history, both acknowledging the Chinese legacy and yet insisting on the autonomy and equal dignity of Vietnamese culture.

Buddhism came to Vietnam during the period of Chinese control, and Zen as a distinctive style of Buddhism started in China. The TDTL clearly recognizes the Chinese connections of the founders of Vietnamese Zen. According to the TDTL, Vinitaruci came from India to China, where he became a disciple of the third Chinese patriarch of Zen, Sengcan. The story tells that at Sengcan's direction, Vinitaruci proceeded on to Vietnam (then the Chinese commandery of Jiaozhou) to link up with potential students of the Dharma there. Master Vô Ngôn Thông, the traditional founder of the other line of Vietnamese Zen, was originally from Guangdong (in south China). He studied with the great Chinese teacher Baizhang before coming to Vietnam in 820 and passing the Zen teaching on to a Vietnamese disciple.

In its section on Thông Biện, in which Thông Biện gives an account of the history of Buddhism,

the TDTL balances this recognition of the Chinese origin of the Zen school with an affirmation of Vietnamese equality with China in terms of Buddhist development. Thông Biện quotes a dialogue between the (Chinese) Dharma teacher Tanqian and the Emperor Sui Wen Di [r. 580–611], the second great unifier of China, who was also an ardent patron of Buddhism. After noting how many temples and *stupas* he has had built, the Chinese emperor says: "Although Jiaozhou [i.e. Vietnam] belongs to China, we still need to bind it to us, so we ought to send monks renowned for their virtue there to convert everyone and let them all attain enlightenment." Tanqian then reminds the emperor:

> The area of Jiaozhou has [long] been in communication with India. Early on, when the Buddha Dharma came to China, it also came there and flourished. Temples were built, monks were ordained, scriptures were translated. Because of this prior connection, there were already [eminent] monks and nuns there. In our time there is the venerable Pháp Hiền, who received the transmission from Vinitaruci, and who is now spreading the school of the Zen patriarchs. Pháp Hiền is a bodhisattva living among humans . . . Thus [the situation of Buddhism in Vietnam] is no different from China. . . . There are already Buddhist teachers there: we do not have to go to convert them.

In several TDTL stories, Buddhist adepts defend Vietnam by impressing Chinese envoys as men of culture, thus demonstrating to them that Vietnam is a highly civilized nation not to be trifled with. The biography of Viên Chiếu contains this story: At the end of the eleventh century, the Vietnamese emperor Lý Nhân Tông gave a copy of a work by Zen master Viên Chiếu to the Chinese envoy, who sent it along to the Song emperor Zhezong. Zhezong summoned a Chinese Buddhist master to explicate the book.

When he had read it, he joined his palms and bowed in homage and said, "In the south a flesh-and-blood bodhisattva has appeared in the world, and he is well able to expound the Dharma. How could I add or subtract anything?" Emperor Zhezong then had a copy made to keep for himself, and sent the original back to Vietnam. . . . Emperor Lý Nhân Tông was very pleased and rewarded Viên Chiếu handsomely.

In other tales in the TDTL, Zen masters use their magical powers to repel Chinese aggression.

In 986 the Chinese army of the Song regime invaded Vietnam. When the Emperor was informed of this, he ordered Khuông Việt to pray [for national salvation]. The enemy army took fright and fled to the Ninh River in Bảo Hựu. Wild waves sprang up, raised by the wind, and flood-dragons appeared leaping and prancing about. The Chinese army fled in complete disarray.

In another tale, the Vietnamese adept takes steps to reverse the damage wrought by the Chinese invaders, and to safeguard the future of the nation.

When La Quí An was about to die, he said to his disciple Thiền Ông: "Formerly, [the Chinese magician-general] Gao Pian constructed a fortress by the Su Li River because he knew that our territory of Cổ Pháp [in that vicinity] has an imperial aura about it, the energy of a place where kings come from. To suppress this energy, he had rivers and lakes rechanneled and dammed up in nineteen places. I have already advised [the local Vietnamese lord] Khúc Lãm to have [the water-courses] rebuilt as they were before. In addition, at Minh Châu Temple I have had a cotton tree planted to secure all these disrupted sites. You should know that in the future a true king

is sure to appear [to rule Vietnam] and support our True Dharma.

La Quí An went on to predict the rise of the Lý dynasty, which consolidated Vietnam's independence from China. (Cổ Pháp was the home area of the Lý family.)

The TDTL sums up the always ambivalent relation of Vietnam with China with particular charm in a story in the TDTL section on Không Lộ:

Zen master Không Lộ journeys to the capital of China in search of copper from which to cast four great ritual vessels. Dressed as a monk, he waits patiently in front of the palace until summoned by the Emperor. When the Emperor asks him what his business is and where he comes from, Không Lộ replies: "I am a poor monk from a small country. . . . My present wish is to cast four vessels for Vietnam, but my strength is not sufficient to accomplish my intention. Therefore, I did not shrink from the long journey: I have come here in the humble hope that the Sagely Emperor will show his mercy and give me a little fine copper to use to cast the vessels."

The Emperor asks how many men Không Lộ has brought along to help him transport the copper, and Không Lộ answers: "There's only me. Please fill my bag and I will carry it myself. That will be enough." The Emperor says: "Take as much copper as your strength allows. Such a trifling matter is not worth discussing."

Không Lộ starts filling his bag with copper coins and takes more and more until he has used up all the copper in the Chinese treasury; still his bag is not full. "People gaped in amazement and shook their heads. The matter was reported to the palace, and the Emperor was astounded. He regretted that he had already given his permission [for Không Lộ to take all he could] and there was nothing he could do about it."

The Chinese Emperor offers Không Lộ an escort back to Vietnam, but Không Lộ declines, saying, "I can carry this one bag of copper myself. Don't bother to accompany me." Then he returns to Vietnam in a twinkling on an eye, using his magic powers. Back home, he uses the copper to cast buddha-images, a *stupa*, a large cauldron, and several giant bells for famous temples in Vietnam. Then he composes a verse:

> Crossing the ocean on my straw hat
> A thousand mile journey in one breath
> Filling my bag with all Song's copper
> My arm can heft ten tons!

The message of the story is clear. On the one hand, Vietnam has undeniably accepted much from China in culture and religion. After all, the TDTL was written in Chinese, and Zen Buddhism itself originated in China. Không Lộ must travel to China for copper: "His family was poor and their strength was limited. One day he got the idea that in the great land of Song, there must be a lot of fine copper that could be used for casting." On the other hand, resisting Chinese claims of hegemony, Vietnam has accepted the Chinese legacy only on Vietnam's own terms. Không Lộ outwits the mighty Song Emperor and makes off with his majesty's wealth by means of his own unsuspected powers, to use it to embellish the temples of Vietnam. "I can carry this one bag of copper myself. Don't bother to accompany me." Represented by the redoubtable Không Lộ, the Vietnamese have taken the "copper" (the literary culture and Zen style of Buddhism) of China and made it their own.

Buddhism and the State

The TDTL gives many examples of the prestige of certain Zen masters among the social elite. Buddhist adepts were received at court, attracted patronage from emperors and courtiers, and sometimes functioned as advisors to the throne. Many of the Zen masters whose stories appear in the TDTL were involved with the Vietnamese imperial court:

"When Khuông Việt was in his forties, his fame reached the royal court. Emperor Đinh Tiên Hoàng [r. 968–979] summoned him for an audience. The Emperor was pleased with him and honored him with the rank of 'General Supervisor of Monks.' In 971 the Emperor granted him the sobriquet 'Great Teacher Who Brings Order to Vietnam.' Emperor Lê Đại Hành [r. 980–1005] honored Khuông Việt even more. He was consulted in all military and court affairs."

Emperor Lý Thái Tổ [r. 1009–1028] often visited the temple of Zen master Thiền Lão. After one conversation with Thiền Lão, the Emperor "suddenly had insight." When Thiền Lão died, the Emperor "deeply mourned his passing and personally composed verses expressing his grief. He sent an envoy to arrange a vegetarian feast [at Thiền Lão's funeral] and to pay his respects."

Zen master Cứu Chỉ lived in seclusion in the mountains, but "his reputation as a teacher reached the imperial court. Emperor Lý Thái Tông [r. 1028–1054] invited him to the capital several times, but Cứu Chỉ did not come. The Emperor paid three visits to his temple to inquire after him. The Imperial Tutor Lương Văn Nhậm also greatly respected Cứu Chỉ."

After hearing Thông Biện's explanations of Buddhist history and the Buddhist Teaching in 1096, the Empress Dowager Phù Thành Cảm Linh Nhân "honored him with the title 'Chief Monk' and gave him a purple robe. She gave him the sobriquet 'National Teacher of Consummate Eloquence' and rewarded him richly. Subsequently, she revered him so much that she summoned him into the palace, and paid homage to him as National Teacher. She inquired into the essential teachings of Zen and had a deep appreciation of its message."

"The Emperor Lý Nhân Tông [r. 1072–1127] and the Empress Dowager Cảm Linh Nhân were turning toward the study of Zen in those days, so they built a temple next to Cảnh Hưng Palace and invited Mãn Giác to live there, so that it would be easier for them to see him and ask him questions. They did not call him by name, but [as a mark of respect] always addressed him as 'Elder.' . . . The Emperor conferred upon him the rank of 'Inner Palace Teacher of Enlightenment' and the sobriquet 'Purple-Robed Great Monk.'"

Relations between Zen teachers and the court were not always so smooth:

"When Princess Nam Khương wanted to renounce the mundane world, she secretly asked Tịnh Không to ordain her as a nun. When the imperial court discovered this, a decree was issued to arrest Tịnh Không. When he was brought to court, his countenance was calm and serene. The Emperor respected him deeply, and revered him as a noted monk of great virtue. Tịnh Không firmly denied all invitations to serve at court."

"Emperor Lê Đại Hành had invited Zen master Maha to court many times to question him [about Buddhism], but the master would only join him palms and bow his head. After the Emperor pressed him repeatedly, Maha replied, 'I am just a crazy monk from Quan Ái Temple.' The Emperor became very angry. He ordered Maha to be held in custody in the palace and assigned men to guard him. The next morning Maha was seen outside the monks' quarters, even though the door [of his cell] remained locked as before. The Emperor thought this most uncanny, and ordered Maha freed."

Many Zen adepts were reluctant to come to court, though imperial invitations were hard to refuse:

"Emperor Lý Anh Tông [r. 1137–1175] had heard about Trường Nguyen and admired his religious life. He wanted to meet him, but Trường Nguyên refused, so the Emperor ordered the master's old friend Border Minister Lê Hối to bring him back to the palace. While they were staying the night at a guest house of a temple [en route], Trường Nguyên regretted [that he had consented to come to court] and escaped hack into the mountains."

"Emperor Lý Huệ Tông [r. 1210–1225] admired Hiện Quang's lofty conduct and invited him to the capital with full ceremony many times. Hiện Quang went into hiding and sent an attendant to reply [on his behalf] to the imperial envoy: 'A poor wayfarer, I was born in his majesty's land and I eat his majesty's provisions. I have lived in the mountains serving Buddha, but after passing many years, I have not yet achieved any merit. . . . What reason is there to invite me to the capital?' From then on, Hiện Quang never left the mountain."

On occasion Zen teachers did accept a role in high politics:

Đa Bao, who had predicted the rise of the Lý dynasty while Lý Thái Tổ' was still a boy, was often invited to court and "consulted about all court and political matters."

Another instance was the case of Viên Thông, who came from a family of mong-officials. "In 1130, Emperor Lý Thần Tông [r. 1127–1137] summoned Viên Thông to Sùng Khai Palace to ask him about the principles of political order and disorder and national prosperity and decline.

"Viên Thông said [in a classical Confucian vein]: 'The realm is like a vessel. Put it in a safe place and it will be safe. Put it in a perilous place and it will be in peril. It all depends on how the ruler conducts himself. If his benevolence is in harmony with the hearts and minds of the people, then they will love him as a parent and look up to him as the sun and moon. This is how to put the realm in a condition of peace and safety.

"'Whether there is order or chaos also depends on the officials. If they win the people's loyalty, then there is political order. If they lose the people's loyalty, then there is chaos. I have observed the rulers of previous generations. None of them succeeded without employing true gentlemen, humane, moral men. None failed unless he employed petty men, shallow, self-seeking men. When we trace the origins of how [political success or failure] came about, it did not happen suddenly overnight; rather, it developed gradually. . . . The [apparent] sudden rise and fall of rulers necessarily depends on a gradual [prior] process of doing good or evil. . . .

"'To bring the people peace means to respect those who are below, to be a chary as someone riding a horse holding worn-out reins. If a ruler can be like this, he cannot but flourish; if not, he cannot but perish. . . .'

"The Emperor was pleased and appointed Viên Thông General Capital Superintendent of Monks and Magistrate for Religion. Viên Thông would approach the Emperor in a relaxed manner and offer policy suggestions, and the Emperor never went against his advice." Later Viên Thông was given the title Guest of the Court. He was appointed as an executor of Lý Nhân Tông's will: "The Emperor entrusted all affairs to Viên Thông." Viên Thông also participated in the regency for the heir to the throne, who was still a child.

In its many anecdotes bearing on the relationship of Zen teachers to the social elite and court politics, the TDTL adheres closely to the traditional attitude of the Zen school in this area. Zen adepts were typified by their detachment from the attractions of worldly fame and profit. It was axiomatic that authentic Zen masters only came to court when it would serve a legitimate altruistic purpose: either to further the Buddhist Teaching or to perform some other public service.

While the high esteem of emperors and courtiers for certain Zen masters is a prominent theme in the TDTL, the book gives only passing references to institutional arrangements relating to Buddhism. It may be that these were common knowledge; familiar details too taken for granted to be worthy of much note. The scant mention made of institutional matters in the TDTL might be meant to convey the message that this aspect was tangential to the real functioning of the Buddhist Teaching.

There are items that suggest that the Vietnamese emperor, as supreme feudal lord, could and did allocate labor and land and other wealth for the benefit of Buddhist temples.

In the biography of Thiền Lão, who was often visited by Emperor Lý Thái Tổ, it is related that after Thiền Lão's death, "the Emperor had [Thiền Lão's] temple enlarged and refurbished, and assigned people to take care of the upkeep and supplies of the temple." In the story of Đa Bảo, another favorite of Lý Thái Tổ, it is related that the Emperor issued a royal decree that Đa Bảo's temple be rebuilt. This decree presumably obligated the local people to furnish the labor and building supplies for the project. Emperor Lý Nhân Tông granted Mãn Giác, whom he and his mother often consulted about Zen, various titles as well as tax exemptions for fifty of his kinsmen.

In the section on Viên Thông, who had served as a political advisor to Emperor Lý Nhân Tông, it says that when Viên Thông retired to his native district and built a temple there, "the revenue from three villages was provided for him by the National Treasury."

After Không Lộ was able to exorcise a newly built palace, Emperor Lý Nhân Tông "rewarded him with a thousand pounds of gold and five hundred acres of farmland to provide for ceremonial expenses." After Không Lộ cured the crown prince, the emperor "rewarded him with a thousand pounds of gold and a thousand acres of land for his temple's permanent endowment, tax-free."

Given the situation in contemporary China, Korea, and Japan, it is reasonable to assume that many of the major temples in Vietnam enjoyed some degree of tax-exemption and drew income from lands that had been donated to them by aristocrats or by imperial authority. The TDTL notes that certain masters (e.g., Tịnh Không, Chân Không, Tĩnh Thiền, Y Sơn) attracted many donors. It is likely that Buddhist temples themselves were also the beneficiaries of donations made by pious nobles and commoners: gifts of money, supplies, and land.

Prophesy, Curing, and Magic

The TDTL is permeated with accounts of the supernatural powers of its heroes, the great Zen masters of old Vietnam. There are stories of prognostication, exorcisms and cures, rainmaking, battles of magic, rapport with wild animals, command over spirits, levitation, and deliberately directed rebirth. Taken together, these tales make up a unique collection of data about popular beliefs among the medieval Vietnamese. Those who study Vietnamese folk religion in the period of French domination will recognize many familiar motifs already in evidence in this thirteenth century work.

Many of the TDTL's tales of prophesy relate to affairs of state.

The following story is from the biography of Đa Bảo, a disciple of Không Việt: "When Lý Thái Tổ [the founder of the Lý dynasty] was still a hidden dragon [living as a child with his family], Đa Bảo met him and said, 'This boy has uncommon physiognomy. In the future he will be a king.' The Lý family were greatly shocked and said, 'At the present time our king is still reigning and the country is at peace. How can you say something that could get our whole family executed?' Đa Bảo said, 'The mandate of heaven has already been decided. Even if you wished to avoid it, it would be impossible to do so. If these words prove correct, please do not forsake me.' When Lý Thái Tổ ascended to the throne, he often invited Đa Bảo to court to ask him for lessons in Zen and he would reward him with generous donations."

When the Emperor Lê Đại Hành asked Vạn Hạnh how to handle a Chinese invasion, Vạn Hạnh accurately predicted that the Chinese would withdraw. When Lê Đại Hành and his courtiers could not decide whether to invade Champa, Vạn Hạnh "memorialized the throne advising the Emperor to act quickly and not miss the opportunity. As it turned out, the Vietamese were victorious."

When weird events were reported during the reign of the tyrant Lê Ngọa Triệu, Vạn Hạnh correctly interpreted them as omens of the imminent collapse of the Lê regime and the rise of the Lý dynasty. Vạn Hạnh was able to inform the uncles of the Lý founder in advance of their nephew's successful coup d'etat against the Lê in the capital.

There are other stories in the TDTL of predictions of purely personal matters:

When Viên Chiếu was a youth, before he had left home to become a monk, he went to visit an elder adept in physiognomy who lived in his home area. "The elder looked him over thoroughly and said, 'You have a karmic connection to the Buddha Dharma. If you leave home you are sure to become a great bodhisattva among humans. If not, it is hard to guarantee how long you will live.'"

Vạn Hạnh was able to foresee a plot against himself: he sent word to his enemy that he knew an attack was coming, and the man was afraid and desisted. The TDTL comments: "There were many other such instances of Vạn Hạnh having prior knowledge of events and being able to see into the past." The ability to predict the future was a mark of the religious adept in old Vietnam, proof of his special powers.

The TDTL also contains several stories of the Zen masters using their healing powers to help win people over to Buddhism.

The section on Đạo Huệ relates this incident: "In 1161 the Imperial Concubine Thụy Minh fell ill. The Emperor sent an envoy to summon Đạo Huệ to the capital to cure her. . . . When Đạo Huệ reached the palace, the moment he arrived just outside the concubine's door, her illness was cured. The Emperor Lý Anh Tông was very pleased and lodged Đạo Huệ at Báo Thiên Temple. Within a month countless numbers of admirers had arrived, both courtiers and religious men. Đạo Huệ opened a teaching hall and began to propound the Dharma and convert people."

Zen master Maha used his powers as a healer to influence a community of hunters who worshipped demons and spirits. "The local people told him, 'For a long time in this area there have been many people who die of leprosy. All the healers and sorcerers have been helpless [to deal with it]. If you can cure this disease, we will listen to your advice.' Maha then blessed some water with mantras and sprayed it from his mouth over those suffering from the disease. The sick ones were immediately cured. Although the local people were moved to submit to Master Maha, because of their deeply ingrained habits, it was not possible for him to convert them right away."

The biography of Đạo Hạnh says that under the influence of Zen master Sùng Phạm, "Đạo Hạnh's Dharma-power increased and his karmic affinity with Zen became more and more mature. . . . He blessed water with mantras and used it to cure the sick. Everything he did was effective."

Another curing story that could be taken as a political metaphor involves the Zen magician Không Lộ: "When [the crown prince] Lý Thần Tông was twenty-one, he suddenly changed into a tiger. He would crouch down and bite at people, acting like a horrifying wild monster. [His father] the Emperor had a golden cage made to keep him in. . . . The Emperor ordered one of his commanders to take a dragon boat and bring Không Lộ [to the capital]. When the commander came to his hut, Không Lộ laughed and said, 'Isn't it the tiger business?' The commander said, 'How did you know?' Không Lộ said, 'Thirty years ago I knew this would happen.' Không Lộ came to the palace and sat peacefully [in front of the emperor and his caged tiger-son]. In a sharp voice he said, 'Let the officials bring a great cauldron of oil right away, put a hundred needles in the cauldron, and light a great fire under it.' [When the oil was boiling], Không Lộ reached into the cauldron with his hand and took out the hundred needles. He stuck them into the prince's body while pronouncing a spell: 'How noble to be the son of heaven!' The hair and tail and claws and fangs fell away spontaneously and the prince was returned to his human form."

There are stories in the TDTL of cures effected by the power of supernatural beings, cures which help the religious seeker to advance on the Path. Tịnh Giới was from a poor family, but sincere and earnest by nature. "When he was twenty-six, he fell seriously ill. In a dream he saw a god who gave him some medicine. When he awoke, he had been abruptly cured. So he decided to leave home to become a monk. . . ." In the section on Viên Chiếu, it is related how the master's study of the Dharma was greatly advanced by a visionary curing experience: "One night when Viên Chiếu was in *samādhi*, he saw the bodhisattva Manjuśri take a knife to him, cut open his stomach, and wash out his guts. Then Manjuśri gave him some medicine. After this, what Viên Chiếu practiced

in his mind seemed preordained to mesh [with reality], and he had deep attainment in the *samādhi* of words, expounding the Dharma most eloquently."

In a familiar pattern in Buddhist legend, the TDTL shows adepts using magical powers to gain entree for the Buddhist teaching: "One day Emperor Lý Nhân Tông said to Giác Hải, 'May we hear something about your supernatural powers of movement by according with Reality?' Giác Hải then worked magical transformations; he projected his body up into the air fifty or sixty feet above the ground and then suddenly descended again. The Emperor and his courtiers all applauded in admiration and acclaimed Giác Hải. He was rewarded and given free access to the palace."

For an agricultural society like medieval Vietnam, adequate and timely rainfall was a life-and-death concern. In droughts the imperial authorities offered prayers for rain and enlisted the help of religious adepts.

Tĩnh Giới's biography relates this story: "In 1177 there was a summer drought. The Emperor Lý Cao Tông ordered all the eminent monks to pray for rain, but to no avail. The Emperor had heard reports of the master's renown for a long time, so he dispatched an envoy to bring Tĩnh Giới to Báo Thiên Temple in the capital. Tĩnh Giới stood in the courtyard there at midnight and burned incense, and immediately rain began to fall. [After this] the Emperor honored and esteemed him deeply, always referring to him as the 'Rain Master.'" Tĩnh Giới also had the power to stop the rain: "In 1179 . . . there was very heavy rain which flooded the roads and interfered with the harvest. Tĩnh Giới stood praying for seven days at a ritual gathering to stop the rain, and the rains became normal again."

Thiền Nham, after long years of chanting dharanis and practicing asceticism, also had the power to make rain: "In the Thiên Thuận era [1128–1132] there was a drought. Thiền Nham was summoned to the capital by imperial edict. He prayed for rain and immediately got results."

Another motif that occurs frequently among the occult qualities of the Zen masters in the TDTL is uncanny power over wild animals. The adepts have recovered the rapport with nature that the inhabitants of ordinary society have lost.

The biography of Đạo Huệ relates: "The feeling that emanated from Đạo Huệ moved the apes and monkeys so much on the mountain [where he lived] that they would come to listen to him." When Đạo Huệ was about to leave to answer an imperial summons, "the apes and monkeys on the mountain cried sadly as if they felt grief and reluctance to let him depart." When Hiện Quang was living in the mountain forest as an ascetic he "began to dress in leaves and stopped eating rice for ten years. . . . Wherever he stopped to sit or lie down, all the wild animals that saw him became tame." After his teacher died, Pháp Hiền practiced meditation on Mount Từ Sơn. "His body was like a dried-out tree; for him, things and self were both forgotten. The birds of the air came to him as if tame and the beasts of the field approached him with familiarity."

"One day while Zen master Trí was sitting in meditation [in the forest on Mount Từ Sơn], he saw a tiger chasing a deer coming toward him. Trí admonished them: 'All sentient beings cherish their lives—you should not harm each other.' The tiger bowed its head to the ground [as a person would when] taking refuge [from a teacher] and went away [letting the deer escape]." When Trí was away from his retreat, "huge tigers would crouch in front of the gate, so no one would dare to rob the place."

Popular Beliefs and Magic: A Zen Perspective

Why would a Zen book like the TDTL include so many stories of supernatural powers and magic? The TDTL was written for an audience and in a milieu where the existence of such things was taken for granted. In the context of the popular beliefs of the time and place, one way to establish the sanctity and authority of a religious figure was to attribute to him powers beyond the reach of ordinary people: the power to foretell the future, to cure disease, to exorcise evil, to direct his own rebirth, to travel long distances in the twinkling of an eye. To the popular mind in medieval Vietnam, these were prime marks of the person of true attainment.

To establish the credentials of Zen masters and draw attention to their Zen lessons, what better way than for the TDTL to depict their supernatural abilities and superhuman powers? Since to Zen adepts no particular forms were sacred, they were free to work within any locally recognized forms by which communication could be facilitated.

The TDTL demonstrates clearly that in old Vietnam belief in magic, omens, and supernatural powers extended through the highest levels of the social hierarchy, the court nobility. From a Buddhist perspective, the common denominator of vulgar religion is not the social class or even the intellectual level of the believers. The mark of vulgar religion is the underlying attitude that religious means can be used to manipulate the supernatural to serve worldly motives. According to the Buddhist criterion, what sets apart the genuine religious elite is their selfless approach to religion as a means of realizing truth for its own sake. Members of this elite can be and have been recruited from all walks of life. By stressing the lowly origins and foreign ethnicity of some of its most illustrious teachers, the Zen tradition made a special point of rejecting the social and ethnic prejudices that assume that religious merit coincides with social standing or cultural affiliation.

When the TDTL colors its accounts with tales of magic, it is in an attempt to communicate with people for whom magic was accepted as real. The Zen masters in the TDTL use magic for altruistic purposes, not for personal gain. Following its consistent design, among dozens of stories of supernatural powers and magic, the TDTL makes oblique comments from the perspective of the Zen school, putting the whole topic in its place.

In the biography of Đạo Hạnh, in which magical elements play a prominent role, there is a clear implication that magical powers are not the ultimate goal of religious practice. After his arduous struggle to learn magical arts in order to avenge his father's death at the hands of a sorcerer, when "his magic powers were now complete," and his vengeance has been accomplished, Đạo Hạnh finally goes to seek instruction from a Zen teacher. Đạo Hạnh states his dilemma in a verse:

> Long mixed up among the dusts of the
> ordinary world,
> I have not recognized the real gold
> I do not know where true mind is
> Please point it out truly to me, extend
> your skill in means
> Let me fully comprehend thusness and
> stop this painful seeking.

An anecdote in the section on Khánh Hỷ delivers a message to the same effect, by using a sorcery ceremony as a metaphor for wishful thinking and futile reliance on mechanical acts:

"One day while Khánh Hỷ and [his teacher] Bổn Tịch were on their way to a donor's house to receive offerings, Khánh Hỷ asked, 'What was the true intent of the Zen patriarchs?' Just then they heard the sounds of a sorcery ceremony coming from someone's house. Bổn Tịch said, 'Are these not the words of a sorcerer calling down spirits?' Khánh Hỷ said 'Don't tease me, Master.' Bổn Tịch said, 'I never play tricks.'"

Here Bổn Tịch makes use of a fortuitous circumstance to challenge Khánh Hỷ for his rote approach to Zen. Bổn Tịch intimates that by asking the age-old question (as if the true intent of the Zen ancestors could be put in words and an appreciation of it could be directly conveyed, with no effort on the learner's part), Khánh Hỷ is behaving simple-mindedly, like a sorcerer who thinks that the mechanical invocation of magic words will beckon the spirits.

The Zen Message

Zen was an integral part of Mahāyāna Buddhism. As such, it taught that all people are inherently endowed with the potential for enlightenment, a potential that can be brought to life by breaking through the shell of conditioned perceptions that encases ordinary people. The Zen school incorporated as its theoretical basis Mādhyamika and Yogācāra Buddhist philosophy and the worldview of the Avatamsaka Sūtra. Zen became the intellectual spearhead of Buddhism in East Asia, exercising a powerful influence on religious practice, philosophy, and aesthetics among the cultured elite. Zen teachers "appeared in the world" and by their personal example and mastery of the Dharma offered proof that the enlightenment of the buddhas was not something superhuman, existing only in the realm of myth. By the startling originality of its rich and intricate literature, the Zen school commanded the attention of cultured people in China, Korea, Vietnam, and Japan.

The utterances of the Zen masters contain multiple layers of meaning and structure that are designed to interact with the mentalities of the listeners, open them up, and transform them. Contrary to the notion that most Zen sayings are irrational paradoxes meant only to assert the futility of rational thought, Zen discourse can be readily read, by those who know its codes, to contain a wide range of messages fully consonant with the theory and practice of Mahāyāna Buddhism.

To illustrate this point, and to show the real identity of the TDTL as a masterpiece of the Zen school, let us turn to some of its Zen-style teachings. Explanatory comments follow each passage.

> Someone asked Viên Chiếu, "'When mind and phenomena are both forgotten, inherent nature is real.' What is real?"
> Viên Chiếu said, "The raindrops on the cliffside flowers are the tears of a goddess. The wind hitting the bamboo in the courtyard is the master musician's lute."

According to Buddhist ontology, there is only one reality; all particular phenomena are manifestations of the one reality. Delusion occurs when people reify the constructs they project upon the phenomenal world, in particular, when they accept their conditioned minds as their real selves and the phenomena they perceive as independently existing entities. To the enlightened eye, the multiplicity of the natural world bespeaks the absolute reality immanent in it.

> Vân Phong asked his teacher Thiện Hội, "When birth-and-death comes, how can we avoid it?"
>
> Thiện Hội said, "Where there is no birth-and-death, we are sure to avoid it."
>
> Vân Phong asked, "Where is the place where there is no birth-and-death?"
>
> Thiện Hội said, "You must comprehend it right in the midst of birth-and-death."

Birth-and-death is *samsāra*, the cycle of suffering and affliction brought on by ignorance and the actions ignorance engenders. The elementary teaching of Buddhism offers a way out of birth-and-death by the ending of ignorance and desire: *nirvāna* as the antithesis of *samsara*. The advanced teaching of Buddhism shifts to the absolute viewpoint, which recognizes that birth-and-death only exists from the viewpoint of delusion; from the enlightened viewpoint, there is no duality between *samsāra* and *nirvāna*. This truth enables the bodhisattvas to experience the absolute while engaged in the relative world as compassionate teachers of enlightenment.

> Someone asked Viên Chiếu, "What is the meaning of [the Zen formula] 'seeing inherent nature and becoming buddha'?"
>
> Viên Chiếu said, "When spring comes the withered trees are adorned all over with flowers. The wind blows a thousand miles carrying their divine perfume."
>
> The man said, "I do not understand. Please instruct me again, Teacher."
>
> Viên Chiếu said, "The fruit tree has been around for ten thousand years. Its dense branches reach to the clouds."

"Spring" denotes the activation of the inherent potential for enlightenment which is our inherent nature. "Flowers" represent the compassionate actions of the enlightened. "The fruit tree" is the tradition of enlightening teachings.

> Viên Chiếu said, "What a pity that having choked once, you sit here hungry and forget to eat."

Here Viên Chiếu was addressing a pupil who had failed at first to understand his message, became discouraged, and neglected to notice further "nutrition" offered by the teacher.

> Viên Chiếu said, "We laugh at the person who clings in vain to his real nature and is drowned in midstream."

The goal of Zen is not to sink into the peace and bliss and emptiness of the absolute, "clinging to real nature": this is only a waystation, "midstream," not the final destination. The Great Vehicle goal is to return to function as a bodhisattva in the world of the relative, now immune to delusion.

> Cứu Chỉ said to his disciples as he was about to die:
>
> "All Dharma-gates, all Buddhist methods, originally come from your own inherent nature. . . . All the afflictions that bind you are empty. Misdeeds and merits right and wrong, are all illusions. There is nothing but cause and effect. In the realm of karma, do not differentiate: if you do, you will not find freedom. [With freedom], you see all phenomena, but without any objects of seeing. You know all phenomena, but without any objects of knowing. You know that all phenomena have interdependent origination as their basis. You see that all phenomena have true reality as their source. Even amidst defilement, you understand that the world is like a magical apparition. You clearly comprehend that the true identity of

sentient beings is the One Reality—there is no other reality. You do not abandon the karmic realm: you use the proper skillful means to show the uncreated Dharma in the realm of the created, but without differentiating and without the marks of creation. This is because desire is ended, self is forgotten, and conceptual judgments are abandoned."

This passage is a clear example of the underlying unity of Zen and scriptural Buddhism.

> Bảo Giám spoke this verse:
> Wisdom is like the moon shining in
> the sky
> Its light encompasses countless
> worlds, shining to infinity
> If you want to know it, you must pick
> it out with care
> The dense thickets on the mountain
> are locked in the evening mist

Wisdom is omnipresent and eternal, but people locked up in conditioned perceptions, the "mist," overlook it and see only the conventional image of reality they have been trained to see.

> Nguyện Học said to his disciples: "The Path has no image or form. It is right before your eyes, not far away. Turn back and find it in yourself. Don't seek to get it from others. Even if you could get something from them, it would not be real . . . ."

"The Path" here means reality itself. Each person ultimately must experience it for herself.

> As he was about to die, Thường Chiếu spoke this verse:
> Fundamentally the Path has no face
> Yet it shows its freshness day after day
> In the galaxy of thousands of worlds
> No place is not its home
> Huệ Sinh said:
> If a person knows this Dharma
> Then sentient beings and Buddha are
> the same

> Quiet and still, the moon over Lanka
> Utterly empty, the boat that crosses
> the ocean
> If you know emptiness, through
> emptiness you awaken to being
> Then you are free to go everywhere
> while still in *samādhi*

For one who knows reality, and sees the real nature of things, there is no dualism between sentient beings and Buddha, because the real nature of sentient beings is their buddha-nature. "The moon over Lanka" represents the one reality. The "empty boat" is the personality purified of ignorance, craving and anger, which "crosses the ocean" of phenomenal existence. "Samādhi" is stable meditative concentration.

> A monk asked Chân Không, "What is the wondrous Dharma?"
> Chân Không said, "You will know only after you have awakened."
> The monk said, "I have not been able to understand your previous instructions, so how can I understand your present teaching?"
> Chân Không said, "If you go to the deep caves where the immortals dwell, you will be able to bring back the elixir that will transform you."
> The monk asked, "What is the elixir?"
> Chân Không said, "Through eons of ignorance, you do not comprehend it, but the morning of enlightenment you open up into illumination."
> The monk asked, "What is illumination?"
> Chân Không said, "Illumination shines through the whole world, [revealing that] all sentient beings are together in a single family."

Study Questions

H.Appendix 1 J.C. Cleary, Buddhism and Popular Religion in Medieval Vietnam

Compose your own study questions and give a short answer to each of them.

H.APPENDIX 2

The Viêtnamese Doctrine of the Human Souls and the Rituals of Birth and Death

Chánh Công Phan

Introduction

The purpose of this paper is to examine three philosophical and ritual issues related to the dialectic of life and death as conceived in the Đạo of Viêtnamese Ancestral Worship (Đạo Thờ Cúng Tổ Tiên). They are the Ontology of Human Hồn (Souls), the Rituals of Birth and Death, and the Protective Divine Powers of Human Hồn. These three issues are very essential for understanding the daily life, philosophy, and folk religion of the Viêtnamese people. They therefore deserve a new scholarly treatment which can help generate future field research in rural Viêt-Nam so that certain theoretical reconstructions can be empirically tested.

Research Sources

The first kind of research sources for this paper are the Viêtnamese popular beliefs regarding the existence of human souls and the conduct of the rituals of birth and death that I have experienced myself since childhood.

The second kind of research sources are a number of important ethnological works such as *Việt Nam Văn Hóa Sử Cương* (An Outline History of Viêtnamese Culture) by the encyclopaedian Đào Duy Anh;[1] *Việt Nam Phong Tục* (Viêtnamese Customs) by the ethnologist Phan Kế Bính;[2] *Nếp Cũ Tín Ngưỡng Việt Nam* (The Old Forms of Viêtnamese Religions),[3] and *Nếp Cũ Con Người Việt Nam* (The Old Traits of Viêtnamese People) by the ethnologist Toan Ánh;[4] and *Tư Tưởng Việt Nam: Tư Tưởng Triết Học Bính Dân* (Viêtnamese Thoughts: Popular Philosophy) by Nguyễn Đăng Thục.[5]

The third kind of information are the systems of geometrical symbols and pictorial images on the early Viêtnamese bronze drums (Heger Type I), used in conjunction with the old Viêtnamese creation myth.[6] The early Viêtnamese bronze drums of Heger Type I, especially, the model drum Ngọc-Lũ I, are now established by Viêtnamese and western archaeologists to have been the most culturally representative archaeological artifacts

Source: "The Viêtnamese Concept of the Human Souls and the Rituals of Birth and Death." Extracted from *Southeast Asian Journal of Social Science*, Vol. 21, No. 2 by Chanh Cong Phan. ISSN 0303-8246, © 1993 Times Media Private Limited. Published by Times Academic Press, an imprint of Times Media Private Limited. E-mail: te@tpl.com.sg. Website: http://timesone.com.sg/te

of the Vănlangian Civilization. The Vănlangian Civilization (traditionally dated 2879–258 BCE), which was formerly known as the "Đôngsơnian Culture" (after its first typesite "Đông Sơn" in northern Việt-Nam), is the singular Southeast Asian civilization that flourished during the Bronze Age and thus paralleled the Shang and Chou civilizations of northern China in historical time.[7] The early Việtnamese bronze drums, which are dated to have been manufactured between 800 BCE and 400 BCE, belong to the group of Heger Type I bronze drums that are found widely distributed not only in northern Việt-Nam but also in southern China and throughout Southeast Asia.[8]

The Vănlangian Civilization ended at its cultural nuclear centre (Red River Delta of northern Việt-Nam) in 258 BCE when the last Hùng King was overthrown by An Dương Vương who founded the Âu Lạc Quốc (258–179 BCE). In 179 BCE the Âu Lạc Quốc was taken over by the Ch'in general Triệu Đà (c. Chao T'o) who founded the Nam Việt Quốc (c. Nan Yüeh) which was in turn destroyed by the Han Chinese in 111 BCE. Northern Việt-Nam became a rebellious province of the new Han Empire and succeeding Chinese dynasties until 939 CE, when it was finally liberated by Ngô Quyền, who created the Việtnamese nation that has continued to exist to the present day. The Vănlangian Civilization (traditionally dated 2879–258 BCE) is nostalgically considered by the Việtnamese to be the "Golden Age" (Thời Đại Vàng Son) of their history in contrast to the "First Period of Northern Domination" (Thời Kỳ Bắc Thuộc Lần Thứ Nhất), which is normally viewed as the "Dark Age" of Việt-Nam (between 111 BCE and 939 CE).[9]

The Việtnamese Civilization (CE 939–Present) is believed by the Việtnamese people to have had its ancient cultural roots in the Vănlangian Civilization (2879–258 BCE) and to have had its culturo-political links with the Chinese Civilization even before the fateful year of 111 BCE when northern Việt-Nam became a province of the Han Empire. The Việtnamese people and their ancestors have therefore shared with the Chinese (especially southern Chinese) and their ancestors many common pre-Han cultural and philosophical traditions (pre-200 BCE) that came to shape the very contents and forms of the Han Empire (northern China, southern China, and northern Việt-Nam).

The historical formation and reformations of the early phases of the Chinese Civilization from 206 BCE to 939 CE can be considered to have been based on the cultural crystallizations of three main pre-Han cultural traditions, namely, the Chou tradition of northern China, the Báchviệtian (c. Pa Yüeh) tradition of southern China, and the Vănlangian tradition of northern Việt-Nam. The formation and reformations of the Han-Việt culture in northern Việt-Nam during the Han-Chinese rule (BCE 111–939 CE) can be considered to have been based on the cultural crystallizations of three main traditions, namely, the Vănlangian tradition of northern Việt-Nam, the Báchviệtian tradition of southern China, and the Han-Chinese tradition that characterized the lives and views of the Han-Chinese rulers and immigrants residing in northern Việt-Nam.[10]

As a result of these cultural crystallization processes, the Việtnamese and the Chinese have shared many common cultural traits and philosophical ideas, including the tradition of ancestral worship and the concept of human souls. Given the numerous common cultural sources that the Việtnamese and Chinese have shared and the many new and different features they have developed for their respective civilizations, I shall focus my paper on the Việtnamese concept of human souls and the rituals of birth and death which can be considered similar to those of the Chinese in the light of the above-mentioned common cultural traditions and national cultural innovations.

An Ontology of Human Souls

The Ontological Essence of Viêtnamese Culture

"What is the *moral* essence of Viêtnamese philosophy, religion, and cultural life?" The answer can be safely given as follows: The moral cornerstone of the Viêtnamese philosophy, religion, and cultural life is the "Đạo of Ancestral Worship" (Đạo Thờ Cúng Tổ' Tiên).[11]

It is this moral cornerstone that Confucius and his early successors used to construct the ethical foundation of their Confucian philosophies.[12] However, when asked about the phenomenon of death and how to serve "the spirits of the dead," Confucius said that if we do not yet know how to serve the living, why bother with the problem of serving "the spirits of the dead" and about death itself![13]

The lack of metaphysical concern about the issues of birth, death, body, and soul on the part of Confucius himself is due in part to his Northern Mongoloid cultural background, which had historically been non-metaphysical.[14] As a conceptual result, his humanistic ethics of filial piety in particular and his moral philosophy in general are completely devoid of a firm ontological and cosmological foundation that they should possess. However, this is apparently not the case with Đạoism (c. Taoism) and the Viêtnamese moral philosophy because they belong to the Southern Austroasiatic philosophical tradition which is known to have historically been metaphysical and cosmological all along the cultural march of time.[15]

If the Đạo of Ancestral Worship is the *moral* quintessence of Viêtnamese philosophy, religion, and cultural life, then, we should ask this next metaphysical question: "What is the ontological essence of the Đạo of Viêtnamese Ancestral Worship (Đạo Thờ Cúng Tổ' Tiên)?" The answer to this metaphysical question can be suggested as follows: The ontological essence of the Đạo of Viêtnamese Ancestral Worship is the sacred belief of the Viêtnamese people in the existence,

immortality, and unfathomable protective powers of their "Divine Ancestral Souls" (Linh Hồn Tổ' Tiên).

A Typology of the Divine Ancestral Souls

The Divine Ancestral Souls (Linh Hồn Tổ' Tiên) that the Viêtnamese have worshipped are of five types. They are (1) the divine ancestral souls of each family (linh hồn tổ' tiên gia đình), (2) the divine ancestral souls of each clan (linh hồn tổ' tiên gia tộc), (3) the divine primordial souls of the entire Viêtnamese people (linh hồn thủy tổ' dân tộc), (4) the superior divinities of the whole nation-state (anh linh quốc gia), and (5) the divine souls of vocational patriarchs and matriarchs (linh hồn sư tổ' bổn nghề).

A. Linh Hồn Tổ' Tiên Gia Đình (Ancestral Family Souls)

They are normally worshipped at the ancestral altar (bàn thờ tổ' tiên) in each individual family. As a general architectural rule, the family ancestral altar is placed in front and against the wall in the central compartment of the house. (Fig. 01). The Ancestral Family Souls that a family worships normally include its deceased parents and deceased grandparents. But the family male head of the oldest branch of a given clan must worship all the "four generations of great ancestors" (tử đại) above him, namely, the "divine souls" (linh hồn) of his deceased parents (Cha Mẹ), grandparents (Ông Bà Nội), great grand parents (Ông Bà Cổ' Nội),and great great grandparents (Kị Nội).

B. Linh Hồn Tổ' Tiên Gia Tộc (Ancestral Clan Souls)

They include all the "higher great great ancestors" (Cao Cao Tổ') above the fifth rank of the male household head such as the great great grandparents (Kị Nôi) and ultimately the first pair of "primal clan ancestors" (Thủy Tổ' Họ Tộc) from whom all posterity has genealogically descended. All the ancestral clan souls are worshipped collectively in the Ancestral Clan Shrine (Từ Đường) under the care of the elder of the clan's "oldest major branch" (tộc trưởng) who performs annual sacrifices and memorial rites of longer time scales.

C. Linh Hồn Thủy Tổ' Dân Tộc
(People's Primordial Ancestral Souls)

There is a sacred national festival which is popularly called the "Lễ Giỗ Tổ'" (Memorial Rite for the Primordial Ancestors) and which has been celebrated annually on the tenth of the third month of the Eastern Calendar. The Lễ Giỗ Tổ'has normally been conducted by the head of the Việtnamese national government in the national sacred Shrine of the Hùng Kings (Đền Hùng Vương located on the holy Núi Nghĩa Lĩnh (Mountain of Righteousness in Command) in the present-day province of Vĩnh Phú), and attended by both government officials and devoted pilgrims from other surrounding provinces.

The Lễ Giỗ Tổ' is still being celebrated annually in Việt-Nam and by many overseas Việtnamese communities in Australia, North America, and Western Europe on the same day. It is nowadays dedicated to the commemoration of the founding Hùng Kings and all the subsequent heroes and heroines, known and unknown, who had sacrificed their lives for building and defending Việt-Nam. But modern archaeological evidence tends to support the possibility that in ancient times the Lễ Giỗ Tổ' had probably been observed by the Hùng Kings (2879–258 BCE) in the Hùngvươngian Shrine to commemorate both the Dragon Father Lạc Long Quân and the Fairy Mother Âu Cơ as the "Primordial Ancestors" (Thủy Tổ') not only of their own Vănlangian peoples but also of the whole human race.[16] It is also logical to *so* assume because the national primeval ancestors of the Việtnamese or of any other people for that matter must have been descended from the "Primordial Ancestors" of the entire human race.

The "Primordial Ancestors" that the Hùng Kings had commemorated on the Vănlangian Lễ Giỗ Tổ' had probably been the primordial divine souls of the first original human world-couple, the Founding Father and Founding Mother, from whom all the "100 Clans" (Trăm Họ) of the Vănlangian nation and of the world had genealogically descended. The original Founding Father and Founding Mother can be considered to have been the "Dragon Father Lạc Long Quân" (Bố' Rồng Lạc Long Quân) and the "Fairy Mother Âu Cơ" (Mẹ Tiên Âu Cơ) whom the Việtnamese people have revered as their own "Primordial Ancestors" until today.

It is recollected in the most sacred Việtnamese human creation myth, the "Story of the Sac of One Hundred Eggs" (Bọc Trăm Trứng), that Fairy Mother Âu Cơ gave birth to a sac of 100 eggs, and then, the 100 eggs were transformed into 100 children. These 100 children were believed to be the ancestors of the Bách Việt (c. Pa Yüeh, Hundred Tribes of Việtians) who are recorded in old Chinese and Việtnamese texts to have had populated southern China and northern Indochina. Among the Bách Việt (Hundred Việtians) were the Lạc Việt (c. Lo Yüeh) who are traditionally considered by the Việtnamese to be their own ancestors whose Vănlangian Civilization was destroyed after the Han-Chinese conquest in 111 BCE and the 1000 year-long Chinese rule ("Northern Domination") that followed (111 BCE–939 CE). The Bách Việt (Hundred Tribes of Việtians) can be reconstructed, as I shall attempt later on, to be the numerological symbol to represent all the "100 Clans" the human race as a whole, all being born from the common World-Parents (Dragon Father Lạc Long Quân and Fairy Mother Âu Cơ).

D. Anh Linh Dân Tộc
(People's Superior Divinities)

There is the fourth type of national ancestral souls that the Việtnamese have also worshipped and prayed for their divine protective interventions in times of great national crisis and personal calamities. This group of national ancestral souls is commonly known under the general title of "Anh Linh Dân Tộc" (People's Superior Divinities) or "Hồn Thiêng Sông Núi (Holy Souls of Mountains and Rivers). The Anh Linh Dân Tộc (People's Superior Divinities) or the Hồn Thiêng Sông Núi (Holy Souls of Mountains and Rivers) are the superior divine souls of those national heroes. heroines, and village founders who had achieved timelessly great merits in their tasks of building and defending the Việtnamese nation-state. Most famous and divine among the People's Anh Linh are the "Four Great Immortals" (Tứ Bất Tử) who are (1) God Tản Viên (Thần Tản Viên), (2) Sage Gióng (Thánh Gióng), (3) God Chử Đồng Tử' (Thần Chử Đồng Tử), and (4) Divine Mother Liễu Hạnh (Thánh Mẫu Liễu Hạnh).[17] Among the Anh Linh Dán Tộc we should also name Trần Hưng Đạo who is one of the most revered national heroes because he defeated all the three powerful waves of the Chinese-Mongol invading forces against Việt-Nam (1284–1288) without ever thinking of furthering his own political ambition.[18]

E. Souls of Vocational Patriarchs or Matriarches (Linh Hồn Sư Tổ' Bổn Nghề)

Finally, there is a fifth type of divine souls that most villages, professional guilds, or certain families, especially in northern Việt-Nam, have worshipped religiously. These are the divine souls of vocational patriarchs or matriarches or what the Việtnamese and the Chinese call the "Teachers-Founders" (Sư Tổ') of their own professions and vocational expertise. It can be said that the practitioners of practically every profession and every vocational expertise (agriculture, carpentry, bronze technology, blacksmith, lacquer, martial art, etc.) worship their own "Teacher-Founder" (Sư Tổ').

The Dual Life-World

The culturally well-entrenched sacred tradition of worshipping the four types of divine ancestral souls reveals the fact that the Việtnamese people have religiously believed in the existence, immortality, and protective powers of the divine souls of all their past ancestors. Such a tradition of ancestral worship necessarily presupposes the existence of an empirically invisible spiritual realm of the dead amidst the empirically visible realm

of the living. Like the Chinese, Japanese, and Korean peoples, the Việtnamese also conceptualize that the dialectic of life and death has always been unfolding between these two biologically and spiritually interrelated realms. The realm of the living is called the "cõi dương" (yang realm) because in part it is empirically visible and biologically existential. The realm of the ancestors is called the "cõi âm" (yin realm) because in part it is empirically invisible and spiritually existential.

Life and Death are thus conceived to be a dialectical process that links the two realms together into one biologically and spiritually unified world. This metaphysical concept is best expressed in the following extremely popular Việtnamese poetic saying: "Sống gởi, Thác về!" It can be rendered into English as follows: "Life is a temporary stay, death is a return!" "Life" to which this saying refers is not human life in general but that of each individual in the empirically visible realm. It is one's personal life that is biologically "temporary" like "the shadow of a horse galloping by a small window!" Death is that which terminates the temporariness of one's biological life on the one hand, and makes one's return to the spiritual realm of one's ancestors possible on the other hand.

The notion of "return" raises a number of metaphysical questions. The first question concerns what really dies at one's death? And the second question concerns what really returns after one's death? The answers to these two metaphysical questions can be found in another extremely popular poetic saying: "Chết là thể phách, còn là tinh anh".[19] This poetic verse can be translated into English in this way: "That which dies is the body (thể) and (its) sense-cons-ciousnesses (phách), and that which remains is the superior quintessence (tinh anh)."

The answers that appear to be apparently inherent in the above-cited poetic verse raise at least three more metaphysical questions that need to be discussed. The first question can be phrased as follows: What is the "superior quintessence" (tinh anh) of a human that really "returns" and "remains" in the spiritual realm? The second question is: What are the "sense-consciousnesses" (phách) that belong to one's body that actually "die" at one's death? And the third question concerns the existentially functional relationship that the Việtnamese people conceive to have biologically existed between one's body (thể xác), one's sense-consciousnesses (phách), and one's superior quintessence (tinh anh) when one lives phenomenally. I shall now discuss these questions by examining the numerological composition of the human hồn so that we may understand the specific way in which the Việtnamese have conceived the existence, immortality, divine powers, and nature of the human souls.

Numerology of the Human Souls

That which is called the "tinh anh" (superior quintessence) of any human being is also popularly called the "hồn" by the Việtnamese people. "Hồn" is a Sino-Việtnamese term which like its Mandarin equivalent "c. hun" means "soul." It is popularly stated in the daily conversations of the Việtnamese people (especially the common masses) that each human being has "three souls" (ba hồn) and a system of "phách" which can be rendered into English as a system of "sense-consciousnesses." The "three souls" (hồn) are commonly believed to be the "superior quintessence" (tinh anh) of any human being since they constitute one's own divine triple life-force which "lives temporarily" (sống gởi) in one's physical body (thể xác).

The three hồn (souls) of any human are said to take abode in what is called the "Tam Tiêu" (Three Transformers) which correspond with the three areas of one's physical body (thể xác). The Tam Tiêu (c. San Chiao), which constitute as one of the " Lục Phủ" (6 Bowels) in relation to the "Ngũ Tạng" (5 Viscera), are vertically divided into the "upper transformer" (thượng tiêu), the "middle transformer" (trung tiêu), and the "lower transformer" (hạ tiêu).[20] The "upper transformer" (thượng tiêu) corresponds to the whole area stretching from one's chin to one's stomach. The "middle transformer" (trung tiêu) corresponds to the upper abdomen which embraces one's whole stomach area. And the "lower transformer" (hạ tiêu) corresponds to the area stretching from the end of one's stomach's duodenum to one's anus. Before discussing what the "Tam Tiêu" (Three Transformers) are and how they are related to the three souls and the body, we must examine the system of phách, which is the biological counterpart of the system of the three hồn (souls).

Numerology of the Phách

In functional association with the three hồn (souls) is a system of sensory, perceptive, reproductive, and excretory powers which is either called the "phách" (c. p'o) in the Sino-Việtnamese language tradition or "vía" in the Việtnamese Quốc Ngữ tradition.[21] Both women and men have their phách or vía, but the total number of phách (vía) that each sex has is different. It is popularly known among Việtnamese adults that each male has seven phách (vía) which correspond to the seven sensuous and perceptive faculties on his face. These faculties are called the "seven holes" (thất khiếu) which are his two eyes (visual faculty), his two ears (audial faculty), his two nostrils (olfactory faculty), and his mouth (gustatory faculty).

Being a much more complex and mystical masterpiece of Nature, each woman is said to have nine phách (vía), which correspond to the "cửu khiếu" (nine holes) of her body. The "nine holes" (cửu khiếu) of each female consist of the seven sensuous and perceptive faculties on her face plus her anus and reproductive path.

It is theoretically apparent here that a functional distinction is made between the human sense-organs (lit. "holes") and the sensory and perceptive powers which define the specific natures of the former. And there is also a numerological distinction that is made between the two sexes since each woman is credited to have a total of "nine holes" in contrast to a total of "seven holes" that each man is said to have, in spite of the biological fact that he actually possesses also nine holes! This arbitrarily determined numerological distinction between women and men must therefore have some special theoretical significance beyond that which is involved with the highly complicated reproductive functions that women are endowed by Nature to perform.

The Hồn-Phách-Body Relationship

What is the relationship between the seven or nine phách (vía) and the three hồn (souls)? Many sinologists have posed this bio-ontological question and have not found good ethnological information in the popular Chinese religious tradition to explain their numerological significance. Some of them have argued in .favor of the collective existence of the "ten souls" (3 + 7 = 10) or the "twelve souls" (3 + 9 = 12) rather than just the three souls, as maintained by others.[22]

This numerological problem does not seem to exist in the Viêtnamese formulation because the three hồn (c. hun) are metaphysically different from the phách (vía). The three hồn (souls) are the unified divine spiritual power or the "tinh anh" (superior quintessence) that "temporarily" lives in one's body. The existence, growth, operation, and protection of one's own souls and body are apparently conceived to depend, firstly, on the sensory and perceptive powers of the seven phách (if male) or nine phách (if female); and secondly, on the reproductive, digestive, excretory, and mental powers of the tam tiêu (three transformers).

Given the seven sense-organs of the male, or the nine sense-organs of a female in which the phách (vía) are biologically embodied, we can see that the phách are not the sense-organs themselves but their functionally inherent sensory, perceptive, excretory, and reproductive powers. Thus thanks to the visual phách of our eyes we can see, the audial phách of our ears we can hear, the gustatory phách of our mouth we can taste, the reproductive phách of our sexual organs we can experience erotic pleasure and reproduce ourselves biologically, etc.

The Viêtnamese tend to believe that there is a direct relationship between the hồn and the phách

and that the tranquility of the hồn depends on the safety and soundness of the phách which in turn depend on the stability and healthiness of the sense-organs. It is commonly believed that one could disturb one's hồn and scatter one's vía (phách) around in case of facing physical danger and terror, especially infants who are frightened or fall down violently. This belief, which is also common to the Chinese, Korean, and Japanese, can be illustrated by this popular Sino-Viêtnamese utterance to dramatize one's fear when faced with physical danger: "[One's] hồn (souls) were trembling and my phách scattered" (hồn xiêu phách lạc)!

When their babies fall down to the ground in panic, Viêtnamese mothers normally perform the ritual of "hốt vía" (lifting up the vía) or "hú vía" (calling the vía back together) at those places where their infants fall forcefully. The hồn-phách restoration rituals consist, among other things, of calling the fragile hồn of the panic-stricken baby three times, and then, seven times (if male) or nine times (if female) in accordance with the numerology of his or her hồn and phách respectively.[23]

The organic relationship between the three hồn (souls) and the body seems to be maintained through the structural and functional mediation of the tam tiêu (three transformers) and their internal organs (5 viscera and 5 bowels). The three hồn (souls) are anatomically attached to the tam tiêu (three transformers) of the body where the three areas of the internal organ systems are structured and at work. The three areas of internal organ systems consist of the respiratory and circulatory systems (namely the lungs and heart), which corresponds to the "upper transformer" (thượng tiêu); the upper digestive system (mainly the stomach and small intestines), which corresponds to the "middle transformer" (trung tiêu); and the lower digestive, excretory, and reproductive systems, which corresponds to the "lower transformer" (hạ tiêu).

What are the "tam tiêu" (three transformers) then? The tam tiêu (c. san chiao) are known in Sino-Viêtnamese medical science as one of the "lục phủ" (c. liu fu, six bowels). The exact functions of the tam tiêu are understood differently among physicians of traditional Sino-Vietnamse medicines. Recent Viêtnamese medical studies have rightly considered that the tam tiêu are not any particular internal organ systems but some types of co-ordinating energies that regulate all the internal organ systems themselves that the human body possesses.[24]

The tam tiêu can therefore be interpreted to be the "energy command centers" (trung tâm năng lực chỉ huy) which co-ordinate, regulate, unify, and syncronize the harmonious functions of all the internal organs of the body. Thus the upper tiêu regulates the respiratory and cardio-vascular systems. The central tiêu regulates the upper digestive system. And the lower tiêu controls the lower digestive, excretory, and reproductive systems. It appears that through the tam tiêu the three hồn (souls) of a living human being operate during the whole lifespan when they temporarily reside in one's body as its existentially unified divine "tinh anh." And it is through the powers of the phách and their respective sense-organs that one's hồn interact with the external world and protect themselves from all physical dangers coming from without.

The Bio-Cosmological Foundation of Human Souls

What is the meaning of the numerology of the three human souls (hồn) as believed in Chinese and Viêtnamese religious traditions? What is the meaning of the numerology of the seven phách (vía) for each male in contrast to the existence of the nine phách (vía) in each female in their relation to the three hồn (souls)? Are the three human hồn conceived in the same functionalistically Platonic way or not? A definite answer to these ontological questions is almost impossible because of the total lack of empirical and textual evidence. Nevertheless, we cannot just dismiss the numerology of the hồn and the phách (vía) to be merely "peasant superstitions," as many

sinologists and viêtologists have done. The numerology of the three hồn and seven phách of the male (3 + 7 = 10) or the three hồn and the nine phách of the female (3 + 9 = 12) must have some deeper meanings which cannot be theoretically reconstructed without tracing them back to the general numerology of East Asian and Viêtnamese ontology and cosmology.

The general numerology of East Asian and Viêtnamese mythology, which contains some ontological and cosmological elements of significance for our purpose here. The second source is the systems of geometric symbols and pictorial images on the oldest Heger Type I Vănlangian bronze drums (formerly Đôngsơnian bronze drums) found throughout southern China, Viêt-Nam, and Southeast Asia. And the third source is the system of philosophical principles and religious rituals of Đaoism (c. Taoism) and the Dịch Lý (c. Yih Li, Philosophy of Change).[25]

These three sources seem to give support to the following thesis: the three human Hồn (souls) are the numerological expression of the three types of natural life-forces (v. sinh lực tự nhiên). The three types of natural life-forces are the, celestial life-energies, the terrestrial life-energies, and the biological life-energies. After the celestial and terrestrial life-energies had been cosmically generated and had come to interact with one another, the cosmic conditions for the generations of all the possible forms of biological life-forces were well-structured and well-prepared. The generation of the three human Hồn (souls) and their human Tinh Khí (quintessential fluids) can be considered to be the final phase of the whole cosmo-biological evolutionary processes.

The final generation of the primal human Hồn and their human Tinh Khí can be reconstructed to have been conceived in either of the two cosmobiological directions. In the first direction of evolution, the celestial and terrestrial life-energies had fused together to generate the common biological life-energies. Then the common biological life-energies eventually diversified themselves into the primal three human

Hồn and their primal human Tinh Khí which constituted the distinctly human life-force in relation to all other non-human life-forces. In the second direction of evolution, it might have been the fusion of the celestial and terrestrial life-energies that directly gave birth to the primal human life-force.

The primal human life-force contains in its very ontological being the two indivisible self-existing and self-creating components which are the three Hồn (souls) and their Tinh Khí (quintessential fluids). The primal three human Hồn constituted the self-moving spirit which was inherently embodied in the living human Tinh Khí which were the self-creative substances of the former. The primal human Tinh Khí, which can be compared with the modern scientific concept of the human DNA, constituted in turn the materialistically self-creative substances of their own inherent self-animating Hồn.

The numerology of the three human Hồn can therefore be interpreted to represent all three forms of cosmically universal life-energies which might have been conceived to he either the celestial, the terrestrial, and the biological or the celestial, the terrestrial, and the human. In either direction of the evolutionary processes, it was the human life-force (Hồn-Tinh Khí which eventually came to evolve biologically (organically) into the first cosmic "Man" (Nam) and the first cosmic "Woman" (Nữ) as they are called in the "Tự Quái Truyện" (c. Tsa Kua Chuan [Miscellaneous Notes on Hexagrams]) of the *Chu Dịch Kinh* (Classic of Universal Changes) or into the Dragon Father "Lạc Long Quân" and the Fairy Mother "Âu Cơ" as they are romanticized in the Việtnamese creation mythology.[26]

Concerning the existence of the "hồn" (c. hun) in relation to the "tinh khí" (c. ching ch'i), the anonymous authors of the "Hệ Từ Truyện" (c. Hsi Tz'u Chuan, Great Treatise) in the *Chu Dịch Kinh* explain as follows:

> The holy sages, looking upwards, contemplated the celestial figures (thiên văn); looking downwards, they examined

the terrestrial forms (địa pháp). Thus they came to know the cause of the dark and the light. By retracing things to their beginnings and following them to their very ends, they came to know the rationality of birth and death. The union of the *tinh khí* (quintessential fluids) produces all things and the journey of the *hồn* (souls) brings about their *dịch* (changes). Through this they came to know the realities of all the *thần* (divinities).[27]

It is said here that the phenomenal existence of any given biological being begins when the "tinh khí" (c. ching ch'i [male-female reproductive fluids]) of a female (mother) and a male (father) are united in their sexual act of reproduction. As the body of any biological being has lived its phenomenally existential life and finally disintegrates, its self-embodying "hồn" takes off, and the biological being ceases to function. It is this dialectic of life and death that the authors of the "Hệ Từ Truyện" (c. Hsi Tz'u Chuan) examined and came to know the realities of all the spiritual powers and life-forces (thần lực [c. shen-lei]) in all the spheres of Being and Non-Being.

It is not stated in the "Hệ Từ Truyện" itself nor in the *Chu Dịch Kinh* as a whole that each human being has "three hồn" as believed in the Sino-Việtnamese ancestral worship traditions. But the three components of the human Hồn, namely, the celestial, the terrestrial, and the human as I have theoretically reconstructed, appear to correspond to the three principles of the ontological ĐẠO (c. TAO). The ontological ĐẠO is conceived in the "Hệ Từ Truyện" to be constituted of a self-governing Lý (c. Li [Principle]) and two primordial Khí (c. Ch'i [Material Forces]). The two primordial Khí are the "Âm Khí" (c. Yin Ch'i [Female Material Force]) and the "Dương Khí" (c. Yang Ch'i [Male Material Force]). In order to exist and continue to exist in itself, by itself, and for itself as the eternal Universal Life-Force, the ontological ĐẠO, which Lão Tử (c. Lao Tzu) also calls the Mother of the

Ten Thousand Entities, is theorized in the "Hệ Từ Truyện" to have had transformed itself into Heaven (v. Thiên) and Earth (v. Địa) whose erotic interactions had given birth to the male and female sexes of the Ten Thousand Entities (v. Vạn Vật). (Fig. 02).

The two sexes of the human race in particular and those of all the other living species in general are conceived to have been generated out of the life-energies of Heaven and Earth. Thus the three components of the human Hồn can be interpreted to correspond with the celestial life-energies and the terrestrial energies which had fused to generate the human life-energies. The celestial, terrestrial, and human life-energies are conceived to be the phenomenally existing manifestations of the three principles of the ĐẠO, namely, its self-governing Lý (c. Li), Dương Khí (c. Yang Ch'i), and Âm Khí (c. Yin Ch'i) as they have now been existing and operating at the cosmic and biological levels of their self-reproductions and self-transformations.

Let us now turn our attention to the Việtnamese creation mythology. The cosmological mythology of ancient Việt-Nam, which is recollected in the "Truyện Hồng Bàng" (Story of Great Vermillion Immensities), contains the famous Vănlangian myth of human creation which is popularly known as the "Story of the Sac of 100 Eggs" (Truyện Bọc Trăm Trứng). This famous Vănlangian myth has been orally handed down to the Việtnamese from the Vănlangian time when the Hùng Kings ruled the Văn Lang Quốc (Kingdom of Civilized Peoples) around four thousand years ago (2879–258 BCE).[28]

The human creation myth contains the two fabulous life-giving images, the Dragon Father Lạc Long Quân and the Fairy Mother Âu Cơ. They fused their "female and male quintessential fluids" (v. tinh khí âm dương [c. yin yang ching ch'i]) or their "seeds of life" (giống), and eventually, Mother Âu Cơ gave birth to "a sac of 100 eggs" (bọc trăm trứng). It was these primordial 100 eggs that were finally hatched into the 100 children, all being healthy, beautiful, talented, and intelligent.

Dragon Father Lạc Long Quân and Fairy Mother Âu Cơ can be considered at the biosocial level as the Việtnamese equivalents of the Judaeo-Christian Adam and Eve. And the "sac of 100 eggs" is the image of the theoretically universalized human womb (đồng bào) which represents the whole human race being born free into existence. This interpreted possibility is quite in harmony with the later Việtnamese concept of humanity and the cosmogonic contents of the systems of pictorial images and geometric symbols on the early Việtnamese bronze drums.[29]

The biological and physical symbols of Father Lạc Long Quân and Mother Âu Cơ seem to indicate that the human race is the best possible fusion of the quintessences of Heaven and Earth and all living things (tinh khí trời đất cùng vạn vạt). Father Lạc Long Quân is symbolized by the biological image of the male "dragon" and the physical image of water. These two images are ontologically, cosmologically, and biologically significant because the Dragon and Water are the symbols that represent all the unfathomable creative and nourishing powers of the terrestrial realm (Earth) in symbolic association with the Phoenix and Fire symbolizing all the divine transforming powers of the celestial realm (Heaven).

Thus Fire as a physical symbol can be considered to represent all the self-transforming creative life-energies of the celestial realm in functional association with the physical symbol Water which represents all the nourishing creative life-energies of the terrestrial realm. And the Phoenix and the Dragon as the cosmo-biological symbols can be interpreted to have been intended by the Vănlangians to represent the female (âm) and male (dương) types of the primal human life-force that had biospiritually emerged out of the cosmic fusions either between the celestial and terrestrial life-energies or between the celestial, terrestrial, and biological life-energies. It is within this final phase of the cosmo-biological processes that the âm (c. yin) and dương (c. yang) types of the primal human life-force came to be generated and eventually gave birth to the First Cosmic Woman and the First Cosmic Man. They were thus symbolically called by the cosmically honorific titles "Dragon Father Lạc Long Quân" and the "Fairy Mother Âu Cơ" as recollected in the Vănlangian creation myth of the "Story of the Sac of 100 Eggs" (Truyện Bọc Trăm Trứng). The whole human race was therefore artistically and poetically romanticized as the "Con Cháu Tiên Rồng" (Children and Grandchildren of Fairy-Dragon-like Quintessences of Being and Non-Being). (Fig. 07).

This mythologically majestic image of the children and grandchildren of the Fairy Mother Âu Cơ and the Dragon Father Lạc Long Quân can now be found to have been expressed in artistic form on the Ngọc-Lũ I and on many other early Vănlangian bronze drums found in northern Việt-Nam, southwestern China, and Laos. (Figs. 06a-06b). The artistic form of the image of the "Con Cháu Tiên Rồng" was symbolized in two artistic ways.

The first artistic way reveals the symbolism of heavenly fairyhood (Tiên) through the beautiful three-dimensional feather clothes that human dancers and musicians were shown to wear. The feather clothes were shown to have been designed in the mode of the two wings of birds and in harmony with the elaborate feather headdresses designed after the shape of bird heads and the image of dragon heads. (Fig. 03). The human dancers, musicians, and warriors, who were shown to wear feather clothes and fantastic bird-like headdresses, dragon-like headdresses, or mixed ones (bird-dragon), can be interpreted to have been intended to concretize the abstract image of the "Children and Grandchildren of Tiên Rồng."

The second artistic way reveals the technoartistically unified symbolism of the "Children and Grandchildren of Tiên Rồng" through the modality of dragon-phoenix loveboats. Each loveboat was designed to be half phoenix in the image of a birdhead-shaped stern and half dragon in the image of a dragon-shaped prow. The dragon-shaped prow of each loveboat contains a very artistically sophisticated

symbolism of the Children and Grandchildren of Tiên Rồng which reveals itself in the eroticism of lovebirds penetrating deep into the mouths of lovedragons. (Figure 04).

The Vănlangian creation myth that mythologized the cosmobiological generation of the primal human life-force as it is revered in Việtnamese mythology seems to have also been expressed in a very interesting artistic form on the earliest Vănlangian-Việtnamese bronze drums (Heger Type I). (Figs. 06a-06b)

The artistically sophisticated systems of geometric and pictorial images on the early Vănlangian bronze drums reveal the symbolism of the one cosmically unified life-generating centre where all types of living species, which are represented by the humans, cervides and birds, are graphically shown to be born into Being and returning into Non-Being unendingly.

The artistically graphic representation of the erotic harmonizations of the male and female reproductive organs (âm-dương [c. yin-yang]) in the central design of each Vănlangian bronze drum seems to reveal clearly the three main phenomena of Nature and Life: (1) the self-existence of the universal Life-Force of Being and Non-Being in the symbolism of the central geometrical disc, (2) the cosmically universal evolution of life from the very beginning of space-time when all biological self-creating Tinh-Khí had been bio-cosmologically generated out of the life-energies of Heaven and Earth, and (3) the dialectic of life and death is biologically self-perpetuating, as the females and males of all species fuse their own tinh khí (quintessential fluids) to reproduce themselves phenomenally.[30] (Figs. 05-06a).

The artistic imagery of the dialectic of life and death appears to be similar to what the authors of the "Hệ Từ Truyện" in the Chu Dịch Kinh conceptualized philosophically as "sinh sinh chi vị dịch" (productions and reproductions constitute the processes of change). Lão Tử (c. Lao Tzu) observes the same dialectic of life and death when he writes: "The ten thousand things rise and fall while the Self watches their return. They grow and flourish and then return to the source. Returning to the source is stillness, which is the way of nature. The way of nature is unchanging."[31]

The technoartistic symbolism on the tympanum of the Ngọc-Lũ I clearly reveals all the three main phenomena of Nature and Life, and especially the cosmically unified dialectic of life and death of Humanity, that I am particularly concerned with here. First, the artists of the Ngọc-Lũ I showed two concentric zones of 55 birds either flying in the sky or standing on earth under the radiating sun at the center of the drum's tympanum.

Second, they showed a circle of 10 couples of kỳ lân (deer-like quadrupeds) running circularly on the surface of the earth.

Third, they showed 35 humans dancing and playing music all around the innermost concentric zone of the drum tympanum under the shining sun.

And fourth, they showed the geometrical symbolism of the central disc in the form of the erotic harmonizations of fourteen pairs of female and male reproductive organs taking place eternally at the unified centre of Heaven and Earth. (Fig. 05).

It can be said that the artists of the Ngọc-Lũ I have successfully revealed the cosmically unified evolutionary dialectic of life and death of the human race as well as of all other living species. This universal dialectic of life and death was shown by the artists of the Ngọc-Lũ I to have been unfolding non-endingly from time immemorial and organically linked with and structurally sustained by Heaven and Earth within one singular cosmically unified framework of biological reproductions and self-transformations. (Fig. 06a).

This cosmically evolutionary dialectic was artistically shown to have originated from one common primordial Life-Force which constitutes Itself simultaneously as the Ultimate Reality of curved Time-Space and as the dynamically self-sustaining power of phenomenal existence as well. The cosmically common primordial Life-Force was artistically represented by the purely geometrical symbolism of the whole central

disc of the Ngọc-Lũ I or of any other early bronze drum of either ancient Việt-Nam, ancient southern China, or ancient Southeast Asia. The central disc of the Ngọc-Lũ I or that of any other early Vănlangian bronze drum was intended to serve as the cosmically universal Centre of Space-Time as well as the Ultimate Reality of Being and Non-Being. (Fig. 05).

The central geometrical disc of every early Vănlangian bronze drum can therefore be compared to the "Source" (ontological ĐẠO) to which Lão Tử (c. Lao Tzu) refers in his *Đạo Đức Kinh* (c. *Tao Te Ching*) since all living things were shown to be born from the Source and to return to the Source non-endingly. The universal Life-Force can also be considered to be ontologically similar to the ĐẠO which is textually discussed in the *Chu Dịch Kinh* (c. *Chou I Ching*) and the *Đạo Đức Kinh* (c. *Tao Te Ching*). It was technoartistically shown to have unfolded itself into Heaven, Earth, Humanity, and All Living Things, and to have remained *ontologically immanent* in all the former and *biophysically existing* as the former.

What is philosophically common to these traditions is the ontocosmologically evolutionistic idea that postulates that, in order to exist phenomenally and eternally, the primordial Life-Force had completely transformed itself into Heaven, Earth, and the Ten Thousand Entities, and has been existing and functioning as the latter in both form and essence. (Figs. 06a-07).

It can be summed up here that the number "3" in the numerology of the human self might have not been intended to represent the three functional components of human souls (the rational, the spirited, the appetitive) as they were conceived by Plato. Instead, the number "3" had probably been intended to represent all the three types of theoretically formulated universal life-energies, namely, the celestial, the terrestrial, and the biological. If such a theoretical possibility were in fact the original case, then, the numerology of the three human Hồn might have been conceived to reveal the cosmo-biological basis of the human souls and to show how the three human Hồn are linked to the living energies of Heaven and Earth. The first hồn represents the living energies of Heaven (the Celestial), the second hồn symbolizes the living energies of Earth (the Terrestrial), and the third hồn represents either the living energies of Humanity (the Human) or the common biological life-energies which eventually diversified into the Human.

If this cosmo-biological foundation of humanity were in fact conceived in the ancient numerology of the human Hồn, then, I think it is possible for us to better appreciate the ontologically profound *raison d'être* of the Việtnamese and East Asian ancestral worshippers who have believed in the immortality and divine protective powers of their ancestral souls and have worshipped them religiously.

Since the natural evolution and biological reproduction of the human life-force (hồn-animated tinh khí) have been an integral part of the cosmic processes, the numerology of the human Hồn and human Phách appears to be related to the numerology of the sexagenary system of the Eastern Calendar. The sexagenary system of the Eastern Calendar is based on the numerology of the 10 Celestial Stems and the 12 Terrestrial Branches.[32]

If we add the three hồn and the seven phách that each male is supposed to have, we obtain the number 10 (3 + 7 = 10). The collectivity of the male three hồn and seven phách thus corresponds to the ten stems of Heaven. If we add the three hồn and the nine phách that each female is conceived to have, we obtain the number 12 (3 + 9 = 12). The combination of the three female hồn and the nine female phách equals the twelve branches of Earth. Now if we add the 10 celestial stems and the 12 terrestrial branches that form the Eastern Calendar's sexagenary system, we obtain the total number 22 (10 + 12 = 22). It is interesting to note that the total of the celestial stems and terrestrial branches thus equals the combination of the male and female hồn and phách of humanity (3 + 7 + 3 + 9 = 22).

The above numerological correlation between the sexagenary cycle, which governs the cosmic processes, and the system of human Hồn and Phách can be considered to be either merely coincidental or philosophically related. A discussion of the philosophical and cultural connections between the two numerological systems is certainly beyond the scope of this paper. But one can suggest that the said numerological correlation points to some cosmic inter-connectedness that might have been conceived to exist between the macrocosm (Heaven and Earth) and the microcosm (Women and Men), whose existences were believed to be biocosmologically interrelated.

Different Honorific Titles for the Human Souls

I have noticed that there is a rather free usage of the Sino-Việtnamese term "linh hồn" (c. ling hun [divine souls]) among sinologists who have studied Chinese religion. This term is used to indicate the "souls" of each human during one's biological life as well as one's after-life.[33] Such a free usage of the term "linh hồn" may not be proper in describing the Việtnamese tradition because there are different honorific titles that are used to indicate the three phases of the spiritual transformation of one's souls during one's "return" to the spiritual realm of one's ancestors.

In phase one of the phenomenal existence of one's three hồn, the Việtnamese use the word "hồn" (souls), or "hồn người" (human souls), or "thần hồn" (godlike souls) to identify them. One's three hồn are believed to reside concretely and temporarily in one's "godlike body" (thần xác) as one's own superior quintessence (tinh anh). Owing to this phenomenal concretization and individuality of each person's hồn, it is popularly recommended that "One should protect one's own souls" (Hồn ai người ấy giữ!). It is also believed that the ancestral "linh hồn" of each family line would always protect their own morally good offspring (posterity) which are the direct reproductions of the souls and bodies of the former. Because of this onto-biological foundation, the Viêtnamese ancestral worshippers always and primarily rely upon and pray to their own deceased fathers, mothers, grandparents, or their most favourite deceased person for their divine protections just like when they were biologically alive. They are therefore quite reluctant to believe in the direct divine protection of a universally "Supreme Being," like most Christians do in their God or most Hindus in their favourite divinities (be that Vishnu, Shiva, Krishna, or Mahadevi).

In phase two of their purely spiritual existence, the hồn of a newly deceased human are conceived to go through a process of self-transformation beginning at the death of the biological body, and are thus called by different honorific titles denoting their chronological transformations and spiritual qualities. When an adult, male or female, dies of a natural death due to sickness or old age, one's hồn (souls) are conceived to undergo their first spiritual self-transformation in the act of escaping from their dying body. The fate of the self-escaping hồn is determined by circumstantial situations, which can be of two kinds.

In the first situation, if the standard rituals of death are performed by the children or relatives of the deceased, then, the now wandering hồn are called back home to reside in the human-figure-shaped white cloth (hồn bạch) that is normally made for this very purpose. From the moment of the second spiritual self-trans-formation, the hồn of the deceased are called the "Hồn Bạch" (White Souls) after the human-figure-shaped white cloth (hồn bạch) in which they reside. They are called the "Hồn Bạch" because of their pure spirituality and noncorporeality (being completely free from the unpure body) and are thus represented by the colour "white" (bạch). In harmony with this purely spiritual quality of the self-transformed hồn, all funeral clothes that are worn have to be white and coarse (vải thô tẳng). And so should the memorial funeral headband (khăn tang) be made of the white

cotton fabric and be worn constantly (except bedtime) for the whole three-year-long mourning period. A modern educated son in mourning normally prefers to wear a rectangular piece of black fabric on their sleeves instead.

After the carefully coffined corpse is buried "under the three layers of soil" (dưới ba tấc đất) in accordance with the traditional funeral rites, the "Hồn Bách" are to go through the third spiritual self-transformation, the human-figure-shaped white cloth (hồn bạch) is replaced by the "thần chủ" (tablet of the deceased) on which the name, age, and title of the deceased is normally written. The "Hồn Bạch" are now called the "Thần Chủ (Godlike or Divine Master) and are welcomed home again in the family of either their wife or eldest son for worship. The "Thần Chủ" will be worshipped at the sacred family ancestral altar (bàn thờ tổ' tiên) according to the established rites of mourning for a period of three years.

After the completion of the three-year-long mourning period (ba năm tang chế), the Thần Chủ goes through the final spiritual self-transformation and is then called "Linh Hồn" (Unfathomably Divine Souls) by their posterity in prayers for their "miraculous" protection and guidance in times of personal crisis and family misfortune. If a prayer is answered in some miraculous way, it is believed that the "Linh Hồn" of one's deceased parent are really "linh" (unfathomably divine or miraculous). The term "Linh Hồn" is gender-free and generally used for both the female and male deceased. But the proper honorific title that should be and is normally used for the female deceased is called "Hương Hồn" (Perfumed Souls) in contrast to "Anh Hồn" (Superior Souls) for the male deceased.

If the Linh Hồn of one's deceased parent were not "linh ứng" (i.e., did not respond to one's prayers and manifest in a spiritually divine and miraculous way to protect their posterity), then, it would be interpreted that there must be something fundamentally wrong with the way their posterity have conducted their moral lives and have treated the Linh Hồn. The succeeding head of the deceased's family should firstly rectify his/her own moral life and that of his/her whole family, and secondly, should ask a geomancer ("địa lý" master) to carefully check whether or not the ecological conditions of the grave and its surrounding environment might have in fact been disturbed the peace and safety of the bones (xương cốt) of the deceased. If the judgment of the địa lý master were negative, then, certain concrete measures should be taken, such as the physical modifications of the existing grave and its ecological environment, or sometimes a second burial at a geomantically determined new place would be a must!

In the second situation, if no rituals of death are performed because the deceased has no posterity or relatives, one's hồn (souls) would wander after escaping one's dying body and eventually become what the Việtnamese call the "hồn ma" (ghost souls), and ultimately the "ma" (ghost). Mạnh Tử (c. Meng Tzu) said: "There are three things which are unfilial, and the greatest of them is to have no posterity" (*Mencius IV*: A: 26). Mạnh Tử does not, however, explain the reason why having no posterity is the greatest unfilial act for the male of a given bloodline.

For most Việtnamese, however, the reason is either personal, clanistic, or patriotic in nature because they certainly would not wish that their own family (gia đình), their own clan (gia tộc), or their own nation (quốc gia) would be onto-biologically terminated! If that unfortunate eventuality should happen, then, their own souls and those of their family, clan, or nation would necessarily become homeless wandering "ma" and "quỷ" (ghosts and demons) who would not only suffer all imaginable misfortunes but also would disturb and harm the living! The biological perpetuation of one's family line, which presupposes that of one's clan, and one's whole nation, is thus held to be spiritually sacred in one's own erotically ritualistic act of onto-biological procreation which is also popularly called "performing the đạo of Heaven and Earth" (làm cái đạo Trời Đất).

The vital link that binds the living and the dead together for eternity is what the Việtnamese call "giống nòi" (the refined seeds of life) which are biologically perpetuated whenever wives and husbands erotically harmonize their female and male "tinh khí" (quintessential fluids) or "giống" (seeds) to reproduce themselves onto-biologically. Getting married, having children, and educating them to become morally principled humans have thus always been conceived to be morally imperative and onto-biologically sacred in the Việtnamese and other East Asian traditions of ancestral worship.

In the case of a violent death, the hồn (souls) of any unfortunate person would wander around the place where their body physically perished! It is believed that the bodily detached hồn would wander around the "death spot" where their body's blood was shed because their phenomenal existence was being cut short immaturely, before the predetermined time. The wandering hồn would become the "hồn ma" if no redemption rites were made to welcome them back home for worship, and they would eventually become the homeless wandering "ma" (ghost).

If a dead person who was a person oh great virtues and good merits, whose hồn are believed by most Việtnamese to be *linh* (spiritually powerful and divine), but this person has no posterity to carry on the necessary worship, his/her wandering hồn will know how to survive in the after-life. The wandering "hồn ma" of the said deceased would normally select a good living person whom they could trust and manifest themselves in some special "linh" ways, such as in the form of a dream, to promise divine protections in return for their worship. Then that chosen person would organize the redemption rites and welcome the said wandering hồn home for worship as a friend, a brother, a sister, or a parent depending on his respective age.

There is also a special type of divine souls which is not called by the term "linh hồn" but is honoured instead by the honorific title "Anh Linh Dân Tộc" (The People's Superior Divinities). The term "Anh Linh Dân Tộc" is used to indicate the collectivity of divine souls of all those great national achievers such as national heroes, heroines, village founders, etc. In addition to the term "Anh Linh Dân Tộc" (The People's Superior Divinities), the term "Hồn Thiêng Sông Núi (Holy Souls of Rivers and Mountains) is used to refer collectively to all powerful divine souls of great national leaders of Việt-Nam. The prayers for their divine interventions are known to be done by most secret revolutionary groups at their founding rites or pre-battle ceremonies, and also by many kings of feudal Việt-Nam in times of national crisis and national memorial festivals.

The Rituals of Birth

It seems desirable for me to briefly discuss the rituals of birth in association with the rituals of death because they are connected with the numerology of the human Hồn and Phách. Furthermore, the two types of rituals represent one unified dialectic of life and death through which the hồn of a person are conceived to live the two stages of their divine existence.

Like the Chinese, Korean, and Japanese peoples, the Việtnamese conceptualize the dialectic of life and death to have been unfolding around two biologically and spiritually interrelated realms. The first is the phenomenally visible realm of the living, which is called the "cõi dương" (yang realm). The second is the spiritually invisible realm of the dead, which is called the "cõi âm" (yin realm). It is ancestral worship that links the phenomenal realm of the living to the spiritual realm of the dead. The two realms thus constitute one single unified life-world.

It is now necessary to discuss briefly the use, significance, and logic of numbers in the Việtnamese tradition as they are related to the numerology of the human souls and the rituals of birth and death. It shall become apparent later that the Việtnamese rituals of birth and death, and most other aspects of the Việtnamese Civilization are based on certain numerical systems and principles. Numbers have in fact played pivotal roles in all aspects of Việtnamese life and culture. Each person is believed to be born with one's "destiny number" (số mệnh), which determines the path and character of one's life, namely, how long or how short one lives, how healthy or sick one is, whether one is rich or poor, noble or base, etc. The phenomenal unfolding of one's life from birth to death and the return of one's souls to the spiritual realm of one's ancestors is therefore governed by a numerical system which provides time, order, structure, and process for the former to unfold as numerologically predestined. Of the Việtnamese numerological system, that of the Dịch Lý (c. Yih Li), odd numerals are organizational numbers, especially the number "three" (3) as exemplified in the Việtnamese rituals of birth and death, in the design of the Eight Trigrams, etc.

Thus every human is born to possess, for example, three hồn and seven phách (if male) or nine phách (if female). To be in harmony with this trinity of the deceased's souls, the various rites of the funeral rituals must be performed accordingly. The calling of the departed souls of the deceased must therefore be made three times and the food offerings to the deceased must be divided into three portions and led three times to the deceased's mouth. In harmony with the three years it takes for the deceased's copse to be completely decomposed, the mourning time must therefore be observed for a total of three years. One's birth and death as well as all the events taking place in between are believed to be predetermined and numerologically timed accordingly. So it takes a total of nine months and ten days for a conceived "watery egg" (trứng nước) to develop into a baby and to be born. It then takes three months for the baby to begin moving waveringly, seven months crawling, and nine months walking clumsily.

Given the metaphysical nature and practical functions that numbers are conceived and established to have played in the Việtnamese culture in general and the Việtnamese rituals of birth and death in particular, I would like to proceed with the discussion of the latter now.[34] Furthermore, for the purpose of rethinking about possible applications of numerology in the organizations of Việtnamese daily life activities, and examining how consistent or unconsistent the numerology of human Hồn and Phách in particular is observed or not observed in the rituals of birth and death, I would like to renumerologize the numbers of things used in rituals in numerical equations and place them in square brackets. It is hoped that this peculiarity will be viewed accordingly.

When a child is successfully born into the world (which is described as a good state of "round mother and square child", mẹ tròn con vuông), one notices a special sign hanging in the front gate of its happy family. The sign consists of 1 taro leaf (lá môn), 1 charcoal stick, and 7 coins (if boy) or 9 coins (if girl). The "isolation time" lasts 7 days if a boy and 9 days if a girl, during which no visitor is welcome. On the seventh day (if boy) or ninth day (if girl), a mini "Thanksgiving for the Midwives" (Lễ Cúng Mụ) is observed by the parents to express their gratitude for the great birth-giving works of the 12 divine Midwives (12 Bà Mụ, 12 = 1 + 2 = 3). The offerings for the Twelve Midwives consist of 12 pairs of shoes and 12 pieces of delicious areca-betel.[35]

Then the "Rite of the First Full Month" (Lễ Đầy Tháng) is specially held to officially express the parents' joy and deepest gratitude for the "Twelve Midwives" (12 Bà Mụ). The offerings consist of (1) seven boiled and red-colored eggs (if boy) or nine (if girl); (2) seven red-colored glutinous rice cakes (if boy) or nine (if girl); and (3) seven boiled sea crabs (if boy) or nine (if girl).

As the first birthday comes, the "Rite of One Full Year of Age" (Lễ Đầy Tuổi Tôi) parents to express thanks to their ancestors (ancestral family linh hồn) and to mark the, child's humanhood. After the performance of this rite, the child is officially regarded as a "human being" (con người) having the basic "human nature" (nhân tính). If the infant would die before the completion of one year, it would not become a "ma" (ghost) but a "ranh" which can be translated into English as a "little demon".

Thus a child less than one year old is not considered by the Việtnamese to possess any authentic human souls yet. Unlike the hồn of a one-year-old child or older who dies, the "ranh" (little demon) is believed to have the capacity to reincarnate itself if not handled correctly in a ritualistic manner. Each reincarnation of a given "ranh" would result necessarily in a miscarriage which then prepares the time lap for its new reincarnation and so forth. The cycle of a ranh's reincarnations could be terminated by a powerful shaman (thầy phù thủy) who would perform a ranh-killing ritual.[36]

The one-year-old celebration rite is also intended to test the career choice of the child and to mark the initial successes of the baby in its numerologically conceived process of growth and functional development. As the saying goes: "In three months it knows how to move waveringly, in seven months it knows how to crawl, and in nine months it knows how to walk clumsily with falling steps" (Ba tháng biết lẫy, bảy tháng biết bò, chín tháng lò dò biết đi!).[37]

The Rituals of Death

The rituals of death are considered by the Việtnamese to be the most important act of filial piety that one should perform in honour of one's parents as they leave the "cõi dương" of the living (yang realm) and return to the "cõi âm" of the dead (yin realm). The rituals of death in the Việtnamese tradition also carry some great metaphysical significance that the living must grasp in order to truly comprehend the dialectic of life and death, for, as the Việtnamese say "Life is a temporary stay, death is a return" (Sống gởi, Thác về). The rituals of death are thus supreme in importance and complex in procedure so that the return of the souls of a deceased should be properly prepared in form and truly spiritual in nature. For the benefit of simplicity, I shall focus on some major rites among the various rituals of death that I have experienced myself as well as those that are discussed in the works of Đào Duy Anh, Phan Kế Bính, and Toan Ánh.

Pre-Death Rites (Lễ Tiền Vong)

As the farewell time of a fully grown human being, say a father, is finally at hand, his children carry him on his deathbed to rest at the centre of the house with the head facing the East, which is the direction of eternal return.[38] Before he breathes his last breath, a holy name, which is called the "tên thụy" or "tên hèm," is selected for and made known to the dying father. After the father is declared to be physically dead, his deathbed is then moved to the centre of the house. The positioning of his deathbed at the centre of the living room after he physically dies is intended to show that he died a good natural death rather than an unfortunate one. A new 7-metre-long white cloth is carefully placed over the face of the deceased and eventually folded into a human figure. This human-figure-shaped white cloth is called the "hồn bạch" (white souls) in which the wandering hồn (souls) of the deceased are believed to return for residence after they are being called back. The children of the deceased then carry and place the corpse on the floor for an instant before returning it to his deathbed. According to Phan Kế Bính, this is done with the view to symbolize the fact that the body comes from earth and back to earth it returns.[39] But Đào Duy Anh explains that it is done for a more practical reason, i.e., the hope that the dead would resurrect if it were to be animated by the earthly ether.[40]

If it were consciously done with such a practical reason in mind as Đào Duy Anh explains, then, this ritualistic practice and hope may reveal the historically lost metaphysical belief in the ontocosmological character of the human Hồn as expressed in the numerology that I reconstructed above. That is to say, death is conceived to be the biological distentegration of the three hồn of a person, namely, the celestial, the terrestrial, and the human. The ritualistic practice of placing the corpse of the deceased on the floor can be considered to be an attempt to re-establish the existential unity of its three hồn which was broken down at the moment of the deceased's physical death.

Rite of Calling the Hồn to Return Home (Lễ Phuc Hồn)

After knowing for sure that the father is dead, one of the deceased's children (normally the eldest son), holding the collar and backside of the shirt of the deceased with his left and right hand respectively, and climbing up onto the. front roof, calls on to the wandering souls of his parent "3 times," as follows:

Việtnamese: "3 Hồn 7 Vía . . . Bố đâu? Về với con!" (3 times)
English (3 times): 3 Hồn and 7 Vía . . . **Where are Thee Father? Please return home with thine children!**

When the deceased is a mother, then, the calling would be as follows:

Việtnamese: **3 Hồn 9 Vía . . . Cái đâu? Về với con! (3 times)**
English (3 times): **3 Hồn and 9 Vía . . . Where are Thee Mother? Please return home with thine children!**

After performing his soul-calling act, he climbs down from the back roof into the house. This is called the "Lễ Phục Hồn" (Rite of Calling the Hồn to Return Home). It is only after the completion of this rite that the deceased's children and grandchildren could cry out, change their clothes to wear the white coarse funeral clothes (quần áo tang), remove all their jewelry, walk barefoot, unwrap their knotted hair, and eat plain rice soup for their meals. All these acts are to show their filial piety (hiếu), reverence, love, remorse, and sorrow for the deceased.

Rite of Feeding the Deceased (Lễ Phạm Hàm)

Next they proceed to wash the body of the deceased father and to put new white clothes on him. Then the ritual "Lễ Phạm Hàm" is observed, in which two kinds of offerings are made in harmony with the numerology of the three hồn (souls): 1 bowl of carefully washed glutinous rice (gạo nếp), and 3 carefully polished coins placed in a plate (1 + 1 + 3 + 1 = 6:2 = 3). The rice and coins are divided into 3 parts which are carefully fed into the mouth of the deceased father for 3 consecutive times. A wealthy family would substitute these offerings with 9 pearls and 3 pieces of gold (9 + 3 = 12:4 = 3).

Rite of Shroudings (Lễ Liệm Xác)

Next comes the "Small Shrouding Rite" (Lễ Tiểu Liệm), which consists of wrapping 1 strip of white cloth over the corpse vertically and 3 strips horizontally, and then the "Great Shrouding Rite" (Lễ Đại Liệm), which consists of wrapping 1 strip vertically and 5 strips horizontally (1 + 3 + 1 + 5 = 10). The shrouding ritual proceeds with this numerological rule until the corpse is well wrapped. We should here notice that a round plate of special wood which bears 7 holes representing the image of the North Star is placed in the coffin. This wood plate is called the "Wood of the 7 Stars" (Ván Thất Tinh). This ritual, which is also observed by certain southern Chinese, may be related to a Việtnamese cosmological belief that the "God of the North Star" (Thần Bắc Đẩu) is in charge of keeping the "Death Records" (Sổ Tử) of all humans, while the "God of the South Star" (Thần Nam Tào) keeps their "Birth Records" (Sổ Sinh).[41]

After the shrouding ceremony, the "holy coffin" (linh cửu) is finally moved to position at the centre of the house whose floor along the two sides of the coffin is covered with rice straws. The holy coffin is attended at all times (day and night) by all the children and grandchildren of the deceased, taking their turns, women on the right hand side, and men on the left, in accordance with the âm-dương (c. yin-yang) principle.

Rite of Welcoming the White Souls (Lễ Triều Tịch Điền)

People erect a "well-furnished holy bed" (linh sàng) in the Eastern quadrant of the house and a "holy offering altar" (linh tọa) in the front gateway of the house. And everyday the children and grandchildren perform the ritual "Lễ Triều Tịch

Điền". This rite includes the caring, welcoming, feeding, and leading the "Hồn Bạch" (white souls of the deceased residing in the human-figure-shaped white cloth) in the morning from the Eastern Holy Bed (linh sàng) to the front Holy Altar (linh tọa), and returning the Hồn Bạch to rest in the Eastern quadrant for the night. During all this time, there is a special band of professional musicians which is charged to conduct funeral music (especially playing reed-organs khèn and leather-drums) and to sing songs concerning the meaning of existence in relation to the special life and career of the deceased. These ceremonial activities are intended to please the Hồn Bạch (White Souls) and to express the dao of filial piety observed by posterity for the deceased parent.

Rite of Informing the Ancestors (Lễ Yết Tổ)

Before the funeral procession (đám tang, phát dẫn), the "Ceremony of Informing the Ancestors" (Lễ Yết Tổ) is performed for the purpose of taking the "Hồn Bạch" (White Souls) to the Ancestral Clan Hall (tử đường, linh đường) so that all the high ancestral clan linh hồn can be informed of the deceased's return and the deceased can pay his respects to them. In order to demonstrate their filial piety (hiếu) and to allow sufficient time for the deceased's resurrection, the children and wife of the deceased would keep his corpse for many days, many weeks, or even many months. The tradition of keeping the corpse for possible resurrection is no longer followed by the Việtnamese today.

Rites of Funeral Procession (Lễ An Táng or Tang Lễ)

The funeral procession (đám tang) is attended and carried out by 7 groups of children, grandchildren, and blood relatives (all wearing white coarse cotton clothes) with the support of funeral professionals. Most significant is the second group in line, which carries honour flags whose characters read "TRINH THUẬN" (Chastity and Devotion) for a mother or "TRUNG TÍN" (Loyalty and Trustworthiness) for a father.

The role of the fifth group in line, tending the "holy hearse" (linh xa), is to later lead the "Hồn Bạch" (white souls of the deceased) back home again.

Facing the holy coffin (linh cửu) are the sons of the deceased who walk backwards with the "round" bamboo canes (gậy tre tròn) in their left hands if the deceased is their father and with the "square" erythrine canes (gậy vông vuông) in their right hands if the deceased is their mother. The geometrical shape of the cane, designed to be either "round" (tròn) or "square" (vuông), is to reveal the gender of the deceased to strangers and also to concretize the cosmological principle of Round Heaven and Square Earth.[42]

This ritualistic aspect of the funeral procession seems to testify to the metaphysical belief in the cosmic character of the three non of the deceased as discussed in my reconstruction of the bio-cosmological foundation of the human souls. The male component of a deceased father's hồn, which corresponds to Heaven, is celestial in nature. That is the cosmological reason why the deceased father is represented by the celestially round cane, which is also intended to symbolize the roundness of Heaven and fatherly virtues. By the same cosmological principle, the deceased mother is represented by the terrestrially square cane, since squareness is the nature of Earth and motherly love.

Behind the coffin are the daughters who walk inside a "white covering curtain" (bạch mạc). In some other variations, sons and daughters of the deceased have to roll their bodies in front of the holy hearse to express their "filial piety" (bày tỏ "chữ hiếu") to their deceased parent.

Rite of Making Offerings to the God of Soil (Lễ Tế Thổ Thần)

Before lowering the holy coffin to rest in the grave, the "offering rite to the God of Soil" (Lễ Tế Thổ Thần) is performed. And a "square" mound of earth is built on the grave surrounded by a raised earth ring whose mouth houses the tomb tablet which contains at least the name and the dates of birth and death of the deceased.

Rite of Welcoming the "White Souls" Home

Finally, after the burial is completed, the rite of welcoming the "Hồn Bạch" (White Souls) home is initiated, so that they will ride the holy hearse back home to the newly constructed holy altar (linh toa) in the house. The "Hồn Bạch" is then proclaimed "Thần Chủ" (Divine Master) of the family.

Rite of Reweeping (Lễ Phản Khốc)

The "rite of reweeping" (Lễ Phản Khốc) is performed once the "Thần Chủ" (Divine Master) is at home residing at a special altar. This altar is placed by the side (left if father, right if mother) of the family ancestral altar if the "linh hồn" (divine souls) of the deceased's grandparents are already worshipped in the central altar area. It is from this time onwards that the souls of the deceased are addressed in worshipping ceremonies as the "Vong Hồn" (Bodily Detached Souls), and sometimes "Linh Hồn" (divine souls), even though they are not yet fully capable of manifesting their miraculous protective powers in support of their posterity.

Rite of Praying for the Peace of the Deceased (Tế Ngu)

There follows a special three-phased rite called "Tế Ngu" (Praying for the Peace of the deceased) which is performed three times with prayers and reciting hymns during the first three days after the funeral. The Tế Ngu is conducted because it is believed that the deceased may suffer greatly from the trauma of death when the existential bonds between his hồn, phách, and body (xác) are physically and spiritually dissolved, and that each of these components is subject to its natural process of self-transformation and dissolution respectively. The observation of the Tế Ngu is also aimed to prevent wandering ghosts and demons (ma quỉ) from harassing or harming the deceased while his souls are going through the process of spiritual self-transformation.

Rite of Opening the Tomb Gate (Lễ Mở Cửa Mả)

At the completion of the first three days after the funeral, all children of the deceased observe the "Rite of Opening the Tomb Gate" (Lễ Mở Cửa Mả). Prayers and ritual offerings (which include fruits, incense (traditional), and flowers (modern) are made to the deceased at the grave. Animal sacrifices (white cock or black dog) are also made to the God of Earth for his protection of the body of the deceased against the harassment of ghosts and demons.

Other Rites During the Three-Year Mourning Period

During the first one hundred days after the funeral, daily "meal offerings" (cúng cơm) are made to the Thần Chủ (deceased) at breakfast, lunch, and dinner. Tea and fresh fruits are normally offered for breakfast, while favourite dishes that were well-liked by the deceased when alive are served for lunch and dinner. It is a general rule that the main dishes are first reverently offered to the Thần Chủ to enjoy before they are brought down for the family to share.

There are other rites observed to mark the temporal periodizations of the post-funeral self-transformations of the hồn, and the gradual dissolutions of the phách and body of the deceased. These rites are characterized by worshipping rituals and expensive feasts that unite all members of the paternal side of the family together in collective mourning. At the completion of the first 49 days after the funeral, the "Observance of the 50 Day Period" (Lễ 50 Ngày) is marked, and at the end of the first 100 days, the "Observance of the 100 Day Period" (Lễ 100 Ngày) is held. The latter rite officially marks an end of all crying by the deceased's children and blood relatives.

On the first anniversary, the "Small Commemoration Rite" (Lễ Tiểu Trường) is performed. The "Great Commemoration Rite" (Lễ Đại Trường) is performed at the end of the second year. As a total of 27 months has fully unfolded, the "Final Completion Rite" (Lễ Đoạn Tất) is organized to mark the termination of the three year mourning period. It is only after the observation of the "Final Completion Rite" that all funeral white coarse clothes are removed and completely burned.

At the end of the three-year mourning period, the hồn of the deceased are believed to have attained the full status of "Linh Hồn" (Divine Souls) and to have become capable of manifesting their divine powers in the protection of their offspring.

Annual Memorial Rite (Lễ Kỵ)

Every year before and after the end of the three-year mourning period, there is an annual memorial rite (Lễ Kỵ) which is in principle organized by the eldest son for the benefit of the linh hồn of the deceased parent and is strictly observed by all members of the family. The ritual offerings will depend on the financial status of the family. But the essential offerings that are made must include the following elements: one bowl of cooked glutinous rice (cơm nếp) on whose oval upper side lies one cooked egg and which is then covered by another bowl on which lies one pair of chopsticks (1 bowl + 1 rice + 1 egg + 1 bowl + 2 chopsticks = 6:2 = 3).[43] The annual memorial rite (Lễ Kỵ) is organized until the deceased has reached the rank of the "fifth great ancestor" (great great grandparent). By then, the linh hồn of the deceased shall be worshipped together with all the other older ancestral souls of the clan in the Ancestral Clan Shrine (linh đường).

Rite of Reburial (Lễ Cải Táng)

After the three-year mourning period, normally comes the "Lễ Cải Táng " (Rite of Reburial), which is conducted under the authority of a geomancer (thầy địa lý). All the bones of the deceased are carefully collected, washed, and finally preserved in a special jar (cái tiểu sành) for reburial in a new tomb. The capping mound of the new grave now takes a "round" shape which is encircled by an elevated ring of earth, in contrast to the "square" shape of the previous tomb. The change of the shape of the tomb mound from "square" to "round" is made in harmony with the cosmological principle of "Round Heaven" (Trời Tròn) and "Square Earth" (Đất Vuông) so as to show the complete dissolution of the body and its phách back to Earth on the one hand, and the complete purification of the hồn to become truly spiritual in harmony with the non-corporeal nature of Heaven on the other hand.

The bones of the deceased are believed to be unfathomably divine and sacred because they constitute the materially imperishable essence of the deceased's former biological being (thể phách). It is also believed that the linh hồn of the deceased parent would interact with and care for their own bones. If the bones are. disturbed or damaged, then great misfortunes would happen to one's posterity as a sign of disapproval or punishment since the peace of the deceased is being ignored and threatened. Normally, repeated occurrences of family misfortunes would necessitate subsequent reburials in the hope of preventing further calamities.

Sometimes the rite of reburial is not advised if the children of the deceased are to enjoy a good life during the three-year mourning period since the deceased is interpreted to be happy with his gravesite. The following three "good signs" (tường thụy) would call for the immediate termination of any reburial project if found in the grave or the coffin. The first good sign is the appearance of a "yellow snake" (con rắn vàng) when the digging of the grave is under way. The yellow snake is taken to be the "snake dragon of vital ether" (long xà khí vật), which is normally interpreted as the medium for the divine manifestation of the deceased's linh hồn. The second one is the web of pink silk-like threads found inside the coffin which is interpreted as the "crystallization of earth" (kết đất). And the third is earth found to be really dry and warm in the grave or the presence of water condensed into crystal-clear particles around the grave wall. If these three auspicious signs are found, then there should be no reburial and the reopened grave should be carefully returned as truly as possible to its pre-reburial condition.

Unity of the Two Realms of Human Existence

We have discussed some theoretically significant aspects of the complex funeral rites which are performed in honour of the great "return" (về) of the hồn of one's parent back to the spiritual realm of ancestors (thế giới thần linh của tổ tiên). It is within the dương (c. yang) realm of their biologically living children and grandchildren that the linh hồn of the "great four generations of ancestors" (tứ đại) interact with and protect their own four succeeding generations of posterity. And it is to the âm (c. yin) realm of their spiritually living ancestors that the biologically living offspring return after leaving the daang realm behind to a new generation for the perpetuation of their family line in space-time. Procreation is thus biologically and spiritually sacred and imperative for each generation to fulfill. The Đạo of Ancestral Worship is the vital link that unifies the two realms of human existence together into one single life-world. Marriage and family are the necessary institutions by which procreation and ancestral worship are to be maintained.

The life-world of "any great clan lineage" (đại họ tộc) is actually divided into "nine generations." Taking a husband and a wife, forming one parental couple with a status of the concerned Subject (Bản Thân), they have to conscientiously demonstrate their filiality (hiếu) to the upper four great generations (tứ đại) on the one hand, and maintain their moral leadership responsibilities to the lower four generations of their posterity on the other hand. The nine generations are patterned after the organizational number 9 as follows:

1. Cao Tổ Phụ Mẫu or Kị (Great Great Grandparents)
2. Tằng Tổ Phụ Mẫu or Cụ (Great Grandparents)
3. Tổ Phụ Mẫu or Nội (Grandparents)
4. Phụ Mẫu or Cha Mẹ (Parents)
5. Bản Thân (Subject)
6. Tử or Con (Children)

7. Tôn or Cháu (Grandchildren)
8. Tằng Tôn or Chắt (Great Grandchildren)
9. Huyền Tôn or Chít (Great Great Grandchildren)

It is precisely in the dương realm of the living and at the sacred ancestral altar (bàn thờ tổ tiên) in the central hall of each family that the linh hồn of the four upper great generations (tứ đại) are directly, reverently, and duly worshipped as "divinely protective gods" (thần linh tổ tiên). The direct ancestral worship in each family (gia đình), in each sublineage (chi tộc), or in each greater lineage (đại gia tộc) is called "the business of incense and fire" (việc hương hỏa or hương hỏa tự), which must be performed by the family head (gia trưởng), the sublineage head (trưởng chi tộc), or the lineage head (trưởng tộc), respectively, as his sacred responsibility.

What has helped shape all the members of a family, a village, or a society into morally good citizens and spiritually elevated human beings is the belief in (1) the existence of the spiritual realm of the ancestral linh hồn to which all members of one family line (gia tộc) "return" either with honour or with shame; (2) the immortality of all ancestral linh hồn; (3) the unfathomable protective powers of ancestral linh hồn to protect their posterity; (4) the sacred duty and pragmatic necessity to maintain the đạo of ancestral worship; (5) the "eternal curse" that their family line will biologically perish; and (6) the prestige and lasting perpetuation of the lineage through its members' great moral and professional achievements (đại nghiệp).

Protective Divine Powers of the Ancestral Linh Hồn

Most Việtnamese, especially peasants, worship and believe in the divine protective powers of their ancestors, in particular deceased grandparents, parents, older brothers, sisters, uncles, aunts or best friends. They normally pray to their favourite ancestors for divine protection to overcome practically every problem that they encounter in their lives. However, most East Asian philosophers and peasants agree that humanity is endowed with the best qualities of the cosmos. This view is symbolically expressed in the Vănlangian and Việtnamese traditions by the mythologically majestic image of "the Children and Grandchildren of Tiên Rồng" or "the Children and Grandchildren of the Fairy Mother Âu Cơ and the Dragon Father Lạc Long Quân" (Con Cháu Tiên Rồng).

The human Hồn and human Tinh Khí are thus unfathomably divine and cosmobiologically quintessential. The ancestral linh hồn are believed to be capable of helping their own offspring in some miraculous ways. Many Việtnamese have told me of incredible miracles their ancestors have performed to protect them in life-or-death situations. Such reports among the Việtnamese are too numerous to discuss here. Moreover, various written accounts also recorded the divine interventions of many known or unknown "Anh Linh Dán Tộc" (People's Superior Divinities) on behalf of the political leaders of Việt-Nam. The following is one such account:

The *Báo Cực Record* contains the story of the First Lady of Good Earth. Upon arriving at the port of Hải Hoàn in his southern campaign against the Kingdom of Chiêm Thành (Charnpa-ccp), King Lý Thánh Tông encountered violent winds, heavy rains, and powerful waves which threatened to sink his dragon command ship. The king was frightened.

In the moments of confusion (during his dream-ccp), the king suddenly saw a girl about 20 years old, walking toward him and smiling, her face was beautiful like a peach flower, her eyebrows were dark like willow leaves, her eyes were bright like stars. She wore a white dress and green pants with a belt around her waist. Gracefully, she spoke to the king:

"I am the Tinh (Quintessence) of the great territory of the Southern Nation. I have long lived in the village of Thùy Vân since my death, awaiting for the right time to commit myself for a good cause. Now in the shadow of your dragon vision, I am fully satisfied, and wish you to achieve a complete victory in this campaign. Being fragile like a willow plant, I would do my best to support you, your majesty. I shall be waiting here for your victorious return."

She vanished into thin air upon speaking her last word. Being shaken upon awakening, but quickly regaining his good spirit, and summoning his entourage, the king told them his dream. Senior monk Huệ Lâm Sinh said: "The Goddess did reveal that she died and has been residing on a tree in the village of Thùy Vân. Let's search for her sign on trees or any other divine manifestations."

The king considered that idea to be sound and sent his bodyguards on a search along the riverbank. Verily, they found a tree whose top resembles the head of a person and has an old mark of paint like the one seen in the king's dream. The king proclaimed the Goddess "The First Lady of Good Earth" (Hậu Thổ Phu Nhân) and ordered an altar of worship to be set up inside the king's command ship. Suddenly, the winds and waves ceased, and trees stopped shaking to their roots.

Arriving in Chiêm Thành, the king, engaging his troops to the battle, and feeling as if being supported by the Goddess, won a great victory. Anchoring at the old port upon his victorious return, the king ordered the building of a temple for the Goddess' worship. Suddenly, powerful winds and heavy rains broke loose as in the past. Senior monk Huệ Lâm Sinh suggested to the king: "Order an oracle and build a temple in the Capital upon our return!"

The oracle was positive and the winds and rains ceased instantly. Upon his return to the Capital, the king ordered his geomancist to select the location and then had a temple built for the Goddess' worship in the village of An-Lãng. The temple became quite a divine place since those who dared to blaspheme (against the Goddess-ccp) suffered immediate misfortunes.[44]

How should we interpret this account of the manifestation of the linh hồn of one unknown heroine in the shape of a "beautiful young girl" and her divine intervention in support of the Viêtnamese King Lý Thánh Tông (1054–1072)? At least two interpretations are theoretically possible. From an ideologically rational standpoint, I would interpret that the dream and the subsequent ritualistic acts undertaken by both King Lê Thánh Tông, and his closest advisor, Senior Monk Huệ Lâm Sinh, were invented to serve at least three main political objectives.

First of all, given the religious belief of the. Viêtnamese during the reign of Lê Thánh Tông, the violent storm was probably interpreted by the soldiers to be an omen that indicated either certain "holy souls of mountains and rivers" (hồn thiêng sông Núi) were not in favour of the military campaign or that the military campaign would be ended in great defeat. Since his first objective was to counterattack this inauspicious omen, King Lê Thánh Tông revealed to the soldiers that the Goddess assured them of her divine protection, which was perceived to have caused the immediate end of the violent storm.

Secondly, the dream and subsequent miraculous events helped the King to achieve a second objective of drumming up the fighting spirit of his soldiers by making them believe that they were supported by a divine Goddess who embodied the invincible "Tinh (Quintessence) of the great territory of the Southern Nation" (Viêt-Nam). The factually perceived proof of such divine protection was the instant termination of the powerful winds, great rains, and violent waves that were about to swallow up the whole naval fleet. The divine power of the Goddess would have been interpreted by the soldiers to have been either the real cause of the powerful storm or to have prevailed over that of any other divinity that might have originally caused it.

The report of divine events finally helped the King to achieve his third political objective: to justify the invasion of Champa by proving both to his external enemies and any domestic critics that the invasion was approved by the divine "Tinh (Quintessence) of the great territory of the Southern Land."

A second interpretation of the story, however, is that King Lý Thánh Tông did in fact have an auspicious dream and the events actually happened as textually recorded, and that he himself and his soldiers were convinced of the Goddess' divine protection for their military campaign against the fierce fighters of Champa.

It is not possible to know which of the two interpretations is true. But the account tells us that the divine manifestations of the Goddess did help legitimize the invasion and boost military morale and discipline which apparently assured the great victory of the military campaign against Champa. This and many other stories show that the Viêtnamese soldiers and peasants at that and subsequent times not only had a strong religious belief in the existence of their ancestral linh hồn but also experienced their divine protective powers and direct interventions on their behalf. This spiritual tradition of ancestral worship and cults of heroes and heroines has continued among the common people of Viêt-Nam until today, despite the anti-religious propaganda and repressions of communist authorities since 1945.

Conclusions

I have presented the Viêtnamese conceptions of the human Hồn and human Tinh Khí as well as the rituals of birth and death, which together constitute the biometaphysical foundation and the ritual expression of the Đạo of Vietnamese Ancestral Worship. Given the philosophical and ritualistic aspects of the Đạo of Vietnamese Ancestral Worship, the Vietnamese, like the Chinese, Japanese, and Korean, seem to have considered the nature of the human Hồn to be characterized by their self-motion, incorporeality, immortality, and divine powers (as revealed for example in the cited story). The first three characteristics of the human Hồn, self-motion, incorporeality, and immortality, are also found in the views of Socrates, Plato, Aristotle, etc. But unlike Socrates and Plato, for example, the Vietnamese people do not talk about the rational, spirited, and appetitive capacities of the human Hồn because the Hồn are the spiritual power of life, not the forces of thought, passion, or desire, which are considered functionally different from the former because they are derivative from the Tinh Khí of the human self.

The intellectual, emotional, and instinctual capacities of the human self are apparently conceived in the Viêtnamese tradition to be primarily and functionally related to the human body since they are developed out of the human Tinh Khí rather than out of the human Hồn. If this were the way the Viêtnamese have in fact conceived, then, the Viêtnamese belief in the divine powers of the dead would be seriously questioned because their linh hồn would not know how to protect nor to harm their posterity if they should so wish. A satisfactory answer to this ontological problem of humanity requires further researches.[45]

The Viêtnamese concept of the human Hồn that I have discussed seems older than and distinct from the Buddhist concept of the human "divine consciousness" (thần thức) to which most Vietnamese Buddhists also adhere and which is sometimes found religiously mixed with the former. Ontologically alien to the Viêtnamese concept are the two distinctive ideas of the Buddhist concept of the human soul: (1) the reincarnation of one's "thần thức" in one of the six forms of rebirth due, to one's negative or positive karma, and (2) the release of one's "thần thức" into Nirvana as the final liberation from samsara. The Buddhist notion of forms of rebirth (divine, hellish, etc.), which presupposes karmic reward and punishment, are therefore absent in and alien to the traditional Đạo of Việtnamese Ancestral Worship.

Instead of paradise and hell or nirvana and samsara, the destination of the dead's hồn is believed to be "returning" (về) to the âm realm of their clan ancestors where they would face some kind of moral judgments from their own "tử đại" ancestors, and probably also from their deceased neighbours as it were done in the dương realm of the living. A Việtnamese ancestral worshipper would try to abstain from immorality or evilness, not because of the fear of lower rebirth in samsara, as in the Hindu and Buddhist views, but because of one's fear of violating "đạo hiếu" (filiality) by displeasing and shaming both the living in the dương realm as well as the dead in the âm realm. In addition, in a closely knit society like that of traditional Việt-Nam, one's internal sense of guilt for being unfilial is normally heightened and maintained by waves and waves of social condemnation throughout one's biological life and beyond. Most Việtnamese are thus taught to remind themselves and to be reminded about the lasting effect of one's behaviour as follows: "After death, a tiger leaves behind its skin, and a person leaves behind one's name and reputation!" (Cọp chết để da, người ta chết để tiếng!)

Furthermore, Việtnamese ancestral wor-shippers would try to abstain from committing evil acts because of the greater fear of being held personally responsible for causing the biological termination of their family bloodline (tuyệt tự) due to their childlessness. The disappearance of one's family bloodline also destroys the entire din realm of one's ancestors and consequently scatters all ancestral linh hồn into wandering ghosts and demons (ma quỷ). The effects of one's moral virtues or one's evilness are believed by the Việtnamese, not to be acting back upon one's own linh hồn for either rebirth or liberation after death, as maintained by most Buddhists and Hindus, but to be transmitted directly to one's own offspring and to act directly upon their fate. Thus, it is said:

"Đời cha ăn mặn, đời con khát nước!" (In his lifetime, if the father eats salty foods, his son(s) shall be thirsty for water in their lifetimes!)

The logic of Việtnamese ethics is thus different from the Buddhist, Hindu, Christian, and Greek ones. It is neither the hope of salvation not-the fear of condemnation of one's own hồn that leads one to live a morally good life, but the perpetuation or the termination of one's own family bloodline which either sustains or destroys the entire âm realm of one's ancestral linh hồn. It is assumed here that one's own moral life or one's own immoral life that directly determines the destiny of one's own souls as well as those of one's ancestral linh hồn. Every person is held morally responsible for maintaining the human status of one's own souls and that of all one's ancestral linh hồn in the human world or for destroying the human status by pushing theta into the non-human world of wandering ma quỷ (ghosts and demons)!

Like other peoples in the world, the Việtnamese have recognized the commonality and universality of human Hồn, believing all human beings on earth were directly derived from one common human genesis. But unlike many other peoples, the Việtnamese have chosen evolutionism over creationism to explain the common genesis of humanity. And unlike the Hindus and Buddhists who have blurred the demarcation between humans and other biological beings in their theories of rebirth (or orthodox Christians, who refuse to recognize the biological commonality between humans and living things), the Việtnamese have recognized the cosmobiological foundations of space-time to be fundamental and common to all life-forms on the one hand, and the uniqueness of humanity on the other hand. Furthermore, the Việtnamese have also considered nationality (ethnicity), tribality, genealogicity, familiality, and individuality to be fundamental characteristics of the human Hồn and human Tinh Khí, as they have biologically and culturally diversified themselves into different families, clans, tribes, and nations. To recognize the commonality of humanity is a philosophically conscious act transcending the particularities of one's own finite existence. To affirm, maintain, and to be genuinely proud of one's own unique individuality, familiality, genealogicity, and tribality or nationality is to recognize the uniqueness of one's own humanhood. To be philosophically conscious of the dialectical relationships between the universals and the particulars and to live one's own life as such, one transcends oneself to reach the ideal of being the "Con Cháu Tiên Rồng" (Children and Grandchildren of the Fairy-Dragon-like Quintessences of Being and Non-Being).

Notes

1. Đào Duy Anh, *Việt Nam Văn Hóa Sử Cương* (An Outline History of Viêtnamese Culture). Reprint. Sài Gòn: Bốn Phương. 1961.

2. Phan Kế Bính, *Phong Tục Việt Nam* (Viêtnamese Customs). Reprint. Fort Smith, AR: Sống Mới, 1983.

3. Toan Ánh, *Nếp Cũ Tín Ngưỡng Việt Nam* (The Old Patterns of Viêtnamese Religions), 2 vols. Reprint. Lancaster, PA: Xuân Thu, not dated.

4. Toan Ánh, *Nếp Cũ Con Người Việt Nam* (The Old Traits of Viêtnamese People). Reprint. Lancaster, PA: Xuân Thu, not dated.

5. Nguyễn Đăng Thục, *Tư Tưởng Việt Nam: Triết Lý Bình Dân* (Viêtnamese Thoughts: Popular Philosophy). Sài Gòn: Khai Trí, 1964.

6. The Viêtnamese sacred creation myth is recollected in the "Truyện Hồng Bàng" which is contained in the famous *Lĩnh Nam Chích Quái* (Incredible Stories of Lĩnh Nam). This collection of ancient Viêtnamese mythology was compiled from oral literature between the 11th and 15th centuries. For the Viêtnamese versions, see *Lĩnh Nam Chích Quái*, translated by Lê Hữu Mục (Sài Gòn 1960), or by Đinh Gia Khánh and Nguyễn Ngọc San (Hà-Nội 1960).

7. On the Vănlangian Civilization, see Nguyễn Phương, *Việt Nam Thời Khai Khai Sinh* (Việt Nam in Primeval Times) (Huế, 1965); Văn Tân et al., *Thời Đại Hùng Vương* (The Hùngvương gian Epoch) (Hà-Nội, 1973); Phan Huy Lê et al., *Lịch sử Việt Nam* (Viêtnamese History), vol. I. (Hà-Nội, 1983); *Hùng Vương Dựng Nước* (Kings Hùng Built the Nation) 4 vols. (Hà-Nội, 1970–1974); Nguyễn Phúc

Long, "Les nouvelles recherches archéologiques au Việtnam." *Arts Asiatiques* 31 (Numéro special), pp. 3–154; Peter Bellwood, *Man's Conquest of the Pacific. The Prehistory of Southeast Asia and Oceania* (New York, 1979).

8. On the studies of the bronze drums of Việt Nam and South East Asia, see A. J. Bernet Kempers, *The Kettledrums of Southeast Asia* (Rotterdam, Netherlands: A. A. Balkema, 1988); Bleckman W. Ralph, "Some Dongson Motifs: Their Iconographical Analysis and Identification in Related Cultures" (Ph.D. dissertation, University of Pittsburgh, 1972); Chánh Công Phan, "The Đạo of Universal Change" (Ph.D. dissertation, University of Chicago, 1986); and Pham Minh Huyền et al., *Trống Đông Sơn* (The Đôngsơnian Bronze Drums), Hà-Nội: NXB Khoa Học Xã Hội, 1987.

9. On this question, see Keith Weller Taylor, *The Birth of Vietnam* (Berkeley and Los Angeles, 1983).

10. On cultural relations in southern China and northern Việt Nam, see Wolfram Eberhard, *The Local Cultures of South and East China* (Leiden, 1968); L. Aurousseau, "Le Première Conquête chinoise des pays annamites." *Bulletin de l'École Francaise d'Extrême-Orient* 23 (1923), pp. 137–264.

11. On this question, see Chánh Công Phan, "The Đạo of Viêtnamese Family Governance" (1989, being revised for publication). For the Viêtnamese sources, see Đào Duy Anh, *Việt Nam Văn Hóa Sử Cương*, pp. 182–207; Phan Kế Bính, *Việt Nam Phong Tục*, pp. 23–54.

12. On early Confucian ethics, see *A Source Book in Chinese Philosophy*, translated and compiled by Wing-Tsit Chan (Princeton: Princeton University, 1972), pp. 14–135.

13. Confucius, *The Analects* XI: 11.

14–15. Confucianism and Moism, two philosophical schools of the northern region of the mainland of ancient East Asia (now North China), are completely non-metaphysical. Only the Dịch Lý (c. Yih Li) in the famous *Chou I Ching* and early Đạoism (c. Taoism) are ontological in nature. But the cultural roots of Dịch Lý are still a major issue of intellectual history to be determined even though the *Chou I Ching* is said to have been the work of the Chou founders. There is no hard archaeological evidence to substantiate the North China origin of the *Chou I Ching* even up to this point in time. It appears quite certain that early Đạoism did emerge in the wet-rice region of the ancient "Southern Barbarians" (Nam Man of South China). On this question, see N. J. Girardot, *Myth and Meaning in Early Taoism* (Berkeley: University of California, 1983). "Confucius" or some old "Master" (Tử) of great merit is quoted in the *Trung Dung* (c. Chung Jung, Doctrine of the Mean, X:1–4) to have recognized for example one of many cultural differences between the ancient North and the ancient South as follows: "Tsze-lu asked about energy (cường-ccp). The Master said, 'Do you mean the energy of the South, the energy of the North, or the energy which you should cultivate yourself? To show forbearance and gentleness in teaching others; and not to revenge unreasonable conduct: this is the energy of Southern regions, and the good man makes it his study. To lie under arms; and meet death without regret: this is the energy of Northern regions, and the forceful make it their study'." *The Chinese Classics*, vols. I & II, translated by James Legge (Shanghai: Oxford University Press, 1935; Reprint Taipei: SMC Publishing Inc., 1991), pp. 389–90.

16. I have re-examined this possibility in my article "The Philosophy of Tiên Rồng" (1989) which I am revising for future publication.

17. Nguyễn Đăng Thục, *Tư Tưởng Việt Nam: Triết Lý Bình Dân*, pp. 148–187.

18. Ibid., pp. 159–171.

19. The second metaphysical premise is a verse found in the singular masterpiece of the Việtnamese elite literature of all times, *Truyện Kiều* (The Story of Kiều), written by the famous Việtnamese poet and statesman Nguyễn Du. Like the first premise, the second one, which can be considered to have been part of the older peasant poetry (ca dao tục ngữ) and borrowed by Nguyễn Du like so many other verses of his *Truyện Kiều*, is also so often used in the daily conversations of the Việtnamese masses and intellectuals alike.

20. On the "Five Tạng" and the "Six Phủ," see *A Barefoot Doctor's Manual*, revived and enlarged edition, prepared by the Revolutionary Health Committee of Hunan Province (Seattle: Madrona Publishers, 1977). The term "Tam Tiêu" in the Sino-Việtnamese language or "San Chiao" in the Mandarin is difficult to translate into English

because no such internal organs are found in western anatomy. In fact the translator of *A Barefoot Doctor's Manual* did not attempt to translate the term "San Chiao" (Tam Tiêu). Since the word "tiêu" (chiao) has the meanings to "digest", "absorb", "dissolve by fire", and "transform", and with the medical functions of the "Tam Tiêu," I feel that the term "transformer" is most appropriate.

21. The word "vía" is more common among the Việtnamese peasants than its Sino-Việtnamese (Nho) term "phách" (c. p'o). The word "vía" appears in my opinion to be more archaic than the Nho term "phách" (c. p'o).

22. On this debate, see Stevan Harrell, "The Concept of Soul in Chinese Folk Religion," *Journal of Asian Studies*, XXXVIII, 3 (May 1979): 521–523.

23. Toan Ánh, *Nếp Cũ Con Người Việt Nam* (Old Traits of the Việtnamese People). Reprint (Lancaster, PA: Xuân Thu, n.d.), p. 44.

24. *Giản Yếu Y Học Dân Tộc* (The Essentials of National Medical Science), prepared by the Discipline of National Medical Science, Medical University of Hà Nôi, Pharmaceutical University of Hồ Chí Minh City (Hà-Nội: NXB Y Học, 1988), p. 21.

25. The Dịch Lý (c. Yih Li) is best contained in the famous *Chou I Ching* (The Classic of Universal Changes). The best exposition of this classic in English is *The I Ching or Book of Changes*, the Richard Wilhelm translation rendered into English by Cary F. Baynes (Princeton: Princeton University, 1979). But Wilhelm's interpretation is too Sinocentric.

26. The "Tự Quái Truyện" (Hsu Kuan Chuan [Sequence of the Hexagrams]) explains the processes of world-generation as follows: "After there are heaven and earth, there are the individual things. After individual things have come into being, there are the two sexes. After there are male and female, there is the relationship between husband and wife. After the relationship between husband and wife exists, there is the relationship between father and son. After the relationship between father and son exists, there is the relationship between prince and servitor. After the relationship between prince and servitor exists, there is the difference between superior and inferior. After the difference between superior and inferior exists, the rules of propriety and of right can operate." *The I Ching or Book of Changes*, the Richard Wilhelm translation rendered

into English by Cary F. Baynes, 16th printing (Princeton: Princeton University Press, 1979), pp. 540–541.

27. For the Richard Wilhelm translation, see op cit., p. 294.

28. For a detailed analysis of this creation myth, see Chánh Công Phan, "The Viêtnamese Đạo of Family Governance" (1989) and "The Philosophy of Tiên Rồng" (1989). Unpublished monographs.

29. See Chánh Công Phan, op. cit.

30. On this issue, see Chánh Công Phan, "The Cosmology of the *Vănlangian Bronze Drums* and Its Semantic Relationship to the *I Ching*". Paper presented at the Asian Studies on the Pacific Coast: A Regional Conference of the Association for Asian Studies, Honolulu (30 June–2 July, 1989).

31. Lao Tzu, *Tao Te Ching*. Translated by Gia-Fu Feng and Jane English (New York: Vintage Books, 1972), p. 18 (ch. 16).

32. On the method of combining of the 10 celestial stems and 12 terrestrial branches to make the Cycle of Sixty, see the "Cycle of Sixty" in C.A.S. Williams, *Outlines of Chinese Symbolism & Art Motives* (New York: Dover Publications, Inc., 1976), pp. 104–107; and William F. Mayers, *The Chinese Reader's Manual*, reprint ed. (Taipei: Ch'eng Wen Publishing Company, 1978), pp. 348–349 (no. 296, Pt. II).

33. For the problematics regarding the Chinese concept of human souls, see Stevan Harrell, op. cit., pp. 519–528.

34. All the information on the rituals of birth and death is taken from Đào Duy Anh, *Viêt Nam Văn Hóa Sử Cương*, pp. 182–186. Most of these practices are still current in many Viêtnamese families in Viêt-Nam or even in certain traditionally-minded Buddhist families in North America. If any piece of information that was not taken from Đào Duy Anh's book, I provide its bibliographical source.

35. On the myth of the Twelve Midwives, see Nguyễn Đồng Chi, *Lược Khảo Thần Thoại Viêt Nam* (An Outline Study of the Viêtnamese Mythology) (Hà-Nội: Ban Nghiên Cứu Văn Sử Địa, 1956), pp. 80–83.

36. This is the tradition practised in my village of Sơn Thượng, district of Quế-Sơn, province of Quảng-Nam that I was often told during my boyhood and youth.

37. The child's parents would display many kinds of toys on the floor, whatever toy that the child should pick up first would be the indication of his/her future career.

38. This is the direction determined by the Dịch Lý (c. Yih Li [Philosophy of Change]) and East Asian and Viêtnamese geomancy (*The I Ching or Book of Changes*, the Richard Wilhelm translation, p 270.)

39. Phan Kế Bính, op. cit., p. 42.

40. Đào Duy Anh, op. cit., p. 194.

41. Nguyễn Đồng Chi, *Lược Khảo Thần Thoại Viêt Nam* (An Outline Study of the Viêtmamese Mythology) (Hà-Nội: Ban Nghiên Cứu Văn Sử Địa, 1956), pp. 84–85.

42. The cosmological concept of "Round Heaven" and "Square Earth" is fundamental in East Asian cosmology and derived from the Dịch Lý (c. Yih Li). This concept is commonly considered to be Chinese in origin even though there is no hard archaeological evidence until the Han time. However, this concept is well represented in the system of geometric and pictorial images on the earliest bronze drums of Viêt-Nam, South China, and South East Asia. This archaeological evidence thus gives support to the formation of this cosmological concept back to the Vănlangian time of northern Viêt-Nam (2879–258 BC) as contained in the Vănlangian "Story of the Bánh Dày and Bánh Chưng" (a pair of cakes: a round cake representing Heaven and a square cake symbolizing Earth). This famous pair of cakes is still made by the Viêtnamese in Viêt-Nam and Viêtnamese refugees in North America in most major festivals, especially the New Year Tết celebration. This pair of cakes is also used among the worship offerings to the dead.

43. These two basic offerings are intended for the dead to "enjoy the fragrance of the sacrificial food" (hưởng mùi thơm của đồ cúng). But the number of offering elements might have been intended to symbolize some onto-biological numerology about the origin of life itself. The egg inside two embracing bowls with a pair of chopsticks on top recalls the "Sac of 100 Eggs" (Bọc Trăm Trứng) which was born free from the womb of Fairy Mother Âu Cơ germinated by the male power of Dragon Father Lạc Long Quân.

44. Ứng Thiên Hóa Dục Nguyễn Trung Hậu Thổ Địa Kỳ Nguyên Quân (Chuyện Hậu Thổ Phu Nhân)

(Story of the Earth Goddess) in Lý Tế Xuyên, *Việt Điển U Linh Tập* (Records of the Unfathomable Vietian Realm), translated by Lê Hữu Mục (Sài Gòn: Khai Trí, 1960), pp. 97–98.

45. I myself think that the human soul(s), if by that we mean the life-energy or living energy inherent in every living being, cannot exist apart from the body of a living person or any living thing. Since reproduction is the way of Nature, then, the soul(s) and body of any living person should be biologically reproduced first in the form of either sperms or ova (eggs), and then in the actual form of one's offspring. Therefore, when a person dies one's physical death, which also terminates the life of one's own soul(s). One's physical and spiritual death can be the actual and total end of one's own existence if one has failed to reproduce oneself biologically and spiritually (having offspring). But if one has successfully reproduced oneself into the actual form of one's offspring, then, one's death is just a phase in the evolution of one's total being (hồn and xác). But given the natural law of biological reproduction, namely, one sperm fuses with one ovum, it would probably take about five consecutive generations of offspring before one's own being (hồn-animated DNA) is finally diluted back into the common pool of human genes.

Study Questions

H. Appendix 2 Chánh Công Phan, The Việtnamese Doctrine of the Human Souls and the Rituals of Birth and Death

Compose your own study questions and give a short answer for each of them.

BIBLIOGRAPHY

Branigan, Michael. 2000. *The Pulse of Wisdom: The Philosophies of India, China, and Japan.* Second edition. Belmont, California: Wadsworth.

Buhler, G., trans. 1886. *The Laws of Manu, Sacred Books of the East,* vol. XXV. London: Oxford University Press.

Burton Watson, trans. 1968. *The Complete Works of Chuang Tzu.* New York: Columbia University.

Burtt, E. A., ed. 1955. *The Teachings of the Compassionate Buddha.* New York: The New American Library of World Literature.

Capra, Fritjof. 1975. *The Tao of Physics.* Boulder: Shambhala.

Chalmers, Lord, trans. 1927. *Further Dialogues of the Buddha,* II, *Sacred Books of the East,* VI. Oxford University Press.

Chan, Wing-Tsit, trans. 1963. *A Source Book in Chinese Philosophy.* Princeton: Princeton University Press.

Chan, Wing-Tsit, trans. 1963. *The Way of Lao Tzu, a Translation and Study of the Tao-te ching.* New York: Bobbs-Merrill.

Chan, Wing-Tsit, ed. 1963a. *The Platform Scripture: The Basic Classic of Zen Buddhism.* St. John's University Press.

Cleary, J. C. Buddhism and Popular Religion in Medieval Vietnam. *Journal of the American Academy of Religion,* LIX/1.

Conze, E., and Horner, I. B., eds. 1964. *Buddhist Texts Through The Ages.* New York: Harper & Row.

De Bary, Wm. Theodore, Chan, Wing-Tsit, and Watson, Burton, eds. 1960. *Sources of Chinese Tradition.* Vol. I. New York: Columbia University Press.

Easwaran, Eknath, trans. 1985. *The Upanishads.* Tomales, California: Nilgiri Press.

Easwaran, Eknath, trans. 1985. *The Bhagavad Gita.* Tomales, California: Nilgiri Press.

Embree, Ed. Ainslie, ed. 1958. *Sources of Indian Tradition.* Vol. I, 2nd edition. New York: Columbia University Press.

Feer, Léon, ed. 1890. *The Samyutta-Nikaya* 3:132–35. London: Pali Text Society.

Fung Yu-Lan. 1947. *The Spirit of Chinese Philosophy.* London: Routledge & Kegan Paul Ltd.

Fung Yu-Lan. 1952. *A History of Chinese Philosophy.* Vol. I. Princeton: Princeton University Press.

Girardot, N. J. 1983. *Myth and Meaning in Early Taoism.* Berkeley: University of California Press.

Graham, A. C. 1989. *Disputers of the Tao: Philosophical Argument in Ancient China.* La Salle, Illinois: Open Court.

Hoff, Benjamin. 1983. *The Tao of Pooh.* New York: Penguin Books.

Hume, R. E., trans. 1921. *The Thirteen Principal Upanishads.* London: Oxford University Press, Humphrey Milford.

Kessler, Gary F. 1995. *Voices of Wisdom: A Multicultural Philosophy Reader.* Belmont: Wadsworth Publishing Company.

Koller, John, and Koller, Patricia. 1998. *Asian Philosophies.* Upper Saddle River, New Jersey: Prentice Hall.

Koller, John, and Koller, Patricia. 1991. *A Sourcebook in Asian Philosophy.* New York: MacMillan Publishing Company, 1991.

Meacham, William. 1983. "Origins and Development of the Yueh Coastal Neolithic: A Microcosm of Culture Change on the Mainland of East Asia." In *The Origins of Chinese Civilization,* ed. David N. Keightley. Berkeley: University of California Press. Pp. 147–75.

Legge, James, trans. 1885. *The Sacred Books of China: The Texts of Confucianism* (Part IV), *Sacred Books of the East*, vol. 28. Oxford University Press.

Legge, James, trans. 1893. *The Chinese Classics*, volumes I–II. London: Oxford University Press.

Lo Kuan-Chung. 1976. *Three Kingdoms. China's Epic Drama.* Moss Roberts, trans. & ed. New York: Pantheon Books.

Macdonell, A. A., trans. 1922. *Hymns from the Rigveda* (X.129). London: Oxford University Press and Calcutta: Association Press, 1922.

Mascaro, Juan, trans. 1965. *The Upanishads*. New York: Penguin Books.

McNeill, Ed. William, and Sedlar, Jean, eds. 1970. *Classical China*. Vol. 5. Ed. William H. McNeill and Jean W. Sedlar. New York: Oxford University Press.

Muller, M., editor. 1881. *The Mahavagga* 1.6, 17–22, *Sacred Books of the East*, volume XIII. Oxford University Press.

Nguyêñ, Du. 1983. *The Tale of Kiều*. Trans. Huỳnh Sanh Thông. New Haven: Yale University Press.

Nishida, Kitaro. 1990. *An Inquiry into the Good*. Trans. Masao Abe and Christopher Ives. New Haven and London: Yale University Press.

Phan, Công Chánh. 1993. "The Vietnamese Concept of the Human Souls and the Rituals of Birth and Death." *Southeast Asian Journal of Social Science*, volume 21, number 2.

Pine, Red, trans. 1987. *The Zen Teaching of Bodhidharma*. San Francisco: North Point Press.

Radhakrishnan, trans. 1958. *The Bhagavad Gita* with an Introductory Essay, Sanskrit Text, English Translation and Notes by Radhakrishnan.

Radhakrishnan, Sarvepalli and Moore, Charles, eds. 1957. *A Sourcebook in Indian Philosophy*. Princeton: Princeton University Press.

Reps, Paul, comp. *Zen Flesh, Zen Bones*. New York: Doubleday, n.d.

Rosenberg, Jay F. 1996. *The Practice of Philosophy*. Third edition. Upper Saddle River: Prentice Hall.

Schumacher, F. E. 1973. *Small is Beautiful: Economics As If People Mattered*. HarperCollins Publishers.

Sénart, Emile, ed. *Mahavastu* 3:330–334. 1897. Paris: Imprimirie Nationale.

Slingerland, Edward (Ted). "The Conception of Ming in Early Confucian Thought." *Philosophy East & West*, volume 46, number 4 (October 1996).

Slingerland, Edward (Ted). 2001. "Introduction and Translation." In *Readings in Classical Chinese Philosophy*. Ed. Philip Ivanhoe and Bryan Van Norden. New York and London: Seven Bridges Press.

Strong, John S. 1995. *The Experience of Buddhism. Sources and Interpretations*. Belmont, California: Wadsworth Publishing Company.

Suzuki, D. T. 1948. *An Introduction to Zen Buddhism*. London.

Thich Nhat Hanh. 1991. *Old Path White Clouds*. Berkeley: Parallax Press.

Thich Nhat Hanh. 1992. *The Diamond That Cuts Through Illusion. Commentaries on the Prajnaparamita Sutra*. Berkeley: Parallax Press.

Thich Thien-An. 1975. *Zen Philosophy, Zen Practice*. Emeryville, California: Dharma Publishing.

Thomas, Edward J. 1923. *Vedic Hymns*. London: HWV, Ltd.

Trenckner, Ed. V. 1888. *The Majjhima-Nikaya*, volume I. London: Pali Text Society.

Warren, H. C., trans. 1915. *Buddhism in Translations*, Harvard Oriental Series, vol. III. Cambridge: Harvard University Press, 6th issue.

Watson, Burton, trans. 1968. *The Complete Works of Chuang Tzu*. New York: Columbia University Press.

Watson, Burton, trans. 1967. *Basic Writings of Mo Tzu, Hsun Tzu, and Han Fei Tzu*. New York: Columbia University Press.

Xunzi: A Translation and Study of the Complete Works, Vol. II, Books 7–16. Stanford: Stanford University Press, 1973.

Zaehner, R. C., trans. 1966. *Hindu Scriptures*. London: J. M. Dent & Sons Ltd.